Seaforth

WORLD NAVAL REVIEW

2013

Seaforth WORLD NAVAL REVIEW 2013

Editor
CONRAD WATERS

Seaforth
PUBLISHING

Frontispiece: The Irish Naval Service on exercises. The service is proud that the Irish Government has recognised the importance of the fleet by maintaining a programme of replacement construction in spite of the country's financial difficulties. A detailed review is provided in chapter 2.4A. *(Defence Forces Ireland)*

The editor welcomes correspondence and suggestions from readers. Please contact him via Seaforth at **info@seaforthpublishing.com**. All correspondence should be marked **FAO: Conrad Waters**.

Copyright © Seaforth Publishing 2012
Plans © John Jordan 2012

First published in Great Britain in 2012 by
Seaforth Publishing
An imprint of Pen & Sword Books Ltd.
47 Church Street, Barnsley
S Yorkshire S70 2AS

www.seaforthpublishing.com
Email info@seaforthpublishing.com

British Library Cataloguing in Publication Data
A CIP data record for this book is available from the British Library

ISBN 978-1-84832–156-4

Typeset and designed by Stephen Dent
Printed and bound in China through Printworks International Ltd

CONTENTS

Note on Tables: Tables are provided to give a broad indication of fleet sizes and other key information but should be regarded only as a general guide. For example, many published sources differ significantly on the principal particulars of ships, whilst even governmental information can be subject to contradiction. In general terms, the data contained in these tables is based on official information updated as of June 2012, supplemented by reference to a wide range of secondary and corporate sources, such as shipbuilder websites.

1 OVERVIEW

INTRODUCTION

'He who knows when he can fight and when he cannot will be victorious,' wrote the famous Chinese military strategist Sun Tzu, author of the influential *The Art of War*. This maxim appears to be exerting particular influence on 'Austerity America's' military – and maritime – strategy as it embarks upon a period of retrenchment to rebuild government finances dented by the global financial crisis and drained by the long 'war against terror', most notably in Iraq and Afghanistan.

The United States defence budget continues to dwarf that of any other nation by a considerable factor, as demonstrated by the comparative data set out in Table 1.0.1. Equally, the country's armed services face an underlying decline in defence spending at a time when that of likely rivals, particularly that of China and Russia, is displaying a markedly upward trajectory. Total US defence expenditure, including both base funding and war costs, is currently planned to drop by over 20 per cent from its 2010 peak after taking account of inflation.[1] This holds out the prospect of a steady diminution of US military hegemony to an extent not seen since the height of the Cold War.

Whilst the United States' response to this threat to its supremacy has been multi-faceted, the overall result has been a significant shift in priorities that will have considerable implications for the world naval balance in the years ahead. A common theme that is steadily emerging is a hard-headed focus on maintaining investment in defence assets which are most critical to US military superiority whilst giving priority to those potential theatres of operation that are paramount to the country's global political inter-ests. At the same time, missions where the US is unlikely to achieve ultimate success, and regions that are perceived as having only peripheral significance to its interests are being de-emphasised. This approach is most evident in the rapid drawdown of US Department of Defense supplemental funding for 'Overseas Contingency Operations', as the expense and impracticality of imposing a military solution on countries such as Afghanistan gives rise to alternative approaches. This is being accompanied by a more fundamental realignment of force struc-tures away from the land-based forces required for protracted stabilisation operations.

The overall reduction in US defence resources means that the traditional 'two-war' force structure that had shaped post Cold War force levels has been abandoned in favour of a configuration which is designed to deter conflict in one region whilst the military is actively engaged in another. This places a premium on power projection type assets that are capable of rapid deployment. Consequently, the US FY2013 defence budget request largely protects investment in air and naval assets with these attrib-utes, such as aircraft carriers, large deck amphibious ships, submarines and long-range bombers. These are seen as being essential in ensuring US victory in any future conflict.

Although the US military will continue to contribute to security globally, the new US Presidential Strategic Guidance issued in January 2012 makes it clear that the rebalancing of its capa-bilities towards the Asia-Pacific region, which is already well underway, will continue.[2] This clear statement of priorities followed President Barack Obama's November 2011 address to the Australian Parliament, when he declared that 'the United States will play a larger and long-term role in shaping this region and its future'. Indeed, the last twelve months have seen a steady stream of initiatives designed to counter the perceived threat to US regional interests

Table 1.0.1: COUNTRIES WITH HIGH NATIONAL DEFENCE EXPENDITURES – 2011

RANK	COUNTRY	TOTAL: US$	SHARE OF GDP: %	CHANGE 2010–11
1	United States	711.4bn	4.7%	-1.2%
2	China	142.9bn	2.0%	6.7%
3	Russian Federation	71.9bn	3.9%	9.3%
4	United Kingdom	62.7bn	2.6%	-0.4%
5	France	62.5bn	2.3%	-1.4%
6	Japan	59.3bn	1.0%	0.0%
7	India	48.9bn	2.6%	-3.9%
8	Saudi Arabia	48.5bn	8.7%	2.2%
9	Germany	46.7bn	1.3%	-3.5%
10	Brazil	35.4bn	1.5%	-8.2%
	World	**1,738.0bn**	**2.5%**	**0.3%**

Information from the Stockholm International Peace Research Institute (SIPRI) – http://milexdata.sipri.org
The SIPRI Military Expenditure Database contains data on 171 countries over the period 1988–2011.

Notes:

1 Spending figures are at current prices and market exchange rates.

2 Figures for China, Germany and the Russian Federation are estimates.

3 Data on military expenditure as a share of GDP (Gross Domestic Product) relates to GDP estimates for 2011 from the IMF World Economic Outlook, September 2011

4 Change is real terms change, i.e. adjusted for local inflation.

posed by an emergent China. These have doubtless been given added impetus by the Chinese People's Liberation Army Navy's (PLAN's) progress in refurbishing the former Soviet carrier *Varyag*. The ship's lengthy progress towards completion took a major step forward in August 2011 when she finally embarked on initial sea trials.

Prominent amongst recent US moves to reinforce its Asia-Pacific presence has been the arrival of an initial contingent of US Marines at Darwin in Australia's Northern Territory in April 2012. This forms part of a plan that could eventually see up to 2,500 troops being based there on rotational training deployments by 2017. Meanwhile, the first US littoral combat ship, *Freedom* (LCS-1) will arrive in Singapore in spring 2013 for berthing trials that could herald four of the new warships being assigned to work with the island republic's navy. There have also been discussions with the Philippines about an enhanced American presence, whilst Australia's Cocos Islands have been mooted as a base for unmanned surveillance drones. Most of these initiatives – involving comparatively modest force levels – have limited military significance in their own right. Instead, they should be seen more as confidence-building measures in respect of US commitment amongst key regional partners.[3] Transfers of military technology, such as former US Coast Guard cutters to the Philippines, as part of measures to build partner capacity, can be regarded in a similar light. The true

The first US Navy nuclear-powered aircraft carrier, *Enterprise* (CVN-65) pictured with other ships of her carrier strike group whilst transiting the Atlantic Ocean on 22 March 2012 during her final deployment. Whilst *Enterprise* will be withdrawn from service at the end of 2012, recent US defence decisions continue to place heavy emphasis on the importance of carrier strike groups. *(US Navy)*

The United States' steady increase in focus on the Asia-Pacific region could see littoral combat ships such as *Fort Worth* (LCS-3) – pictured left during pre-commissioning sea trials – forward deployed to Singapore. In addition, friendly navies are being strengthened through the transfer of surplus equipment such as the Philippines' *Gregorio del Pilar*, formerly the Coast Guard's high endurance cutter *Hamilton* (WHEC-715). Both measures are intended to encourage confidence in US commitment to the region rather than impacting the military balance in their own right. *(Lockheed Martin, Mrityunjoy Mazumdar)*

Table 1.0.2: MAJOR FLEET STRENGTHS 2011-2012

COUNTRY	USA		UK		FRANCE		ITALY		SPAIN		RUSSIA[2]		INDIA		CHINA[2]		JAPAN		S KOREA	
Year[1]	2011	2012	2011	2012	2011	2012	2011	2012	2011	2012	2011	2012	2011	2012	2011	2012	2011	2012	2011	2012
Aircraft Carrier (CVN/CV)	11	11	–	–	1	1	–	–	–	–	1	1	–	–	–	–	–	–	–	–
Support Carrier (CVS/CVH)	–	–	1	1	–	–	2	2	1	1	–	–	1	1	–	–	2	2	–	–
Strategic Missile Sub (SSBN)	14	14	4	4	4	4	–	–	–	–	15	15	–	–	3	3	–	–	–	–
Attack Submarine (SSGN/SSN)	57	58	7	7	6	6	–	–	–	–	20	20	–	1	5	5	–	–	–	–
Patrol Submarine (SSK)	–	–	–	–	–	–	6	6	4	3	20	20	14	14	55	55	16	16	12	12
Battleships/Battlecruisers (BB/BC)	–	–	–	–	–	–	–	–	–	–	2	1	–	–	–	–	–	–	–	–
Fleet Escort (CGN/CG/DDG/FFG)	111	107	19	19	17	17	16	15	10	10	30	30	19	21	50	55	40	40	20	20
Patrol Escort (DD/FFG/FSG/FS)	2	2	–	–	15	15	8	8	–	–	55	55	8	8	30	25	6	6	23	21
Missile Attack Craft (PGG/PTG)	–	–	–	–	–	–	–	–	–	–	50	50	12	12	75	75	6	6	5	9
Mine Countermeasures (MCMV)	14	14	15	15	14	14	12	10	6	6	45	45	8	7	20	20	30	30	9	9
Major Amph (LHD/LPD/LPH/LSD)	30	28	6	6	4	4	3	3	3	3	1	1	1	1	2	3	3	3	1	1

Notes:
1 Data refers to fleet strengths as of mid-year 2011 and 2012.
2 Figures for Russia and China are approximate. The table in *Seaforth World Naval Review* 2012 contained an error in respect of China's patrol escorts, which has now been corrected.

blueprint underlying US war-fighting potential in Asia-Pacific remains the development of integrated air and naval forces that underpins the Air-Sea Battle concept and its ability to counter Chinese anti-access/area-denial (A2/AD) capabilities.[4]

Elsewhere, Iran's nuclear ambitions and their potential to lead to a conflict impacting freedom of navigation in the Persian Gulf have continued to exert considerable attention on the maritime thinking of the United States and its allies. This is also a region where deployment of the new littoral combat ships is being considered. News reports suggest that up to eight of the vessels are being earmarked for operation from the troubled island state of Bahrain in due course. By way of contrast, Europe is becoming steadily less significant from a maritime perspective. This reflects both a low level of imminent threat and the region's diminishing influence as the Eurozone crisis continues to impact both its economic and naval potential. Efforts to reconfigure European naval forces to the post Cold War environment have been making progress. However, there is ongoing reliance on the United States for the provision of certain key capabilities, as NATO's involvement in the Libyan conflict demonstrated. Confirmation in November 2011 that four Aegis-equipped US Navy warships will be forward

The US Navy's *Los Angeles* (SSN-688) class nuclear-powered attack submarine *Tucson* (SSN-770) pictured berthing at Polaris Point, Guam on 31 May 2012. The island's naval and air force facilities are becoming increasingly important for US forces as the so-called 'Pivot to the Pacific' and development of the Air-Sea Battle concept places added emphasis on secure bases in the region. *(US Navy)*

The Asian navies continue to grow in numerical strength and technological capability. India, particularly, is benefiting both from the delivery of long-delayed indigenous construction and the fulfilment of previous orders from Russia. This is the newly delivered Russian Project 971 'Akula II' type nuclear-powered attack submarine *Chakra,* seen off the Indian Coast in April 2012. *(Indian Navy)*

The US Coast Guard national security cutter *Waesche* (WMSL-751) operating with the US Navy destroyer *Lassen* (DDG-82) and Royal Thai Navy ships in May 2012. Whilst less sophisticated than front-line warships, the Coast Guard's new national security cutters provide a useful complement to US warships in lower intensity missions. *(US Navy)*

Developments in fixed wing aviation over the past year have been dominated by the US Joint Strike Fighter programme, which seems to be making some headway in spite of numerous problems. F-35B short take off and landing (foreground) and F-35A carrier (background) variants are pictured in this line up at Naval Air Station Patuxent River in February 2012. *(Lockheed Martin)*

deployed to Rota in Spain by 2015 as part of plans to develop a European-wide theatre ballistic missile defence (TBMD) network provide further evidence of this dependency. It seems unlikely the situation will change any time soon given ongoing pressure on European defence budgets that is even more severe than that experienced by the United States.

FLEET REVIEWS

The current estimates of fleet strengths for the leading navies that are set out in Table 1.0.2 reflect the decline in the naval strength of the traditional 'Western' maritime powers compared with that of many of the developing nations. Whilst the prior year's comparative data is not sufficient to show longer term trends clearly, the overall picture of a slow but steady shrinkage in force levels maintained by the four main European navies is apparent. This contrasts with the steady or growing numbers of increasingly capable ships deployed by emergent powers such as China, India and South Korea. The following detailed observations are also worthy of note:

■ By virtue of its nature as a snapshot at a given point in time, the table gives little indication of future changes in fleet strength that will feed through during the rest of the decade as new construction is completed. This is likely to have a

particularly marked impact on India, which will see long-delayed indigenous construction programmes start to deliver new ships at the same time as orders from Russian yards are fulfilled. Equally, the US Navy's surface fleet will increasingly transition to a two-tier force of oceanic DDG-51 class destroyers and smaller littoral combat ships of the LCS-1 and LCS-2 variants as many late Cold War era ships are retired.

■ A number of second-rank navies are growing the breadth and depth of their capabilities to an extent that they are likely to supplant some of the major fleets currently listed within the foreseeable future. For example, Turkey already operates the largest submarine force in Western Europe and has ambitious plans for new amphibious shipping and air defence destroyers. In Latin America, Brazil also has an expansionary naval agenda, including construction of the continent's first nuclear-powered submarine.

■ The full impact of the crisis impacting many Eurozone countries has not yet fully filtered through to force levels maintained by many European fleets. For example, recent reports suggest that Spain is considering withdrawing its sole carrier, *Príncipe de Asturias,* and two *Santa María* class frigates from active service as an economy measure. Similarly, sharp cuts are

planned in the Italian Navy's frigate, corvette and minehunter flotillas to preserve investment elsewhere.

In view of the particular financial pressures currently facing the European navies, the two specific Fleet Reviews both focus on the naval forces maintained by countries particularly impacted by Eurozone sovereign debt concerns. Richard Beedall's chapter on the Irish Naval Service demonstrates how this small but effective constabulary navy has managed to demonstrate its value to the extent that its programme of replacement shipbuilding has continued in spite of near universal cutbacks in state spending. Meanwhile, Enrico Cernuschi and Vincent O'Hara's historical review of post-war Italian naval strategy indicates how the *Marina Militare*'s active role in recent operations off Libya also appears to have secured the survival of key maritime capabilities. Most notable are those provided by the new carrier *Cavour* and her planned air group of F-35B Joint Strike Fighters.

SIGNIFICANT SHIPS

Another important Italian naval programme is that for the acquisition of the new Franco-Italian FREMM type multi-mission frigates. The opening chapter of our second major section, examining significant new warship designs, looks at this project

The Royal Australian Navy frigate *Anzac* and the British Royal Navy frigate *Richmond* were both deployed to the Persian Gulf in support of US-led coalition operations in Iraq. The United States wants to encourage burden-sharing amongst its main partners in the face of falling defence expenditure but many allies are also cutting back on military capabilities. (*Royal Australian Navy*)

from the French perspective. With orders for eleven French ships in two different configurations already confirmed, this programme is central to the future of the *Marine Nationale*'s surface fleet. In particular, it allows modernisation of a wide spectrum of capabilities at acceptable cost. *Aquitaine,* the lead French ship, was completing builders' sea trials at the time of writing prior to delivery to the navy in the second half of 2012. The class's land attack capabilities give it particular relevance in littoral warfare scenarios, an environment that is also central to the requirements driving Germany's K-130 *Braunschweig* class corvette design. All five of this class, which will replace legacy Cold War fast attack craft that have largely been retired already, should now be commissioned by the start of 2013 following delays caused by faulty gearboxes. Guy Toremans' chapter describes the class's importance in the context of the *Deutsche Marine*'s increasingly broad geographical operations. He also highlights some of the technology that allows operation by a core crew of less than sixty personnel.

Lean manning is less of a requirement in the Indian Navy, where personnel costs are relatively low. Nevertheless, India's new Project 17 class stealth frigates feature a notable increase in automation compared with previous indigenous Indian warships. They also mark the first widespread use of stealth features in a locally-built ship. Mrityunjoy

Mazumdar's chapter reviews the class's sophisticated key design features, as well as the reasons behind delays in delivery that have also been common to many other Indian programmes. The US Coast Guard's new *Bertholf* (WMSL-750) 'Legend' class cutters are at the other end of the capability spectrum, being designed with a primary patrol mission in mind. However, Scott Truver's chapter explains how the class provide an important complement to the US Navy's front-line warships, particularly in low intensity scenarios.

TECHNOLOGICAL DEVELOPMENTS

As usual, our final section focuses on technological developments. Fixed wing naval aviation continues to be dominated by the giant F-35 Joint Strike Fighter programme. Accordingly, it features prominently in David Hobbs's annual overview of the naval aviation scene. The new fighter has been dogged by problems resulting from the now discredited concept of concurrent design and production, a philosophy that previously also adversely impacted earlier stages of littoral combat ship construction.[5] However, the last twelve months appear to have seen real progress achieved in bringing the design closer to maturity. This has included initial 'at sea' trials of the F-35B short take off and vertical landing (STOVL) variant from the amphibious assault ship *Wasp* (LHD-1). Meanwhile, maritime deployment

of anti-ballistic missile defence capabilities is being actively considered by an increasing number of nations in view of the proliferation of nuclear and chemical weapons and associated delivery systems, not to the mention the much-reported arrival of China's new Dong-Feng DF-21D 'carrier-killing' ballistic missile.[6] Norman Friedman's concluding chapter, examining the development of ballistic missile defence technologies in the US Navy, is therefore particularly pertinent.

SUMMARY

The last twelve months have been something of a transitional year with respect to naval developments. The United States has taken tangible steps to reconfigure its force structure to acknowledge budgetary constraints. It appears to be making logical choices in terms of focusing on priority theatres of operation and capabilities, both of which have tended to favour maritime forces. This welcome pragmatism has been reflected elsewhere amongst its allies, for example in terms of the stability brought to a diminished United Kingdom military through the financially sustainable, ten-year equipment procurement budget announced on 14 May 2012. However, there is a real prospect of further significant reduction in planned US defence expenditure that would likely overturn the current, well-considered plans with a need to find hasty and damaging short-term savings.[7] These, in turn, would further diminish the post-war naval supremacy enjoyed by the US Navy and allied forces. Further pressure could result from seemingly opportunistic savings being implemented by traditional partner nations in the face of financial challenges. A good example is the previously unexpected real terms ten per cent reduction in Australia's defence budget also announced in early May 2012 and the associated decision to accelerate a rewriting of the 2009 Defence White Paper. The contrast with China's steady and patient approach to investing in its military potential, including its steady acquisition of true oceanic naval capabilities, is quite marked.

ACKNOWLEDGEMENTS

Seaforth World Naval Review continues to rely on a large number of people, not least its contributing authors, to achieve its core aim of providing a comprehensive summary of annual naval developments at an affordable price. In addition to recognising the quality of design provided by Steve Dent and publishing editor Rob Gardiner's ongoing support, particular acknowledgement is due to John Jordan for his considerable work on line drawings. The generosity of Maurizio Brescia, Derek Fox and Bruno Huriet in supplying photographs has also been invaluable. Amongst a large number of industry representatives and defence attachés, the willingness of Solen Dupy of DCNS, Commodore S K Grewal of the Indian Navy, Paul Haccuria of OCCAR, Ester Benito Lope of Navantia, Craig Taylor of Rolls Royce and of Frank van de Wiel of Thales Nederland to 'go the extra mile' to obtain information and imagery deserves particular note. I need also to reference the remarkable patience of my family in accepting the commitment required to making *Seaforth World Naval Review* a reality, not to mention my wife Susan's help with initial proofreading.

Readers' comments, criticisms and suggestions are noted with interest and appreciation. This year's edition reflects feedback received on earlier volumes, most notably in the omission of the index and a slight reduction in the number of chapters to allow larger reproduction of imagery. Please continue to forward any observations to the editor via the contact address, which is detailed opposite the contents page.

Conrad Waters, Editor
30 June 2012

Germany is one of a number of countries considering development of an anti-ballistic missile defence capability, which would be based around Standard SM-3 missiles deployed on the F124 *Sachsen* class frigates. The class are currently armed with the Standard SM-2 air defence missile, seen here being fired by *Sachsen* herself in September 2011. *(German Navy)*

Notes:

1. This figure is based on information provided at the time of the US Department of Defense Budget Request for FY2013. For further analysis, please refer to *Defense Budget Priorities and Choices, January 2012* (Washington DC, Department of Defense, 2012).

2. The strategic guidance was set out in *Sustaining US Global Leadership: Priorities for 21st Century Defense* (Washington DC, Department of Defense, 2012). As well as stressing the key importance of ensuring stability in the Asia-Pacific region, the document referenced the maintenance of a US and allied presence in the Middle East and an active approach to countering violent extremists as major objectives. Whilst the continued importance of Europe and NATO was also referenced, the US presence there will evolve towards greater pooling of assets and the provision of specialised capabilities. Elsewhere, American security objectives will primarily be met by 'low-cost and small-footprint approaches'. Subsequently, on 2 June 2012, Secretary of Defense Leon Panetta reinforced this approach whilst speaking at the annual Shangri-La Dialogue, indicating that sixty per cent of US Navy assets would be deployed in the Pacific by 2020.

3. A good overview of the emerging US response to China's rise as a regional power is contained in Andrew Davis and Benjamin Schreer's *Whither US forces? US military presence in the Asia-Pacific and the implications for Australia* (Canberra, Australian Strategic Policy Institute, 8 September 2011). The web link http://www.aspi.org.au/publications/publications_all.aspx can be used to search for all the institute's publications.

4. Originated late in 2009, the Air-Sea Battle concept envisages greater inter-operability of US Force and US Navy assets to combat the restriction on US power projection that would otherwise arise from potential adversaries expanding A2/AD capabilities. An Air Sea Battle Office was formed during 2011 to give the concept practical effect. Although not officially targeted at a specific potential adversary, most commentators acknowledge that it was developed with China and, to a lesser extent, Iran in mind.

5. A debate continues as to the extent to which concurrency – the actual production of a weapons system whilst design elements are still being completed – is a

flawed concept. An interesting overview is provided by Donald Birchler, Gary Christle and Eric Gross in 'Investigating Concurrency in Weapons Programs', *Defense AT&L* – September–December 2010 (Fort Belvoir, VA, Defense Acquisition University, 2010), pp.18–21.

6. In addition to the Netherlands' announcement in November 2011 that it would modify its *De Zeven Provinciën* class's SMART L surveillance radars to incorporate an extended range ballistic missile tracking capability, Germany is also considering modifications to its similar *Sachsen* class frigates that would also see them being equipped with Standard SM-3 missiles to act in 'shooter' mode. See Nicholas de Larrinaga's 'Germany considers SM-3 BMD capabilities', *Jane's Defence Weekly* – 16 May 2012 (Coulsdon, IHS Jane's, 2012), p.13.

7. The threat of further substantial reductions in American security expenditure is largely driven by the possibility of across the board cuts to most elements of US government expenditure under the sequestration process contained in the US Budget Control Act of 2011. This is explained further in Chapter 2.1.

2.1 REGIONAL REVIEW

NORTH AND SOUTH AMERICA

Author:
Conrad Waters

INTRODUCTION:

Recent naval developments in the Americas have inevitably been dominated by increasing pressures on US Navy force levels and future procurement as the post 9/11 era of buoyant defence spending comes to an end. The switch in emphasis towards the Asia-Pacific region highlighted in the introductory chapter is taking place against the backdrop of a FY2013 Defense Budget request that will reduce core expenditure by US$259bn over five years and by US$487bn over ten years in comparison with previous plans to meet the constraints of the 2011 Budget Control Act. The five-year reduction represents a decline of as much as nine per cent against previous assumptions, although the actual real reduction compared with the current FY2012 budget over the same period is more manageable at less than two per cent overall.[1] When taken in conjunction with the underlying emphasis on naval and air power contained within the new US Presidential Strategic Guidance, sufficient funding has been provided to maintain US Navy personnel levels at c.320,000 and protect the core force of eleven carrier strike groups on which the navy's power projection capabilities depend. Nevertheless, the US fleet has had to accept some significant pain. This includes a material reduction in short-term procurement plans and a fall in planned force levels as a number of older Aegis cruisers and amphibious transport ships are retired early.

There are also reasons to fear that the ultimate outcome for future US naval force levels will be worse than the current plans suggest. The long-range construction programme suggests a need to significantly increase annual shipbuilding spend from around the end of the decade if an anticipated battle force of around three hundred warships is to be achieved. Unfortunately, it is by no means clear that the money required to pay for these ships will be forthcoming. Additionally, previous assessments by the independent Congressional Budget Office have suggested that US Navy estimates of likely construction costs have been notably optimistic, particularly in later plan years. However, the main threat is the so-called sequestration process under the 2011 Budget Control Act, which mandates across the board government spending cuts equivalent to a further US$1,200bn through to FY2021. These are to be split equally between security and other programmes.[2] If no alternative agreement is forthcoming, this could result in further annual reductions to defence funding of about US$55bn per annum or roughly as much again as those already being implemented. Given limited flexibility in reducing ongoing operating and personnel costs, it is likely that procurement would be particularly badly impacted. The situation is being exacerbated by the inevitable uncertainties posed by a US Presidential election year and a marked reluctance by Department of Defense leaders to accept – and plan for – an outcome with an impact ranging from the disruptive to the potentially devastating.

Meanwhile, in Latin America, the thirtieth anniversary of the start of the Falkland Islands War in April 2012 brought about an unwelcome return to tensions in the South Atlantic. Renewed Argentine claims to the British-held territory driven by a combination of President Cristina Fernández de Kirchner's nationalist agenda and an increased likelihood of exploitable oil and gas reserves being discovered around the islands have received considerable political support from other Latin American states but seem unlikely to be backed by Argentine military force. Even so, the rhetoric was sufficient to result in the powerful British Royal Navy destroyer *Dauntless* being sent to the region on her maiden deployment to reinforce the local naval presence headed by the offshore patrol vessel *Clyde* and newly commissioned ice patrol ship *Protector*. The unconfirmed presence of a Royal Navy nuclear-powered *Trafalgar* class attack submarine in the region lent the response additional weight. Whilst Argentina's military expenditure has been on a sharply upward trajectory over the past few years in line with that of many other Latin American countries, this has not yet been sufficient to make good the damage caused by decades of previous neglect. Consequently, most commentators believe that the depleted Argentine navy – and air force – would be unlikely to repeat the initially successful invasion of the islands achieved in 1982 in the face of a much enhanced local British military garrison.[3]

Table 2.1.1 provides a summary of major fleet strengths in both North and South America as of mid 2012.

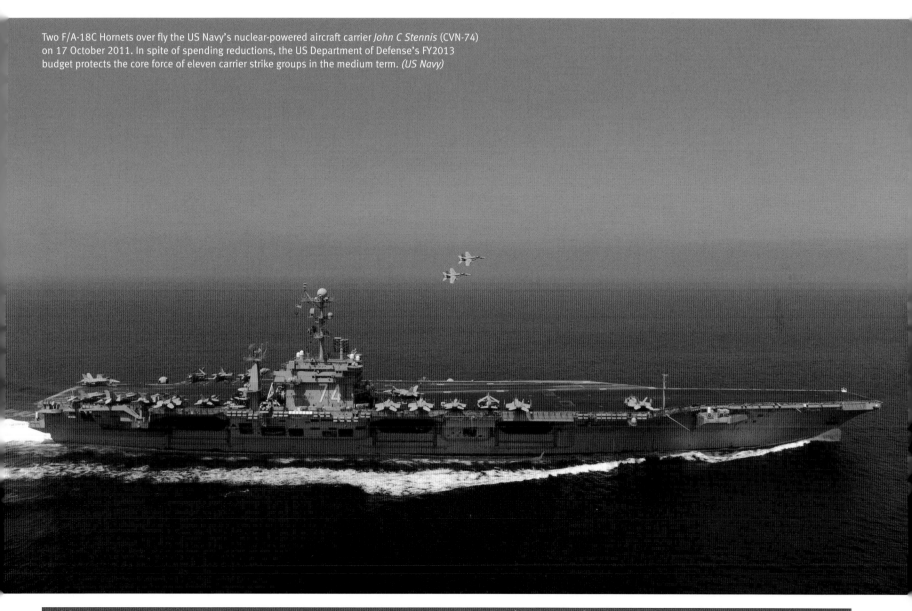

Two F/A-18C Hornets over fly the US Navy's nuclear-powered aircraft carrier *John C Stennis* (CVN-74) on 17 October 2011. In spite of spending reductions, the US Department of Defense's FY2013 budget protects the core force of eleven carrier strike groups in the medium term. *(US Navy)*

Table 2.1.1: FLEET STRENGTHS IN THE AMERICAS – LARGER NAVIES (MID 2012)

COUNTRY	ARGENTINA	BRAZIL	CANADA	CHILE	ECUADOR	PERU	USA	VENEZUELA
Aircraft Carrier (CVN/CV)	–	1	–	–	–	–	11	–
Strategic Missile Submarine (SSBN)	–	–	–	–	–	–	14	–
Attack Submarine (SSN/SSGN)	–	–	–	–	–	–	58	–
Patrol Submarine (SSK)	3	5	4	4	2	6	–	2
Fleet Escort (CG/DDG/FFG)	4	9	15	8	2	9	107	6
Patrol Escort/Corvette (FFG/FSG/FS)	9	5	–	–	6	–	2	–
Missile Armed Attack Craft (PGG/PTG)	2	–	–	7	3	6	–	6
Mine Countermeasures Vessel (MCMV)	–	6	12	–	–	–	14	–
Major Amphibious Units (LHD/LPD/LPH/LSD)	–	2	–	1	–	–	28	–

The Royal Canadian Navy frigate *Vancouver* pictured passing the Rock of Gibraltar in January 2012. Canada's hard-worked frigate fleet is in the course of receiving midlife modernisations pending construction of a planned new single-class surface combatant. *(Royal Canadian Navy)*

The Royal Canadian Navy's much reviled purchase of former Royal Navy *Unicorn* class patrol submarines was one of the few programmes to make good progress in the last twelve months and three boats should be operational by 2013. This is *Victoria* pictured during diving trials off Esquimalt in February 2012. *(Royal Canadian Navy)*

MAJOR NORTH AMERICAN NAVIES – CANADA:

Table 2.1.2 lists key statistics for current principal Royal Canadian Navy units, there being no change from the previous year.

The last twelve months have seen mixed fortunes for Canada's naval service, which reverted to its historic Royal Canadian Navy title following a decision announced on 16 August 2011. The symbolic change, which reverses the use of the Maritime Command nomenclature introduced in 1968 when the Canadian forces were unified under a central command structure, has been sought by veterans for a number of years and is seen as a way of reinforcing links between the current navy and its distinguished heritage.

A more substantive decision was revealed on 19 October 2011 when the names of the shipyards selected to carry out the vast bulk of Canada's National Shipbuilding Procurement Strategy were made public. This strategy has mandated that future construction of major vessels – those displacing more than 1,000 tons – for the Canadian government will be allocated to two domestic yards. The big winner was Irving Shipbuilding Inc of Halifax, Nova Scotia. It has been earmarked for a package of work estimated at c.C$25bn (US$24bn) to build the navy's future combat vessels, encompassing Arctic offshore patrol vessels and future surface combatants, following the allocation of a leading 82.8 per cent score under an independent shipyard evaluation process. The runner up was west-coast-based Vancouver Shipyards, which is part of the Seaspan group. It was selected for a work package estimated at around C$8bn (US$7.7bn) to build large non-combatant ships, including up to three planned JSS joint support ships, after an independent evaluation of 74.9 per cent. The Quebec facility of Davie Yards was the loser in the three-way selection process but remains eligible to bid for work constructing smaller ships.

Although umbrella agreements with both firms were subsequently confirmed in January 2012, it is important to note that specific contracts for the various construction programmes have yet to be awarded. In addition to the inevitable uncertainties resulting from likely changes to government priorities and funding availability with respect to work that will extend to more than twenty years into the future, negotiation of detailed contracts for more immediate elements of the programme could result

Table 2.1.2: CANADIAN NAVY: PRINCIPAL UNITS AS AT MID 2012

TYPE	CLASS	NUMBER	TONNAGE	DIMENSIONS	PROPULSION	CREW	DATE
Principal Surface Escorts							
Destroyer – DDG	**IROQUOIS**	3	5,100 tons	130m x 15m x 5m	COGOG, 29 knots	280	1972
Frigate – FFG	**HALIFAX**	12	4,800 tons	134m x 16m x 5m	CODOG, 29 knots	225	1992
Submarines							
Submarine – SSK	**VICTORIA** (UPHOLDER)	4	2,500 tons	70m x 8m x 6m	Diesel-electric, 20+ knots	50	1990

in further slippage to projects that have already experienced significant delays. The most advanced is that for the Arctic offshore patrol vessels. Between six and eight of these are to be built at a cost of c.C$3.1bn (US$3bn) to an essentially constabulary design specification drafted by BMT Fleet Technology. An order was expected in 2012 for delivery of the first ship by 2015 but the latter date has recently been pushed back to 2018. This might, in turn, further postpone initiation of work on the planned single-class surface combatant, which should see the fifteen existing *Iroquois* and *Halifax* class escorts replaced from the middle of the next decade. The latter vessels are being modernised under the combined *Halifax* Class Modernisation/Frigate Life Extension (HCM/FELIX) upgrade package, encompassing enhanced radar, command and control systems and electronic countermeasures. However, the three remaining *Iroquois* class destroyers will all have passed their fortieth birthdays by the end of 2012 and it appears likely they will be withdrawn from service as the *Halifax* class complete their refits, leading to an overall drop in fleet numbers.[4]

The fleet's two *Protecteur* class replenishment oilers are even older than the *Iroquois* destroyers but their JSS replacements have also been beset by delays. A bespoke 'in-house' design drawn up by BMT Fleet Technology has been selected for further development in competition against a variant of Germany's Type 702 *Berlin* class. A decision on which design to select is expected by early 2013 prior to the award of a C$2.6bn (US$2.5bn) construction contract to Vancouver Shipyards. This should allow completion of the first ship by 2017, although many commentators believe this schedule is overly aggressive given the fate of other programmes. A key example is the C$3.2bn (US$3.1bn) maritime helicopter programme, which is to deliver twenty-eight Sikorsky CH-148 Cyclones to replace the existing Sea King helicopters operated from the country's surface escorts and other

ships. Only one interim-fit Cyclone has been delivered thus far, with a further five expected in the second half of 2012. This compares with an initially expected 2008 handover date.

Given the extent of current procurement problems, it is a little ironic that the one Canadian naval programme that does seem to be making good progress is the *Victoria*-In Service Support Contract (VISSC) for the often reviled submarines acquired from the United Kingdom in 1998. The submarine fleet is finally expected to achieve full operational

capability during 2013, when three boats will be available for operations. One high-readiness submarine will be maintained on both the east and west coasts. *Victoria* – formerly the British Royal Navy's *Unseen* – carried out the class's first successful test firing of a US Mk48 torpedo in March 2012 as part of these plans, following completion of an extended docking period the previous September. *Windsor* and *Chicoutimi* are also scheduled to complete planned docking periods during 2012, with the former being undocked on 11 April 2012. The

All three of Canada's remaining *Iroquois* class destroyers will have passed their fortieth birthdays by the end of 2012 and it therefore seems likely there will be a gap between their withdrawal and the commissioning of replacements. This is *Algonquin* on a visit to San Francisco in summer 2011. *(Mrityunjoy Mazumdar)*

A picture of the torpedo room of the Royal Canadian Navy submarine *Victoria*. She carried out the class's first successful test firing of a US Mk48 torpedo in March 2012. *(Royal Canadian Navy)*

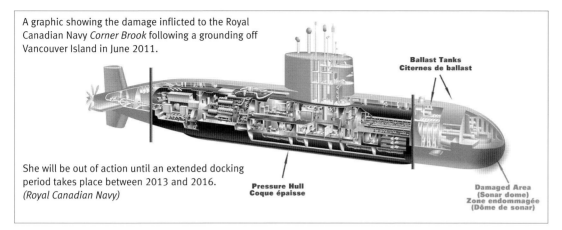

A graphic showing the damage inflicted to the Royal Canadian Navy *Corner Brook* following a grounding off Vancouver Island in June 2011.

She will be out of action until an extended docking period takes place between 2013 and 2016. *(Royal Canadian Navy)*

Ballast Tanks
Citernes de ballast

Pressure Hull
Coque épaisse

Damaged Area
(Sonar dome)
Zone endommagée
(Dôme de sonar)

fourth boat, *Corner Brook*, ran aground on 4 June 2011 whilst conducting officer training off Vancouver Island, causing damage to the forward sonar dome. Repairs will be carried out as part of the boat's own extended docking period, which is scheduled for 2013–16.

MAJOR NORTH AMERICAN NAVIES – UNITED STATES

In spite of the significant changes to both the strategic and budgetary outlook already referenced, the US Navy has remained remarkably consistent throughout the last decade in planning for an overall medium-term battle fleet of a little over three hundred ships. This consistency is evident in the Long-Range Shipbuilding Plan for FY2013 presented to Congress in April 2012, which references a battle force goal reduced only slightly to *around* three hundred warships and which contains numbers that add up to between 310–316 vessels.[5] However, a new force structure assessment is

currently underway in light of the recently revised strategic guidance and it is conceivable that this could impact total force constituents or individual components once completed.

Unfortunately, another recurring theme of recent US Navy planning has been near-term force projections that fall some way short of this ultimate target. This trend has been reinforced by the FY2013 budget reductions. As demonstrated by Table 2.1.3, the projected number of battle force ships will struggle to reach the three hundred mark before the end of the decade and is also significantly lower throughout the intervening period than expected this time last year. In the early years, this is largely the result of early decommissioning of current warships, with seven *Ticonderoga* (CG-47) class Aegis cruisers and two *Whidbey Island* (LSD-41) dock landing ships slated for withdrawal from late 2012 onwards. Later in the decade, cutbacks in warship procurement also start to take effect, having a particularly marked impact on the construction of smaller vessels.

The revised FY2013–2017 shipbuilding plan has been significantly reduced from previous expectations, encompassing a total programme of just forty-one battle force ships compared with the fifty-seven ships envisaged in FY2012. Nine of the sixteen-ship reduction relates to ships that have been totally eliminated from future construction plans and will no longer be built. The remaining seven have been deferred beyond FY2017. Table 2.1.4 confirms the fact that most of the reduction has fallen on smaller ships, most notably the termination of construction of joint high speed vessel (JHSV) troop transports at just ten units in FY2013. A total of over twenty of these high-speed, intra-theatre transports was previously planned – including a further seven in the FY2013–2017 period – under a joint US Army/Navy programme. Whilst acquisition of larger warships has been much less impacted, some orders have been slowed. In addition, construction times for new aircraft carriers appear to have been stretched out by as much as two years, largely to ensure the carrier fleet does not grow beyond the required eleven carriers over the next decade.

Current fleet numbers are slightly reduced year-on-year at around 285 vessels. This largely reflects the retirement of FFG-7 class frigates and older amphibious ships at faster rates than replacements are being commissioned. Table 2.1.5 provides a summary of the main units currently in commission, whilst further granularity on recent developments in terms of major ship categories are summarised below.

Aircraft Carriers: The US Navy's carrier force will temporarily fall to ten vessels in the course of the next year following completion of the *Enterprise*'s (CVN-65) final deployment. The carrier, which cele-

Table 2.1.3: REVISIONS TO PROJECTED US NAVY BATTLE FORCE LEVELS: FY2012 PLAN COMPARED TO FY2013 PLAN

SHIP TYPE	FY2013		FY2014		FY2015		FY2016		FY2017		FY2018		FY2019		FY2020	
FY2012 Plan/**FY2013 PLAN**	2012	**2013**	2012	**2013**	2012	**2013**	2012	**2013**	2012	**2013**	2012	**2013**	2012	**2013**	2012	**2013**
Aircraft Carrier (CVN)	10	**10**	10	**10**	11	**11**	11	**11**	11	**11**	11	**11**	11	**11**	12	**11**
Strategic Missile Submarine (SSBN)	14	**14**	14	**14**	14	**14**	14	**14**	14	**14**	14	**14**	14	**14**	14	**14**
Attack Submarine (SSGN/SSN)	59	**59**	59	**59**	58	**58**	56	**57**	54	**54**	54	**55**	55	**55**	53	**52**
Fleet Escort (CG/DDG)	84	**80**	85	**78**	86	**78**	90	**80**	91	**82**	93	**84**	95	**86**	97	**87**
Patrol Escort / Minehunter (FFG/LCS/MCMV)	35	**35**	30	**30**	26	**26**	31	**30**	32	**32**	36	**35**	36	**39**	40	**37**
Amphibious Unit (LHA/LHD/LPD/LSD)	30	**31**	30	**29**	30	**28**	31	**29**	33	**30**	33	**31**	33	**31**	33	**31**
Other	55	**56**	58	**59**	61	**61**	64	**63**	66	**62**	70	**62**	72	**64**	73	**63**
TOTAL	287	**285**	286	**279**	286	**276**	297	**284**	301	**285**	311	**292**	316	**300**	322	**295**

brated her fiftieth birthday in November 2011, will be withdrawn from service at the end of the year prior to formal decommissioning in March 2013. Work on her replacement, *Gerald R Ford* (CVN-78), is reportedly progressing reasonably well and it was claimed that she was over seventy-five per cent structurally complete when her lower bow section was joined to other keel sections on 24 May 2012.[6] Launch from Huntington Ingalls Industries' (HII's) Newport News yard is scheduled for 2013 prior to delivery in 2015. The new carrier has a similar hull form to the previous *Nimitz* (CVN-68) class design but incorporates a significant amount of new equipment, notably the Electromagnetic Aircraft Launch System (EMALS), Advanced Arresting Gear (AAG) and a new dual-band active phased array type radar. These and other 'first-of-class' issues, as well as considerable growth in material costs, have pushed estimated procurement costs up to over US$12.3bn and delayed planned delivery by several months. Lessons learned will be incorporated in the fabrication of the second *Ford* class vessel, *John F Kennedy* (CVN-79), which is already under construction. Improvements envisaged include greater block lifting capability and an increase in the level of pre-launch outfitting. The ship's construction will be extended out to 2022 (previously 2020) as a result of the changes outlined in the FY2013 budget, with estimated acquisition cost amounting to US$11.4bn.

Surface Combatants: The US Navy's fleet of surface combatants will steadily transition to a two tier fleet of *Arleigh Burke* (DDG-51) variant destroyers and *Freedom* (LCS-1) and *Independence* (LCS-2) type littoral combat ships over the coming years as older, Cold War era ships are steadily decommissioned. The rate of withdrawal of the remaining *Oliver Hazard Perry* (FFG-7) class frigates is accelerating, with a further five ships scheduled to be withdrawn from service in 2013 to add to the four decommissioned during calendar year 2012. This will leave fewer than twenty in service. The numbers of *Ticonderoga* class Aegis cruisers will also rapidly reduce following the FY2013 budget request to deactivate a further seven of the class, with just fifteen remaining operational. The ships slated for deletion encompass the six members of the class that have not been modernised for ballistic missile defence and newest member of the class, *Port Royal* (CG-73), which was damaged in a grounding off Hawaii in 2009.

Construction of the original sixty-two *Arleigh*

Table 2.1.4: USN FY2013 FIVE YEAR SHIPBUILDING PLAN (FY2013-FY2017)

SHIP TYPE	FY2012: ACTUAL	FY2013: REQUEST	FY2014: PLAN	FY2015: PLAN	FY2016: PLAN	FY2017: PLAN
Aircraft Carrier (CVN-78)	Nil	1 (1)	Nil (Nil)	Nil (Nil)	Nil (Nil)	Nil (Nil)
Attack Submarine (SSN-774)	2	2 (2)	1 (2)	2 (2)	2 (2)	2 (2)
Destroyer (DDG-51)	1	2 (2)	1 (2)	2 (2)	2 (1)	2 (2)
Littoral Combat Ship (LCS-1/2)	4	4 (4)	4 (4)	4 (4)	2 (3)	2 (3)
Amphibious Assault Ship (LHA-6)	Nil	Nil (Nil)	Nil (Nil)	Nil (Nil)	Nil (1)	1 (Nil)
Amphibious Transport Dock (LPD-17)	1	Nil (Nil)	Nil (Nil)	Nil (Nil)	Nil (Nil)	Nil (Nil)
Dock Landing Ship (LSD-X)	Nil	Nil (Nil)	Nil (Nil)	Nil (Nil)	Nil (Nil)	Nil (1)
Joint High Speed Vessel (JHSV-1)	2	1 (2)	Nil (2)	Nil (2)	Nil (1)	Nil (2)
Mobile Landing Platform (MLP-1)	1	Nil (1)	1 (Nil)	Nil (Nil)	Nil (Nil)	Nil (Nil)
Replenishment Oiler (TAO(X))	Nil	Nil (Nil)	Nil (1)	Nil (1)	1 (1)	Nil (1)
Fleet Tug (TAFT)	Nil	Nil (Nil)	Nil (Nil)	Nil (1)	2 (Nil)	Nil (1)
Surveillance Ship (TAGOS)	Nil	Nil (1)	Nil (Nil)	Nil (Nil)	Nil (Nil)	Nil (Nil)
Total	11	10 (13)	7 (11)	8 (12)	9 (9)	7 (12)

Notes

1 Figures in brackets relate to previous FY2012 Budget Request and Shipbuilding Plan.

2 Figures relate to Ship Battle Forces – other ships are not included.

The FY2014 MLP mobile landing platform ship will be built as an afloat forward staging base (AFSB) variant.

The US Navy's battle force will fall below previous plans during the rest of the decade as Cold War era ships are retired early. *Normandy* (CG-60) is set to survive the reductions but seven of her Aegis-equipped sisters in the *Ticonderoga* (CG-47) class will be withdrawn before the end of 2014. (*Conrad Waters*)

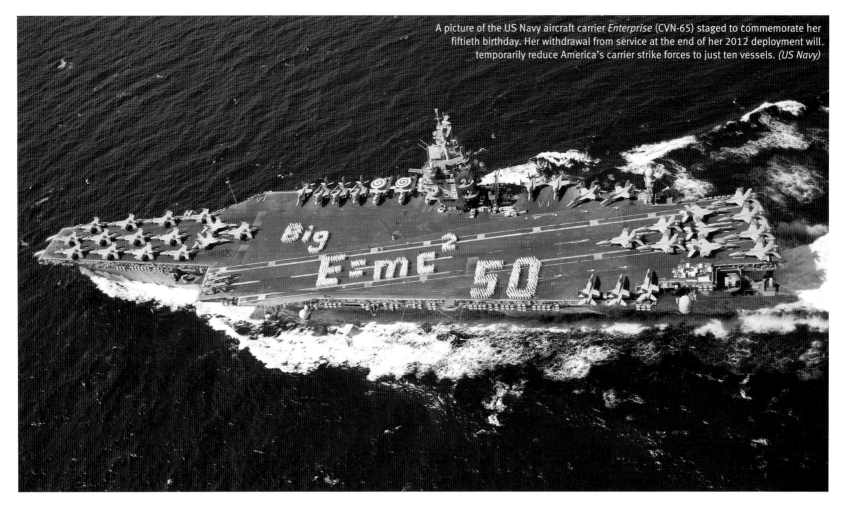

A picture of the US Navy aircraft carrier *Enterprise* (CVN-65) staged to commemorate her fiftieth birthday. Her withdrawal from service at the end of her 2012 deployment will temporarily reduce America's carrier strike forces to just ten vessels. *(US Navy)*

Two pictures of the lead *Gerald R Ford* (CVN-78) class carrier under construction at Huntington Ingalls Industries' Newport News shipyard. She was claimed to be over seventy-five per cent structurally complete by May 2012 and should be launched before the end of 2013. *(Huntington Ingalls Industries)*

Burke class destroyers has now come to an end. The final ship, *Michael Murphy* (DDG-112), was delivered to the navy in May prior to a formal commissioning ceremony planned for 6 October 2012. However, orders have now been confirmed for resumption of Flight II-A *Burke* class construction, with *John Finn* (DDG-113) and *Ralph Johnson* (DDG-114) being allocated to HII's Ingall's division and *Rafael Peralta* (DDG-115) and *Thomas Hudner* (DDG-116) assigned to General Dynamics' Bath Iron Works. A further six ships are planned through to FY2017, when construction will transition to the proposed Flight III variant, which will incorporate a new Air and Missile Defence Radar (AMDR) system. There are, however, increasing concerns that the basic 1980s DDG-51 design is simply too cramped to accept the size and power requirements of the new radar system without a substantial redesign that could add significantly to the c.US$2.5bn cost estimate for the new ships. There have therefore been suggestions that reversion to the previous plan of a new design might be more cost-effective in the longer term, perhaps based on the larger *Zumwalt* (DDG-1000) class hull form.[7]

The DDG-1000 programme was truncated at just three ships due to cost overruns but progress on the remaining destroyers appears to be going to plan. Construction contracts for the second and third vessels were awarded to Bath Iron Works on 15 September 2011, which also performed a ceremonial keel-laying for the first of class in November. *Zumwalt* is now estimated to be over 60 per cent complete and should be delivered to the US Navy in the course of 2014.[8] Current plans envisage *Michael A Monsoor* (DDG-1001) will follow in December 2015, with the newly named *Lyndon B Johnson* (DDG-1002) completing the trio in September 2018.

Meanwhile, the all-important littoral combat ship programme has also experienced a good year, with orders continuing to be placed under the multi-year procurement arrangement negotiated in 2010. This saw contracts awarded under the FY2012 programme on 16 March 2012 for LCS-1 variants *Little Rock* (LCS-9) and *Sioux City* (LCS-11) and for LCS-2 type ships *Gabrielle Giffords* (LCS-10) and *Omaha* (LCS-12) to Lockheed Martin and Austal USA respectively. Construction of earlier ships is also proceeding to plan, with *Fort Worth* (LCS-3) scheduled for commissioning in September 2012 following successful completion of navy acceptance

A picture of the *Ticonderoga* (CG-47) class cruiser *Port Royal* (CG-73) in the course of salvage after she ran aground on a reef off Hawaii in February 2009. Although subsequently repaired, it would seem this was not entirely effective and she is one of seven cruisers slated for early withdrawal. *(US Navy)*

Michael Murphy (DDG-112), the last of the initial production run of sixty-two *Arleigh Burke* (DDG-51) class destroyers to be completed, is scheduled for commissioning in New York in October 2012. *(General Dynamics Bath Iron Works)*

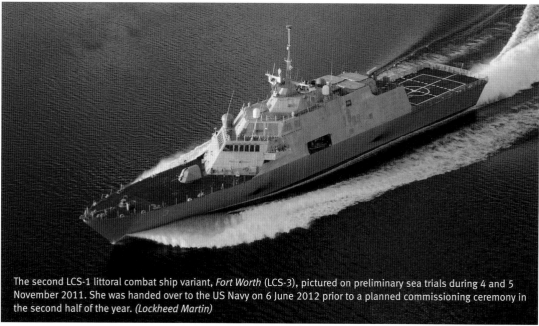

The second LCS-1 littoral combat ship variant, *Fort Worth* (LCS-3), pictured on preliminary sea trials during 4 and 5 November 2011. She was handed over to the US Navy on 6 June 2012 prior to a planned commissioning ceremony in the second half of the year. *(Lockheed Martin)*

Table 2.1.5: UNITED STATES NAVY: PRINCIPAL UNITS AS AT MID 2012

TYPE	CLASS	NUMBER	TONNAGE	DIMENSIONS	PROPULSION	CREW	DATE
Aircraft Carriers							
Aircraft Carrier – CVN	**NIMITZ** (CVN-68)	10	101,000 tons	340m x 41/78m x 12m	Nuclear, 30+ knots	5,700	1975
Aircraft Carrier – CVN	**ENTERPRISE** (CVN-65)	1	93,000 tons	342m x 41/76m x 12m	Nuclear, 30+ knots	5,900	1961
Principal Surface Escorts							
Cruiser – CG	**TICONDEROGA** (CG-47)	22	9,900 tons	173m x 17m x 7m	COGAG, 30+ knots	365	1983
Destroyer – DDG	**ARLEIGH BURKE** (DDG-51) – Flight II-A	34	9,200 tons	155m x 20m x 7m	COGAG, 30 knots	380	2000
Destroyer – DDG	**ARLEIGH BURKE** (DDG-51) – Flights I/II	28	8,800 tons	154m x 20m x 7m	COGAG, 30+ knots	340	1991
Frigate – FFG	**OLIVER HAZARD PERRY** (FFG-7)	23	4,100 tons	143m x 14m x 5m	COGAG, 30 knots	215	1977
Littoral Combat Ship – FS	**FREEDOM** (LCS-1)	1	3,100 tons	115m x 17m x 4m	CODAG, 45+ knots	<50[1]	2008
Littoral Combat Ship – FS	**INDEPENDENCE** (LCS-2)	1	2,800 tons	127m x 32m x 5m	CODAG, 45+ knots	<50[1]	2010
Submarines							
Submarine – SSBN	**OHIO** (SSBN-726)	14	18,800 tons	171m x 13m x 12m	Nuclear, 20+ knots	155	1981
Submarine – SSGN	**OHIO** (SSGN-726)	4	18,800 tons	171m x 13m x 12m	Nuclear, 20+ knots	160	1981
Submarine – SSN	**VIRGINIA** (SSN-774)	9	8,000 tons	115m x 10m x 9m	Nuclear, 25+ knots	135	2004
Submarine – SSN	**SEAWOLF** (SSN-21)	3[2]	9,000 tons	108m x 12m x 11m	Nuclear, 25+ knots	140	1997
Submarine – SSN	**LOS ANGELES** (SSN-688)	42	7,000 tons	110m x 10m x 9m	Nuclear, 25+ knots	145	1976
Major Amphibious Units							
Amph Assault Ship – LHD	**WASP** (LHD-1)	8[3]	41,000 tons	253m x 32/42m x 9m	Steam, 20+ knots	1,100	1989
Amph Assault Ship – LHD	**TARAWA** (LHA-1)	1	40,000 tons	250m x 32/38m x 8m	Steam, 24 knots	975	1976
Landing Platform Dock – LPD	**SAN ANTONIO** (LPD-17)	6	25,000 tons	209m x 32m x 7m	Diesel, 22+ knots	360	2005
Landing Platform Dock – LPD	**AUSTIN** (LPD-4)	1[4]	17,000 tons	171m x 25m x 7m	Steam, 21 knots	420	1965
Landing Ship Dock – LSD	**WHIDBEY ISLAND** (LSD-41)	12[5]	16,000 tons	186m x 26m x 6m	Diesel, 20 knots	420	1985

Notes:

1 Plus mission-related crew.   **2** Third of class, SSN-23 is longer and heavier.   **3** LHD-8 has many differences.
4 In addition, PONCE has been converted to an interim AFSB   **5** Includes four LSD-49 HARPERS FERRY variants.

trials in May and with *Coronado* (LCS-4) christened on 14 January 2012. The seaworthiness and general suitability of the two prototype lead ships has continued to attract criticism, with *Freedom* (LCS-1) suffering structural problems and leaks that put her in dock for much of the past year. However, she subsequently passed a special INSURV inspection between 22 and 24 May 2012 following completion of remediation work, and was declared fit for duty prior to her planned deployment to Singapore in 2013.[9] In the longer term, the LCS-1 type's excellent manoeuvrability could see it being deployed to the enclosed waters of the Gulf and less-developed port facilities of Africa, with the greater endurance and aviation capabilities of the LCS-2 type making it more suitable for the open spaces of the Pacific.

Amphibious Shipping: The amphibious force has suffered notable shrinkage over the past year, as the last elderly *Austin* (LPD-4) class amphibious transport docks have fallen due for retirement. *Cleveland* (LPD-7) and *Dubuque* (LPD-8) were both decommissioned during 2011 but *Ponce* (LPD-15) received a last minute reprieve. She has been converted as an interim afloat forward staging base prior to completion of purpose-built construction, departing Norfolk, Virginia on 1 June 2012 for African waters and her new assignment with the US Central Command. This leaves just *Denver* (LPD-9) of the original twelve-strong class serving in her designed role.

The replacement *San Antonio* (LPD-17) class seem to be leaving past construction problems behind, but completion is not quite keeping pace with the rate of withdrawals of the older ships. The sixth member of the class, *San Diego* (LPD-22), was commissioned on 19 May 2012, whilst *Anchorage* (LPD-23) has finished builders' sea trials and should be delivered before year-end. A further three ships are currently in various stages of construction, with *Somerset* (LPD-25) launched from HII's Avondale yard on 14 April 2012. She is likely to be the final ship built at the Texas facility, which will close when the ship is completed. Authorisation for the eleventh and final class member was included in the FY2013 budget request but she will be built at the company's Pascagoula, Mississippi, facility, where the group's non-nuclear shipbuilding activities are being concentrated.

In the meantime, HHI received a US$2.4bn contract on 31 May 2012 to construct the second

The former amphibious transport dock *Ponce* (AFSB(I)-15) has been converted as an interim afloat forward staging base prior to the completion of new mobile landing platforms. She is seen here departing Norfolk Virginia on 1 June 2012 on deployment to African waters. *(US Navy)*

The LPD-17 amphibious transport dock programme seems to have left previous construction problems behind it and new ships are being completed at regular intervals. This is pre-commissioning unit *Anchorage* (LPD-23) on trials in May 2012. *(Huntington Ingalls Industries)*

A graphic of the mobile landing platform intended to facilitate the transfer of US troops and equipment from transport vessels to the shore along with a picture of the new Austal-built joint high speed vessel *Spearhead* (JHSV-1) that will make use of the concept. The latter programme has been truncated at ten vessels due to budget cuts. *(General Dynamics NASSCO, Austal)*

America (LHA-6) amphibious assault ship, which will be named *Tripoli* (LHA-7). In contrast to earlier ships of the type, the two new ships sacrifice their well deck for an enhanced aviation capability, including F-35B joint strike fighters and V-22 Osprey tilt rotors. With a full load displacement of c.45,000 tons and a length of 257m, the ships exceed that of most other countries' aircraft carriers, approaching the British Royal Navy's new *Queen Elizabeth* class in size. The lead ship is running behind her original construction schedule but was launched on 4 June 2012 for delivery around the end of 2014. Construction of the third ship in the class, the unnamed LHA-8, has been deferred to FY2017. She is to be redesigned to reinstate the internal docking capability.

Orders have also been placed for the first two specialised mobile landing platforms, which will be named *Montford Point* (T-MPL-1) and *John Glenn* (T-MPL-2). The former ship's keel was laid on 19 January 2012 at General Dynamics' NASSCO yard in San Diego and is likely to be operational by 2015. Based on a commercial 'Alaska' class tanker design, the new ships will be operated by the Military Sealift Command and are intended to facilitate the transfer of equipment and troops from transport vessels such as the joint high speed vessels and roll-on/roll-off ships to the shore by acting as a staging hub for landing craft air cushion (LCAC) operations. Three LCAC lanes are provided in the initial design, which could be extended, e.g. to support helicopter operations. Meanwhile, the truncated JHSV programme

is also starting to deliver results, with the first ship *Spearhead* (JHSV-1) completing builders' trials in April 2012, prior to delivery to the military sealift command in the second half of the year. Orders for the sixth and seventh vessels of the US$1.6bn ten-ship programme were finalised on 30 June 2011, with contracts for JHSV-8 and JHSV-9 following in February 2012.

Submarines: The construction of the *Virginia* (SSN-774) class nuclear-powered attack submarines continues to be one of the US Navy's major procurement success stories, with the boats being consistently delivered early and within budget. A new record was set with the ninth class member, *Mississippi* (SSN-782), which was delivered almost a year ahead of schedule by General Dynamics' Electric Boat division on 2 May 2012 prior to commissioning a month later on 2 June. Fabrication of *Minnesota* (SSN-783), the tenth boat and final Flight II unit, is also progressing well at Newport News in line with planned delivery in 2013. Focus will then switch to the revised Flight III type, which incorporate a revised bow sonar arrangement and twin multiple launch canisters instead of the individual launch tubes on earlier boats. The boats requested in the FY2013 budget will be the seventh and eighth Flight III submarines, all procured under a 'block-buy' multi-year procurement contract split between Electric Boat and Newport News. Subsequent orders will be for a slightly revised Flight

IV design prior to incorporation of further significant changes in a Flight V type around the end of the decade. These will attempt to replicate some of the firepower incorporated in the modified *Ohio* (SSGN-726) guided missile submarines through installation of a c.30m Virginia Payload Module (VPM) containing four additional, larger-diameter launch tubes for up to twenty-eight additional Tomahawk cruise missiles or equivalent. Replacement of the fourteen remaining *Ohio* class submarines retaining their original strategic deterrent role is also being considered, although the FY2013 budget has pushed back funding for the first boat until 2021. The so-called SSBN(X) type will feature a common missile compartment that will also be installed in the United Kingdom's *Vanguard* class 'Successor' replacements.

Pending the arrival of more *Virginia* class boats, the remaining, modernised *Los Angeles* (SSN-688) class submarines continue to comprise the core of the US Navy's underwater capabilities. Numbers have remained stable over the past year but there were initial fears that *Miami* (SSN-755) might be declared a total loss following a severe fire in her forward sections on 23 May 2012 shortly after she commenced refit at Portsmouth Naval Shipyard in Maine. The blaze was extinguished with only minor injuries to firefighters and, although damage was extensive at an estimated US$400m, the fact that the nuclear power plant was unscathed suggests repair will be cost-effective.

Operationally, the US Navy has remained extremely busy over the past year in spite of the absence of naval missions of similar intensity to the initial March 2011 strikes on Gadaffi loyalist forces in Libya. In addition to the increased commitments involved in the so-called 'pivot to the Pacific', continued tensions arising from Iran's nuclear ambitions have kept naval forces in the Gulf region on high alert. Indeed, some concerns have been raised about the extent to which cannibalisation has been used to maintain operational effectiveness, a clear sign of a fleet under short-term pressure. In addition to day-to-day tasking, considerable effort continues to be expended in support of longer-term objectives, most notably the missile defence programme. This has included tests of the more capable Block 1B variant of the Standard SM-3 ballistic missile interceptor. The new missile carried out its first successful interception of a target weapon from the cruiser *Lake Erie* (CG-70) on 9 May 2012 after a rare failure in its first trial the preceding September. At the other end of the scale, *Jane's Defence Weekly* has reported the creation of a new US Navy Coastal Riverine Force (CORIVFOR) from previous riverine and expeditionary security force components as a bridge between sea- and land-based operations.[10]

The US Coast Guard's recapitalisation plans continue to move forward. Steady arrival of the new *Bertholf* (WMSL-750) 'Legend' class national security cutters is allowing a start to be made on withdrawing the 1960s vintage *Hamilton* (WHEC-715) class. However, a reduction in planned orders from eight to six ships could result in a capability gap at the 'high end' of the Coast Guard's fleet.[11] At the other end of the spectrum, the first new 'Sentinel' fast response cutter *Bernard C Webber* (WPC-1101) was commissioned on 14 April 2012. A further eleven of the type are under construction or on order from Bollinger Shipyards following exercise of an option for a further four in September 2011 and up to fifty-eight may eventually be built. Based on the Dutch Stan 4708 design, they displace around 350 tons, have a maximum speed of 28 knots and are armed with a 25mm chain gun and heavy machine guns. Progress has also been made towards soliciting a request for proposals on the intermediate Offshore Patrol Cutter, which is likely to have a similar armament to the 'Legend' class but a simpler diesel or diesel-electric propulsion plant. Up to US$8bn could be spent on building up to twenty-five ships to the design that is ultimately selected.

OTHER NORTH AND CENTRAL AMERICAN NAVIES

Only the *Armada de México* has any real significance amongst the other remaining North and Central American naval forces. Its attentions are being increasingly focused on domestic concerns as it becomes more and more drawn in to combating the country's endemic organised crime problem. This has extended to significant internal policing operations, most notably the temporary assumption of naval control over the port city of Veracruz in December 2011 following disbandment of the local police department as part of moves to root out corruption. Whilst a small flotilla of elderly former US Navy frigates provides some limited war-fighting capabilities, it is inevitable that recent investment has been focused on modernising constabulary assets. There is considerable focus on local construction, with recent deliveries of *Oaxaca* class patrol boats now being supplemented by a class of indigenous 3,500-ton logistical support ships of LST type appearance. The

The *Los Angeles* (SSN-688) class submarine *Miami* (SSN-755) seen entering Portsmouth Naval Shipyard in Maine on 15 March 2012 for a scheduled overhaul. A subsequent fire on 23 May 2012 caused an estimated US$400m of damage to the boat's forward sections. *(US Navy)*

The Mexican frigate *Hermenegildo Galeana*, the former US Navy *Bronstein* (FF-1037), pictured from the US Navy's *Independence* (LCS-2) on 28 April 2012 whilst the two ships were exercising together. Whilst the Mexican Navy maintains a token force of front-line warships, most current investment is being directed towards constabulary assets. *(US Navy)*

first of the new ships, *Montes Azules,* was launched in August 2011 and commissioned the following February. The keel for a second vessel was laid on the same day the first ship was launched. Continued deliveries of licence-built 'Polaris' CB-90 type fast assault craft are also being made, whilst the navy's aviation branch has obtained four CN-235-300 Persuader maritime patrol aircraft from EADS under a c.US$150m US Foreign Military Sales agreement.

MAJOR SOUTH AMERICAN NAVIES – ARGENTINA

In spite of increased rhetoric over the long running Falkland Islands dispute and a marked increase in government defence spending, Table 2.1.6 indicates that there has been no change to the main constituents of the *Armada Argentina* year-on-year. To an extent, this reflects the need to refurbish existing assets and the supporting infrastructure of the Argentine Naval Industrial Complex (CINAR) after years of neglect, particularly as development of local yards is a key government objective. An important indication of progress in this area is expected by the end of 2012, when the TR-1700 patrol submarine *San Juan* should complete sea trials following a lengthy refit at the Astillero Almirante Storni facility. There are ongoing reports that her unfinished sister, *Santa Fe,* will then enter the yard for completion, possibly even as a test bed for a mooted nuclear propulsion plant. The technical – and financial – challenges such a programme would present are enormous and possibly beyond the capacity of Argentina's economy.

Also expected to return to operational service during 2012 is the fire-damaged ice breaker *Almirante Irizar,* which is close to completing a protracted period of repair and modernisation at the Tandanor yard. Current plans envisage that she will be completed for deployment during the 2012/13 Antarctic summer, although recent reports suggest

there have been problems refurbishing her elderly radar system. Funding is in place for the yard to commence construction of the German Fassmer-designed OPV80 offshore patrol vessels that were approved back in 2010 but contracts had not been finalised as of mid-year.

MAJOR SOUTH AMERICAN NAVIES – BRAZIL

The principal units of the *Marina do Brasil* are set out in Table 2.1.7. The country's main current procurement effort is the PROSUB (*Programa de Desenvolvimento de Submarinos*) programme to replace its submarine fleet with French-designed Scorpène type boats under an agreement announced in December 2008. The transaction includes four stretched, diesel-electric 'Scorpène' variants and a nuclear-powered derivative with an entirely Brazilian-developed nuclear plant. Work on the aft section of the first submarine commenced at the local Itaguaí Construções Navais joint venture between France's DCNS and Brazil's Odebrecht in July 2011. The forward section is being constructed by DCNS in Cherbourg and will be shipped to Brazil towards the end of 2012 to allow assembly to be completed.

The above-water counterpart to PROSUB is PROSUPER (*Programa de Obtenção de Meios de Superfície*), the programme to recapitalise Brazil's increasingly elderly surface fleet. Original plans envisaged the acquisition of five surface escorts, five oceanic patrol vessels and a replenishment ship in conjunction with an overseas partner as the initial phase of a longer-term twenty-year strategic maritime plan. However, it seems that the plan may be split into several parts following the January 2012 announcement that Brazil has acquired three offshore patrol vessels built in the United Kingdom for Trinidad and Tobago by BAE Systems. These had been put up for sale after political changes in the Caribbean state. The £133m (US$205m) deal will

see two of the vessels delivered in 2012 and the last in 2013 following completion to Brazilian specifications.[12] Whilst not officially changing the overall scope of PROSUPER, the transaction could also see the oceanic patrol vessel part of the programme met by licence-built production of the type in a Brazilian yard. BAE is also pitching its Type 26 global surface combatant for Brazil's surface escort requirement.

The Brazilian Navy also has an active programme of construction of smaller, 500-ton patrol vessels that are being licence built to CMN's 'Vigilante' 400 design. Two ships – *Macaé* and *Macau* – have already been completed and a further four are at various stages of construction. An additional contract for a seventh vessel was ordered at the end of 2011. Maritime patrol activities are being further enhanced by modernisation of air force P-3 Orion aircraft under an agreement with Airbus.

Operationally, the Brazilian Navy is becoming increasingly ambitious in the extent of its deployments, doubtless reflecting a broader national agenda to enhance Brazil's global status. There has been a particularly significant commitment to the maritime component of the United Nations' UNIFIL stabilisation mission in Lebanon. Following assumption of command of the UN's maritime task force in the region early in 2011, Brazil has despatched two frigates to support the mission, with *Liberal* replacing *Uniäo* on station in May 2012. Less positively, Brazil's presence in the Antarctic suffered a setback in February 2012 when an explosion and fire seriously damaged the country's naval-manned research base in the region, killing two naval personnel.[13]

MAJOR SOUTH AMERICAN NAVIES – CHILE

Chile's principal units are listed in Table 2.1.8.

The *Armada de Chile* remains one of the most proficient in the region following the wholesale

Table 2.1.6: ARGENTINE NAVY: PRINCIPAL UNITS AS AT MID 2012

TYPE	CLASS	NUMBER	TONNAGE	DIMENSIONS	PROPULSION	CREW	DATE
Principal Surface Escorts							
Destroyer – DDG	**ALMIRANTE BROWN** (MEKO 360)	4	3,600 tons	126m x 14m x 4m	COGOG, 30 knots	200	1983
Frigate – FFG	**ESPORA** (MEKO 140)	6	1,800 tons	91m x 11m x 3m	Diesel, 27 knots	100	1985
Corvette – FSG	**DRUMMOND** (A-69)	3	1,200 tons	80m x 10m x 3m	Diesel, 24 knots	95	1978
Submarines							
Submarine – SSK	**SANTA CRUZ** (TR 1700)	2	2,300 tons	65m x 7m x 7m	Diesel-electric, 25 knots	30	1984
Submarine – SSK	**SALTA** (Type 209)	1	1,200 tons	54m x 6m x 6m	Diesel-electric, 22 knots	30	1974

Table 2.1.7: BRAZILIAN NAVY: PRINCIPAL UNITS AS AT MID 2012

TYPE	CLASS	NUMBER	TONNAGE	DIMENSIONS	PROPULSION	CREW	DATE
Aircraft Carriers							
Aircraft Carrier – CV	SÃO PAULO (FOCH)	1	33,500 tons	265m x 32/51m x 9m	Steam, 30 knots	1,700	1963
Principal Surface Escorts							
Frigate – FFG	GREENHALGH (Batch I Type 22)	3	4,700 tons	131m x 15m x 4m	COGOG, 30 knots	270	1979
Frigate – FFG	NITERÓI	6	3,700 tons	129m x 14m x 4m	CODOG, 30 knots	220	1976
Corvette – FSG	INHAÚMA	4	2,100 tons	96m x 11m x 4m	CODOG, 27 knots	120	1989
Corvette – FSG	BARROSO	1	2,400 tons	103m x 11m x 4m	CODOG, 30 knots	145	2008
Submarines							
Submarine – SSK	TIKUNA (Type 209 – modified)	1	1,600 tons	62m x 6m x 6m	Diesel-electric, 22 knots	40	2005
Submarine – SSK	TUPI (Type 209)	4	1,500 tons	61m x 6m x 6m	Diesel-electric, 22+ knots	30	1989
Major Amphibious Units							
Landing Ship Dock – LSD	CEARÁ (LSD-28)	2	12,000 tons	156m x 26m x 6m	Steam, 22 knots	345	1956

Brazil's *Niteroi* class frigate *Independência* in May 2012. Members of the class are being deployed to the Mediterranean to participate in the United Nation's maritime task force off Lebanon in a sign of the leading Latin American navy's growing ambitions. *(US Navy)*

Brazil has purchased the three *Port of Spain* offshore patrol vessels initially built by the UK's BAE Systems for Trinidad and Tobago. This picture of *Port of Spain* – reportedly to be renamed *Amazonas* – was taken in November 2011 before the ships received Brazilian colours. *(Conrad Waters)*

Table 2.1.8: CHILEAN NAVY: PRINCIPAL UNITS AS AT MID 2012

TYPE	CLASS	NUMBER	TONNAGE	DIMENSIONS	PROPULSION	CREW	DATE
Principal Surface Escorts							
Frigate – FFG	ALMIRANTE WILLIAMS (Batch II Type 22)	1	5,500 tons	148m x 14m x 5m	COGOG, 30+ knots	260	1988
Frigate – FFG	ALMIRANTE COCHRANE (Type 23)	3	4,800 tons	133m x 16m x 5m	CODLAG, 28 knots	185	1990
Frigate – FFG	CAPITÁN PRAT (L class)	2	3,800 tons	131m x 15m x 4m	COGOG, 30 knots	200	1986
Frigate – FFG	ALMIRANTE RIVEROS (M class)	2	3,300 tons	122m x 14m x 4m	CODOG, 30 knots	160	1992
Submarines							
Submarine – SSK	O'HIGGINS ('Scorpène')	2	1,700 tons	66m x 6m x 6m	Diesel-electric, 22 knots	30	2005
Submarine – SSK	THOMSON (Type 209)	2	1,400 tons	60m x 6m x 6m	Diesel-electric, 22 knots	35	1984
Major Amphibious Units							
Landing Platform Dock – LPD	SARGENTO ALDEA (FOUDRE)	1	12,000 tons	168m x 24m x 5m	Diesel, 20 knots	225	1990

The Peruvian Type 209 submarine *Antofagasta* docking at US Naval Submarine Base King's Bay on 20 September 2011. Peru may turn to Korea for modernisation of her ageing submarine force. *(US Navy)*

Colombia is contemplating an expansion of its underwater arm through the purchase of two of the German Type 206A submarines that were prematurely decommissioned in 2010. These would complement her existing pair of Type 209 boats of similar vintage. This picture shows *U15* shortly before decommissioning. *(German Navy)*

modernisation of surface and submarine forces over the last decade supported by so-called 'Copper Law' funds.[14] The recent focus has therefore been on strengthening other naval capabilities, most notably the recapitalisation of the amphibious flotilla through the purchase of the surplus French amphibious transport dock *Foudre*. She was transferred at the end of 2011, being welcomed to her new home in March 2012 by a presidential reception. She has taken the name *Sargento Aldea* in Chilean service. Chile's long coastline and vulnerability to tsunamis means that she will have an important secondary role as a relief vessel. The navy has also been acquiring additional helicopters to operate from the new ship, with two additional Eurocopter AS332L Super Pumas joining the naval aviation branch in May to boost the existing five-strong Super Puma/Cougar fleet.

Offshore surveillance assets are also being strengthened. Work has started on a third Fassmer OPV80 type offshore patrol vessel of the *Piloto Pardo* class following signature of a contract with the local ASMAR yard on 27 December 2011. The new

ship is scheduled for delivery in 2014 and will feature improvements over the existing ships, including a larger 76mm gun and a reinforced hull to aid Antarctic operations. Modernisation work also continues on other vessels, including improvements to the trio of Type 23 frigates acquired second-hand from the British Royal Navy. Enhancements planned include upgrades to the Type 911 tracking radars used in conjunction with the Seawolf missile system, as well as procurement of Thales Type 2087 CAPTAS-4 towed arrays.

MAJOR SOUTH AMERICAN NAVIES – PERU

There has been little in the way of material developments with respect to *Marina de Guerra de Perú* in recent years and Table 2.1.9 continues to show a static position. Recent procurement has focused on the modernisation of existing assets, expansion of aerial maritime patrol assets and acquisition of Griffon 2000TD hovercraft to patrol the country's Amazonian borders with Brazil. In January 2012, Griffon Hoverwork announced that it had received

an order for five more of the craft, which are able to transport a two-ton payload at up to 35 knots. This increases Peru's total inventory of the type to seven.

An interesting announcement from Korea's Daewoo Shipbuilding and Marine Engineering (DSME) in April 2012 could, however, herald a more active procurement policy. It was reported that the company had signed a memorandum of understanding with the Peruvian defence ministry that put it in pole position to be selected for joint construction of new submarines and logistic support vessels. The announcement is logical in the context of DSME's recent export successes for both types of vessel and Peru's position as Latin America's largest submarine operator.

OTHER SOUTH AMERICAN NAVIES

Of the other Latin American Navies, **Columbia** continues to have the most active procurement programme.[15] The country currently has the second largest defence budget in South America after Brazil. Whilst most of this is devoted to land-based forces (including over 20,000 Marines), enough funding

Table 2.1.9: PERUVIAN NAVY: PRINCIPAL UNITS AS AT MID 2012

TYPE	CLASS	NUMBER	TONNAGE	DIMENSIONS	PROPULSION	CREW	DATE
Principal Surface Escorts							
Cruiser – CL	ALMIRANTE GRAU (DE RUYTER)	1	12,200 tons	187m x 17m x 7m	Steam, 32 knots	950	1953
Frigate – FFG	CARVAJAL (LUPO)	8	2,500 tons	112m x 12m x 4m	CODOG, 35 knots	185	1977
Submarines							
Submarine – SSK	ANGAMOS (Type 209)	6	1,200 tons	54m x 6m x 6m	Diesel-electric, 22 knots	30	1980

has been available to support ongoing modernisation of existing assets and some significant acquisition projects. The most interesting recent development has been the possible acquisition of two of the German Type 206A coastal patrol submarines that were prematurely decommissioned in August 2010 and which have previously been subject to abortive sale discussion with Thailand. The boats would reinforce the two existing German-built Type 209 submarines of similar vintage already in Colombia's inventory. Meanwhile, domestic construction of Fassmer OPV80 type vessels has made satisfactory progress, with *20 de Julio,* commissioned in February 2012. She is the first of a planned total of between four and six ships, with fabrication of the second already reportedly well advanced at the COTECMAR shipyard. Whilst German companies appear to be gaining the lion's share of modernisation work, Colombia is another market where Korean naval industries are attempting to expand. The reported gift of a decommissioned Korean *Po*

Hang class corvette, the former *Kun San*, is apparently part of moves to strengthen the country's local market position.

Neighbouring **Venezuela** has now received all four of the 2,400-ton POVZEE oceanic patrol vessels ordered from Navantia with the arrival of *Kariña* in May 2012 following delivery on 23 April. Three of the four smaller 1,500 ton 'BVL' littoral patrol vessels have also been handed over but there have been tough discussions as to whether the local Dianca yard has the technical capability to complete the in-country build of the fourth vessel, *Tamanaco.* A further unit of each type may be ordered if a satisfactory conclusion is reached. The *Armada Nacional Bolivariana de Venezuela* is also taking delivery of logistic landing ships from the Dutch Damen group's Cuban affiliate. The second Type 209 submarine modernisation should be completed with the recommissioning of *Caribé* around the end of the year, whilst the long-discussed acquisition of new Russian-built boats is apparently attracting renewed attention.

Spanish yard Navantia's construction of offshore patrol vessels for Venezuela is coming to an end with the delivery of the fourth and final POVZEE type vessel *Kariña* in Spain on 23 April 2012. These images show here subsequent arrival in Venezuela in May. Three smaller BVL littoral patrol vessels have also been delivered from Spain, whilst debate continues over local completion of a fourth ship. *(Navantia)*

Notes:

1. Mastering the complexities of US defence and security budgeting, with expenditure split between several accounts and with war costs allocated to a separate 'Overseas Contingency Operations' (OCO) heading, is not for the faint-hearted. However, a good summary of the background to the FY2013 budget request is provided by Stephen Dagett and Pat Towell in their *FY2013 Defense Budget Request: Overview and Context* (Washington DC, Congressional Research Service, 2012). Figures quoted here relate to the base Department of Defense budget, excluding OCO.

2. The reasons for the structure of the sequestration process are far beyond this book's scope. It reflects a compromise solution to the need to slow the growth in US government debt in the face of deep political divisions as to whether this should be achieved by tax rises or by spending cuts.

3. A good overview of the current military balance in the South Atlantic is provided by Tim Ripley in 'A New South Atlantic War?', *Jane's Defence Weekly* – 28 March 2012 (Couldson, IHS Jane's, 2012), pp.22–3.

4. The first four *Halifax* class frigates undergoing refit and modernisation (*Halifax, Calgary, Fredericton* and *Winnipeg*) will receive additional upgrades to accommodation and communications systems to undertake the command and control functions currently exercised by *Iroquois* class pending delivery of replacement surface combatants.

5. Please refer to *Annual Report to Congress on Long-*

Range Plan for Construction of Naval Vessels for FY2013 (Washington DC, Office of the Chief of Naval Operations, 2012). Following legislative action, this report is again being produced every year. A useful analysis of the plan is contained in Ronald O'Rourke's regularly updated *Navy Force Structure and Shipbuilding Plans: Background and Issues for Congress* (Washington DC, Congressional Research Service). Mr O'Rourke, a Congressional Research Office specialist in naval affairs, produces regular reports on US Navy programmes and other issues that can be accessed via the Federation of American Scientist's website at http://www.fas.org/sgp/crs/. Amongst recent reports at the time of writing was a fascinating study on US Navy ship-naming conventions.

6. Although the ship was structurally well-advanced at this time, the seventy-five per cent figure does not reflect the considerable outfitting and integration work still requiring completion.

7. More detail on the potential problems associated with the Flight III DDG-51 design is contained in Michael Fabey's 'Flight Fight: Cost, schedule challenges rock US Navy's DDG-51 Flight III program', *Defense Technology International* – May 2012 (Washington, The McGraw-Hill Companies Inc, 2012), pp.36–7.

8. The DDG-1000 is being built to a modular design, with much sub-system work subcontracted to other contractors. For example, Ingalls Shipbuilding is fabricating the ship's composite superstructure modules in Mississippi before shipping them to Maine. As such, a considerable amount

of work is completed before keel-laying takes place.

9. A full report on the INSURV examination and the issues behind it is found in Christopher P Cavas's 'Hunt says LCS Freedom is "fit for service"', *Navy Times* – 30 May 2012 (Springfield VA, Gannett Government Media, 2012).

10. More detail is provided in Kate Tringham's 'NECC creates Coastal Riverine Force', *Jane's Defence Weekly* – 23 May 2012 (Couldson, IHS Jane's, 2012), p.10.

11. Please refer to chapter 3.2 for a detailed review of the 'Legend' class national security cutter programme.

12. The new ships will reportedly take the names *Amazonas, Apa* and *Araguari* in Brazilian service. The first ship was delivered at Portsmouth on 29 June 2012.

13. For further reading, the Portuguese language Poder Naval website at www.naval.com.br remains an excellent source of information on Brazilian naval developments.

14. Chile's Copper Law mandates that 10 per cent of export revenues earned by state-owned copper company Coldelco should be earmarked for military procurement. The law is in the course of replacement by a more transparent funding mechanism.

15. The Spanish language *Base Naval* website at www.basenaval.com provides a broad range of press reports and other news from which some of the material used for this summary of the minor Latin American fleets has been drawn.

2.2 REGIONAL REVIEW

ASIA AND THE PACIFIC

Author: **Conrad Waters**

INTRODUCTION:

The ongoing advance in the capability and proficiency of China's People's Liberation Army Navy (PLAN) inevitably continues to drive the pace of naval developments in the Asia-Pacific region. The most newsworthy event in the past year was undoubtedly the long-awaited emergence of the former Soviet carrier *Varyag*, reportedly renamed *Shi Lang*, from Dalian on preliminary sea trials on 10 August 2011. Finally proving China's ambitions to deploy a carrier strike force, the short four-day trial has been succeeded by several more, each interspersed with bouts of further outfitting and remediation activity. In truth, *Varyag's* progress towards delivery has more of a symbolic than tangible impact on the balance of naval power in the region; the more so given that many commentators doubt she will ever enter full operational service. Of much greater consequence is the conspicuous productivity of China's broader shipbuilding industry. Here a second batch of Type 052C *Lanzhou* class air-defence destroyers and an entirely new Type 056 littoral corvette class are supplementing ongoing production of general purpose frigates and increasingly advanced patrol submarines.

The key question remains China's intended use of its new-found naval prowess. Certainly, the contrasting trajectory of the PLAN's rising ambitions with the steady decline of the traditional European maritime powers that are increasingly focusing on constabulary 'soft power' projection is noteworthy. As recently noted by one pair of leading PLAN analysts, 'As one civilization vacates the

oceans, another is crowding the seas and skies with ships and warplanes that bristle with offensively oriented weaponry'.[1] Unsurprisingly, therefore, the last twelve months have seen continued tensions in disputed areas of the resource-rich South China Seas. These have included a naval stand-off between China and the Philippines during April 2012 over alleged illegal fishing in waters around Scarborough Shoal. There have also been reports of harassment of US and Indian naval vessels in international waters close to Vietnam. One consequence has been a growth in links between a number of Asian nations and the United States as the latter implements its 'Pivot to the Pacific' already highlighted in the opening chapter. President Barack Obama's call in June 2012 for clear rules to resolve maritime disputes in the South China Seas was just one further sign of US resolve to counterbalance perceived Chinese expansionary inclinations.[2] Another result has been an overall rise in collective regional defence expenditure as China's neighbours have sought to boost their own capabilities, particularly in the maritime domain. The relative resilience of the Asian economies during the world's economic troubles has supported this trend.

The growth in Asian economic – and maritime – influence is also accelerating a trend touched upon in the inaugural *Seaforth World Naval Review* of 2010. This is the emergence of Asian shipyards as significant producers of naval vessels for both domestic and export markets as the region's indigenous technological capabilities expand. Although not yet approaching Asia's dominance in the field of

merchant shipping construction, the last year has provided clear evidence that a number of Asian countries are now forces to be reckoned with as warship manufacturers.

At one end of the spectrum, the Chinese shipbuilding industry is becoming adept at finding a market for inexpensive, if relatively unsophisticated, surface vessels. For example, the first half of 2012 saw contracts announced with both Algeria and Nigeria for, respectively, light frigates and offshore patrol vessels. These vessels added to previous similar orders from Pakistan, Bangladesh and Namibia. Moreover, Asian yards are also gaining a reputation for construction of more sophisticated warships. This has, perhaps, been most clearly demonstrated by Indonesia's December 2011 selection of neighbouring South Korea's Daewoo Shipbuilding and Marine Engineering (DSME) in preference to European and Russian facilities to build new Type 209 submarines. Singapore's much smaller shipbuilding industry has also had its successes. The delivery of an *Endurance* class amphibious transport dock to the Royal Thai Navy on 3 April 2012 was swiftly followed by ST Marine's announcement of an order for four advanced 75m offshore patrol vessels from Oman. Interestingly, Singapore beat off competition from Dutch and Indian yards to secure the contract. Whilst Europe's naval construction sector still enjoys an edge with respect to exports of the most advanced warship types, the steady progress of Asia's maritime sway is evident here, as elsewhere.

Table 2.2.1 provides a summary of the more significant regional fleets as of mid 2012.

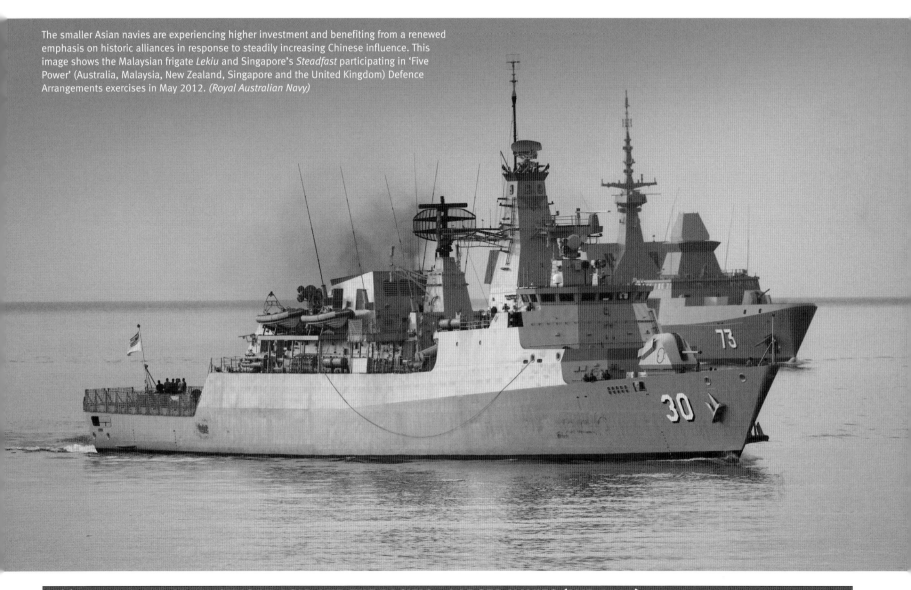

The smaller Asian navies are experiencing higher investment and benefiting from a renewed emphasis on historic alliances in response to steadily increasing Chinese influence. This image shows the Malaysian frigate *Lekiu* and Singapore's *Steadfast* participating in 'Five Power' (Australia, Malaysia, New Zealand, Singapore and the United Kingdom) Defence Arrangements exercises in May 2012. *(Royal Australian Navy)*

Table 2.2.1: FLEET STRENGTHS IN ASIA AND THE PACIFIC – LARGER NAVIES (MID 2012)

COUNTRY	AUSTRALIA	CHINA	INDONESIA	JAPAN	S KOREA	SINGAPORE	TAIWAN	THAILAND
Support/Helicopter Carrier (CVS/CVH)	–	–	–	2	–	–	–	1
Strategic Missile Submarine (SSBN)	–	3	–	–	–	–	–	–
Attack Submarine (SSN)	–	5	–	–	–	–	–	–
Patrol Submarine (SSK/SS)	6	55	2	16	12	5	4	–
Fleet Escort (DDG/FFG)	12	55	6	40	20	6	26	8
Patrol Escort/Corvette (FFG/FSG/FS)	–	25	24	6	21	6	–	11
Missile Armed Attack Craft (PGG/PTG)	–	75	8	6	9	–	c.50	6
Mine Countermeasures Vessel (MCMV)	6	20	12	30	9	4	8	6
Major Amphibious Units (LHD/LPD/LSD)	–	3	5	3	1	4	1	1

Note: Chinese numbers approximate; Taiwanese fast attack craft numbers are fluctuating as new KH-6 class replaces many of the existing 'Hai Ou' type.

In spite of recent defence spending reductions, the Royal Australian Navy is benefiting from upgrades to existing units that have already been approved, including the extension of anti-ship missile defence upgrades to all eight *Anzac* class frigates. This image shows the prototype conversion, *Perth*, visiting San Francisco in June 2012. In addition to the prominent CEAFAR radar system, some non-standard garden furniture can be seen on the upper deck! *(Mrityunjoy Mazumdar)*

MAJOR REGIONAL POWERS – AUSTRALIA:

The Royal Australian Navy's recent development has been governed by Australia's 2009 White Paper on defence and the 'Force 2030' structure contained therein. This included plans for a doubling of the submarine flotilla to twelve boats (project SEA 1000); the replacement of the *Anzac* class frigates on a one-for-one basis (project SEA 5000); and the construction of twenty smaller offshore combatants for constabulary patrol and mine warfare roles (project SEA 1180). These ambitious requirements supplemented previous orders for three F-100-derived *Hobart* class air-warfare destroyers and two *Juan Carlos I* type amphibious assault ships. If achieved in its entirety, the naval element of 'Force 2030' would undoubtedly maintain the Royal Australian Navy's position as a leading Asian fleet.

However, events in the past year make it increasingly unlikely that the naval force structure envisaged in 2009 will be achieved. In May 2012, the Australian government announced significant defence spending reductions as part of efforts to balance the federal budget. These included an immediate real-terms cut of around 10 per cent in the 2012 defence budget; the deletion of a total A$5.5bn (US$5.5bn) from previous spending plans over four years and a further reallocation of A$2.9bn (US$2.9bn) of funds within the military account to meet emerging cost pressures.[3] The majority of the cuts will fall on procurement expenditure. The government also announced that it would advance production of a new Defence White Paper to 2013, when major changes to the 2009 blueprint are likely to be revealed.

The former British Royal Fleet Auxiliary *Largs Bay* was recommissioned as *Choules* on 13 December 2011, providing a major upgrade to Australia's depleted amphibious fleet. This picture shows the ship operating landing craft from her well deck during exercises in March 2012. The newly-installed helicopter shelter is also evident. *(Royal Australian Navy)*

Table 2.2.2: ROYAL AUSTRALIAN NAVY: PRINCIPAL UNITS AS AT MID 2012

TYPE	CLASS	NUMBER	TONNAGE	DIMENSIONS	PROPULSION	CREW	DATE
Principal Surface Escorts							
Frigate – FFG	**ADELAIDE** (FFG-7)	4	4,200 tons	138m x 14m x 5m	COGAG, 30 knots	210	1980
Frigate – FFG	**ANZAC**	8	3,600 tons	118m x 15m x 4m	CODOG, 28 knots	175	1996
Submarines							
Submarine – SSK	**COLLINS**	6	3,400 tons	78m x 8m x 7m	Diesel-electric, 20 knots	45	1996

In the short term, the Royal Australian Navy has emerged comparatively unscathed from the immediate reductions. Indeed, it has even the equivalent of almost US$1bn over four years redirected to its maintenance accounts. This will boost sustainment of the existing force of somewhat troubled *Collins* class submarines and improve overall fleet availability, which has been a problem in recent years. The fleet structure outlined in Table 2.2.2 should therefore benefit from improvements in overall availability.[4]

The navy is also starting to benefit from upgrades to existing units that have already been approved. The most notable of these is the November 2011 decision to extend the ASMD anti-ship missile defence upgrades under Project SEA 1448 Phase 2 to all eight *Anzac* frigates by 2017. This followed successful trials of the locally-developed CEAFAR active phased array and associated CEAMOUNT illuminators on *Perth*. The modification allows simultaneous engagement of multiple airborne targets compared with the single channel of fire currently available. Other recent enhancements have included the delivery of the former British Royal Fleet Auxiliary's dock landing ship *Largs Bay*. She was recommissioned as *Choules* on 13 December 2011.[5] The amphibious flotilla will also gain temporary use of the offshore support vessel *Skandi Bergen* pending arrival of the two new amphibious assault ships from 2014 onwards. These additions provide a degree of compensation for the premature withdrawal of the two former *Newport* class amphibious transports. *Kanimbla,* the last of the pair in service, joined sister *Manoora* on the disposals list following decommissioning on 25 November 2011.

Construction of the amphibious assault ships, which are being built by Navantia in Spain before being barged to Australia for final outfitting, is reportedly progressing well. *Canberra,* the first of class, was launched in 2011 and should arrive in Australia for final outfitting by BAE Systems in Melbourne during the second half of 2012. Launch of sister ship *Adelaide* is scheduled for early July 2012. An order for twelve LCM-1E landing craft to operate from the new ships was awarded to Navantia in October 2011. Navantia has also gained additional block construction work for the *Hobart* class destroyers being constructed to its F-100 design following the problems that emerged in late 2010 with the central keel block being constructed at Melbourne. It will now undertake significant block construction work on the third and final ship,

mirroring the arrangement previously agreed for ship two. The initial problems have delayed *Hobart's* scheduled delivery. It is likely she will enter service around the end of 2015.

The longer-term outlook is much more uncertain following the lower priority accorded to defence that is apparent from the May 2012 announcement. The most significant element of the naval part of 'Force 2030' – perhaps, even, of the overall plan – is the renewal and expansion of the underwater force. This is potentially a hugely expensive undertaking. The Australian government explicitly confirmed its commitment to the programme at the time the defence reductions were announced and A$214m of funding for detailed design studies has been approved. However, expectations of the development of a specific Australian design have been watered down with the decision to invite DCNS, Navantia and ThyssenKrupp's HDW to submit modified versions of their existing submarines for consideration. Kockums, designer of the existing *Collins* class, will also undertake studies with respect to an updated version. These proposals will be considered against the option of an entirely new design. Cost and time considerations suggest an upgrade of an existing submarine is the most likely outcome.

MAJOR REGIONAL POWERS – CHINA:

The remarkable ambition of China's current warship construction programme has already been referenced in the opening remarks to this chapter, encompassing at least three classes of major surface combatant, submarines and other specialised shipping. The extent of work underway inevitably makes it difficult to keep track of the progress of individual projects. As such, Table 2.2.3 outlining principal fleet units should be regarded as giving only a broad indication of the current state of affairs. In addition, an assessment of the major projects currently underway is provided below.[6]

Major Surface Combatants: The PLAN currently has three classes of major surface vessel under construction covering air-defence, general purpose and littoral warfare requirements. The most potent are the air defence destroyers of the Type 052C 'Luyang II' class, of which *Lanzhou* is the lead ship. Two of the class were commissioned during 2004/5 as part of a programme comprising three alternate destroyer designs, after which there was a significant gap before further ships of the type started to be launched from 2010 onwards. There are at least four additional destroyers in this second batch, with a

Although media attention has focused on trials of the former Soviet aircraft carrier *Varyag*, modern destroyers and frigates such as the increasingly numerous Type 054A 'Jiangkai II' class form the core of the Chinese fleet. This picture shows *Chao Hu* in 2010 during her deployment to the Indian Ocean as part of China's fifth anti-piracy escort flotilla. *(NATO)*

Table 2.2.3: PEOPLE'S LIBERATION ARMY NAVY: PRINCIPAL UNITS AS AT MID 2012

TYPE	CLASS	NUMBER	TONNAGE	DIMENSIONS	PROPULSION	CREW	DATE
Principal Surface Escorts							
Destroyer – DDG	Type 051C **SHENYANG** ('Luzhou')	2	7,100 tons	155m x 17m x 6m	Steam, 29 knots	Unknown	2006
Destroyer – DDG	Type 052C **LANZHOU** ('Luyang II')	4	6,500 tons	154m x 17m x 6m	CODOG, 28 knots	280	2004
Destroyer – DDG	Type 052B **GUANGZHOU** ('Luyang I')	2	6,000 tons	154m x 17m x 6m	CODOG, 29 knots	280	2004
Destroyer – DDG	Project 956E/EM **HANGZHOU** (Sovremenny)	4	8,000 tons	156m x 17m x 6m	Steam, 32 knots	300	1999
Destroyer – DDG	Type 051B **SHENZHEN** ('Luhai')	1	6,000 tons	154m x 16m x 6m	Steam, 31 knots	250	1998
Destroyer – DDG	Type 052 **HARBIN** ('Luhu')	2	4,800 tons	143m x 15m x 5m	CODOG, 31 knots	260	1994
Plus c.10 additional obsolescent destroyers of Type 051 **JINAN** ('Luda') class							
Frigate – FFG	Type 054A **XUZHOU** ('Jiangkai II')	11	4,100 tons	132m x 15m x 5m	CODAD, 28 knots	190	2008
Frigate – FFG	Type 054 **MA'ANSHAN** ('Jiangkai I')	2	4,000 tons	132m x 15m x 5m	CODAD, 28 knots	190	2005
Frigate – FFG	Type 053 H2G/H3 **ANQING** ('Jiangwei I/II')	14	2,500 tons	112m x 12m x 5m	CODAD, 27 knots	170	1992
Plus c.25 additional obsolescent frigates of Type 053 H/H1/H1G/H2 **XIAMEN** ('Jianghu') classes							
Submarines							
Submarine – SSBN	Type 094 ('Jin')	2+	9,000 tons	133m x 11m x 8m	Nuclear, 20+ knots	Unknown	2008
Submarine – SSBN	Type 092 XIA ('Xia')	1	6,500 tons	120m x 10m x 8m	Nuclear, 22 knots	140	1987
Submarine – SSN	Type 093 ('Shang')	2+	6,000 tons	107m x 11m x 8m	Nuclear, 30 knots	100	2006
Submarine – SSN	Type 091 ('Han')	3	5,500 tons	106m x 10m x 7m	Nuclear, 25 knots	75	1974
Submarine – SSK	Type 039A/Type 041 ('Yuan')	8	2,500 tons	75m x 8m x 5m	AIP, 20+ knots	Unknown	2006
Submarine – SSK	Type 039/039G ('Song')	13	2,300 tons	75m x 8m x 5m	Diesel-electric, 22 knots	60	1999
Submarine – SSK	Project 877 EKM/636 ('Kilo')	12	3,000 tons	73m x 10m x 7m	Diesel-electric, 20 knots	55	1995
Plus c.20 obsolescent patrol submarines of the Project 033 ('Romeo' class) and Type 035 ('Ming' class) designs. A Type 039B/Type 43 'Qing' trials submarine has also been commissioned.							
Major Amphibious Units							
Landing Platform Dock	Type 071 **KULUN SHAN** ('Yuzhao')	3	18,000 tons	210m x 27m x 7m	CODAD, 20 knots	Unknown	2007

fifth ship in the early stages of fabrication possibly forming an improved Type 052D variant.

The backbone of the 'blue water' surface fleet is comprised of the Type 054A 'Jiangkai II' frigates, which have been in series production at two yards since the middle of the last decade. Eleven of the type were in commission as of mid 2012, with at least a further five at various stages of construction. The same Hudong-Zhonghua and Huangpu facilities are also starting to turn out the new Type 056 corvettes, which are likely to replace the elderly 'Jianghu' class frigates and supplement the Type 022 'Houbei' fast attack catamarans in defence of littoral waters. Images of the new ships suggest they will displace in the region of 1,000–1,500 tons and include a 76mm gun, surface-to-surface and point defence missile systems and landing facilities for an anti-submarine helicopter or unmanned aerial vehicles. At least four of the class were under construction as at June 2012, with the second ship, *Huizhou*, floated out at the start of the month. The programme supports contentions that the PLAN is as focused on devel-oping A2/AD capabilities in its littoral waters as much as pursuing broader oceanic ambitions.

Submarines: There has been a marked lack of tangible news in respect of China's nuclear-powered attack and strategic submarines since the emergence of the new Type 093 'Shang' and Type 094 'Jin' classes in the second half of the last decade. This has resulted in a number of commentators concluding that the PLAN has been dissatisfied with the performance of both types, suspending construction in favour of rumoured Type 095 and Type 096 vari-ants incorporating lessons learned from the earlier boats. If this assessment is correct, clearer evidence of the new classes is likely in the year ahead.

By way of contrast, delivery of conventional diesel-electric submarines has been maintained at round three units per annum, comprising incre-mental improvements of the established Type 039A/Type41 'Yuan' design. Around eight of the type are currently in service and production is likely to continue for a while yet to allow retirement of the obsolescent Type 035 'Ming' type to second line duties. Most construction is centred on the inland port of Wuhan, although the Jiangnang yard in Shanghai can also produce the type. The PLAN reportedly has around eight boats in each of the two patrol submarine flotillas assigned to the three main fleets. This suggests a total requirement of approxi-mately forty-eight modern boats against the thirty to thirty-five currently completed.

The effectiveness of the submarine force is also being boosted by the delivery of new submarine tenders, with two further Type 926 support vessels fitting out following completion of the first ship in 2010. The lead ship is equipped with a LR7 subma-rine rescue vehicle acquired from the United Kingdom, significantly enhancing the PLAN's ability to rescue stranded submariners at depths of 300m and more.

Other Warships: Although progress with the carrier *Shi Lang*'s refit is attracting the most headlines, the development of a much broader range of maritime capabilities is also being supported by new construction. For example, amphibious forces will soon be supplemented by the commissioning of a third Type 071 amphibious transport dock. Construction of a Type 081 amphibious assault ship that appears broadly similar in size and capability to France's *Mistral* type has also been reported. Other programmes include additional replenishment vessels, whilst mine-warfare capabilities are getting a much-needed enhancement with new minehunter and minesweeper classes in the course of production. However, perhaps the most interesting development has been the deployment of the so-called 'lifestyle' ship, offering medical, sporting and other leisure facilities for the crews of ship on lengthy 'out of area' deployments. The ship's introduction is reportedly a reflection of the difficulties China faces in attracting the skilled crew required to operate increasingly complex warships, as well as the need to find a way of providing recreational facilities in the absence of a network of foreign bases.

The arrival of significant quantities of new ships is finally allowing withdrawal of obsolescent warship types. For example, at least two 1970s vintage 'Luda' class destroyers have been decommissioned over the last year. In addition, many earlier 'Jianghu'-series frigates are either being transferred abroad or downgraded to subsidiary duties. Overseas deployments are almost exclusively in the hands of the more recent surface vessels, with a Type 054A frigate seemingly invariably being paired with one of the Type 052 series destroyers and a supporting replenishment vessel for these duties. February 2012 saw the departure of the eleventh anti-piracy escort flotilla to the Indian Ocean. China's Northern Fleet provided the task group's constituent warships for the first time. The deployments have ensured a virtually permanent Chinese presence along a critical sea line of communication since the inaugural mission at the end of 2008. Equally, an ongoing process of rotation has allowed a steadily increasing number of units – and their personnel – to grain practical experience of blue water operations.

MAJOR REGIONAL POWERS – JAPAN:

The medium term outlook for Japanese defence strategy was determined by the publication of the government's National Defence Programme Guidelines for FY2011 and beyond and the related 2011–15 Japanese Mid Term Defence Programme in December 2010. Continued instability in North Korea and the rise in China's maritime power remain key strategic considerations. The challenge for Japan is to maintain and modernise its armed forces to counter these potential threats on a static defence budget.

The new guidelines envisage a projected strength of forty-eight major surface vessels and twenty-two submarines for the Japan Maritime Defence Force (JMSDF). Whilst destroyer numbers are broadly stable, the planned submarine strength represents a significant uplift from the level set out in the current fleet summary provided in Table 2.2.4. Construction of only three new major surface ships is envisaged during the life of the five-year plan, one of which is the second of two large 22DDH 'helicopter carrying destroyers' that will replace the much smaller *Shirane* (DDH-143) class. The first of these – authorised during the previous five-year plan – was laid down in January 2012 at IHI Marine United. Her sister has been included in the FY2012 defence budget at a cost of Yen 115.5bn (US$1.5bn).[7] The new ships are essentially much-enlarged variants of the existing *Hyuga* (DDH-181) class.

Given the limited extent of surface ship construction, resort is being made to the life extension of older ships to maintain surface flotilla numbers.

Table 2.2.4: JAPAN MARITIME SELF-DEFENCE FORCE: PRINCIPAL UNITS AS AT MID 2012

TYPE	CLASS	NUMBER	TONNAGE	DIMENSIONS	PROPULSION	CREW	DATE
Support and Helicopter Carriers							
Helicopter Carrier – DDH	HYUGA (DDH-181)	2	18,000 tons	197m x 33m x 7m	COGAG, 30 knots	340	2009
Principal Surface Escorts							
Helicopter Destroyer – DDH	SHIRANE (DDH-143)	2	7,500 tons	159m x 18m x 5m	Steam, 32 knots	350	1980
Destroyer – DDG	ATAGO (DDG-177)	2	10,000 tons	165m x 21m x 6m	COGAG, 30 knots	300	2007
Destroyer – DDG	KONGOU (DDG-173)	4	9,500 tons	161m x 21m x 6m	COGAG, 30 knots	300	1993
Destroyer – DDG	HATAKAZE (DDG-171)	2	6,300 tons	150m x 16m x 5m	COGAG, 30 knots	260	1986
Destroyer – DD	AKIZUKI (DD-115)	1	6,800 tons	151m x 18m x 5m	COGAG, 30 Knots	200	2012
Destroyer – DDG	TAKANAMI (DD-110)	5	5,300 tons	151m x 17m x 5m	COGAG, 30 knots	175	2003
Destroyer – DDG	MURASAME (DD-101)	9	5,200 tons	151m x 17m x 5m	COGAG, 30 knots	165	1996
Destroyer – DDG	ASAGIRI (DD 151)	8	4,300 tons	137m x 15m x 5m	COGAG, 30 knots	220	1988
Destroyer – DDG	HATSUYUKI (DD-122)	7 (3)	3,800 tons	130m x 14m x 4m	COGOG, 30 knots	200	1982
Frigate – FFG	ABUKUMA (DE-229)	6	2,500 tons	109m x 13m x 4m	CODOG, 27 knots	120	1989
Submarines							
Submarine – SSK	SORYU (SS-501)	4	4,200 tons	84m x 9m x 8m	AIP, 20 knots+	65	2009
Submarine – SSK	OYASHIO (SS-590)	11	4,000 tons	82m x 9m x 8m	Diesel-electric, 20 knots+	70	1998
Submarine – SSK	HARUSHIO (SS-583)	1 (2)	3,300 tons	77m x 10m x 8m	Diesel-electric, 20 knots+	75	1990
Major Amphibious Units							
Landing Platform Dock – LPD	OSUMI (LST-4001)	3	14,000 tons	178m x 26m x 6m	Diesel, 22 knots	135	1998

Note: Figures in brackets refer to trials or training ships.

Provision was made for modernisation of two *Asagiri* (DD-151) class destroyers in the FY2012 defence budget. It also allocated funds for provision of long-lead items for future upgrades of a further six *Asagiri*, *Hatsuyuki* (DD-122), *Abukuma* (DE-229) and *Hatakaze* (DDG-171) type ships. Although the life-extension programme should buy the JMSDF some time, it is difficult to envisage how destroyer numbers will be maintained in the longer term without a major increase in the construction programme given the substantial proportion of the surface fleet that is now more than twenty years old.

Current Japanese defence strategy places a high priority on ballistic missile defence (BMD) given the potential threat from North Korea's missile and nuclear weapons programmes. Japan's four *Kongou* (DDG-173) class Aegis-equipped destroyers have already been equipped with Standard SM-3 missiles and associated Aegis upgrades as part of the US Navy's broader missile defence programme.[8] The five-year plan included provision for the modifications to the two more recent *Atago* (DDG-177) class ships. Funding for both was included in the 2012 budget at a cost of Yen 36bn (US$460m). Japan's defence electronics industry is heavily involved in a joint project with the US to develop an improved SM-3 Block IIA missile and this should enter service in the Japanese ships during the second half of the decade. Japanese electronics are also conspicuous in the new *Akizuki* (DD-115) class destroyers, the first of which was commissioned in March 2012. Fitted with the FCS-3A weapons system developed from an earlier variant first installed on the *Hyuga* and Evolved Sea Sparrow Missiles (ESSM), the new class can provide a local air defence capability for the

Aegis destroyers when the latter are focused in the BMD role. Other equipment includes a 127mm gun, ASROC anti-submarine and Type 90 surface-to-surface missiles, Phalanx close-in-weapons systems and a helicopter.

Submarine construction continues to be focused on progressively enhanced variants of the *Soryu* class air-independent propulsion (AIP) equipped types, which feature Kockums' Stirling engine propulsion. Four of the class are now in commission following delivery of *Kenryu* in March 2012, whilst an eighth was authorised in the 2012 budget. She will be equipped with improved torpedo countermeasures. Current plans envisage submarine construction continuing at one unit per annum through to FY2015 as part of measures to increase the submarine force from the current sixteen active boats. This is also likely to see existing members of the *Oyashio* (SS-590) and *Harushio* (SS-583) classes maintained in service for longer than the previous standard sixteen years.

MAJOR REGIONAL POWERS – SOUTH KOREA

The Republic of Korea Navy has been experiencing something of an identity crisis since the sinking of the corvette *Cheonan* in March 2010. The ship's destruction, which a panel of international experts concluded was caused by a North Korean torpedo, resulted in calls for the navy to change its focus towards deterrence of its northern neighbour's littoral forces at the expense of a previous approach that emphasised a steady accretion of 'blue water' capabilities. This has seen investment shift towards, for example, anti-submarine and mine warfare

equipment, including the potential purchase of latest model Seahawk or Lynx Wildcat helicopters. This has been accompanied by a much greater emphasis on anti-submarine warfare training. However, it is apparent that there remains a significant school of thought within the navy's hierarchy that clings to aspirations of global power projection and this is starting to reassert itself as the immediacy of *Cheonan*'s loss passes. A symbolic development was reported by the local *Korea Times* in February 2012 in an article referencing the revival of the slogan 'Korean Ocean-Going Navy' on official documents. This could have a significant impact on future naval programmes, particularly the navy's ambitions to acquire further Aegis-equipped destroyers.

Another symbol of Korean 'blue water' ambitions has been the construction of an entirely new naval base on the Volcanic island of Jeju, which lies south of the mainland straddling sea lanes between China and Japan. The US$1bn project aims to provide an operating base for the navy's major warships in a key strategic location and is slowly being pressed forward in spite of considerable opposition on both environmental and political grounds since it was first announced in 2007. Physical construction commenced in 2011 and work was said to be approaching 20 per cent completion as of mid 2012 in spite of ongoing protests. The base will reinforce South Korea's presence in the East China Sea, where the country's territorial claims overlap with those of China and Japan.

Existing construction programmes for both oceanic and littoral warships are also making headway. The third and final KDX-III class destroyer *Ryu Sung-ryong* should be delivered by the

Table 2.2.5: REPUBLIC OF KOREA NAVY: PRINCIPAL UNITS AS AT MID 2012

TYPE	CLASS	NUMBER	TONNAGE	DIMENSIONS	PROPULSION	CREW	DATE
Principal Surface Escorts							
Destroyer – DDG	KDX-III **SEJONGDAEWANG-HAM**	2	10,000 tons	166m x 21m x 6m	COGAG, 30 knots	300	2008
Destroyer – DDG	KDX-II **CHUNGMUGONG YI SUN-SHIN**	6	5,500 tons	150m x 17m x 5m	CODOG, 30 knots	200	2003
Destroyer – DDG	KDX-I **GWANGGAETO-DAEWANG**	3	3,900 tons	135m x 14m x 4m	CODOG, 30 knots	170	1998
Frigate – FFG	**ULSAN**	9	2,300 tons	102m x 12m x 4m	CODOG, 35 knots	150	1981
Corvette – FSG	**PO HANG**	21	1,200 tons	88m x 10m x 3m	CODOG, 32 knots	95	1984
Submarines							
Submarine – SSK	KSS-2 **SON WON-IL** (Type 214)	3	1,800 tons	65m x 6m x 6m	AIP, 20+ knots	30	2007
Submarine – SSK	KSS-1 **CHANG BOGO** (Type 209)	9	1,300 tons	56m x 6m x 6m	Diesel-electric, 22 knots	35	1993
Major Amphibious Units							
Amph Assault Ship – LHD	LPX **DOKDO**	1	18,900 tons	200m x 32m x 7m	Diesel, 22 knots	425	2007

end of 2012 and will be followed shortly afterwards by the lead FFX patrol frigate *Incheon*. A further two frigates are believed to be under construction at lead yard Hyundai Heavy Industries but orders for other units may be placed with rival shipbuilders Daewoo and STX. This is seemingly in line with a policy of spreading warship construction amongst the country's major yards. These ships will feature differences from the frigates already ordered, with Rolls-Royce reporting on 26 June 2012 that its MT30 turbine had been selected for the first of eight 'Batch II' ships. Up to twenty of the FFX type may be eventually commissioned to replace existing light frigates and corvettes, which are reaching the end of their service lives and are already starting to be withdrawn. Also entering service are PKX class missile fast attack craft following apparent resolution of previous design issues with the propulsion system. Around nine expected to be in service by the second half of 2012, with orders being split in batches of four between Hanjin Heavy Industries and STX following completion of the lead ship. Completion of the next batch of Type 214 submarines is further off, with deliveries expected from 2014 onwards.

Table 2.2.5 provides an overview of major constituents of the Republic of Korea Navy as at mid 2012.

OTHER REGIONAL FLEETS:

Brunei: The Royal Brunei Navy's fleet renewal plan has been completed with the commissioning of the third and final *Darussalam* class offshore patrol vessel *Darulaman* at a ceremony in Brunei on 12 December 2011. The 80m Lürssen-built vessels supplement four smaller 40m *Ijhtihad* vessels also built by the German yard.

Burma (Myanmar): Political reforms are leading to Myanmar's return to international acceptance, whilst its strategic location bordering the Indian Ocean make the country of interest to China and India alike. The former has been the navy's main supplier of weaponry in recent years, with elderly Chinese patrol craft supplementing indigenous construction of basic corvettes and lighter units. However, tensions with neighbouring Bangladesh over territorial rights in the Bay of Bengal may well have been the driving force behind the acquisition of more potent warships, as reflected in the arrival of two former PLAN 'Jianghu II' Type 053H1 frigates in April 2012. The 1980s-built *Mahar Bandoola* (ex-

A dramatic view of the South Korean KDX-II type destroyer *Moonmu Daewang* pictured from a US Navy carrier on 21 June 2012. They could be supplemented by similar-sized Aegis-equipped destroyers if funding is provided. *(US Navy)*

The Royal Brunei Navy has completed fleet modernisation plans with commissioning of the third and final *Darussalam* class offshore patrol vessel *Darulaman* in December 2011. This picture shows second of class *Darulehsan* operating with other fleet units in November 2011. *(US Navy)*

Anshun) and *Mahar Thiha Thura* (ex-*Jishou*) are obsolescent by objective standards but give the navy a useful counter to Bangladesh's similar *Osman* and more recent *Bangabandhu*. Meanwhile, India is stepping up joint naval exercises as it attempts to limit Chinese influence in its own 'back yard'.

Indonesia: The Indonesian armed forces are starting to benefit from the end to years of chronic underfunding as a strengthening economy filters through to higher levels of defence spending. Whilst budgets are still tight, sufficient money is becoming available to allow some of the most pressing procurement needs to be met. The most significant sign of progress in the past year was undoubtedly the US$1.1bn order for three submarines from DSME announced in December 2011, reinforcing a relationship which has already seen the Korean company refurbish Indonesia's two existing Type 209 boats. The new submarines are also understood to be Type 209 derivatives, for which the Korean yard holds a construction licence from the original German designers. Two of the new submarines will be built in South Korea, with the third being assem-

bled at the local PT Pal yard in Surabaya. All should be in service by 2018. Indonesia's defence planning envisages a total underwater flotilla of around ten boats by 2024 but this looks challenging from both a financial and manning perspective.

Although the new submarines will provide useful 'high-end' capabilities, Indonesia's greatest need is for a large number of patrol vessels to undertake constabulary duties across the archipelago's vast territorial waters. Recent policy has been to encourage indigenous manufacture of relatively standardised designs to meet this need. This is bringing increasing uniformity to a previously disparate collection of second-hand vessels. Whilst construction of the more complex vessels is reserved to PT Pal in Surabaya, smaller vessels have been ordered from a range of other yards, therefore expanding local building capacity. The private PT Palindo Marine yard in Batam appears to be enjoying particular success with its KCR-40 missile-armed fast attack craft. A second unit, *Kujang*, has now been commissioned and two further vessels are under construction, with plans for a further twenty confirmed, subject to finance.

Meanwhile, PT Pal has finally signed the contract to build a new Dutch-designed 'Sigma' light frigate that was referenced in last year's *Seaforth World Naval Review*. The agreement, concluded on 5 June 2012, provides for the construction of a 105m Sigma PKR 10514 variant displacing around 2,400 tons with a combined diesel and electric propulsion system. Armament will include a 76mm gun, surface-to-air and surface-to-surface missiles and anti-submarine torpedo tubes, all controlled by a Thales Tacticos combat management system. The US$220m contract with Damen Schelde Naval Shipbuilding provides for modules to be fabricated at the company's yards in the Netherlands and Romania as well as at PT Pal in Indonesia. The Indonesian company will be responsible for final assembly and trials. Completion is scheduled for around 2016, when the new ship will join the navy's four existing smaller Sigma type *Diponegoro* class corvettes. Further construction could follow if the project is successful.

Malaysia: Although neighbouring Indonesia's acquisition of additional submarines may ultimately result in further expansion of Malaysia's embryonic underwater flotilla, the immediate requirement is for further surface warships. The troubled and prolonged construction of MEKO A-100 type *Kedah* class offshore patrol vessels (essentially light frigates) was finally brought to a satisfactory conclusion in 2010. However, this only meets six out of an initial twenty-seven ship requirement. Reports at the end of 2011 suggested that DCNS had been successful in pairing with Boustead Naval Shipyard to offer a variant of its 'Gowind' family of ships for the next batch of six ships under a contract reportedly valued at some US$2.8bn. However, it is far from clear that a definitive contract has been signed and negotiations may well be delayed by forthcoming Malaysian elections. If concluded, the deal is likely to be one of the larger, frigate type variants of the 'Gowind' designs, owing as much to the frigate *Aquitaine* as France's smaller offshore patrol vessel *L'Adroit*.

Given the slow progress of domestic construction, consideration is also being given to acquisition of second-hand vessels from overseas to fill the capability gap. In May 2012, *Jane's Defence Weekly* reported that contact had been made with the US Navy to investigate purchase of surplus FFG-7 type frigates and *Whidbey Island* (LSD-41) dock landing ships; some of the latter are being withdrawn early

The Indonesian Navy is reliant on a large fleet of relatively unsophisticated surface vessels to police the archipelago's vast territorial waters. These are supplemented by a handful of more sophisticated warships, notably the Dutch-built, Sigma type *Diponegoro* corvettes. *Sultan Iskandar Muda* of the class is pictured here in company with the indigenous amphibious transport dock *Banda Aceh*. The diminutive nature of the Indonesian vessels is apparent when compared with the accompanying US Coast Guard cutter *Waesche* (WMSL-751), essentially a large offshore patrol vessel. *(US Navy)*

The new Royal New Zealand Navy offshore patrol vessel *Otago* delivered as part of Project Protector has been steadily working up to full operational capacity, recently carrying out initial helicopter landing trials. This mid 2011 image shows her on operations with the Royal Australian Navy. *(Royal Australian Navy)*

The Philippines is one of the countries that feels most exposed to rising Chinese influence but its budget only runs to making minor enhancements to its naval forces. The newly acquired *Gregorio del Pilar*, the former US Coast Guard cutter *Hamilton* (WHEC-715), is already forty-five years old. *(US Navy)*

under recent US defence spending reductions.[9] Malaysia has been without a proper amphibious capability since the destruction of the former *Newport* (LST-1179) class tank landing ship *Sri Inderapura* in a fire on 8–9 October 2009. The surplus US ships would allow a relatively rapid and cost-effective restoration of the lost capacity.

New Zealand: Having previously completed the upgrade of its offshore patrol vessel fleet under Project Protector, the Royal New Zealand Navy is now turning to the renewal of support and aviation assets in line with the 2010 Defence White Paper. This envisages the hydrographic and diving support vessels *Resolution* and *Manawanui* being substituted by a single ship and a one-for-one replacement of the existing replenishment oiler *Endeavour*. In line with these plans, *Resolution* decommissioned on 29 April 2012. However, details of the new vessel have yet to be announced. Equally pressing is renewal of the existing Karman SH-2G Super Seasprite helicopters, which have recently suffered from poor availability. The rotorcraft are operated by the Royal New Zealand Air Force's No 6 Squadron and serve on the two *Anzac* class frigates and the multi-purpose vessel *Canterbury.* Initial flying trials from the new offshore patrol vessel *Otago* were also conducted in May 2012. Recent press reports suggest that New Zealand is contemplating acquiring eleven similar

helicopters rejected as unsuitable by Australia in 2008, which would be refurbished to meet New Zealand's less demanding requirements.

The Philippines: The Philippine Navy probably faces the most challenging backdrop of any of the Asian fleet. In addition to having to find the resources to police a vast network of islands, it also faces growing tensions with its mighty Chinese neighbour over territorial rights in the South China Sea. Given this scenario, the Philippines' move towards a renewed partnership with the United States is undoubtedly a welcome development for local commanders. It improves access to US military assistance for force modernisation and provides a powerful ally should additional support become necessary. Fruits of the former are already becoming apparent with the arrival of surplus American naval equipment. A second US Coast Guard *Hamilton* (WHEC-715) class high endurance cutter, the former *Dallas* (WHEC-716) was acquired on 22 May 2012 and will take the name *Ramon Alcaraz* in Philippine Navy service. She joins *Gregorio del Pilar,* the former *Hamilton* herself, which was formally commissioned in December 2011 and subsequently involved in the April 2012 stand-off with China. A third ship may be transferred in due course as the class is replaced by the new 'Legend' class in US Coast Guard service. Whilst the new vessels represent a welcome

upgrade to the Philippine Navy, the fact that these forty-five-year-old ships will be amongst the most powerful in the fleet reflects the extent of modernisation still required.

Singapore: The Republic of Singapore Navy's rolling, well-funded programme of enhancements is currently focused on modernisation of its submarine flotilla. This is being carried out in conjunction with Sweden's Kockums, which previously upgraded the quartet of *Challenger* (former Swedish A-12 *Sjöörmen*) class boats supplied between 2000 and 2004. The current 'Northern Lights' project is focused on the modernisation of and installation of AIP-equipment in two former A-17 *Västergötland* class submarines, which have been renamed *Archer* and *Swordsman* in Swedish service. The former boat arrived in Singapore on 17 August 2011 for a period of trials in system verification in local conditions before being commissioned at a ceremony attended by Defence Minister Dr Ng Eng Hen the following December. Meanwhile, *Swordsman* is currently undergoing trials in Sweden and should arrive in Singapore before the end of 2012. Sweden has hopes that Singapore will become a partner in the new A26 submarine design. A local joint venture between Kockums and Singapore's ST Marine to support the existing submarines announced in April 2012 may bring this possibility closer.

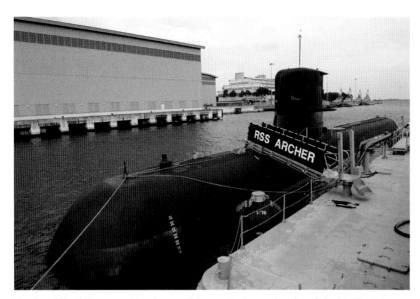

The Republic of Singapore Navy is one of the most advanced and proficient in the Asia-Pacific region, benefiting from a rolling programme of fleet renewal. Its first AIP-equipped submarine, *Archer*, an upgraded Swedish A-17 type, arrived in August 2011. *(Republic of Singapore Navy)*

Following the decision not to progress the creation of a submarine flotilla, Thailand's modernisation of its surface fleet has assumed greater importance. This includes combat system and missile upgrades to the two Chinese-built *Naresuan* class frigates. *Taskin* is seen here in this 2011 image of fleet units at anchor in the main Sattahip naval base. *(US Navy)*

Taiwan: Whilst Taiwan's Republic of China Navy continues to develop asymmetrical force structures to deter any potential aggression from mainland China, a lack of political will, inadequate financial resources and difficulties accessing an appropriate range of technology are all combining to create an increasing capability gap with the ever more sophisticated PLAN.

The most important requirement is renewal of Taiwan's submarine flotilla; a need which has been recognised for a decade or more. The United States has previously agreed to help furnish a flotilla of eight new boats to replace the existing four submarines. However, fulfilment of the programme is dependent on the support of European submarine builders given the US Navy's reliance on nuclear-propulsion. These have proved reluctant to provide the necessary technology given the importance of relations with mainland China. Nevertheless, the ambition to acquire new submarines was reconfirmed during the first half of 2012, with indigenous construction considered a possibility if external assistance is not forthcoming. In the meantime, there have been reports that a long-awaited upgrade of the two existing Dutch-built *Hai Lung* class submarines with Harpoon surface-to-surface missiles will be implemented during 2013.[10]

With new submarine construction still in abeyance, Taiwan's main naval deterrent is effectively in the hands of the surface-to-surface missile armed escorts and fast attack craft that form the fleet's core. The fast attack force has been steadily modernised with the construction of thirty indigenous 'Kuang Hua 6' (KH-6) vessels, the last pair of which were delivered in October 2011. Three of the navy's five missile boat squadrons now comprise KH-6 craft, with the others being constituted from the remaining members of the older 'Hai Ou' type that will be retired soon. The new class are armed with the 130km, sub-sonic Hsiung Feng II (HF-2) missile which provides the navy with its principal anti-ship capability. A supersonic, long-range HF-3 variant has also been developed. This is starting to be retrofitted to existing surface ships and will also arm a new class of 500-ton, twin-hulled stealth corvette. An order for a prototype of the new ship was placed in May 2012 for delivery in 2014.

The United States continues to provide considerable assistance and refurbished PC-3 patrol aircraft are likely to start arriving by the end of 2012. Two former US Navy *Osprey* class minehunters are also in the course of refurbishment for further service with Taiwan. They should be delivered as *Yung Jin* (the former *Oriole*) and *Yung An* (the former *Falcon*) by year-end.

Thailand: The last year has been something of a mixed one for the Royal Thai Navy, with both negative and positive developments. On the negative side, the navy's long-cherished but ambitious plans to establish a submarine flotilla appear to have suffered a stumbling block with failure to conclude previously announced plans to purchase former German Type 206A boats. The rumoured 7.7bn Thai Baht (c.US$250m) deal collapsed in the face of significant naval and political opposition, including reports of royal concerns that submarines might not be suitable for operation in Thailand's shallow offshore waters. The submarines' capabilities will be met by investment in other systems, most notably the current frigate modernisation programme being undertaken in conjunction with Saab.

More positively, the Royal Thai Navy's amphibious capabilities received a major boost with the preliminary acceptance of the modified *Endurance* class amphibious transport dock *Angthong* from Singapore's ST Marine on 3 April 2012. The new ship displaces around 7,600 tons and is capable of deploying around 350 marines from two 23m and two 13m landing craft, as well as from the large flight deck. One large or two medium-sized helicopters can be supported; the latter including two new MH-60S Seahawks delivered from the United States in the second half of 2011. Thailand is

Thailand is placing increased emphasis on local warship construction. This picture was taken shortly after the launch of *Krabi*, based on BAE Systems' 90m *Port of Spain* design, at Bangkok Dock in December 2011. *(BAE Systems)*

The Royal Thai Navy has upgraded its amphibious forces with delivery of the modified *Endurance* class amphibious transport dock *Angthong* from Singapore's ST Marine in April 2012. *(ST Marine)*

the first international customer for the variant. The navy has been reported to be seeking funding for a second vessel of the type but any order will probably have to wait satisfactory initiation of the lead ship. Thailand is also placing increased emphasis on local construction, as evidenced by the launch of the BAE Systems *Port of Spain* type offshore patrol vessel *Krabi* at Bangkok Dock in December 2011. There is a requirement for more vessels if the original contract proves successful.

Vietnam: Disagreements with China over maritime boundaries around the Paracel and Spratly Islands have fuelled increased investment in the Vietnam People's Navy in recent years and a rolling

programme of upgrades continues. The second Project 1166.1 'Gepard' class frigate built by Zelenodolsk was commissioned as *Ly Thai To* on 22 August 2011 and there have been reports that a second pair of ships have been ordered. If confirmed, it is likely that this batch will feature improved anti-submarine capabilities in comparison with the anti-surface orientation of the initial ships.

Local construction of Russian-designed fast attack craft also continues, with the emphasis on coastal defence also being reinforced by delivery of additional mobile K-300 Bastion-P land-based anti-shipping missile systems. Meanwhile, construction of new 'Kilo' class submarines is underway in Russia, with the first deliveries scheduled in around eighteen months.

Notes:

1. See Toshi Yoshihara and James R Holmes, *Red Star Over the Pacific: China's Rise and the Challenge to US Maritime Strategy* (Annapolis, US Naval Institute Press, 2010), p.3.

2. US military engagement with the Philippines is now probably at its closest since the Philippines' senate refused to extend the agreement allowing US use of the Subic Bay Naval Base and Clark Air Base in 1991. President Obama's comments on a rule-based approach to resolving regional maritime disputes were made in the context of a meeting with the country's president, Benigno Aquino, and a US desire to increase access to local military facilities. For further discussion, see Geoff Dyer and Roel Landingin, 'Obama in show of support for Philippines', *Financial Times* – 9 June 2012 (London, Pearson Plc, 2012). US contacts with Vietnam have also been stepped up.

3. A detailed analysis of the Australian 2012 defence budget is contained in Mark Thomson's *The Cost of*

Defence: ASPI Defence Budget Brief 2012–13 (Canberra, Australian Strategic Policy Institute, 2012).

4. A more detailed review of current Royal Australian Navy fleet structure and the impact of authorised procurement programmes can be found in Julian Kerr's 'Wave of the future', *Jane's Defence Weekly* – 18 January 2012 (Couldson, IHS Jane's, 2012), pp.21–7.

5. The ship is named after Claude Stanley Choules (1901–2011), the last First World War combat veteran, who served in both the British Royal Navy and the Royal Australian Navy.

6. The best source of information on ongoing PLAN developments is possibly the analysis and news contained in the China Air and Naval Power blog, which can be found at http://china-pla.blogspot.co.uk. The Chinese Defense Blog at http://china-defense.blogspot.co.uk/ is another useful source of up-to-date news.

7. An English language summary of Japan's defence budget is made available annually and provides much useful information on JMSDF programmes. See *Defense Programs and Budget of Japan: Overview of FY2012 Budget* (Tokyo, Ministry of Defence, 2012), which can be found by searching the ministry's website at http://www.mod.go.jp.

8. An overview of the development of the US Navy's Aegis Ballistic Missile Defence (BMD) system can be found in chapter 4.2.

9. See Dzirhan Nahadzir's 'Malaysia looking to buy surplus US frigates and LSDs', *Jane's Defence Weekly* – 2 May 2012 (Couldson, IHS Jane's, 2012), p.18.

10. The news was reported in Eric Wertheim's regular 'Combat Fleets' update in the April 2012 edition of *Proceedings* (Annapolis, US Naval Institute, 2012).

2.3 REGIONAL REVIEW

Author:
Conrad Waters

THE INDIAN OCEAN AND AFRICA

INTRODUCTION:

Although the Asia-Pacific nations have continued to lead the way in terms of their expanding maritime influence, it is arguable that the waters of the Indian Ocean, Africa and the Middle East rival them so far as operational naval activity is concerned. Developments in the Far East can – simplistically – be explained by growing Chinese sway and regional reliance on rapidly expanding trade. It is more difficult to identify an equally straightforward explanation for the Indian Ocean and Africa's position as a seeming magnet for the world's navies given the region's size and complexity. However, a number of broad, interlinked themes do have a particular influence on the area's significance in an international naval context. These warrant further discussion.

One obvious factor is the region's geographical position astride the main trade routes between Europe and Asia. This is supplemented by ongoing significance as a trading destination in its own right due to the prevalence of local natural resources. Of course, these facts have long influenced naval and political developments. For example, they had considerable impact on driving European maritime ascendancy from the late fifteenth century onwards. Subsequently, they played a leading role in the Victorian colonial 'Scramble for Africa'. However, a new dimension to the dynamic is Asia's own need to secure raw materials for its growing industries. This is inevitably driving a desire to grow regional leverage, most evident in the wave of Chinese investment directed towards many African countries.[1]

Navies have historically played a major role in developing such 'soft influence'. Today is no exception. This is evident not only, for example, in the virtually permanent deployment of Chinese escort flotillas in the Indian Ocean but also from the orders for warships placed with its yards from countries such as Algeria, Namibia and Nigeria. Of course, China is only one of a number of countries increasing their local naval profile. Japan, Malaysia and Singapore are amongst many other Asian countries that have added their warships to the longer-established European and American regional presence.

Another regional theme is an inherent instability probably unparalleled elsewhere in the world. The events of the Arab Spring have now run their course in Libya – assisted significantly by NATO maritime and naval aviation assets – but unrest continues elsewhere. For example, Russia announced in mid June 2012 that it was to deploy amphibious ships to Tartus in Syria to protect Russian nationals in the face of the possible collapse of its last major ally in the Middle East.[2] Meanwhile, little progress has been made in resolving tensions resulting from Iran's nuclear programme. This has resulted in the near-term strengthening of 'Western' naval assets in the Persian Gulf in response to ongoing Iranian threats to block the Straits of Hormuz should conflict erupt, as well as longer-term Israeli investment in a submarine flotilla widely reported to form part of its own nuclear deterrent. Elsewhere, instability in Africa has been more a factor of weak or non-existent governmental infrastructure and the general lawlessness

that this permits. Here, however, there have been signs of progress, notably the African Union's largely land-based successes against the extremist al-Shabab group in Somalia and a reduction in Indian Ocean piracy due to increasingly sophisticated naval operations. These included an inaugural European Union Naval Force strike against land-based targets on 15 May 2012.

The final factor worth considering is the expansion of the region's own naval capabilities. For example, the boost to African economies provided by increased raw material demand is filtering through to renewed naval investment. Consequently, local capacity – particularly with respect to constabulary missions – is improving. At the other end of the scale, countries such as Saudi Arabia and India are already amongst the world's largest defence spenders. The latter country, perhaps unnerved by a plethora of foreign warships transiting the Indian Ocean, has pursued expansionary naval ambitions for some time. Although delays with indigenous and overseas contracts alike have frustrated full realisation of its strategy, 2012 could prove a tipping point in its rise to regional naval ascendancy. More particularly, an embryonic underwater nuclear capability was established with the arrival of the Russian-built *Chakra* on 4 April 2012. Equally, credible fixed-wing maritime aviation should resume with the planned delivery of the carrier *Vikramaditya* at year-end. In a similar fashion to China, India's navy is steadily becoming a force to be reckoned with amongst the world's fleets.

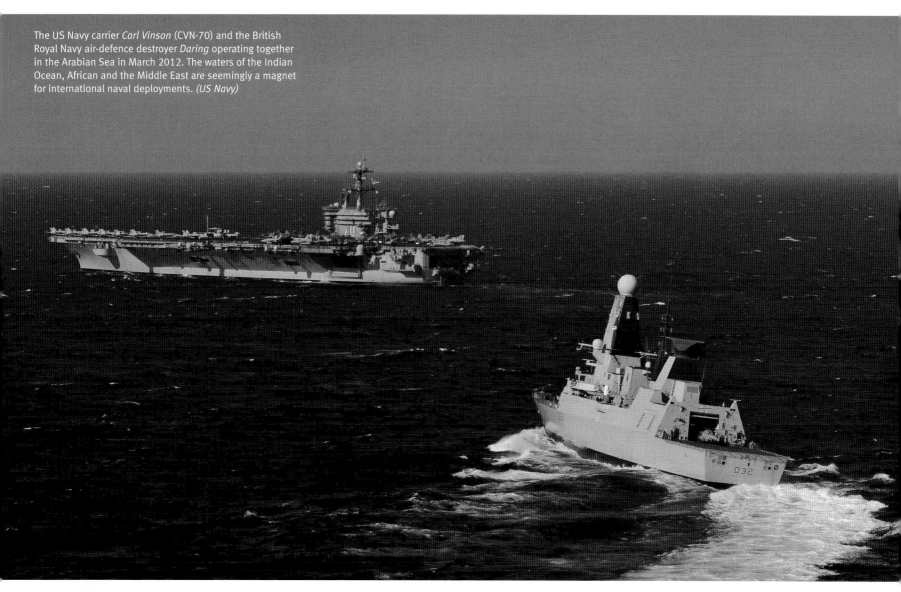

The US Navy carrier *Carl Vinson* (CVN-70) and the British Royal Navy air-defence destroyer *Daring* operating together in the Arabian Sea in March 2012. The waters of the Indian Ocean, African and the Middle East are seemingly a magnet for international naval deployments. *(US Navy)*

Table 2.3.1: FLEET STRENGTHS IN THE INDIAN OCEAN, AFRICA AND THE MIDDLE EAST – LARGER NAVIES (MID 2012)

COUNTRY	ALGERIA	EGYPT	INDIA	IRAN	ISRAEL	PAKISTAN	SAUDI ARABIA	SOUTH AFRICA
Support/Helicopter Carrier (CVS/CVH)	–	–	1	–	–	–	–	–
Attack Submarine (SSN/SSGN)	–	–	1	–	–	–	–	–
Patrol Submarine (SSK/SS)	4	4	14	3	4	5	–	3
Fleet Escort (DDG/FFG)	–	6	21	–	–	10	6[2]	4
Patrol Escort/Corvette (FFG/FSG/FS)	6	4	8	6	3	–	4	–
Missile Armed Attack Craft (PGG/PTG)	12	30[1]	12	24	10	7	9	3
Mine Countermeasures Vessel (MCMV)	–	14	7	–	–	3	7	3
Major Amphibious (LPD)	–	–	1	–	–	–	–	–

Notes:

1 Egyptian fast attack craft numbers approximate.   2 Status of one Saudi Arabian fleet escort doubtful following grounding damage.

INDIAN OCEAN NAVIES

Bangladesh: Although the Bangladesh Navy has ambitious plans to transform itself into a three-dimension force with surface, aviation and underwater elements, only limited progress is being achieved. As is the case elsewhere in much of the developing world, China is the supplier of preference, with recent reports suggesting that obsolescent PLAN 'Jianghu' Type 053H1 frigates may soon be delivered to supplement a pair of new-build missile armed corvettes/fast attack craft under construction in Shanghai. The frigates would join the existing 'Jianghu' type frigate *Osman* currently deployed in support of the UNIFIL maritime mission off Lebanon and allow final retirement of the even older trio of 1950s-built British frigates that, with the more modern *Bangabandhu,* form the core of the surface fleet. There is also a pressing need for modern patrol and survey assets to support the country's influence in the Bay of Bengal, where tensions with Myanmar remain in spite of a United Nations ruling in March 2012 broadly supporting Bangladesh's territorial claims. Second-hand offshore patrol and survey vessels recently acquired from the United Kingdom will meet part of the need, whilst a pair of Dornier 228NG maritime patrol aircraft

manufactured in Germany by RUAG will provide the navy's first fixed-wing capability when they are delivered in the summer of 2013. There has been less news in respect of the sub-surface element of the triad, with successful establishment of a submarine flotilla within the planned end of decade time frame looking increasingly unlikely.

India: Recent years have seen the extent of the Indian Navy's aspirations to transition into a first-rank, blue water force surpassed only by difficulties it has encountered in realising its ambitions. In contrast to the situation in much of the rest of the world, this has not been due to financial constraints. Indeed, the Indian defence budget has been growing at a healthy rate, with projected expenditure for 2012–13 likely to see an increase approaching 20 per cent above the previous year and with naval procurement a particular area of focus. The real issue has been the inability of the domestic shipbuilding industry to achieve anything close to planned output levels, coupled with a series of delays to contracts placed with overseas – largely Russian – yards. Significant efforts are being made to increase the efficiency of the largely state-owned indigenous warship sector. These have encompassed opening up

Indian Navy contracts to the private sector and the promotion of joint ventures between state-owned and commercial yards.[3] Whilst there has not yet been sufficient time to judge whether these steps will have any significant benefit, Russia is now starting to deliver a significant flow of new equipment. Long-delayed indigenous ships are also starting to appear. The combined effect is starting to reverse the decline in fleet numbers seen in recent years, as evidenced by the summary of current principal units provided in Table 2.3.2. Additional detail with respect to specific ship categories is provided below:

Aircraft Carriers: The highlight of the last year has been the departure on trials of *Vikramaditya*, the former Soviet *Admiral Gorshkov*, from the Sevmash yard at Severodvinsk on 8 June 2012. Their commencement marks the final stage of a long-delayed refurbishment, and planned delivery in December 2012 is broadly in line with the revised schedule agreed when the Indian purchase contract was renegotiated in 2010. As of mid 2012, fifteen of the forty-five MiG-29K/KUB jets ordered to operate from the carrier had been delivered. Trial flight operations from the new carrier should commence during 2013. Meanwhile, construction of the first indigenous aircraft carrier *Vikrant* is making slow progress at Cochin Shipyard and the ship's incomplete hull was floated out at a low-key ceremony in December 2011. Delays to the delivery of gearboxes and other key components has put the ship further behind schedule and it seems likely that the current operational carrier *Viraat* (the former British *Hermes*) will be withdrawn before her replacement is completed.

Surface Combatants: The Indian Navy currently has no less than four series of surface escorts under construction. Three of these are being built in Indian yards and the fourth in Russia. All the indigenous programmes are subject to significant delays. The largest vessels are the three 6,800-ton Project 15A *Kolkata* class destroyers. They use the same hull form and propulsion system as the earlier Project 15 *Delhi* class but incorporate improved weapons systems and stealth features. Work on the project commenced as long ago as 2003 at Mazagon Dock and *Kolkata* was launched in March 2006. However, sea trials had yet to commence as of mid 2012. Delays will have a knock-on effect on the follow-on Project 15B series, four of which were approved in 2009. Better progress

The Bangladesh Navy's offshore patrol vessel *Sangu* (formerly the British 'Island' class *Guernsey*) operating with a former British Royal Navy 'Castle' class vessel in September 2011. Bangladesh needs modern patrol and survey assets to protect its interests in the Bay of Bengal. *(US Navy)*

The departure of the refurbished carrier *Vikramaditya*, formerly the Soviet *Admiral Gorshkov*, on trials from the Sevmash facility in Severodvinsk in June 2012 has probably been the highlight of the last year for the Indian Navy. The new carrier will be equipped with Russian MiG-29K jets operating in short take off and assisted recovery (STOBAR) mode and is scheduled for delivery by the end of 2012. These photographs, courtesy of Commodore S K Grewal, the Indian Navy attaché in Moscow, show the new carrier departing Sevmash on 8 June 2012 and during initial sea trials in the course of that month *(Sevmash via Cmde S K Grewal, IN)*

Table 2.3.2: INDIAN NAVY: PRINCIPAL UNITS AS AT MID 2012

TYPE	CLASS	NUMBER	TONNAGE	DIMENSIONS	PROPULSION	CREW	DATE
Aircraft Carriers							
Aircraft Carrier (CV)	**VIRAAT** (HERMES)	1	29,000 tons	227m x 27/49m x 9m	Steam, 28 knots	1,350	1959
Principal Surface Escorts							
Destroyer – DDG	Project 15 **DELHI**	3	6,700 tons	163m x 17m x 7m	COGAG, 32 knots	350	1997
Destroyer – DDG	Project 61 ME **RAJPUT** ('Kashin')	5	5,000 tons	147m x 16m x 5m	COGAG, 35 knots	320	1980
Frigate – FFG	Project 17 **SHIVALIK**	2	6,200 tons	143m x 17m x 5m	CODOG, 30 knots	265	2010
Frigate – FFG	Project 1135.6 **TALWAR**	4	4,000 tons	125m x 15m x 5m	COGAG, 30 knots	180	2003
Frigate – FFG	Project 16A **BRAHMAPUTRA**	3	4,000 tons	127m x 15m x 5m	Steam, 30 knots	350	2000
Frigate – FFG	Project 16 **GODAVARI**	3	3,850 tons	127m x 15m x 5m	Steam, 30 knots	315	1983
Frigate – FFG	**NILGIRI** (LEANDER)	1	3,000 tons	114m x 13m x 5m	Steam, 28 knots	300	1974
Corvette – FSG	Project 25A **KORA**	4	1,400 tons	91m x 11m x 5m	Diesel, 25 knots	125	1998
Corvette – FSG	Project 25 **KHUKRI**	4	1,400 tons	91m x 11m x 5m	Diesel, 25 knots	110	1989
Submarines							
Submarine – SSN	Project 971 **CHAKRA** ('Akula II')	1	9,500+ tons	110m x 14m x 10m	Nuclear, 30+ knots	100	2012
Submarine – SSK	Project 877 EKM **SINDHUGHOSH** ('Kilo')	10	3,000 tons	73m x 10m x 7m	Diesel-electric, 17 knots	55	1986
Submarine – SSK	**SHISHUMAR** (Type 209)	4	1,900 tons	64m x 7m x 6m	Diesel-electric, 22 knots	40	1986
Major Amphibious Units							
Landing Platform Dock – LPD	**JALASHWA** (AUSTIN)	1	17,000 tons	173m x 26/30m x 7m	Steam, 21 knots	405	1971

has been made with Mazagon Dock's other major surface warship programme for Project 17 stealth frigates, with the third and final ship, *Sahyadri*, beind delivered at the end of June 2012 for commissioning in July. A much-modified Project 17A class of seven ships will be split between Mazagon Dock and Garden Reach Shipbuilders & Engineers (GRSE) but formal orders have yet to be placed.[4] Meanwhile GRSE is having its own problems

completing a batch of four 2,500-ton Project 28 *Kamorta* class anti-submarine corvettes intended to upgrade littoral warfare capabilities. Second of class *Kadmatt* was launched in October 2011 but the lead ship is struggling to meet a mid 2012 delivery date.

There is better news with respect to the second batch of three Project 1135.6 *Talwar* class frigates ordered from Russia in 2006. These are slightly modified variants of the earlier three ships, incorpo-

rating the surface-to-surface version of the BrahMos supersonic cruise missile jointly developed by India and Russia. The lead ship, *Teg,* was commissioned at the Yantar yard in Kaliningrad on 27 April 2012 and commenced her two-month delivery voyage to India the following month. The other two ships – *Tarkash* and *Trikand* – will be handed over at roughly six-monthly intervals. Whilst the overall project has been delayed by around a year compared with initial plans, this represents a much better performance than the experience with domestic yards.

Submarines: Russia is also playing an important role upgrading India's underwater forces, most notably through delivery of the Project 971 'Akula II' nuclear-powered attack submarine *Chakra* in April 2012. The submarine is reportedly being leased from Russia under a ten-year contract agreed in the middle of the last decade but delayed due to the accidental release of a gas suppression system during sea trials in November 2008 that killed twenty personnel. The submarine takes the name of an earlier boat leased to India in the late 1980s and is intended to refresh Indian skills in the underwater operation of nuclear propulsion before the deployment of the country's first strategic missile submarine, *Arihant.* Few definitive details of the secretive Advanced Technology Vessel (ATV) are in the public domain but the navy

The Indian Navy's Project 25A corvette *Kulish* pictured with other fleet ships whilst on exercise in the Indian Ocean with a US Navy carrier task group in early 2012. A decline in fleet numbers is starting to be reversed as overseas contracts supplement long-delayed indigenous construction. *(US Navy)*

An image of the Indian replenishment tanker *Shakti*, one of two *Deepak* class vessels delivered by Italy's Fincantieri during 2011. The strengthening of India's fleet train will greatly enhance its ability to sustain 'blue water' deployments. *(US Navy)*

The arrival of the nuclear-powered attack submarine *Chakra* from Russia in April 2012 marked a major step forward in the Indian Navy's steady transformation into one of the leading global fleets. One of the new 'Akula II' class boat's core roles is to give Indian submariners practical experience of operating underwater nuclear propulsion in advance of the arrival of the first indigenous strategic missile submarine *Arihant*. *(Indian Navy)*

seem confident the lead vessel will be delivered in the course of 2013. A second boat, *Aridhaman,* is expected to be launched around 2012 year-end and others are being built. Reports suggest the submarines displace around 6,000 tons, have a length of 112m and are powered by an indigenous nuclear reactor. Initial armament will be the K-15 missile, which has a limited, 700km range. However, longer-range weapons are under development.

The situation with the conventional force of diesel-electric submarines is less positive, as the construction of French-designed 'Scorpène' boats is yet another programme at Mazagon Dock that has suffered delays. The original plan was to start delivering six of the class from 2012 onwards at a cost of c.US$3.3bn but construction of the so-called Project 75 submarines is currently running around three years behind schedule and c.US$1bn over budget. The latest in a series of problems was a flood in July 2011 that submerged prefabricated hull sections with seawater. If the revised schedule is met, the first of the new submarines should start trials by the end of 2013. There have been suggestions that at least some of the follow-on Project 75-I class will be allocated to foreign yards in the hope of avoiding further delays. Meanwhile, refits of existing 'Kilo' class submarines are continuing so as to maintain a core underwater force until new construction is completed.

Other Construction: Delivery of front-line warships is being supplemented by a major programme of secondary construction encompassing offshore and coastal patrol vessels, minehunters, survey ships and fleet replenishment auxiliaries. Most orders have been placed with local yards but a major exception has been the two *Deepak* class fleet replenishment tankers allocated to Italy's

Fincantieri in 2008. The lead ship was commissioned in early 2011 with a sister, *Shakti,* following her into service on 1 October the same year. The 175m-long vessels displace 27,500 tons at full load with two 20MW diesel engines providing a top speed of 20 knots. They are fitted with double hulls in compliance with MARPOL regulations and can replenish four vessels simultaneously. The navy has

In spite of the decline in its fleet numbers starting to reverse, India will continue to operate obsolescent ships until local yards become more adept at delivering new ships. This image shows the destroyer *Ranvir*, which is a modified 1960s Russian design delivered in 1986. *(US Navy)*

Pakistan's missile-armed fast attack craft *Shujaat* is seen here on 23 March 2012. One of four *Jalalat* class vessels delivered between 1997 and 2006, she is being joined by two larger Chinese-designed *Azmat* class ships. *(Mrityunjoy Mazumdar)*

Increasing tensions between the United States and Pakistan over the campaign against Islamic extremists seems to be impacting deliveries of second-hand US naval equipment. As such, the transfer of further FFG-7 type frigates beyond *Alamgir* (ex-*McInerney*), seen here operating with the Royal Australian Navy's *Toowoomba*, are unlikely in the short term. *(Royal Australian Navy)*

lacked an adequate supply train in recent years and operational flexibility will be significantly enhanced by the new ships' arrival. Fleet support is also being bolstered by further investment in shore facilities, most notably the approval for commencement of Phase II-A of Project Seabird that will result in further expansion of the new west-coast naval base at Karwar. When completed around 2017/18, the US$2.5bn expansion will provide berthing and support for over thirty major vessels compared with around ten large units and ten smaller vessels currently based at the facility.

Operationally, the Indian Navy continues to expand its activities beyond the Indian Ocean in pursuit of the country's growing international economic and political interests. For example, June saw a flotilla that included the new frigate *Shivalik* visit Shanghai in the first deployment to China for five years at the same time as another squadron was departing for the Mediterranean for exercises with the French and other fleets. Bilateral exchanges are also being stepped up in the Indian Ocean, with inaugural exercises with Japan's JMSDF another new development in 2012.

Pakistan: Table 2.3.3, summarising current major Pakistan Navy units, reveals no major changes from the position a year ago. The increasing quantitative and qualitative gap with the neighbouring Indian fleet will be eased slightly over the next twelve months with the delivery of a fourth and final Chinese-designed F22P *Zulfiqar* class frigate, *Aslat*, from Karachi Shipyard and Engineering Works (KSEW), as well as the first of a pair of large fast missile-armed fast attack craft ordered from the China's Xingang Shipyard in Tianjin. The 550-ton *Azmat* was inducted into the fleet on 21 June 2012 following delivery in April and will be followed by a second KSEW-built sister in due course. The stealthy, 60m vessels are heavily orientated towards anti-surface warfare, shipping a main armament of eight C-802 (CSS-N-8 Saccade) surface-to-surface missiles supplemented by light anti-aircraft weapons. There have also been discussions with China about the acquisition of further frigates and submarines but it is unclear whether funding for these is available.

Increasing reliance on China for naval equipment reflect a deepening of Sino-Pakistan ties at a time when the country's longer-established relationship with the United States is under pressure from supposed Pakistan state links with radical Islamist elements, and the country's opposition to

Table 2.3.3: PAKISTAN NAVY: PRINCIPAL UNITS AS AT MID 2012

TYPE	CLASS	NUMBER	TONNAGE	DIMENSIONS	PROPULSION	CREW	DATE
Principal Surface Escorts							
Frigate – FFG	ZULFIQAR (F22P)	3	3,000 tons	118m x 13m x 5m	CODAD, 29 knots	185	2009
Frigate – FFG	ALAMGIR (FFG-7)	1	4,100 tons	138m x 14m x 5m	COGAG, 30 knots	215	1977
Frigate – FFG	TARIQ (Type 21)	6	3,600 tons	117m x 13m x 5m	COGOG, 32 knots	180	1974
Submarines							
Submarine – SSK	HAMZA (AGOSTA 90B/AIP)	1	2,100 tons	76m x 7m x 6m	AIP, 20 knots	40	2008
Submarine – SSK	KHALID (AGOSTA 90B)	2	1,800 tons	68m x 7m x 6m	Diesel-electric, 20 knots	40	1999
Submarine – SSK	HASHMAT (AGOSTA)	2	1,800 tons	68m x 7m x 6m	Diesel-electric, 20 knots	55	1979

unmanned drone strikes on militant targets within its boundaries. This has probably put a halt – at least temporarily – to further planned transfers of former US Navy FFG-7 type frigates following the initial transfer of the former *McInerney* (FFG-8) as *Alamgir* in 2010. In spite of this, the navy retains close links with North American and European fleets and remains an active participant in anti-piracy and anti-terrorist operations in the Indian Ocean.

AFRICAN NAVIES

Procurement activity amongst the African navies has been heavily skewed towards the North African coastline in recent years, with resource-rich **Algeria** leading the way. Earlier procurement of additional 'Kilo' class submarines and refurbishment of existing vessels has now been supplemented by further acquisitions, with three major projects confirmed in the last twelve months. The first contract awarded was placed with Italy's Fincantieri in July 2011 for a new amphibious ship that is thought to be a heavily modified variant of the Italian Navy's *San Marco* LPD design. Displacing around 9,000 tons and reportedly equipped with a multifunction radar and MBDA Aster surface-to-air missiles, the new vessel will be capable of deploying around 450 troops from landing craft carried in the well dock and from two helicopter landing spots on the flight deck. First steel was cut in January 2012 and delivery is expected before the end of 2014. Joining the new ship will be up to four MEKO 200 type frigates under a c.US$3bn contract signed with Germany's ThyssenKrupp Marine Systems in March 2012. The agreement, which reportedly covers AgustaWestland Super Lynx helicopters and ongoing support and training, will see two ships constructed at the Blohm & Voss yard in Hamburg followed by licence-built production of further vessels in Algeria. The announcement was closely followed by news of a further contract, this time with China, for a further three corvette-sized vessels. The decision to select such a diverse range of suppliers is even more surprising given Algeria's past reliance on Russian technology and it will be interesting to see how effectively it manages to integrate the new ships into its existing fleet.

Elsewhere along the North African coast, **Morocco** is seeing good progress achieved with construction of the three 'Sigma' class corvettes ordered from the Dutch Damen Schelde Naval Shipbuilding. The first ship, *Tarik ben Ziyad*, was commissioned on 10 September 2011, with the second vessel, *Sultan Moulay Ismail*, following on 10 March 2012. The final ship has also commenced sea acceptance trials and should be delivered in the second half of 2012. Interestingly, the Royal Moroccan Navy has also selected multi-country sourcing for its warship requirements, turning to France for the FREMM type frigate, *Mohammed VI*, and the OPV70 class patrol vessel *Bir Anzaran*. The latter ship was delivered in June 2011 whilst the frigate was floated out in September of the same year and should be delivered during 2013.

The African Spring has curtailed other developments in the region, although construction of 'Ambassador III' fast attack craft continues for **Egypt** at Halter Marine in the United States. A dedication for the first of four units was carried out in October 2011, when the lead ship was named *S Ezzat* after the commander of the Egyptian Navy between 1953 and 1967. Along the coast, **Libya** faces the need to rebuild its navy after the widespread damage inflicted by NATO forces during the civil war, with the core of the remaining fleet being comprised of those ships that defected to the rebel side at the start of the conflict. The immediate priority is to reconstitute an operational patrol capa-

A number of African navies are boosting their constabulary forces to counter the rising threat of piracy and other criminal activity, which has spread far beyond the Indian Ocean. The West African state of Benin is one example, acquiring three new 30m patrol vessels from France's OCEA. They are similar in design to an earlier class built for Algeria, with this image showing the Algerian *Mirfak* in May 2009. *(Bruno Huriet)*

bility and several countries have been approached for assistance in this regard.

Elsewhere on the continent, development of meaningful constabulary patrol capabilities is also the priority. **South Africa** has the most ambitious plans in this regard under the long-awaited Project Biro and significant funding is to be made available from FY2013/14 to take these forward. The project envisages the acquisition of both offshore and inshore patrol vessels to replace existing life-expired assets, with the offshore patrol ship blueprint also likely to be used for a new survey ship under the associated Project Hotel. A foreign design is likely to be selected for local construction, with DCNS, Lürssen and Navantia amongst European builders linking with South African yards to bid for the programme. The new vessels will be based at Salisbury Island in Durban, which will be upgraded to a full naval base for the first time since the naval presence there was dramatically scaled back in 1994. Durban is better situated than Simon's Town for supporting increased patrols off Africa's east coast, where the navy has been active in combating the southward spread of piracy from the Horn of Africa. At the moment these are carried out by the 'Valour' class MEKO A-200 frigates supplemented by the replenishment ship *Drakensberg*. The latter helped catch seven Somali pirates operating in the Mozambique Channel in April 2012 in what was South Africa's first participation in a successful piracy arrest.[5]

Maritime security problems are, however, not limited to Africa's Indian Ocean coastline. For example, West Africa is now rated amongst the world's top ten piracy hotspots. **Nigeria**'s navy is one of the local fleets being renewed to meet the challenge after a long period of neglect. The most significant investment to date was announced in March 2012 with the decision to acquire two 95m, 1,800-ton offshore patrol vessels from China, of which one will – in part – be built locally. Neighbouring **Benin** is also upgrading patrol forces, if on a lesser scale, acquiring three new-build coastal patrol craft from France's OCEA that are similar to previous boats built for Algeria. The vessels have a maximum speed of around 30 knots and carry a 30mm main gun supplemented by lighter weaponry.

MIDDLE EASTERN NAVIES

Israel's navy continues to be the dominant force amongst the Middle East's maritime forces, not least

An unidentified Libyan 'La Combattante' fast attack craft pictured in a burnt-out and half-sunken condition after the collapse of the Gadaffi regime. Libya's Navy will need to be entirely rebuilt following the country's civil war. *(NATO)*

Saudi Arabia's *Tabuk*, one of four *Badr* class corvettes delivered from the United States in the early 1980s, pictured on 24 March 2012. Saudi Arabia is planning a significant modernisation programme for its surface fleet but no final decisions have yet been made. *(Mrityunjoy Mazumdar)*

because of its powerful anti-submarine fleet. This is believed to have a strategic as well as tactical dimension through its Type 800 *Dolphin* class boats' ability to deploy nuclear-armed Popeye Turbo cruise missiles. Existing boats in the three-strong flotilla are currently being put through midlife refits whilst the force's overall size will be doubled in the next few years as additional units are delivered by Germany's HDW. Two of these Batch 2 units were ordered in 2006 and feature an 11m AIP hull plug for extended underwater operation. The first was launched at Kiel on 19 February 2012 and was delivered to its new owners in May for extensive sea trials prior to its departure for Israel in 2013. The other should follow around a year later. An order for a further Batch 2 unit was announced in the first half of 2012, with – as for the previous boats – around one third of the c.US$700m cost being subsidised by Germany. The flotilla gives Israel a theoretical second-strike nuclear capability against Iran through forward deployment to the Indian Ocean, although submarine range and payload provide significant limitations. As such, the flotilla is possibly being used as a signal of strategic intent rather than providing a fully robust operational capability.[6]

Whilst **Iran** is seen as the main threat to regional stability by dint of its own nuclear programme, it is unclear whether its increasingly elderly navy would be capable of causing any lasting disruption to seaborne traffic through the Straits of Hormuz in the event of all-out conflict. Impressive progress has certainly been made in developing an indigenous warship construction and maintenance capability given the lack of outside assistance, with most effort being focused on developing asymmetrical capabilities in spite of the high profile given to more conventional capabilities such as the locally-built

The US Military Sealift Command-chartered M/V *Tern*, a Netherlands semi-submersible transport, pictured transiting the Indian Ocean on 18 June 2012 carrying four US Navy *Avenger* class mine countermeasures vessels to Bahrain. Development of Iranian asymmetrical capabilities in the area of mine warfare is triggering a response from the United States and its allies. *(US Navy)*

frigate *Jamaran*. There has been particular emphasis on the construction of 120-ton 'Ghadir' class midget submarines, which have both torpedo and mine-laying capabilities. Around twenty of these have entered service to supplement the light gun- and missile-armed fast attack boats and coastal missile batteries that are intended to complicate 'Western' planning. Developments in Iranian capabilities are certainly causing a response in terms of American and allied countermeasures, for example, through the deployment of additional minehunters to the region.

Iranian rhetoric – although not necessarily its actual military capability – is also fuelling higher expenditure amongst neighbouring fleets in the Persian Gulf, where buoyant oil revenues are helping fund fleet renewal.[7] **The United Arab Emirates** is currently the most advanced with its procurement activities, with the lead *Baynunah* class corvette constructed by France's CMN likely to be declared operational shortly. A further five vessels were allocated to Abu Dhabi Shipbuilding, which launched the fourth member of the class, *Mezyad,* on 15 February 2012. Delivery is also expected soon of the Italian-built *Abu Dhabi*, a derivative of the Italian Navy's 'Comandanti' class, and two smaller 55m 'Falaj2' patrol ships. The first of these, *Ghantut*, was launched in January 2012, and sister *Qarnen* followed on 8 June. The heavily-armed pair are interesting in having a low top speed of 20 knots, relying on stealth and electronics for effective surveillance and interception.

Elsewhere in the region, **Oman**'s long-delayed Project Khareef seems to be making headway. The lead ship of a trio of three corvettes, *Al Shamikh,* resumed trials in November 2011 after a long delay apparently caused by problems with the seawater cooling system. However, the ship's problems were not entirely over, with the *Daily Telegraph* reporting in March 2012 that three BAE Systems engineers had been injured when a gun misfired during trials off the Dorset coast. The Royal Navy of Oman has decided to turn east for its next major purchase, with Singapore's ST Marine securing a c.US$900m contract for four 75m offshore patrol vessels based on the Republic of Singapore Navy *Fearless* design in April 2012. The quartet are scheduled for delivery between 2015 and 2016. Both **Saudi Arabia** and **Qatar** also have ongoing requirements to replace ageing fast attack craft but final procurement selections have yet to be made.

The Royal Oman Navy's Project Khareef for three *Al Shamikh* class corvettes seems to be back on track following the rectification of problems identified with earlier trials. Following several months in dockyard hands, the lead ship re-emerged for further trials in November 2011 and should be delivered by the end of 2012. *(Conrad Waters)*

Notes:

1. According to a 2011 report in *The Economist,* China's trade with Africa exceeded US$120bn per annum by 2010, whilst the Middle East and Africa accounted for over 30 per cent of the country's entire outward investment in the period between 2005 and 2010. The information is contained in 'Trying to pull together: Africans are asking whether China is making their lunch or eating it', *The Economist* – 20 April 2011 (London, The Economist Newspaper Ltd, 2011).

2. The Syrian port of Tartus is one of Russia's few remaining overseas facilities, providing fuelling and maintenance facilities for warships operating in the Mediterranean. Amongst a number of papers reporting news of the planned deployment was *The New York Times*: see Andrew E Kramer's 'Russian Warships Said to Be Going to Naval Base in Syria', *The New York Times* – 18 June 2012 (New York, The New York Times Company, 2012).

3. Approval for a joint venture between leading state-owned warship builder Mazagon Dock and the private sector Pipavav Shipyard was signed off in May 2012. It has also been reported that Mazagon will form an alliance with another private company, Larsen & Turbo, for the forthcoming Project 75I submarine programme. Private

builders ABG Shipyard and Bharati Shipyard have also been authorised to bid for future warship construction.

4. A more detailed description of the Project 17 series is contained in Chapter 3.4. The Project 15 series was analysed in *Seaforth World Naval Review 2011*.

5. Further details of South African naval developments can be found on the informative *defenceWeb* site at www.defenceweb.co.za.

6. This line of argument was put forward by S Samuel C Rajiv in a paper published by India's Institute for Defence Studies and Analyses. See *Israel's Dolphin Class Submarines: A Potent Deterrent?* (New Delhi, IDSA, June 2012). A copy can be found by searching the http://isda.in/ website.

7. A comprehensive update on naval programmes being undertaken by the Gulf Co-operation Council States, as well as by Iran and Iraq, was published by *Jane's Defence Weekly* in March 2012. See Kate Tringham's 'Building new Capabilities: GCC states maritime update', *Jane's Defence Weekly* – 14 March 2012 (Coulsdon, IHS Jane's, 2012) pp.26–33.

2.4 REGIONAL REVIEW

EUROPE AND RUSSIA

Author:
Conrad Waters

INTRODUCTION:

In overall terms, the prognosis for Europe's fleets remains difficult. The absence of a solution to the crisis in confidence that continues to threaten the financial wellbeing of the Eurozone and its neighbours has extended funding restrictions that will be a theme of defence budgets until financial stability is restored. The long timescales inherent in naval procurement mean that equipment continues to be delivered in accordance with contracts signed before the current financial crisis. However, prospects for new programmes are largely reliant on the need to maintain key industrial capabilities and the opportunities for skilled employment they provide.

The general atmosphere of gloom is not uniform. For example, medium-term prospects for the British Royal Navy appear a little brighter in spite of the short-term damage caused by a 2010 Strategic Defence Review that is starting to look increasingly ill-judged as key components begin to unravel.[1] The shock caused by the extent of the cutbacks and the discipline imposed by a new, financially-astute defence secretary seem to have produced a more-realistic planning framework. This holds out some prospect of matching planned force structures with available funding. In particular, an agreed ten-year £160bn (US$250bn) procurement programme – including contingencies for cost overruns and emerging requirements – is allowing new acquisitions. These have included four long-awaited replenishment tankers under the MARS Military Afloat Reach and Sustainability programme, as well as

investment in design work for the 'Successor' strategic missile submarines.

The Royal Navy has also benefited from implementing planned reductions quickly. This means that it is further advanced than many European peers in establishing a new baseline from which to rebuild capabilities. By contrast, both the Italian and Spanish fleets are only now commencing 'rebalancing' plans that will see significant reductions in existing force levels, as well as the curtailment of future procurement. Prospects for the *Armada Española,* which has built one of the most effective European fleets in recent years, are particularly bleak given the extent of Spain's financial problems. Lack of funding has killed off any prospect for a sixth F-100 class frigate and leaves shipbuilder Navantia facing an increasingly empty order book for its main yard at Ferrol unless additional export work is secured.[2] Meanwhile, French defence priorities will be determined by the new administration of socialist President François Hollande. He assumed office on 15 May 2012 following his election victory over Nicolas Sarkozy. A new White Paper on defence and security is to be published within the next twelve months. This will inform the detailed 2014–20 defence plan and provide further clarity. Closer strategic co-operation between the major European nations has been seen as one way of maintaining the continent's military influence whilst budgets are under pressure. However, prospects for implementation of the 2010 Anglo-French defence treaty are uncertain following co-signatory Sarkozy's ejection from office.[3]

Two trends standing out from the current focus on austerity and financial control – both referenced in 2012's *Seaforth World Naval Review* – are worthy of further note. One is an increasing emphasis on investment in anti-ballistic missile defence (AMD) capabilities. A notable development here was the Dutch announcement in September 2011 that they would modify radars on their *De Zeven Provinciën* frigates to participate in NATO's Active Layered Theatre Ballistic Missile Defence project. Their navy becomes the first European fleet to deploy AMD technology. The Dutch ships will assist US Aegis-equipped vessels to detect and track targets but will not, at least initially, provide 'shooter' capabilities. The other trend is Russia's determination to rebuild its forces after their post Cold War decay; a project given added impetus by Vladimir Putin's re-election to the Russian presidency in May 2012. In similar fashion to India, lack of shipbuilding and technological infrastructure has been a major constraint to achieving these ambitions. For example, the Project 677 'Lada' class submarine programme was essentially put on hold in November 2011 after insurmountable problems with the propulsion and combat management systems installed in the prototype boat. Capabilities are slowly being rebuilt, assisted by experience gained on export work and – to an extent – the import of overseas expertise.[4] Commencement of builder Sevmash's long-delayed trials for the refurbished Indian carrier *Vikramaditya* in June 2012 evidences just another milestone in a process that still represents 'work in progress'.

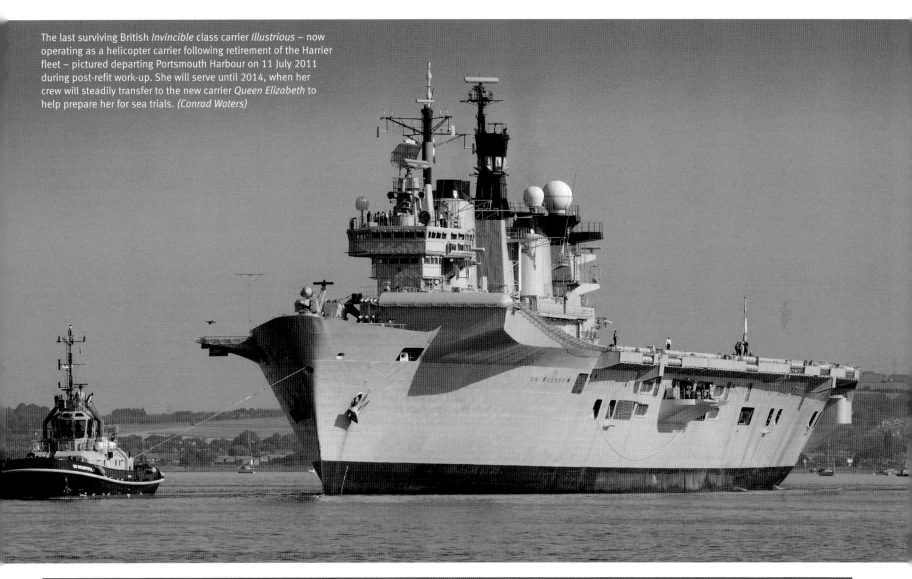

The last surviving British *Invincible* class carrier *Illustrious* – now operating as a helicopter carrier following retirement of the Harrier fleet – pictured departing Portsmouth Harbour on 11 July 2011 during post-refit work-up. She will serve until 2014, when her crew will steadily transfer to the new carrier *Queen Elizabeth* to help prepare her for sea trials. *(Conrad Waters)*

TABLE 2.4.1: FLEET STRENGTHS IN WESTERN EUROPE – LARGER NAVIES (MID 2012)

COUNTRY	FRANCE	GERMANY	GREECE	ITALY	NETHERLANDS	SPAIN	TURKEY	UK
Aircraft Carrier (CVN)	1	–	–	–	–	–	–	–
Support/Helicopter Carrier (CVS/CVH)				2	–	1	–	1
Strategic Missile Submarine (SSBN)	4	–	–	–	–	–	–	4
Attack Submarine (SSN)	6	–	–	–	–	–	–	7
Patrol Submarine (SSK)	–	4	8	6	4	3	14	–
Fleet Escort (DDG/FFG)	17	15	13	15	6	10	17	19
Patrol Escort/Corvette (FFG/FSG/FS)	15	5	–	8	–	–	7	–
Missile Armed Attack Craft (PGG/PTG)	–	8	16	–	–	–	27	–
Mine Countermeasures Vessel (MCMV)	14	17	9	10	6	6	20	15
Major Amphibious (LHD/LPD/LPH/LSD)	4	–	–	3	2	3	–	6

Note: The five new German K-130 corvettes are being progressively brought up to operational status as gearbox repairs are completed.

The new French offshore patrol vessel *L'Adroit* has been funded by DCNS and handed over to the *Marine Nationale* on a three-year loan in the hope of securing both domestic and export orders. This image was taken shortly after she was delivered on 21 October 2011. *(DCNS)*

MAJOR REGIONAL POWERS – FRANCE:

The principal constituents of the *Marine Nationale* are set out in Table 2.4.2. The main change over the last year has been the replacement of the amphibious dock transport *Foudre* with the larger and more capable amphibious assault ship *Dixmude*. Third of the *Mistral* class *bâtiments de projection et de commandement*, *Dixmude* is one of a pair of additional ships included in the 2008 Defence White Paper. She was ordered under an accelerated timescale in April 2009 as part of France's plans to ensure recovery from the early stages of the economic crisis, protecting employment in STX Europe's Chantiers de l'Atlantique yard at Saint Nazaire. She was handed over to France's DGA procurement agency three months ahead of schedule in January 2012 and has already been deployed to the Indian Ocean on training and anti-piracy duties as part of pre-commissioning trials. Current plans envisage the fourth and final ship being delivered by 2020 in replacement for *Foudre*'s sister *Siroco* but this will depend on funds being available. Also entering service are the new EDA-R catamaran landing craft, with three of a first batch of four delivered by June 2012. One of these was deployed on *Mistral* to test inter-operability with US forces during the 'Bold Alligator' exercises off the American coast in early 2012. Another is being carried by *Dixmude* during her training cruise.

TABLE 2.4.2: FRENCH NAVY: PRINCIPAL UNITS AS AT MID 2012

TYPE	CLASS	NUMBER	TONNAGE	DIMENSIONS	PROPULSION	CREW	DATE
Aircraft Carriers							
Aircraft Carrier – CVN	CHARLES DE GAULLE	1	42,000 tons	262m x 33/64m x 9m	Nuclear, 27 knots	1,950	2001
Principal Surface Escorts							
Frigate – FFG	FORBIN	2	7,000 tons	153m x 20m x 5m	CODOG, 29+ knots	195	2008
Frigate – FFG	CASSARD (FAA-70)	2	5,000 tons	139m x 15m x 5m	CODAD, 30 knots	250	1988
Frigate – FFG	TOURVILLE (FASM-67)	1	6,100 tons	153m x 16m x 5m	Steam, 32 knots	300	1974
Frigate – FFG	GEORGES LEYGUES (FASM-70)	7	4,800 tons	139m x 15m x 5m	CODOG, 30 knots	240	1979
Frigate – FFG	LA FAYETTE	5	3,600 tons	125m x 15m x 5m	CODAD, 25 knots	150	1996
Frigate – FSG	FLORÉAL	6	3,000 tons	94m x 14m x 4m	CODAD, 20 knots	90	1992
Frigate – FS1	D'ESTIENNE D'ORVES (A-69)	9	1,300 tons	80m x 10m x 3m	Diesel, 24 knots	90	1976
Submarines							
Submarine – SSBN	LE TRIOMPHANT	4	14,400 tons	138m x 13m x 11m	Nuclear, 25 knots	110	1997
Submarine – SSN	RUBIS	6	2,700 tons	74m x 8m x 6m	Nuclear, 25+ knots	70	1983
Major Amphibious Units							
Amph Assault Ship – LHD	MISTRAL	3	21,500 tons	199m x 32m x 6m	Diesel-electric, 19 knots	160	2006
Landing Platform Dock – LPD	FOUDRE	1	12,000 tons	168m x 24m x 5m	Diesel, 20 knots	225	1990

Note: 1 Now officially reclassified as offshore patrol vessels.

Current construction is focused on series production of the *Aquitaine* class FREMM type frigates and *Suffren* class Barracuda type nuclear-powered attack submarines. Details of the former project, which will see eleven ships delivered at roughly ten-monthly intervals through to 2022, are set out in Chapter 3.1. Delivery of a total of six submarines is planned at roughly two-yearly intervals through to 2027, of which three have been ordered to date. Work on *Suffren* and sister *Duguay-Trouin* is already well-advanced at DCNS in Cherbourg. Meanwhile, the first underwater test firing of the MdCN cruise missile that will eventually equip the new boats took place in June 2011.

The significant sums being spent on these two frontline programmes – around US$20bn in total – means that there is little additional money to allocate to secondary shipping. The situation with respect to corvettes and offshore patrol vessels is particularly concerning and it will be interesting to see whether the three-year loan of the DCNS-built and funded *L'Adroit* to the navy will translate into firm orders. Delivered on 21 October 2011 – less than two years after construction commenced – and formally commissioned in March 2012, the c.1,500-ton offshore patrol vessel is operated by two crews of thirty sailors that alternate every four months. Around 220 sea days are scheduled each year. Initial operations have been conducted from Toulon and have encompassed fishery protection and maritime security missions. The ship is able to operate helicopters up to NH-90 size and has also successfully tested the Schiebel S-100 Camcopter.

Also competing for limited *Marine Nationale* funds is a new class of multi-product logistic support vessels to replace the remaining four *Durance* class command and replenishment ships. The DCNS BRAVE (*bâtiment ravitailleur d'escadre*) will almost certainly be selected for the design, with construction likely to be allocated to STX at Saint Nazaire. The 30,000-ton vessels are 190m long and provide hospital and command facilities as well as a full range of replenishment capabilities. There will also be the capacity to embark up to sixty troops or other personnel in addition to the core crew of around one hundred, whilst a two spot helicopter deck will provide additional flexibility. A range of self-defence options includes remotely controlled light weapons and Mistral surface-to-air missiles. If all goes to plan, delivery of the first ship is anticipated around 2016/17.

The rather battered-looking French command and replenishment vessel, *Somme*, seen on 29 March 2012 after a short stopover at Portsmouth, United Kingdom. Current plans envisage four new multi-product logistic support ships replacing *Somme* and her three French sisters around the 2016/17 timescale. *(Conrad Waters)*

MAJOR REGIONAL POWERS – ITALY:

A full review of the development of Italy's *Marina Militare* from the dark days after the 1943 armistice to the present is contained in Chapter 2.4B, whilst current fleet strength is summarised in Table 2.4.3. Although the Italian Navy's core projects have escaped the worst of recently announced defence cutbacks, current numbers will still fall significantly over the next four years as older vessels are retired without adequate replacement. Front-line units scheduled for withdrawal by 2016 include all four of the unmodernised *Maestrale* class frigates, three or four of the similar *Artigliere* class, six of the *Minerva* class corvettes and at least three of the initial batch of *Lerici* class minehunters. Support and auxiliary shipping will also be impacted by the decommissioning of tugs, replenishment vessels and training units. It is also likely that the submarine flotilla will fall to just four boats as the second pair of Type 212A submarines are commissioned.

The planned withdrawals of 'high-end' units will be largely counterbalanced by progressive delivery of Italian variant FREMM type frigates. Fincantieri has made good progress with these over the past year, with the initial ship, *Carlo Bergamini*, being launched from their Riva Trigoso yard near Genoa on 16 July 2011 prior to commencing sea trials from their Muggiano facility on 6 October. She has been closely followed by the second of class, *Virginio Fasan*, which undertook her maiden voyage on 14 June 2012, less than three months after launch on 31 March. In contrast to the lead ship, she has been built to a specialised anti-submarine specification with a lighter main armament but provision for a towed array and the MILAS torpedo-carrying missile. Both vessels will be delivered during 2013. Four additional ships will be commissioned at roughly annual intervals, of which two are already under construction. The original plan was for ten ships but this seems increasingly unlikely given ongoing financial constraints.

The revised fleet structure will still leave the Italian Navy capable of deploying powerful task groups around the new carrier *Cavour* and amphibious units, particularly if plans for new amphibious assault ships to replace the *San Giorgio* class and *Giuseppe Garibaldi* make it past the design stage. However, the loss of corvettes and mine countermeasures vessels will leave the fleet short of capabilities in these critical areas. New light frigates and offshore patrol vessels are being contemplated to fill the gap but these will also be dependent on the availability of funding.

Table 2.4.3: ITALIAN NAVY: PRINCIPAL UNITS AS AT MID 2012

TYPE	CLASS	NUMBER	TONNAGE	DIMENSIONS	PROPULSION	CREW	DATE
Aircraft Carriers							
Aircraft Carrier – CV	CAVOUR	1	27,100 tons	244m x 30/39m x 9m	COGAG, 29 knots	800	2008
Aircraft Carrier – CVS	GIUSEPPE GARIBALDI	1	13,900 tons	180m x 23/31m x 7m	COGAG, 30 knots	825	1985
Principal Surface Escorts							
Frigate – FFG	ANDREA DORIA	2	7,100 tons	153m x 20m x 5m	CODOG, 29+ knots	190	2007
Destroyer – DDG	DE LA PENNE	2	5,400 tons	148m x 16m x 5m	CODOG, 31 knots	375	1993
Frigate – FFG	MAESTRALE	8	3,100 tons	123m x 13m x 4m	CODOG, 30+ knots	225	1982
Frigate – FFG	ARTIGLIERE	3	2,500 tons	114m x 12m x 4m	CODOG, 35 knots	185	1994
Frigate – FS	MINERVA	8	1,300 tons	87m x 11m x 3m	Diesel, 25 knots	120	1987
Submarines							
Submarine – SSK	TODARO (Type 212A)	2	1,800 tons	56m x 7m x 6m	AIP, 20+ knots	30	2006
Submarine – SSK	PELOSI	4	1,700 tons	64m x 7m x 6m	Diesel-electric, 20 knots	50	1988
Major Amphibious Units							
Landing Platform Dock – LPD	SAN GIORGIO	3	8,000 tons	133m x 21m x 5m	Diesel, 20 knots	165	1987

Away from disposal and procurement activities, the main story impacting the *Marina Militare* over the past year has been the arrest of two marines from the San Marco Regiment by the Indian authorities over the deaths of two fishermen apparently mistaken for pirates. The Italians were part of a six-strong security detachment aboard the Italian-flagged tanker *Enrica Lexie* that fired warning shots towards a suspect vessel on 15 February 2012 whilst off the India coast. The case, which raises significant legal questions both in respect of jurisdiction over foreign naval personnel onboard commercial shipping and also with regards to rights in the extended territorial waters of an exclusive economic zone, has become something of a cause célèbre in both countries. The two marines remain under restricted bail in India until the case is decided.

MAJOR REGIONAL POWERS – SPAIN:

The *Armada Española* has made great strides in the last decade, with the commissioning of new and effective fleet units more than compensating for an overall decline in fleet numbers. The Aegis-equipped F-100 *Álvaro de Bazán* class frigates and *Juan Carlos I* multi-purpose amphibious assault ship provide the core of an effective blue water flotilla, whilst the new BAM (*buque de acción maritima*) offshore patrol ships of the *Meteoro* class will progressively take over a wide range of secondary duties. Construction of four S-80 air-independent propulsion-equipped (AIP) submarines has also escaped cutbacks to date. Launch of the first boat, *Isaac Peral,* is scheduled for mid 2013.

The most important current Italian construction programme is for the Italian variant of the Franco-Italian FREMM multi-mission frigates. These views show the dry launch of second of class, *Virginio Fasin,* at Riva Trigoso near Genoa in 31 March 2012. The incomplete hull of the third ship, *Carlo Margottini,* can also be seen. *(OCCAR)*

Table 2.4.4: SPANISH NAVY: PRINCIPAL UNITS AS AT MID 2012

TYPE	CLASS	NUMBER	TONNAGE	DIMENSIONS	PROPULSION	CREW	DATE
Aircraft Carriers							
Aircraft Carrier – CVS	PRINCIPE DE ASTURIAS	1[1]	16,700 tons	196m x 24/32m x 7m	COGAG, 25 knots	555	1988
Principal Surface Escorts							
Frigate – FFG	ÁLVARO DE BAZÁN (F-100)	4	6,300 tons	147m x 19m x 5m	CODOG, 28 knots	200	2002
Frigate – FFG	SANTA MARIA (FFG-7)	6[1]	4,100 tons	138m x 14m x 5m	COGAG, 30 knots	225	1986
Submarines							
Submarine – SSK	GALERNA (S-70/AGOSTA)	3	1,800 tons	68m x 7m x 6m	Diesel-electric, 21 knots	60	1983
Major Amphibious Units							
Amph Assault Ship – LHD	JUAN CARLOS I	1	27,100 tons	231m x 32m x 7m	IEP, 21 knots	245	2010
Landing Platform Dock – LPD	GALICIA	2	13,000 tons	160m x 25m x 6m	Diesel, 20 knots	185	1998

1. Plans are under consideration to place *Principe de Asturias* and two of the FFG-7 type frigates in long reserve as an economy measure.

Above: Severe budgetary restrictions mean that Spain's *Cristóbal Colón* (*Christopher Columbus*) will be the last F-100 type Aegis frigate delivered to the Spanish Navy. She is seen here departing Ferrol on preliminary sea trials during March 2012. (*Navantia*)

The most important surface vessel currently being built is the fifth and final F-100 class vessel, *Cristóbal Colón*. She commenced sea trials in March 2012 and will be delivered in the second half of the year. She incorporates a number of improvements over the earlier quartet, including enhancements to the combat management system and the incorporation of a bow thruster for enhanced manoeuvrability. The Spanish Navy hopes to receive authority for a follow-on F-110 design – which will replace the existing FFG-7 *Santa Maria* class frigates from the start of the next decade – if the country's financial situation improves. The current baseline design envisages a 5,000-ton mono-hulled ship with combined diesel-electric and gas propulsion and an innovative integrated mast that could house a newly-developed phased array.[5] Capabilities will fall somewhere between the intensive war fighting potential of the F-100 class and the cost-effective, constabulary capacity provided by the BAM design.

Deliveries of the initial batch of BAM type vessels are now well underway. The lead ship, *Meteoro,* was commissioned in July 2011 and a further two had been delivered by mid 2012. This leaves only

Right: A view of the new Spanish 'BAM' type offshore patrol vessel *Meteoro*, which was commissioned into the *Armada Española* in July 2012. A second batch of ships was authorised in 2011 but the financial crisis means that firm orders have yet to be placed. (*Navantia*)

Tornado to be handed over in the second half of the year. The new class are armed with a 76mm gun and are equipped with a hangar and flight deck for helicopter operation. Orders for five more were authorised during 2011 but a contract for their construction has yet to be signed with Navantia, apparently due to budgetary constraints. A new 'Vision 2025' strategy is being developed to determine future procurement priorities but this will inevitably be hindered by the evolving financial situation being faced by the government.

The funding crisis is also impacting existing fleet numbers contained in Table 2.4.4. The existing S-70 *Agosta* type submarine *Siroco* was decommissioned in June 2012 to avoid the costs of a planned refit and will be used as a source of spares for the remaining three boats until they are replaced by the new S-80 class. There have also been press reports that the government is planning to pay off the flagship aircraft carrier *Principe de Asturias* and two FFG-7 type frigates into extended reserve to save refit and operating costs. The former ship's Harriers will be operated from *Juan Carlos I* but it is by no means clear that there will be sufficient money to replace them with F-35B Lightning II Joint Strike Fighters when they fall due for replacement.

MAJOR REGIONAL POWERS – UNITED KINGDOM:

There have been few changes to the principal Royal Navy constituents set out in Table 2.4.5, with nearly all the significant reductions in fleet strength prescribed by the 2010 Strategic Defence Review (SDSR) implemented by June 2011. A more detailed assessment of developments in respect of major warship categories is set out below:

Aircraft Carriers & Amphibious Ships: The major development in the last year has undoubtedly been the May 2012 decision to abandon plans announced in the SDSR to acquire the F-35C carrier variant of the Joint Strike Fighter and to fit one of the two new *Queen Elizabeth* aircraft carriers with catapults and arrester gear to handle the plane.[6] Instead, the UK's Conservative-Liberal coalition will revert to the previous administration's plans to operate the F-35B STOVL variant in a major embarrassment to British Prime Minister David Cameron, who had been a vocal critic of the earlier arrangement. The decision was made when it became apparent that cost of conversion of *Prince of Wales,* the ship earmarked for conversion, had more than doubled to c.£2bn (US$3.1bn), undermining the economic rationale for the scheme outlined in the SDSR. The return to STOVL operation opens up the prospect of both carriers entering service to ensure that one is continuously available for operations as compared with the SDSR intention to 'mothball' or sell the unconverted ship. A final decision will be taken in the next defence review scheduled for 2015, although the modest £60m (US$90m) annual cost of maintaining both ships makes this a likely option. The revised plan will see *Queen Elizabeth* delivered to the Royal Navy in 2017 and commence trial F-35B operations the following year. An operational fixed wing capability will be restored by 2020.

In the meantime, the last remaining *Invincible* class light carrier, *Illustrious,* has completed work-up following her final refit and will serve as the fleet's 'on-call' helicopter carrier until retired in 2014. The other helicopter carrier, *Ocean,* returned home from a seven-month deployment that included successful operations off Libya in December 2011. She has subsequently been assigned a command and control role in support of the 2012 London Olympics before starting a scheduled refit.

Surface Combatants: The replacement of the remaining Type 42 air defence destroyers with their vastly more capable Type 45 *Daring* class replacements continues apace. The fourth ship, *Dragon,* was delivered at Portsmouth on 31 August 2011, swiftly losing the distinctive dragons that had adorned her bow during contractor's sea trials. She was subsequently commissioned in April 2012, effectively replacing the last Batch II Type 42 destroyer, *Liverpool,* which was withdrawn from service on 30 March after just short of thirty years' service. The fifth Type 45, *Defender,* is due to be delivered in July 2012, whilst the sixth and final ship, *Duncan,* should commence trials towards the end of the year. Meanwhile, the first three ships have commenced operational duties. *Dauntless* was tasked with the standing South Atlantic mission and both *Daring* and *Diamond* were deployed, consecutively,

A British Army AH1 Apache helicopter operating from the helicopter carrier *Ocean* as part of Operation Ellamy, the British contribution to NATO's intervention in the 2011 Libyan Civil War. US Pave Hawk search and rescue helicopters can also be seen on deck. *(©UK/MOD Crown Copyright 2012)*

Left: The fourth British Type 45 destroyer, *Dragon*, pictured in the English Channel on 30 August 2011 during her delivery voyage. The distinctive dragon images that adorned her bow during sea trials were painted out immediately after she commissioned to meet the demands of officialdom. *(©UK/MOD Crown Copyright 2012)*

Below: An image of the Type 45 destroyer *Defender* on builder's trials off the Scottish coast in November 2011. She will be delivered in the second half of 2012. *(BAE Systems)*

The final Batch II Type 42 destroyer, *Liverpool*, decommissioned on 30 March 2012 after nearly thirty years' service. One of her final duties before decommissioning was to monitor the movements of the Russian carrier *Admiral Kuznetsov* as she passed close to UK waters in February 2012 on return from a Mediterranean cruise. *(©UK/MOD Crown Copyright 2012)*

to the Persian Gulf. The two latter vessels received various enhancements prior to departing home waters, most notably the installation of Vulcan Phalanx close-in weapons systems and improved electronic support measures technology.

The thirteen Type 23 frigates continue to go through a rolling series of upgrades. The next steps will be integration of the new Artisan radar, scheduled to be installed in *Iron Duke* in 2013, and the Sea Ceptor variant of the Common Anti-Air Modular Missile (CAMM). A £483m (US$750m) development contract for the new missile, which will replace the existing Sea Wolf, was announced in January 2012. Both systems will eventually be trans-

ferred to the replacement Type 26 global combat ship, which has been confirmed as part of the core ten-year procurement programme. Designer BAE Systems have been making strenuous efforts to attract international partners to share development costs but success has proved illusory to date.

Submarines: *Astute*, lead boat of her class of new nuclear-powered attack submarines, has recovered from the setbacks that marked the first year of her career, undertaking a highly successful, 142-day deployment to North America as part of a continuing series of post-acceptance trials. She carried out test-firings of Tomahawk land attack cruise missiles during the course of her mission and also reportedly performed well in war games against the US Navy's new *Virginia* class submarine *New Mexico* (SSN-779). Second of class *Ambush* should leave her builders' hands to join her sister at the Clyde submarine base at Faslane during the second half of 2012, replacing the twenty-eight-year-old *Turbulent* that is scheduled to decommission in July.

Contracts are also being agreed to progress development of the proposed new class of 'Successor' strategic missile-armed submarines, although final confirmation of the programme will not occur until 2016, when a new British government will have been formed. These have included £350m (US$550m) of design contracts announced in May 2012 and a £1.1bn (US$1.7bn) agreement with Rolls-Royce the following month to upgrade reactor production facilities and fund new nuclear cores for both the

Table 2.4.5: BRITISH ROYAL NAVY: PRINCIPAL UNITS AS AT MID 2012

TYPE	CLASS	NUMBER	TONNAGE	DIMENSIONS	PROPULSION	CREW	DATE
Aircraft Carriers							
Aircraft Carrier – CVS	**INVINCIBLE**	1	22,000 tons	210m x 31/36m x 8m	COGAG, 30 knots	1,100	1980
Principal Surface Escorts							
Destroyer – DDG	**DARING** (Type 45)	4	7,400 tons	152m x 21m x 5m	IEP, 30 knots	190	2008
Destroyer – DDG	**MANCHESTER** (Batch III Type 42)	2	5,200 tons	141m x 15m x 4m	COGOG, 30+ knots	290	1982
Frigate – FFG	**NORFOLK** (Type 23)	13	4,900 tons	133m x 16m x 5m	CODLAG, 30 knots	185	1990
Submarines							
Submarine – SSBN	**VANGUARD**	4	16,000 tons	150m x 13m x 12m	Nuclear, 25+ knots	135	1993
Submarine – SSN	**ASTUTE**	1	7,800 tons	93m x 11m x 10m	Nuclear, 30+ knots	100	2010
Submarine – SSN	**TRAFALGAR**	6	5,200 tons	85m x 10m x 10m	Nuclear, 30+ knots	130	1983
Major Amphibious Units							
Helicopter Carrier – LPH	**OCEAN**	1	22,500 tons	203m x 35m x 7m	Diesel, 18 knots	490	1998
Landing Platform Dock – LPD	**ALBION**	2	18,500 tons	176m x 29m x 7m	IEP, 18 knots	325	2003
Landing Ship Dock – LSD (A)	**LARGS BAY**	3	16,200 tons	176m x 26m x 6m	Diesel-electric, 18 knots	60	2006

final *Astute* class boat and the first 'Successor'. The latter will be built to the new, safer PWR3 design selected in May 2012. In the meantime, the rolling programme of refuelling and refit of the existing *Vanguard* class boats has continued, with *Vengeance* replacing her sister *Vigilant* in the submarine refitting complex at Devonport.

A significant step towards full gender equality took place in December 2011 when it was announced that women would be allowed to serve in submarines for the first time in the Royal Navy's history. The decision follows a similar move by the US Navy in February 2010 and was taken after an eighteen-month review looking at a wide range of issues related to the new policy.

Other Categories: The long delayed MARS programme finally moved forward on 9 March 2012 with the signature of a contract with Daewoo Shipbuilding and Marine Engineering (DSME) for four 37,000-ton double-hulled tankers that will be built to a design derived from BMT Defence Services' Aegir concept. The award of the £452m (US$700m) agreement to an overseas yard proved controversial but reflected an absence of British bidders. Domestic industry, including BMT, does, however, stand to gain around £90m or 20 per cent of the main contract, whilst customisation and support work to the value of a further £60m may also be carried out in the UK. The new vessels, with a length of 200.9m and a breadth of 28.6m, are roughly similar in size to the new BRAVE design being considered for the *Marine Nationale*'s replenishment fleet but will lack their command and hospital facilities. Core crew will be sixty-three – with space for a further forty-six personnel – and

three abeam replenishment stations will be provided for the transfer of diesel oil, aviation fuel and fresh water in addition to solid stores transfer capabilities. Other facilities include a single spot helicopter flight deck and maintenance hangar. The four ships will enter service at annual intervals from 2016.

Operationally, the SDSR reductions have left the Royal Navy extremely stretched in meeting a wide range of standing commitments, which include the ongoing deployment of surface escorts and minehunters 'East of Suez' in the Indian Ocean and Persian Gulf as well as patrols in the South Atlantic and Caribbean. The extent of the problem – exacerbated by the Libyan campaign – hit the headlines in November 2011 when several papers reported there was no surface escort available to meet the 'fleet ready escort' role in British home waters. More positively, the new Response Force Task Group (RFTG) concept developed in the aftermath of the temporary loss of a carrier strike capability has worked well in practice, enabling the navy to carry out a range of international exercises during 2011 whilst providing the naval contribution to the Libyan Operation Ellamy.[7]

MID SIZED REGIONAL FLEETS

Germany: The *Deutsche Marine* continues its transformation from a regional force focused largely on the littorals to a more globally deployable, flexible configuration in line with its increased participation in international stabilisation missions. Although Germany's financial situation is better than most in Europe, this is being achieved against the backdrop of a reduction in the military's overall size under the 2010 defence reforms that abolished conscription. For the navy, this will include a reduction to a core of c.13,000 personnel and some shrinkage in overall fleet numbers.

At present, surface forces are being boosted by the delayed entry into operational service of the K-130 *Braunschweig* class following resolution of previous gearbox problems. The class is described in some detail in chapter 3.3. Good progress is also being achieved with the follow-on class of much larger F-125 type stabilisation frigates. A formal keel-laying ceremony for the first, to be named *Baden-Württemberg*, was held on 2 November 2011 and launch should take place during 2013. The new class of four vessels will replace the existing eight F-122 *Bremen* class frigates, which are likely to start to

Revitalisation of the British Royal Fleet Auxiliary has achieved a significant step forward with an order for four new replenishment tankers in March 2012. The ships will be built by South Korea's Daewoo Shipbuilding and Marine Engineering to a British BMT Defence Services Aegir design. *(BMT Defence Services)*

Germany's *Deutsche Marine* will see significant changes over the next few years as many existing classes are replaced by smaller numbers of more capable ships. Amongst ships retiring will be the eight F-122 *Bremen class* frigates – *Emden* is pictured here during a training cruise. *(Conrad Waters)*

A picture of the new Germany Type 702 combat support ship *Bonn* taken in snowy weather in February 2012 whilst fitting out. Delivery is scheduled for September 2012. *(Blohm & Voss, TKMS)*

The fifth German Type 212A submarine was named *U-35* at HDW in Kiel on 15 November 2011. She should start sea trials at the start of 2013. *(HDW, TKMS)*

decommission at approximately annual intervals from the second half of 2012 onwards. Smaller units less suitable for international missions are also being scaled back, with recent withdrawals including two of the Type 143A *Gepard* class fast attack craft and a further two mine-countermeasures vessels. All the remaining fast attack craft will be retired within the next few years, while the mine warfare squadron will be cut to ten boats, possibly supplemented by mine-countermeasures modules deployed on other ships. There will also be a reduction to thirty in the total number of naval helicopters from the current forty-three strong Sea King and Lynx fleet.

The focus on international deployments has resulted in greater emphasis on logistical support. 2012 will see delivery of the third Type 702 *Berlin* class combat support ship, *Bonn,* which was christened in Emden on 17 April. The 20,000-ton ship is similar to the earlier ships with a length of 174m and beam of 24m but features a number of detailed improvements in comparison with her two previous sisters. A wide range of replenishment capabilities are supplemented by a hangar and flight deck facilities for up to two helicopters of Sea King size, whilst a defensive armament includes 27mm cannon and, potentially, RAM surface-to-air-missiles. Top speed is 20 knots. She is able to carry around ninety additional personnel over and above a core crew of 151 and is fitted with extensive control and communications facilities. There is also provision for a containerised hospital. The navy hopes to supplement the class with an additional pair of joint support ships during the next decade if funding is provided. These could potentially be built to a Type 702 derivative design.[8]

Meanwhile progress continues to be made in rebuilding Germany's underwater capabilities following the premature decommissioning of the remaining Type 206A submarines in 2010. *U-35,* the initial boat of the additional pair of Type 212A submarines ordered in 2006, was christened on 15 November 2011 and should start sea trials in January 2013 prior to a planned October delivery. The sixth and final German boat, to be named *U-36,* is also under construction at HDW's facility at Kiel and will complete the *Deutsche Marine* order.

Greece: Although the Hellenic Navy nominally remains one of Europe's major fleets, Greece's economic problems mean that naval development is effectively in abeyance. Whilst there have been no

The Hellenic Navy's fast attack craft *Laskos* and *Xenos* pictured during 'live fire' exercises in May 2012. *Laskos* is a 'La Combattante III' vessel armed with Exocet missiles whilst *Xenos* is a 'La Combattante IIIB' derivative with the Norwegian Penguin missile system. *(Hellenic Navy)*

further official decommissioning ceremonies for principal naval units since the withdrawals announced in the first half of 2011, there are reports that a number of units are being maintained at reduced operational status to provide sources of spares for the active fleet. The status of indigenous construction programmes, particularly the three Type 214 submarines being built at Hellenic Shipyards and the remaining *Roussen* fast attack craft ordered from Elefsis Shipyards is also subject to uncertainty. The navy has also been forced to cut back on international deployments, notably in support of anti-piracy operations in the Indian Ocean. Conversely, activities in the Mediterranean continue at a relatively high level against a backdrop of lingering tensions with Turkey. These have included live fire exercises against the former *Thetis* class corvette *Doxa* in May 2012.

Turkey: In contrast to the fortunes of the neighbouring Hellenic Navy, the Turkish fleet continues to expand quantitatively and – especially – qualitatively. This has been accompanied by an increased emphasis on developing indigenous technology instead of the past reliance on licensed-build of overseas designs, particularly with respect to surface warships and support vessels. The most important domestic programme is undoubtedly that for 'Milgem' type corvettes, which should eventually see a class of twelve vessels commissioned. This project is now starting to yield tangible results. Lead ship, *Heybeliada,* commissioned on 27 September 2011 –

Turkish Navy Day – after an intensive series of sea trials. Second of class, *Büyükada,* was launched from Istanbul Naval Shipyard on the same day. Current plans still envisage series production switching to the private sector, leaving the Istanbul facility to concentrate on the long-anticipated TF-2000 air defence escort class that is likely to enter service around 2020. The United Kingdom had attempted to interest Turkey in a partnership around the Type 26 Global Combat Ship. However, this option has been rejected, possibly in favour of a largely indigenous design supported by technology from the United

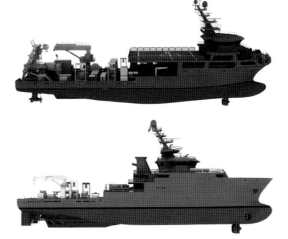

Images of the new Turkish submarine rescue and mother ship and rescue and towing designs that are being built by the Istanbul Shipyard. They feature Rolls-Royce propulsion equipment. *(Istanbul Shipyard via Rolls Royce)*

States' Lockheed Martin. In the meantime, core surface capabilities continue to be provided by the eight MEKO 200 type frigates and eight FFG-7 'G' class frigates, supported by the solitary remaining *Knox* (FF-1052) class escort *Zafer.* It was previously thought she had been decommissioned until an appearance on UNIFIL duties off Lebanon.

Turkey maintains Europe's largest submarine flotilla outside of Russia, with fourteen variants of the German Type 209 currently in commission. In addition, licence-built production of a further six, Type 214 air-independent propulsion equipped boats was confirmed with an announcement from HDW on 1 July 2011 that the requisite advance payment on the €2bn (US$2.5bn) contract had been received. Support infrastructure for the underwater force is also being strengthened, with construction of a submarine rescue and mother ship and two rescue and towing ships contracted with Istanbul Shipyard. The United Kingdom's Rolls-Royce announced a contract for the supply of propulsion equipment for the three ships in May 2012.

Other construction programmes currently underway include the innovative, 400-ton *Tuzla* class coastal patrol ships and the four large *Dost* class offshore search and rescue vessels ordered by the Coast Guard. The first of these ships was originally scheduled for delivery in 2011 but her trials – and those of her two sisters – were still underway in the first half of 2012. News is still awaited on an order for the planned new amphibious ship – officially an amphibious transport dock but likely to be a through-deck amphibious assault ship – with a Chinese Type 081 design, a bespoke BMT design developed for builder RMK and a variant of Spain's *Juan Carlos I* all said to be under consideration.

The Netherlands: The Royal Netherlands Navy has quickly implemented its share of the defence reductions announced in April 2011. The four additional 'Tripartite' type minehunters of the *Alkmaar* class slated for withdrawal were laid up soon after the announcement was made and the elderly combat support ship *Zuiderkruis* followed in February 2012. The other current replenishment ship, *Amsterdam,* will also be decommissioned – in around 2014 – when the new joint support ship *Karel Doorman* is delivered.

More positively, the last year has seen progressive delivery of the four *Holland* class offshore patrol vessels being built by Damen Schelde Naval Shipbuilding at its yards in Vlissingen in the Netherlands and in Galati in Romania. The ships are initially being delivered without their Thales Nederland-built IM400 integrated masts but the first unit was integrated onboard *Holland* in November 2011 prior to an expected formal commissioning ceremony in July 2012. Two additional vessels – *Zeeland* and *Friesland* – have now been handed over to the Dutch Ministry of Defence's Materials Organisation whilst the fourth vessel, *Groningen*, is completing final outfitting. The new ships will provide some relief to the navy's much reduced fleet of *De Zeven Provinciën* and 'M' class frigates which remain extremely active in support both of NATO operations and the Dutch presence in the Caribbean.

Dutch support of NATO initiatives was also demonstrated by the September 2011 announcement that the SMART-L surveillance radars installed in the four *De Zeven Provinciën* class ships would be modified to support a ballistic-missile detection and tracking capability. A contract was subsequently signed in June 2012 for Thales to

A series of images depicting the new Dutch oceanic patrol vessel *Holland* at sea in November 2011 shortly after installation of her Thales Nederland IM400 integrated mast. The integrated mast is a completely different design concept from the sensor layout traditionally seen in warships, with one central mast structure housing radar, optronic and communications systems as well as peripheral equipment. Both building times and ongoing maintenance requirements are reduced in consequence. *(Thales Nederland)*

carry out the relevant upgrades and the necessary modifications should be completed around 2017. The Dutch government has not allocated funding to acquire the SM-3 missiles that would be required to provide an engagement capability but this would be a relatively straightforward future development if the money can be found. However, the next major naval procurement decision will probably relate to successors for the four *Walrus* class patrol submarines. These have been subject to midlife modernisation but will require replacement around the 2025 time frame.

OTHER REGIONAL FLEETS

Black Sea: With the exception of the major regional powers of Russia and Turkey, the Black Sea remains something of a backwater so far as naval procurement activity is concerned. None of the smaller countries have the economic strength to pursue really significant force modernisation. However, both **Bulgaria** and **Romania** have undertaken meaningful naval upgrades in recent years as a result of the acquisition of surplus vessels from Belgium and the United Kingdom following accession to NATO. **Ukraine** is placing significant emphasis on its Project 58250 corvette programme – which is intended to deliver four 2,500-ton ships in the 2016–21 timescale – to revitalise the national shipbuilding sector. The project's financing has been somewhat spasmodic since design work was completed in 2009 but the country's 2012 budget has reportedly provided US$50m of funding to expedite construction of the first vessel. The Ukraine has also re-established an underwater capability with the completion of overhaul work on the country's sole Project 641 'Foxtrot' class submarine *Zaporizhzhya*. Initial sea trials of the 1970s vintage boat commenced in April 2012 with considerable Russian assistance. It has been reported that these were apparently largely successful, although it is not clear to what extent underwater operations were carried out. Whilst there has to be some scepticism of the value of repairing such an elderly unit, the Ukrainian Navy apparently sees the boat as having use training a new cadre of submariners should more extensive modernisation become affordable.

North Sea and Atlantic: Although **Portugal**'s financial crisis has effectively put a halt to further procurement activity by the *Marinha Portuguesa*, a programme of modernisation implemented during the good years has delivered a modern front-line force of five surface escorts and two advanced Type 214 AIP-equipped submarines. These remain active in spite of the country's funding problems. Both the *Vasco da Gama* MEKO 200 and *Bartolomeu Dias* 'M' class frigates have been taking regular turns in support of the European Union's Operation Atalanta anti-piracy operation off the Horn of Africa, with *Vasco da Gama* acting as the mission's flagship for a time during 2011. Meanwhile, the initial Type 214 submarine *Tridente* became the first Portuguese underwater unit to cross the North Atlantic, participating in the War of 1812 Fleet Exercise with the US Navy and other fleets in June 2012. The situation with second-line assets is less positive. In particular, the NPO2000 offshore patrol vessel *Viana do Castelo* remains the sole member of the new class in commission, suggesting problems with delivery of the long-awaited second unit, *Figueira da Foz*. Up to eight NPO2000 vessels in different configurations were originally planned but programme delays mean that Portugal's existing elderly corvettes remain in service for the time being.

Elsewhere in the Atlantic, **Iceland**'s Coast Guard has received a major addition to its fleet with the arrival of the Chilean-built *Thor*, which replaces the decommissioned *Odin* of Anglo-Icelandic Cod War fame. Based on Rolls Royce's UT712 design, the 4,000-ton ship is equipped for constabulary and search and rescue operations.[10] She features a helicopter landing facility as well as a light armament. Built at the ASMAR yard in Talcahuano, Chile, the ship was fortunate to escape severe damage when the facility was impacted by the Chilean earthquake and tsunami of February 2010. Delivered in September 2011, she joins two older *Ægir* offshore patrol

The Portuguese Type 214 class submarine *Tridente* made history in 2012 when she became the navy's first underwater unit to cross the Atlantic during ninety-nine years of submarine operation. *(US Navy)*

An image of the Norwegian *Skjold* class fast attack craft *Storm* at speed. These small but powerfully-armed and exceptionally fast warships are finally starting to enter service after a protracted period of construction and trials. *(Umoe Mandal)*

vessels as the main components of Iceland's most significant paramilitary force.

An overview of **Ireland**'s naval service is contained in Chapter 2.4A.

Scandinavia and the Baltic: The main Scandinavian fleets continue to make headway with modernisation programmes that are largely intended – in similar fashion to Germany's *Deutsche Marine* – to produce smaller forces, better configured for international deployment. Nowhere has this change been more apparent than **Denmark**. Here coastal submarines and Stanflex littoral patrol vessels have been withdrawn and replaced by *Absalon* class command and support ships and *Iver Huitfeldt* class frigates that are more appropriate for 'blue water' operations. Good progress has been achieved with introduction of the latter class over the past year. The lead ship commissioned on 6 February 2012 following installation of her APAR multifunction radar – earlier than originally expected – in November 2011. She is expected to deploy to the Indian Ocean on anti-piracy duties towards the end of 2012. Second of class, *Peter Willemoes*, has already undergone warm weather climate testing in the Caribbean at the end of 2011, whilst the third and final ship – *Niels Juel* – was officially named on 7 November of the same year. The new 6,500-ton ships are of similar size to the previous *Absalon* class vessels but have much-enhanced air defence capabilities.

Sweden's immediate focus remains on bringing the five *Visby* class corvettes into full operational service.[11] *Visby* has been the first ship of the class to be upgraded to the final, 'Version 5', delivery standard, which includes provision of anti-surface and mine clearance capabilities. New equipment installed includes RBS15 surface-to-surface missiles, remotely-operated underwater vehicles, enhanced command and control and communications systems and upgraded electronic countermeasures. An initial test firing of the RBS15 from the modified ship was carried out on 27 June 2012. The navy also hopes for approval for a multi-role support vessel built to civilian roll-on/roll-off standards, although the most important future programme is for new A-26 class submarines, for which international partners are still sought.

One potential partner for the A-26 programme is **Norway**, which reaffirmed its requirement for a submarine force in November 2011. The six existing early 1990s vintage *Ula* class boats will reach the end

The new Icelandic offshore patrol vessel *Thor* was delivered by Chile's ASMAR yard in September 2011. She is an example of one of Rolls-Royce's extensive portfolio of ship designs. *(Rolls-Royce)*

of their life expectancy around 2020 and either life-extension or construction of new submarines will be needed to maintain an underwater capability. At present, a final decision on the way forward is scheduled around 2017, leaving little time to implement its conclusion. In the meantime, the modernisation of surface forces continues with progressive delivery of the *Skjold* class missile-armed fast attack craft, albeit to a protracted schedule. The fourth operational member of the class, *Glimt*, was handed over at the end of March 2012. The two final vessels should be delivered before the end of 2013.

Finland has started to take delivery of the three new *Katanpää* class minehunters ordered from Italy's Intermarine under a €250m (US$310m) contract in 2006. The first vessel was handed over in May 2012 and should arrive in Finland on a heavy lift vessel in the second half of the year. Third of class *Vahterpää* was named in November 2011 and both she and the second vessel should also arrive in Finland by mid 2013. Finland's attention is then expected to turn to replacements for the *Rauma* class fast attack craft and the three minelayers. In line with thinking elsewhere across Scandinavia, construction of a larger, multi-purpose class better capable of international deployment seems to be the preferred option. Across the Baltic, however, **Poland**'s ambitions to deploy a

modern force of surface escorts have been dashed by the decision to abandon the modified MEKO A-100 'Gawron' corvette project and write off the US$130m spent to date on constructing the first unit that was laid down as long ago as 2001. Money allocated to the project is likely to be invested in modernising the country's ageing submarine flotilla.

RUSSIA:

An overview of current Russian fleet strength is set out in Table 2.4.6. As it remains very difficult to assess the true operational status of Russian warships, this should be regarded as providing only a broad estimate of actual fleet capability.

The Russian government has ambitious plans to rebuild the country's naval strength. However, there has long been a significant gap between the hyperbole contained in official statements – perhaps representing a throwback to a past era of Soviet propaganda – and the capacity of a run-down shipbuilding industry to deliver on the politicians' promises. In particular, yards have been extremely slow to deliver new construction and the resulting ships have not always performed to the standards originally expected. As a result, the fleet list continues to be dominated by obsolescent Cold War designs that are increasingly expensive to maintain and have doubtful reliability. The decision to turn to France's DCNS to supply modified *Mistral* class designs to drive forward modernisation of the amphibious fleet is evidence both of the problem's extent but also of a willingness to swallow national pride to resolve the situation. It should, however, also be noted that the steady flow of investment in both orders and infrastructure that has been evident over the last few years is also seemingly having a beneficial impact on domestic warship-building capabilities. As such, the overview of major programmes provided below presents a steadily improving situation:

Submarines: Maintenance of Russia's underwater forces has always been the navy's top priority by virtue of their importance as a key component of the country's strategic nuclear deterrent. Significant effort has been expended over the last decade in developing the new RSM-56 'Bulava' (NATO: SS-

NX-30) submarine-launched ballistic missile and the associated Project 955 'Borey' class strategic missile submarines. The missile's initial development proved troublesome. However, an unbroken series of six successful tests has been achieved from October 2010 onwards following a thorough investigation of the original problems. These included four successful launches from the lead Project 955 submarine, *Yury Dolgoruky*, on 28 June, 27 August, 28 October and 23 December 2011, paving the way for the missile's official adoption for naval service. *Yury Dolgoruky* is likely to be declared fully operational during the second half of 2012, whilst initial test launches from second of class, *Aleksandr Nevsky*, are also scheduled before year end. By this time the third submarine, *Vladimir Monomakh*, should have been launched.

Subsequent production will be focused on the modified Project 955A type, which will feature an enlarged missile-carrying capacity and other

improvements. Preparatory work on the lead boat, *Svyatitel Nikolay*, is already well underway and orders for a further four units were confirmed in May 2012. It seems likely that early units of the 'Borey' class will be deployed to Russia's Pacific Fleet to replace the few remaining, life-expired Project 667BDR 'Delta III' boats. Meanwhile, modernisation of the six Project 667BDRM 'Delta IV' submarines allocated to the Northern Fleet should allow them to remain operational prior to replacement by later 'Borey' class boats around the 2025 timescale.[12] The upgrade will include installation of the R-29RMU2 'Liner' missile, a derivative of the existing 'Sineva', which was first launched from the submarine *Ekaterinburg* in May 2011. *Ekaterinburg* was subsequently badly damaged in a fire whilst undergoing maintenance on 29 December 2011 and expensive repairs will be needed. Previous plans to reactivate laid-up Project 941 'Typhoon' class submarines seem to have been abandoned and the

TABLE 2.4.6: RUSSIAN NAVY: SELECTED PRINCIPAL UNITS AS AT MID 2012

TYPE	CLASS	NUMBER[1]	TONNAGE	DIMENSIONS	PROPULSION	CREW	DATE
Aircraft carriers							
Aircraft Carrier – CV	Project 1143.5 **KUZNETSOV**	1	60,000 tons	306m x 35/73m x 10m	Steam, 32 knots	2,600	1991
Principal Surface Escorts							
Battlecruiser – BCGN	Project 1144.2 **KIROV**	1 (1)	25,000 tons	252m x 29m x 9m	CONAS, 32 knots	740	1980
Cruiser – CG	Project 1164 **MOSKVA** ('Slava')	3	12,500 tons	186m x 21m x 8m	COGAG, 32 knots	530	1982
Destroyer – DDG	Project 956/956A **SOVREMENNY**	c.5	8,000 tons	156m x 17m x 6m	Steam, 32 knots	300	1980
Destroyer – DDG	Project 1155.1 **CHABANENKO** ('Udaloy II')	1	9,000 tons	163m x 19m x 6m	COGAG, 29 knots	250	1999
Destroyer – DDG	Project 1155 **UDALOY**	c.8	8,400 tons	163m x 19m x 6m	COGAG, 30 knots	300	1980
Frigate – FFG	Project 1154 **NEUSTRASHIMY**	2	4,400 tons	139m x 16m x 6m	COGAG, 30 knots	210	1993
Frigate – FFG	Project 1135 **BDITELNNY** ('Krivak I/II')	c.4	3,700 tons	123m x 14m x 5m	COGAG, 32 knots	180	1970
Frigate – FFG	Project 2038.0 **STEREGUSHCHY**	2	2,200 tons	105m x 11m x 4m	CODAD, 27 knots[2]	100	2008
Frigate – FFG	Project 1161.1 **TATARSTAN**	1	2,000 tons	102m x 13m x 4m	CODOG, 27 knots	100	2002
Submarines							
Submarine – SSBN	Project 955 **YURY DOLGORUKY** ('Borey')	1	17,000+ tons	170m x 13m x 10m	Nuclear, 25+ knots	110	2010
Submarine – SSBN	Project 941 **DONSKOY** ('Typhoon')	1	33,000 tons	173m x 23m x 12m	Nuclear, 26 knots	150	1981
Submarine – SSBN	Project 677BDRM **VERKHOTURYE** ('Delta IV')	6	18,000 tons	167m x 12m x 9m	Nuclear, 24 knots	130	1985
Submarine – SSBN	Project 677BDR **ZVEZDA** ('Delta III')	4	12,000 tons	160m x 12m x 9m	Nuclear, 24 knots	130	1976
Submarine – SSGN	Project 949A ('Oscar II')	c.5	17,500 tons	154m x 8m x 9m	Nuclear, 30+ knots	100	1986
Submarine – SSN	Project 971 ('Akula I/II')	c.10	9,500 tons	110m x 14m x 10m	Nuclear, 30+ knots	60	1986
Submarine – SSK	Project 677 **ST PETERSBURG** ('Lada')	1	2,700 tons	72m x 7m x 7m	Diesel-electric, 21 knots	40	2010
Submarine – SSK	Project 877/636 ('Kilo')	c.20	3,000 tons	73m x 10m x 7m	Diesel-electric, 20 knots	55	1981
Major Amphibious Units							
Landing Platform Dock – LPD	Project 1174 **IVAN ROGOV**	1	14,000 tons	157m x 24m x 7m	Gas, 19 knots	240	1978

Notes:

1 Table only includes main types and focuses on operational units: bracketed figures are ships being refurbished or in maintained reserve.

2 Some sources state CODOG propulsion.

test boat *Dimitry Donskoy* is now likely to remain the sole member of class in commission.

Almost as much effort is being devoted to modernising conventionally-armed submarine forces; both nuclear and diesel-electric powered. However, progress has been somewhat mixed. Positively, the lead Project 885 'Yasen' class nuclear-powered attack submarine *Severodvinsk* has spent much of the past year undergoing trials and should be accepted around the end of 2012. Two modified Project 885M are reportedly under construction and others have been contracted for an eventual class of between eight and ten boats. Negatively, the Project 677 patrol submarine programme appears to have encountered major problems, with poor perform-ance of lead boat *St Petersburg*'s command and propulsion systems during nearly five years of trials threatening termination of the entire class. Fabrication of two additional members of the class has reportedly been suspended until a final decision is reached. In the meantime, construction of 'Kilo' class submarines for Russian Navy use has been revived at the famous Admiralty Shipyard, where at least six upgraded, Project 636.3 types are likely to be built. The first of these, *Novorossiysk*, is likely to be launched in 2013 and a second, *Rostov na Donu*, was laid down in November 2011. Refits of earlier 'Kilo' class submarines, as well as of 'Oscar' and 'Akula' type nuclear-powered boats, is also ongoing.

Aircraft Carriers & Amphibious Ships: The contact with France's DCNS to build *Mistral* class amphibious assault ships has moved forward swiftly since signature in June 2011. The keel for the first ship, *Vladivostok,* was laid at STX Europe's St Nazaire yard in February 2012, with delivery expected during 2015. The second ship will follow around a year later. Russian yards will be involved in fabrication of modules for both ships prior to planned construction of a second pair in Russia. The new vessels will form the centrepiece of Russia's amphibious forces, which are also being supple-mented by construction of the Project 11711 *Ivan Gren* tank landing ships. The lead ship was launched from the Yantar yard at Kaliningrad in May 2012 and up to five further class members are planned.

The sole carrier, *Admiral Kuznetsov,* completed another Mediterranean deployment in early 2012, reportedly embarking both SU-33 and MiG-29K fighters as well as Ka-27 helicopters for the three-month voyage. Russia is planning to take delivery of twenty-four MiG-29s by 2015, standardising the carrier's air group on this type. Previous reports suggest *Kuznetsov* herself will enter refit at the Sevmash facility towards the end of 2012 once work on India's *Vikramaditya* has been completed.

Surface Vessels: Commissioning of new surface warships has been particularly badly impacted by deficiencies with Russia's shipbuilding infrastructure and new tonnage is urgently needed to replace existing life-expired vessels. Fortunately some progress is being made in resolving production bottlenecks and the next two years should start to see series delivery of long-awaited classes materialise.

The most important facility for surface escort construction is currently St Petersburg's Severnaya Verf, which has now been nationalised under the control of the United Shipbuilding Corporation after financial difficulties. This has been entrusted with construction of the Project 2235.0 *Gorshkov* class 'blue water' frigates and the smaller Project 2038.0 *Steregushchy* class corvettes. Three of the former type are currently under construction following the keel-laying of *Admiral Golovko* in February 2012 and current contracts are believed to cover a total of eight ships. However, the lead vessel, *Admiral Sergei Gorshkov*, has been badly delayed and is unlikely to be delivered before the end of 2013, at least four years behind initial plans. As such, recourse has been made to adopting the Project 1135.6 *Talwar* class design exported to India for domestic construction. *Admiral Essen* and *Admiral Makarov,* the second and third vessels of an initial batch of three, were laid down by Yantar in July 2011 and February 2012 respectively. In addition, contracts were signed for a second tranche of three ships in August 2011. This would suggest creation of a modern fleet of nearly fifteen blue water frigates

The Russian Pacific Fleet's cruiser *Varyag* pictured on exercises with the US Navy in October 2011. Although Russia is building new frigates and corvettes, the replacement or refurbishment of larger warships poses a major challenge. *(US Navy)*

is achievable by the early years of the next decade.

Better progress has been made with the Project 2038.0 design, with second of class *Soobrazitelny* now commissioned and the fourth ship *Stoiky* launched on 30 May 2012. Severnaya Verf has now progressed to working on the modified Project 2038.5 *Gremyashchy* class but the Far Eastern Amur yard at Komsomolsk is also constructing a pair of the earlier type after laying the keel of a second in February 2012. At least eighteen of the two variants are eventually planned as part of a total force of around thirty-five light frigates.

Other construction is directed towards bolstering Russia's naval presence on the Caspian Sea, including the second Project 1161.1 corvette *Dagestan* and a series of Project 2163.0 'Buyan' type gunboats. At least six of these c.600-ton ships are planned, including a modified Project 2163.1, missile-armed variant. The second ship in the class, *Volgodonsk,* was commissioned in June 2012 and the

Russia's *Admiral Chabanenko* pictured in June 2011. Shipbuilding delays have meant that Cold War era designs have had to remain in service in spite of high maintenance costs and problems with operational availability. *(US Navy)*

third has also been launched. At the other end of the scale, plans exist for refurbishment of the three laid-up Project 1144.2 *Kirov* class, nuclear-powered battlecruisers, as well as a new class of destroyer that could also have nuclear propulsion. The challenges involved with these projects should not be underestimated and their ultimate realisation should be regarded as doubtful.

Notes:

1. Amongst the most notable changes to the original 2010 Strategic Defence and Security Review (SDSR) announced over the past year have been further revisions to British Army size and structure resulting from a growing realisation that the previous determination to minimise land force size reductions were financially unsustainable and a reversion to the F-35B short take off and vertical landing variant of the Joint Strike Fighter. Richard Beedall's 'United Kingdom: Defence Review Reshapes the Royal Navy' in *Seaforth World Naval Review 2012* (Barnsley, Seaforth Publishing, 2011), pp.97–107 provides further detail on the SDSR's original plans.

2. State-owned Navantia is one of Europe's largest shipbuilding groups, specialising in all aspects of non-nuclear powered warship construction. Its Cartagena yard is currently focused on construction of the S-80 submarine class, whilst facilities in the Bay of Cadiz hope for orders for further offshore patrol vessels from Venezuela and, perhaps, Spain. However, utilisation of Ferrol's capacity will run down following completion of the fifth F-100 frigate, *Cristóbal Colón*, and two *Canberra* class amphibious assault ship hulls for Australia

3. A summary of likely future French defence policy was provided by Vivien Pertusot's 'Defence and Foreign Policy under President-elect François Hollande', which was published by the Royal United Services Institute. See http://www.rusi.org/analysis/commentary/ref:C4FA6FCABF 031A/. Reports in late June 2012 suggested the defence budget could be reduced by as much as 7 per cent in the medium term.

4. The most important technological transfer agreed to date is linked to the €1.2bn (c.US$1.7bn at then-current exchange rates) deal with DCNS for *Mistral* class amphibious assault ships agreed in June 2011. The deal includes construction of hull blocks for the first two French-built ships at United Shipbuilding Corporation's historic Baltic Shipyard in St Petersburg and potential construction of an additional pair of vessels in Russia. In addition, details relating to the SENIT 9 combat management system will also be transferred.

5. Detail on the F-110 concept design is provided in Richard Scott's 'Spain outlines ambitions for F-110 frigate', *Jane's International Defence Review* – March 2012 (Couldson, IHS Jane's, 2012).

6. A copy of the defence secretary's statement on the reversion back to the F-35B can be found at http://www. mod.uk/DefenceInternet/AboutDefence/CorporatePublicati ons/PolicyStrategyandPlanning/StatementOnCarrierStrikeC apabilityDefenceSecretary10May2012.htm.

7. The RFTG concept is based around the previous UK Amphibious Task Group and provides a flexible, high readiness maritime force capable of responding to crisis and other world events in rapid order. Constituents normally include an amphibious transport dock in the command role, a helicopter carrier, surface escorts, replenishment vessels, a nuclear-powered attack submarine, a range of navy and army helicopters as well as Royal Marine Commando elements. The addition of a *Queen Elizabeth* class carrier to the group from the end of

the decade will provide an additional fixed wing strike capability.

8. The Type 207 design is a leading contender for the Royal Canadian Navy's joint support ship requirement.

9. An excellent source of information on Turkish naval developments is Devrim Yaylali's Bosphorus Naval News website which can be found at http://turkishnavy.net.

10. Although principally known for its aero-engine business, Rolls-Royce has a large marine division with activities extending far beyond gas turbine propulsion. These include the production of ship designs, most notably the UT-Design family that was originally launched in the 1970s.

11. The *Visby* class was considered in detail by Guy Toremans in last year's *Seaforth World Naval Review*. See 'Sweden's *Visby* Class Corvettes: Stealth At All Levels', *Seaforth World Naval Review 2012* (Barnsley, Seaforth Publishing, 2011), pp.149–65.

12. A number of sources suggest deliveries will be split evenly between the Northern and Pacific Fleets on an ongoing basis but this seems unlikely given the doubtful operational status of the remaining 'Delta III' class boats and the desirability of focusing initial support infrastructure in one location. The alternative viewpoint is contained in a useful update on the Russian Navy in 'Russia's Navy: a fair wind into a storm?', editor David Foxwell, *Warship Technology* – May 2012 (London, RINA, 2012), pp.18–20.

2.4A Fleet Review

IRELAND

The Irish Naval Service: A Model Constabulary Navy

Author: **Richard Beedall**

The Irish Naval Service is the navy of the Republic of Ireland. In Ireland it is generally referred to simply as the Naval Service, or *an tSeirbhís Chabhlaigh* in the Irish language (*Gaelige*).

Whilst the Irish state was established in 1922, it was not until 1938 that the country gained full control of its ports and coastal waters from the United Kingdom.[1] A small Marine Service was then established to help protect the country's neutrality during the Second World War. In 1946 the Marine Service was replaced by the Naval Service (NS), which currently has about one thousand personnel and operates a flotilla of eight major vessels – all essentially patrol ships.

Since its establishment, the NS has focused its activities on patrolling and protecting the coastal and ocean waters under Irish jurisdiction – the latter now stretching 500 nautical miles out into the North Atlantic Ocean. Policing this large area places a heavy burden on the navy's small force of mainly elderly ships, nevertheless in recent years some ships have occasionally ventured further afield and the NS has an ambition to acquire one or two multi-role vessels with much greater capabilities. The economic crisis in Ireland since 2008 has at least delayed these plans, but the NS has still managed to secure funding to build new patrol vessels and is pursuing some innovative ideas and concepts that are of interest to navies of all sizes.

ROLE OF THE NAVAL SERVICE

The Naval Service is one of the three standing branches of the Irish Permanent Defence Forces, along with the Irish Army and the Irish Air Corps. The stated mission of the Defence Forces (DF) is 'to provide for the military defence of the State, contribute to national and international peace and security and fulfil all other roles assigned by Government'.

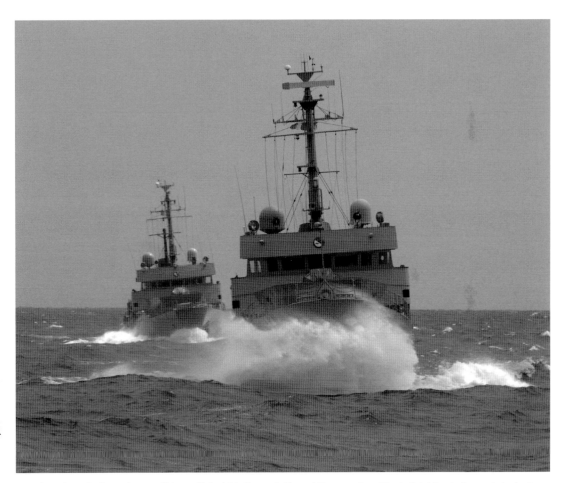

Seen here in typical weather conditions off the Irish Coast, *Aoife* and *Emer* are the oldest of eight patrol vessels tasked with securing Ireland's extensive territorial waters. In spite of Ireland's difficult economic situation, they will be replaced by new construction during 2014/15. *(Defence Forces Ireland)*

In support of this mission, a Defence White Paper published in 2000 designated the Naval Service as the Irish State's principal seagoing agency, and the maritime component of the Defence Forces.[2] Its primary role is to deter and resist armed aggression and provide an armed presence in Irish territorial waters in order to prevent their use by belligerents. It has also been assigned numerous secondary roles including fishery protection, search and rescue, anti-pollution and aid to the civil power (e.g. arms and

Two British BL 6in MkVII coastal defence guns overlooking Lough Swilly at Fort Dunree. Although Irish independence was achieved in 1922, the United Kingdom retained control of the defences of Ireland's three 'Treaty Ports' until 1938, delaying the establishment of an Irish Navy. *(Conrad Waters)*

Commissioned in 2001, *Niamh* is currently the Irish Naval Service's most modern unit. Her main role is policing Ireland's large Exclusive Economic Zone (EEZ), which extends far into the North Atlantic. *(Defence Forces Ireland)*

drugs interdiction). Although peacemaking and peacekeeping operations are an important task for the Irish Defence Force as a whole, the current policy is not to deploy NS ships overseas in support of such operations.

The primary role of the NS can be interpreted as requiring a powerful navy – particularly as 97 per cent of Ireland's trade (by volume) travels by sea – but it has to be considered in the context of a small and geographically isolated county with a policy of neutrality and no obvious military threats from neighbours. Significant protection is also effectively provided by the country's proximity to the United Kingdom and other NATO alliance members. These considerations meant that the Defence White Paper was also able to say: 'Having regard to the defence and security environment assessment … there is no case for a significant shift … towards an enhanced naval contribution. Ireland does not face a maritime-based threat for which the provision of a full naval capability is necessary or for which the huge costs of warships could be justified.' As a result, the NS is able to give a low priority to defensive capabilities that are important to many small

navies, for example coastal defence, anti-submarine warfare and mine warfare. Also, offensive capabilities such as land attack, amphibious operations and special operations are of very limited interest to the Naval Service.

In practice, the training and equipment of the NS is focused upon policing and protecting the country's 3,600 miles of coastline and large Exclusive Economic Zone (EEZ). As well as rich fishing grounds, an estimated US$1 trillion of oil and gas reserves are believed to reside within the EEZ off Ireland's west coast. The EEZ extends up to 200 nautical miles from shore and covers an area of 132,000 sq nm of ocean (16 per cent of EU waters). The Irish State also has associated obligations as a member of the European Union (EU) and with respect to the EU Common Fisheries Policy. Indeed, the EU has – in the past – contributed funding towards the procurement of new vessels by the NS and even towards upgrades and some operational costs.

The NS patrols the entire EEZ 200 nautical mile limit and periodically operates beyond these limits to protect specific fisheries and interests within

Ireland's continental shelf jurisdiction. These patrols are carried out on a regular and frequent basis and are directed to all areas of Irish waters as necessary, including coastal areas. The NS is committed to having at least three vessels on patrol within the Irish EEZ at any one time and to provide a total of 1,480 ship patrol days per annum. All vessels are multi-tasked in so far as they undertake general surveillance security and other duties while conducting their primary day-to-day tasking of providing a fishery protection service. NS patrols are complemented by assistance provided by the Irish Air Corps. The Air Corps' 101 'Maritime' Squadron carries out aerial surveillance of the EEZ using the two CASA CN-235M-100P Persuader Maritime Patrol Aircraft, which are operated from Baldonell Aerodrome in County Dublin.

The demands placed upon the Irish Naval Service became even more onerous when, in April 2007, the country extended its claimed jurisdiction to the west of the island in accordance with the United Nations Commission on the Limits of the Continental Shelf. The new limit extends up to 500 nautical miles offshore, roughly doubling the NS's total area of

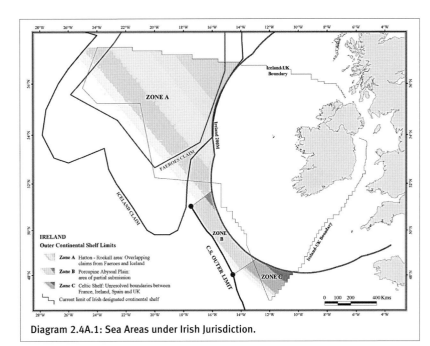

Diagram 2.4A.1: Sea Areas under Irish Jurisdiction.

A Naval Service armed boarding party on exercises on board the large patrol vessel *Róisín* in June 2011. 1,264 actual boardings – leading to ten ship detentions – were carried out in 2011. Providing aid to the civil power, including arms and drug interdiction, is an important naval task. *(Defence Forces Ireland)*

responsibility, as illustrated in Diagram 2.4A.1. The NS does not have sufficient ships with which to police this huge area effectively and its smaller ships are not well suited to the hostile sea states and weather conditions likely to be encountered far out into the North Atlantic. To help stretch its resources, the NS relies heavily upon information technology and satellite information in order to improve the efficiency of its patrols.

Another important and statutory task carried out by the NS is search and rescue (SAR). The NS contributes to the National Search and Rescue Organisation and NS ships are invoked for an average of ten SAR missions per ship per annum.

Finally, as the only state agency with the capability to carry out operations in Irish Waters, the NS is frequently called upon to assist and support the *An Garda Siochána* (civilian police force), the Sea Fishery Protection Authority and the Irish Customs and Revenues organisation in law enforcement at sea.

ORGANISATION

The Naval Service currently has an authorised strength of 1,094 permanent personnel (but is slightly under-strength in practice) and operates a flotilla of eight vessels from the country's only naval base, at Haulbowline Island in Cork Harbour, County Cork. The NS also has four companies of reservists for port security duties and coastal defence

Whilst the Irish Naval Service does not possess any airborne assets of its own, the Irish Air Corps operates two CASA CN-235M Persuader maritime patrol aircraft that provide an important complement to naval patrols of Ireland's waters. *(Defence Forces Ireland)*

Table 2.4A.1: IRISH NAVAL SERVICE PERSONNEL STRENGTH – APRIL 2012

CATEGORY	NUMBER	NOTES
Authorised	1,094	
Trained	946	Includes 67 female personnel: 28 officers, 38 enlisted, 1 cadet.
Untrained	58	Includes 17 officers under training, 14 cadets and 27 recruits.
Sub-Total	1,014	80 (7%) below authorised strength.
Reserves	201	41 in Cork; 59 in Dublin; 51 in Limerick, 50 in Waterford.
Total	1,215	

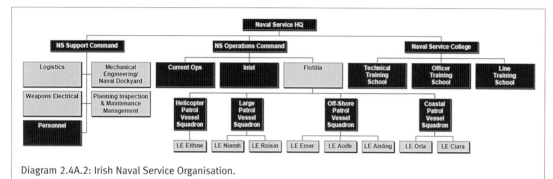

Diagram 2.4A.2: Irish Naval Service Organisation.

A rare view of six Irish Naval Service vessels operating in company during 2011, representing 75 per cent of the entire fleet. The view includes all three *Emer* class offshore patrol vessels, two former British Royal Navy coastal patrol vessels and one of the *Róisín* class large patrol vessels. *(Defence Forces Ireland)*

purposes. The organisational structure of the NS is shown in Diagram 2.4A.2, whilst Table 2.4A.1 provides a breakdown of overall personnel head-count.

The Naval Service, like the other two branches of the Irish Defence Forces, is controlled by the Department of Defence (DOD), with the government's Minister for Justice, Equality and Defence acting as head of the defence department. He is advised by the Defence Forces' Chief of Staff, the country's most senior military officer and a three-star appointment. The DOD has about 380 civil servants and 270 military personnel. The military personnel constitute the joint service Defence Forces Headquarters (DFHQ), which is located in Newbridge in County Kildare.

The Naval Headquarters (NHQ) is co-located with the Naval Operations and Naval Support Commands on Haulbowline Island. The Flag Officer Commanding the Naval Service (FOCNS), who holds the one-star rank of Commodore, operates from NHQ. The post of FOCNS is currently (mid 2012) held by Commodore Mark Mellett. An important responsibility of FOCNS is overall co-ordination of Irish Naval Service strategy, including heading the Naval Strategic Oversight Group and playing a leading role in decisions related to the navy's fleet replacement programme.

The Naval Operations Command is tasked with the conduct of all operations afloat and ashore by the NS. The Officer Commanding Naval Operations Command (OCNOC), who reports to FOCNS, commands the service's operational resources.

Naval Support Command is tasked with the support of the NS afloat and ashore, as well as enabling it to fulfil its operational and training commitments. The Officer Commanding Naval Support Command (OCNSC), who also reports to FOCNS, commands the personnel, logistic and technical support resources at the Haulbowline Naval Base.

A naval college is responsible for the training of all personnel in the NS. The Commandant Naval College reports directly to FOCNS on all matters related to NS training.

THE FLEET

The Irish Naval Service currently operates a flotilla of eight major ships. As set out in Table 2.4A.2, these comprise one helicopter patrol vessel, three offshore patrol vessels, two large patrol vessels and

Table 2.4A.2: IRISH NAVAL SERVICE FLEET COMPOSITION – MID 2012

TYPE	CLASS	NAME	PENNANT	DATE [1]	BUILDER	TONNAGE	NOTES
Helicopter Patrol Vessel	EITHNE	EITHNE	P31	1984	Verlome, Cork	1,900 tons	Flagship of the Irish Naval Service
Large Patrol Vessel	RÓISÍN	RÓISÍN	P51	1999	Appledore, Devon	1,700 tons	
Large Patrol Vessel	RÓISÍN	NIAMH	P52	2001	Appledore, Devon	1,700 tons	
Offshore Patrol Vessel	EMER	EMER	P21	1978	Verlome, Cork	1,000 tons	To decommission January 2014
Offshore Patrol Vessel	EMER	AOIFE	P22	1979	Verlome, Cork	1,000 tons	To decommission 2015
Offshore Patrol Vessel	EMER	AÍSLING	P23	1980	Verlome, Cork	1,000 tons	
Coastal Patrol Vessel	PEACOCK	ORLA	P41	1985 (1988)	Hall Russell, Aberdeen	700 tons	Former Royal Navy SWIFT
Coastal Patrol Vessel	PEACOCK	CÍARA	P42	1984 (1988)	Hall Russell, Aberdeen	700 tons	Former Royal Navy SWALLOW

1: Date in brackets relates to entry into Irish service where the ship served elsewhere previously.

The helicopter patrol vessel *Eithne* is flagship of Ireland's fleet. The last Naval Service vessel built in Ireland; she is seen here on exercises in Irish waters during 2010. *(Defence Forces Ireland)*

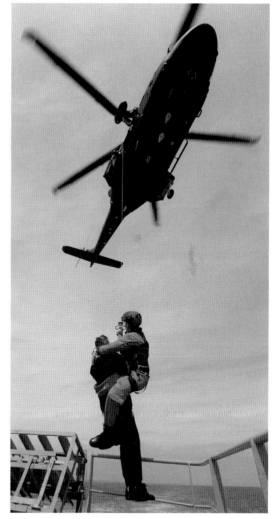

An Irish Air Corps AW-139 helicopter carrying out a rescue exercise with an Irish Naval Service vessel during 2011. The Dauphin rotorcraft previously used on *Eithne* have been retired without replacement. *(Defence Forces Ireland)*

two coastal patrol vessels. The NS also operates several small craft, including passenger launches and sail training vessels.

The NS is proud of its Celtic background and all of its ships are named after famous women from Irish and Celtic mythology. Ship names are proceeded by LÉ (*Long Éireannach*), meaning Irish Ship. The current flagship of the NS is the *Eithne*; commissioned in 1984 she is the service's only helicopter patrol vessel but now rarely conducts helicopter operations. In 1986 two Aerospatiale SA 365Fi Dauphin II helicopters were adapted for service from her, equipped with crash-proof fuel tanks and harpoon deck arrester gear, but these were retired without replacement at the end of 2005. *Eithne* also has the distinction of being the last NS vessel to be built in Ireland; three planned sister ships were never ordered due to budget constraints.[3]

ECONOMIC CHALLENGES

The Naval Service is funded via a budget allocation from Defence Forces central funds. About ten per cent of the budget is normally spent on the NS, although capital expenditure on new ships can increase this percentage temporarily.

The Irish economy boomed during the decade to 2007 and the budget of the Department of Defence increased significantly, reaching a peak of nearly €1.1bn ($1.3bn) in 2008 (albeit this included a large pension element). As a result of the favourable funding situation, it was possible in the middle of the decade to adopt quite ambitious plans to increase the capabilities and reach of the Defence Forces. For example, the Programme for Government 2007–2012 stated that a forthcoming Defence White Paper (originally expected by 2010, but still not published) would 'consider expanding the roles of … the Naval Service. This will include increasing the size of the navy flotilla.' However, since 2008 the Irish economic situation has changed disastrously, and the defence budget has not been immune to the down turn, with annual 3 to 4 per cent cash reductions being imposed. The 2012 Defence Budget was just €902.3m, including a provision of €214m for defence force pensions. The reductions are expected to continue until at least 2014.

The Irish Army has borne the brunt of the resulting cutbacks. For example, it has downsized from three to two brigades. Consequently, although the overall size of the DF is being reduced from 10,500 to 9,500 trained personnel, the establishment of the NS will remain at 1,094. Also, a recent re-examination of the ten-year defence equipment plan has resulted in the continuation of a fleet replacement programme, although at a much slower pace than originally envisaged. Despite these positives, the NS is facing severe budgetary constraints, with fluctuations in fuel prices being a particular challenge – it consumes 40 per cent of all fuel purchased by the DF. The NS has therefore implemented an energy conservation management regime, including a single engine running policy for its ships that has resulted in significant reductions in fuel consumption, and consequent savings. The NS has also worked with the local research community in order to develop dynamic scheduling models for the management of ship refits and patrol planning; these have resulted in substantial efficiency gains.

The NS has halted the high profile, but quite costly, extended overseas naval deployments that it had occasionally undertaken in recent years. The most recent was the 2010 visit by the large patrol vessel *Niamh* to South America. Nevertheless the NS will continue to commit approximately eighty-five to ninety of its annual patrol days to foreign deployments, with operational visits to Lorient and Vigo among those that will be made in 2012.

FLEET REPLACEMENT PROGRAMME

With exception of the two *Róisín* class large patrol vessels, the ships in the NS flotilla are all reaching the end of their nominal thirty-year service lives and are therefore in need of replacement. The highest priority is the *Emer* class OPVs, all three of which have already exceeded this limit.[4] The continued use of older vessels is expensive in terms of both maintenance and repairs. In addition, an increasing number of patrol days are being lost due to technical problems.

Nearly a decade ago a Replacement Working Group began to define the requirements that needed to be met in new warships, and to study the options available. By early 2006 the Naval Vessel Replacement Programme had been developed which identified the need for two types of new ship:

The two smallest ships in the Irish Naval Service's eight-strong fleet are two former Royal Navy *Swallow* class coastal patrol vessels originally built in the 1980s for service off Hong Kong. This is *Orla*, previously the Royal Navy's *Swift*. (Defence Forces Ireland)

■ **Offshore Patrol Vessels (OPVs):** Intended to

Table 2.4A.3: IRISH NAVAL SERVICE: SPECIFICATION OF NEW PATROL VESSELS

TYPE	CLASS	NUMBER	TONNAGE	DIMENSIONS	PROPULSION	CREW	SERVICE DATE
Offshore Patrol Vessel (OPV)	P60 (PV90)	2 building + 1 option	c.1,800 tons	90m x 14m x 4m	Diesel, 23 knots	44+10 spare	January 2014
Extended Patrol Vessel (EPV)	Not Known	Up to 2 planned	c.4,000 tons	130/140m x 16/20m x 4/5m	22/26 knots	Not known	2020+

Right: The *Emer* class offshore patrol vessel *Aísling* at a Presidential Fleet Review held off Cobh, near Cork, in April 2012 to commemorate the one hundredth anniversary of the liner *Titanic's* loss. Cobh, then Queenstown, was *Titanic's* last port of call before her tragic loss. The economic difficulties facing Ireland means that the thirty-two-year-old vessel still awaits replacement. *(Defence Forces Ireland)*

perform a range of duties throughout Irish Waters, including fishery protection, search and rescue, maritime protection, drug interdiction, anti-pollution and maritime security duties, and vessel boarding – 90 per cent of which were expected to relate to fishery protection.

■ **Extended Patrol Vessels (EPVs):** Larger than the OPVs, the EPVs would provide a similar but enhanced patrol capability, being optimised for the adverse weather conditions of the North Atlantic. On limited occasions they would also be used to transport personnel and equipment.

Initial government approval to proceed with the replacement programme was received in July 2007, and on 24 August 2007 a tender was published for the purchase of two OPVs, with an option for a third; plus one EPV, with an option for a second. Responses were received from industry in October 2007. At this time it was expected an order for two OPVs would be placed in late 2008 or early 2009, with delivery likely to take place in 2011 and 2012.

Following a short-listing process, detailed tender responses were returned to the DOD by the shipbuilders on 11 November 2008. In early 2009, the United Kingdom-based company of Babcock Marine was selected as the preferred supplier for the two OPVs, the company offering a design – designated PV90, with a specification as shown in Table 2.4A.3

Right: Ireland's fleet replacement programme is based on a lengthened variant of the STX Canada Marine PV80 *Róisín* class large patrol vessel, two of which were built by the Appledore yard in North Devon, United Kingdom, around the turn of the Millennium. This image shows second of class *Niamh* in gunnery exercises with the inshore patrol vessel *Orla* during 2011. *(Defence Forces Ireland)*

– that had been developed by STX Canada Marine. The design was essentially an enlarged version of the existing *Róisín* (PV80) class large patrol vessels, with a hull extended from c.80m to 90m and given greater draught to cope more effectively with sea conditions in the North Atlantic. There will also be improvements to propulsion arrangements.[5] However, by mid 2009, the replacement programme was being impacted by the difficult economic conditions suddenly facing Ireland, and a report by the country's Special Group on Public Service Numbers and Expenditure Programmes recommended that the new ships' procurement should be extended over a longer time frame. After further extended discussions with Babcock Marine, the cost of building the first two OPVs was finalised at €99m, excluding taxes. An additional €7.8m will be needed for a similar armament outfit to the *Róisín* class.

To the relief of the Naval Service, the government approved the inclusion of funding for the new ships in the 2011 Department of Defence Budget. A contract with Babcock Marine was finally signed in October 2010 and the first payment was made. The contract provided for a revised build schedule compared with that originally planned, with deliveries of the two ships on firm order set for January 2014 and January 2015, and payments extending out as far as 2017. A decision on whether to order the optional third unit is expected by 2014.

Construction of the first new OPV (ship programme number AS194) – still unnamed but allocated the pennant number P61 – commenced on 24 November 2011 at the Babcock Marine Appledore shipyard in North Devon. A formal keel-laying ceremony was subsequently held on 18 May 2012. As of writing (mid 2012) construction is ahead of schedule and her sea trials are expected to commence in September 2013, with delivery in November. Work on the second unit (AS195/P62) will commence in July 2013. If the option on the third unit is taken up, her construction is likely to begin in 2015.

As regards the EPV, Table 2.4A.3 also shows an official indicative specification that was published in 2006. The final specification may differ significantly, as interest in a design with enhanced multi-role capabilities has continued to increase, it being

A computer-generated image of the new PV90 offshore patrol vessel design, which originates from STX Marine in Canada but which is being constructed at the Appledore yard in Devon that built the previous PV80 vessels. Two ships have been ordered under a c.€100m contract and there is an option for a third vessel. *(STX Marine Canada)*

The PV80 *Róisín* class large patrol vessel *Niamh*.
Similarities with the new, enlarged PV90 class are readily apparent. *(Defence Forces Ireland)*

3

Right: The Danish flexible support ship *Absalon* on operations with US Navy units in the Indian Ocean during 2009. Ireland has looked to the design as a possible model for its proposed EPV extended patrol vessel, although it is difficult to envisage the budget being available for such a complex ship. *(US Navy)*

considered that such a vessel would provide substantial 'added value' to the Irish State. Possible roles in addition to patrol duties might include naval transport, disaster relief, humanitarian aid and providing an Irish maritime contribution to international security and peacekeeping operations. The Danish *Absalon* class of flexible support ships are often unofficially cited as a possible model for EPV. One early cost estimate suggested about €48 million for each EPV, but this now seems far too low. The first EPV is intended to replace *Eithne* directly, providing greatly increased capabilities. The option for a second unit might be taken up at a later date.

A key forthcoming decision to be made by the NS and the Irish Department of Defence is whether to prioritise ordering the third new OPV or the first EPV. If the former option is selected, then funding constraints mean that it is unlikely that the first EPV could be ordered any earlier than 2020. This would result in *Eithne* being about forty years old by the time she is decommissioned.

INNOVATION

Given Ireland's economic situation the current Naval Service Strategic Plan, developed in 2011 and dealing with the challenges and commitments that the navy faces out to 2016, inevitably places an emphasis on the navy delivering value for money in relation to defence, security, and other service requirements. Two key projects are seen as facilitating this vision.

First, in 2004, the Irish Naval Service entered into academic partnership with the Cork Institute of Technology (CIT) for the purpose of delivering education and training to both military and merchant seafarers. As a result a new, purpose-built, National Maritime College of Ireland (NMCI) was constructed at Ringaskiddy, adjacent to the naval base on Haulbowline Island, and Irish Naval Service cadets now spend the second year of their training studying there. This unique partnership has proven to be very successful in focusing Ireland's third level maritime education into a single, state-of-the-art location or 'one-stop shop'.

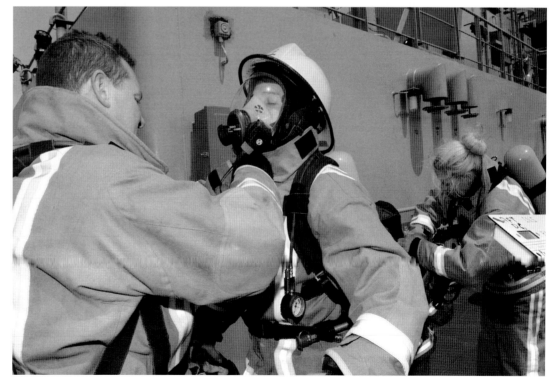

Irish Naval Service personnel engaged in a firefighting exercise. Collaboration with the IMERC maritime research cluster has helped the Naval Service develop wireless technology for tracking firefighters in enclosed spaces. *(Defence Forces Ireland)*

Second, in 2008, a large group of maritime stakeholders met to discuss the possibility of pooling Ireland's maritime industrial research at a single location, adjacent to the NMCI. In 2010 the Irish Maritime Energy and Research Cluster (IMERC) emerged. IMERC represents an integrated institutional arrangement between the Naval Service, CIT and University College Cork that brings together a critical mass of expertise in the fields of energy engineering, maritime operations, maritime technology and ecosystem governance. It has also partnered with more than thirty other organisations and enterprises. From a NS perspective, the IMERC initiative helps it to address technology challenges in a wide range of areas, for example: wireless technology for tracking maritime firefighters in enclosed spaces; the development of unmanned maritime air vehicles; remote underwater vehicle technology; and security technologies for high value items.

The NS is also collaborating with the Marine Institute (a national agency responsible for Marine Research) on sub-surface technologies and countering underwater threats. This is a new area for the NS, but a driver is the interdiction of drug trafficking. The resources available to drug cartels are enormous and – in recent years – they have progressed from delivering narcotics to shore by means of semi-submersible craft transported into Irish waters by merchant ship to delivery by fully submersible underwater vehicles.

In a final example, the NS is assisting UCC, the University of Limerick and IMERC on an initiative called 'Sky Sails'. This uses kites to supplement the power of a ship's main engines and thus save fuel. The technology is of possible interest to the NS in the context of a patrol ship maintaining station in a small area for a long period of time.

CONCLUSION

The Irish Naval Service has less than a thousand trained personnel and only eight vessels with which to police one of the largest maritime jurisdictions in Europe. As such, it is rare that more than one of those vessels can be seen alongside at the service's only naval base on Haulbowline Island.

Unlike many other navies in Europe, the Irish Naval Service has been able to justify its size, role and funding at a time of considerable economic difficulty and budgetary austerity. The continuation of the fleet replacement programme is a matter of particular satisfaction, and represents recognition by

The large patrol vessel *Niamh* pictured at the Presidential Fleet Review in April 2012. The Irish Naval Service is an effective role model for other small constabulary navies around the world. *(Defence Forces Ireland)*

the Irish government of the importance of effective patrolling by the NS of the extensive sea areas to which Ireland claims sovereign control or jurisdiction. However, as only two new patrol vessels have been ordered so far, it seems certain that several existing vessels will have to operate long beyond their normal service life. The NS is partially compensating for this by the innovative use of technology – a significant advantage of its partnering with Irish academia and industry.

Whilst the NS would benefit from more funding for new ships, its equipment, training and approach already provides a model for other small 'constabulary' navies around the world.

Notes:

1. The Anglo-Irish Treaty of December 1921 that established the Irish Free State as a self-governing dominion within the broader framework of the British Empire provided for continued British control of the harbours of Berehaven, Lough Swilly, and Queenstown (now Cobh) near Cork, and associated harbour defences, as well as for ongoing British responsibility for Ireland's coastal defence. The so-called 'Treaty Ports' were not handed over to the newly constituted Republic of Ireland until 1938.

2. Only one Defence White Paper has ever been published by Ireland. Issued in 2000 it was intended to cover the period up to 2010. The economic situation disrupted plans to issue a new White Paper in 2010, but it still seems to be intended. In the absence of a new White Paper, the Department of Defence has published a Strategy Statement 2011–2014. This is a high-level document, with little implementation detail. Both documents can be found by searching http://www.defence.ie.

3. *Eithne* was also the last ship built at Cork's Verolme dockyard, which had previously constructed the Irish Naval Service's other purpose-built offshore patrol vessels but

closed in December 1984 due to lack of follow-on work. Subsequent new-build vessels for the Naval Service have all been contracted to the Appledore yard in Devon, United Kingdom, which is now owned by Babcock Marine.

4. The prototype for the *Emer* or P21 class, *Deidre*, was decommissioned shortly after the turn of the millennium after thirty years' service.

5. The *Róisín* class were, themselves, constructed to the Aker group's (now STX Canada Marine's) PV80 design, which was a non-helicopter-equipped variant of the Mauritian Coast Guard's 'Guardian' class patrol vessel *Vigilant*. This, in turn, traced its origins to a Canadian Coast Guard vessel.

6. There are only limited up-to-date sources of further reading available on the Irish Naval Service. Official websites for the Irish Department of Defence and the Defence Forces can be found at http://www.defence.ie and http://www.military.ie. The latter includes a sub-site for the Naval Service. Useful background to the naval service's development is contained in Aidan McIvor's *A History of the Irish Naval Service* (Dublin, Irish Academic Press, 1994).

Authors:
Enrico Cernuschi
Vincent P O'Hara

ITALY

The Marina Militare:
A Well-balanced Force in Time of Crisis

When the authors commenced this short study of the Italian Navy's current composition and strategic objectives in the autumn of 2011, the task seemed easy. For two generations, the Italian Navy had enjoyed a steady development and practised a consistent policy, with only a pair of minor detours. It had just completed a successful – if little publicised – war cycle off Libya. Then the world economic crisis finally caught up with the Italian military and everything seemed jeopardised.

Fortunately for the service, the *Marina Militare*'s basic policy quickly demonstrated its soundness and resilience. The navy's leadership, confronted by a storm of political chaos worsened by a worldwide journalistic proclivity for drama, asserted itself in a masterful way. This steadfast group, which included the new minister of defence, as well as many former leaders of the fleet, intelligence, submarine and Special Forces commands, and some navy intellectuals, all came from the same Leghorn Naval academy class, the *Dragoni* of 1963–67. This circumstance greatly helped the *Marina Militare*

maintain a common front in the face of the storm.

However, any examination of recent developments requires a much longer journey back in time, beginning from the Italian Navy's darkest days: the months following the country's 8 September 1943 armistice with the Allies during the Second World War.[1]

PROLOGUE: FOUNDATIONS OF A NEW FLEET

On 23 September 1943, the Allied naval commander, Admiral Andrew B Cunningham, and the Italian Navy chief of staff, Admiral Raffaele de Courten, signed a gentleman's agreement about the *Regia Marina*'s participation in the fighting against Germany.[2] This act preceded the Italian Kingdom's declaration of war against its former ally, which followed on 13 October 1943. It therefore confirmed the Italian Navy's status as almost a state within a state, or – at least – the fact that the Allies considered the *Regia Marina* the only Italian institution of real value after the collapse caused by the armistice. Such a dynamic endured during later times of crisis and, arguably, remains true even today.

Nonetheless, in the spring of 1944 the British War Cabinet was still debating whether to disband the *Regia Marina* after the war, in similar fashion to the fate that befell the German and Japanese Navies. The more politically astute Prime Minister, Winston Churchill, however, had already noted that such a proposal was nonsensical. By early 1945, the British government admitted – grudgingly – that a post-war Italian Navy based on a pair of cruisers and a flotilla of destroyers, would be inevitable. Indeed, the fleet's survival became increasingly desirable as the short-lived British alliance with Tito in Dalmatia gave way to the prospect of the old nightmare of a Russian presence in the Adriatic Sea in the name of the common Communist faith.

The Italian *Marina Militare*'s first aircraft carrier, *Giuseppe Garibaldi,* pictured at sea with a complement of Harrier aircraft onboard. She forms a key part of a balanced naval force designed to secure Italy's interests in the wider Mediterranean area. (*Editor's Collection*)

In the immediate post-war era, the new *Marina Militare*'s once formidable battle-fleet was reduced to the two modernised battleships of the *Doria* class, which were largely used for training purposes. *Andrea Doria* herself is shown here. *(Editor's Collection)*

From the beginning, the American point of view was much more generous towards Italy and its navy for a mixture of geopolitical, cultural, and economic reasons. The Italian Navy exploited this difference between the Anglo-American partners, obtaining – before the end of 1945 – the right to save a pair of battleships for post-war service. Italy hoped to recommission the modern *Italia* and *Vittorio Veneto* but got to keep instead the old, if modernised, *Doria* and *Duilio*.[3] However, the military value of these ships – used during the second half of the 1940s and into the 1950s for training and potential shore bombardment – was not what really mattered. The real goal was to maintain formal 'major navy' status and to persuade the new democratic political class in power since mid 1944 not to reduce the naval instrument, but to conserve and renew it.

The immediate post-war shape of the Italian Navy was determined by the Paris Peace Treaty of 10 February 1947, which limited the fleet to 67,000 tons of shipping (excluding the two battleships) and 22,500 personnel, whilst prohibiting ownership of several warship categories.[4] Between 1947 and 1949, the Italian Navy, now the *Marina Militare*, happily bargained or simply violated in all possible ways the limitations of this harsh peace treaty, beginning with the retention and discreet commissioning of a pair of submarines so as to preserve the service's anti-submarine warfare and submarine experience. The navy also deployed fast coastal forces and special attack craft units in violation of treaty provisions.[5]

By 1949, when NATO was created with Italy as one of the founding members, the country's new naval policy had already been planned against a backdrop of the imminent relaxation of peace treaty restrictions. The idea, according to a secret document generated by the chief of staff, was to create two

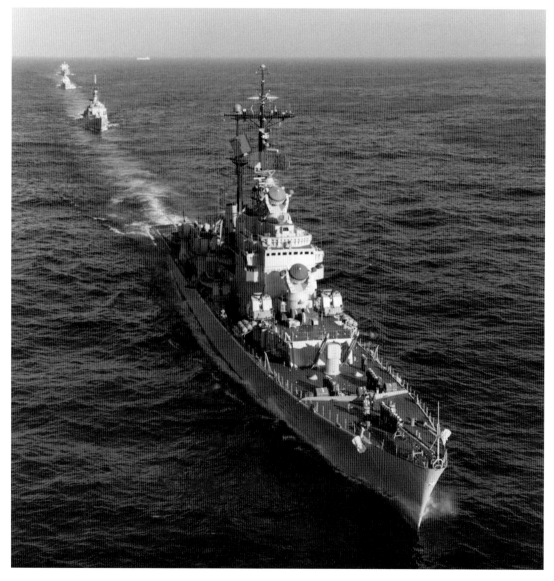

Opposition to fixed wing maritime aviation from the Italian Air Force resulted in the post-war Italian Navy taking an early lead in deploying helicopters at sea. The authorisation of two new *Andrea Doria class* helicopter cruisers in 1957-58 supported the navy's doctrine of operating two escort groups. This is the second *Andrea Doria* to serve with the *Marina Militare*. *(Editor's Collection)*

escort groups, each consisting of a carrier, two anti-aircraft cruisers and a flotilla of modern, 2,600-ton destroyers. The label 'escort group' rather than 'battle group' was a political concession unrelated to the unit's anticipated function. A new generation of escort destroyers and corvettes were also planned to serve in the convoy protection role, while fast coastal forces, minesweeping, and landing craft were also envisaged to meet Italy's coastal warfare requirements.

THE TOOL: FLEET DEVELOPMENT

In 1950 the US Navy offered to the *Marina Militare* an *Independence* (CVL-22) class light carrier and a *Commencement Bay* (CVE-105) class escort carrier, along with one hundred Curtiss S2C-5 Helldivers to equip them, to replace the battleship *Cesare* and the cruiser *Duca d'Aosta* handed over to the Soviets as war reparations. However, while the prospect of carrier task forces delighted Italy's admirals, it horrified their air force counterparts. Citing laws from the 1920s that gave it control over all fixed-wing aviation, the air force scuttled the promised transfer. During the rest of the 1950s economic realities further reduced the navy to a ragbag of modern prototypes and refurbished Second World War vessels.

Despite being apparently defeated by the air force, the navy continued to follow its general vision in ways that were more innovative – and ultimately more fruitful – than the easy adoption of cast-off flat-tops would have been. Starting in 1953, the *Marina Militare* conceived and developed an original helicopter-based doctrine of naval aviation upon the humble foundation of a pair of tiny Bell 47 helicopters purchased for 'agricultural' purposes by a benevolent forestry minister and surreptitiously transferred to navy control. From this unlikely start, the *Marina Militare* developed the first Western missile-armed naval helicopters, which it deployed against the threat of the fast coastal forces being mustered in the Adriatic by Yugoslavia. When the old battleships were finally discarded in the mid-1950s, they were replaced by the *Andrea Doria* class helicopter cruisers authorised in 1957–58. In this way Italy avoided the fate of Argentine, Australian, Canadian and Dutch naval aviation, which faded away once their Second World War carriers ultimately wore out.

In 1989, after thirty years of steady lobbying against both parliamentary and public opinion dominated, as in Fascist times, by the more glamorous air force, the *Marina Militare* was finally able

The light carrier *Giuseppe Garibaldi* pictured operating with NATO units in the North Atlantic during the summer of 2004. The Italian government's purchase of a small batch of AV-8B Harrier aircraft in 1989 marked the culmination of longstanding naval efforts to develop a modern air arm. *(US Navy)*

to acquire AV-8B Harrier aircraft to equip the new light carrier *Giuseppe Garibaldi,* which replaced the first-generation helicopter cruisers. Subsequently, the long-term goal of maintaining two carrier-led battle groups (with their related anti-submarine frigates and logistical support ships) was finally confirmed by the commissioning, in 2009, of the new carrier *Cavour,* which replaced the old helicopter cruiser, *Vittorio Veneto.*[6]

During this same, long season, the submarine force was able, step-by-step, to achieve an average of around half a dozen operational boats. A century-long dream of a true, air-independent submarine operation was finally accomplished with the commissioning of *Salvatore Todaro,* lead Italian unit of the German-designed Type 212A class, in 2006. Meanwhile, coastal forces evolved during the late 1970s from the Second World War-type fast attack units through missile-armed hydrofoils to progressively larger patrol vessels. Special attack units continued to develop both in terms of doctrine and

new weapons, while minesweepers evolved into mine hunters and the auxiliary fleet was funded from the dregs of the budget. Following decisions originating from the 1960s, amphibious forces grew slowly from a short-range Adriatic force to one with high seas capacity. From the late 1980s, Italian marines were carried by the LPD-type dock landing ships *San Giorgio*, *San Marco* and *San Giusto*, handy vessels which were soon to prove their utility.

THE AIM: AN INSTRUMENT OF NATIONAL INFLUENCE

The persistent dream of a modern, balanced navy, cultivated since the days of the armistice, was particularly advanced by this 1961 decision to use some of the scarce funds available to develop a long-range landing force. This decision put in place the final strategic element of today's *Marina Militare* as an instrument capable of projecting national influence.

It is a matter of fact that both Italy's political class and the county's economic interests have always

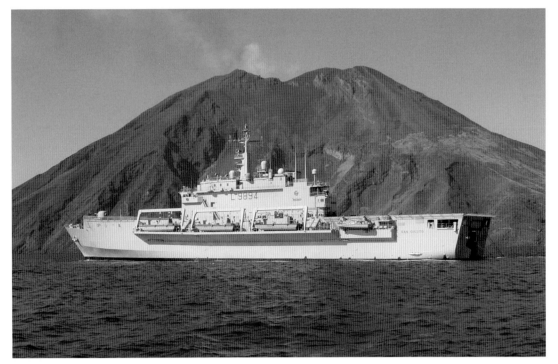

The *Marina Militare* operates three LPD-type amphibious transport docks, the most modern of which – *San Giusto* – is pictured here. The decision to develop a long-range amphibious force was a major step in achieving Italy's aim of developing a modern, balanced navy. *(NATO)*

The Type 212A submarine *Scirè* seen during a deployment to North American waters in the summer of 2009. The *Marina Militare* currently operates two of this air-independent propulsion equipped class and a further two are on order. *(US Navy)*

nourished high ambitions. Even centuries before Italy's 1861 union, its constituents formed one of the world's largest economies. Consequently, the decision of the new post-war Italian political leadership to keep a low profile after the disasters caused by the bombastic Mussolini did not prevent the nation from participating in substantial economic investments throughout the Mediterranean and Africa in the hope of national financial gain, often colliding with similar British and French ambitions. Within the *Mediterraneo allargato* – the area from the Canary Islands to the Indian Ocean (including the Red and the Black Sea) – the *Marina Militare* was discreetly used to project – and increasingly protect – Italian economic interests that underpinned the *Miracolo economico*. Between the 1950s and 1970s, the *Marina Militare* and other elements of Italy's armed forces developed a presence in locations such as Israel, Jordan and Somaliland whilst participating in various United Nations peace missions in diverse locations throughout the world. However, the government's orders during this period were always to maintain a low profile and avoid publicity.

After this period of low-key performance – and with its relevance within the NATO Alliance greatly expanded by the Soviet Navy's accelerating Mediterranean build-up – a renewed *Marina Militare* abandoned its previous 'silent service' policy and a previous focus on NATO duties to become, almost overnight, a more overt player on the world stage. This began with the never fully explained 1979 deployment of the helicopter cruisers *Vittorio Veneto* and *Andrea Doria*, supported by the logistic ship *Stromboli*, to the other side of the globe to rescue boat people in Vietnamese waters. The Italian government decided upon this expedition with less than twenty-four hours' warning to the chief of staff. Subsequently, a series of milestones marked the *Marina Militare*'s increased global presence and operational reach.

These have included naval and air confrontations with Libya off Malta in 1980 and 1986; constant naval patrol activity in the Red Sea since 1982; missions off Lebanon between 1982 and 1984 and,

The *Maestrale* class frigate *Scirocco* operating in the Indian Ocean with NATO forces from Standing Maritime Group 2 (SMG2) in May 2010. From the 1950s onwards, the *Marina Militare* quietly developed a presence in the *Mediterraneo allargato* in support of Italian economic interests. *(NATO)*

Italy's helicopter cruiser *Vittorio Veneto*. Her despatch – along with the cruiser *Andrea Doria* and the replenishment tanker *Stromboli* – to help rescue the Vietnamese boat people in 1979 was a marked step forward in the development of the *Marina Militare*'s global presence. *(Editor's Collection)*

again, since 2006; international minesweeping operations in the Red Sea in 1984; Persian Gulf operations in 1987–88; the war against Iraq in 1991; Yugoslavia from 1991–97; Mozambique in 1993; Somalia from 1991–95; Albania in 1997; Eritrea in 1998; the conflict against Serbia in Kossovo from 1999 (when the AV-8Bs from *Garibaldi* conducted their first bombing missions); Timor in 1999; Afghanistan since 2001 (here again the *Garibaldi*'s air wing participated in combat); Iraq peacekeeping since 2003; and continuous anti-piracy patrols in the Indian Ocean. On 22 November 2011, for example, the new 'Horizon' class destroyer *Andrea Doria* exchanged gunfire with a motor boat suspected of pirate activities eight miles off the Somali coast.

In addition to these special missions, it is worth noting the *Marina Militare* undertakes the less glamorous but vital daily tasks of fishery protection and

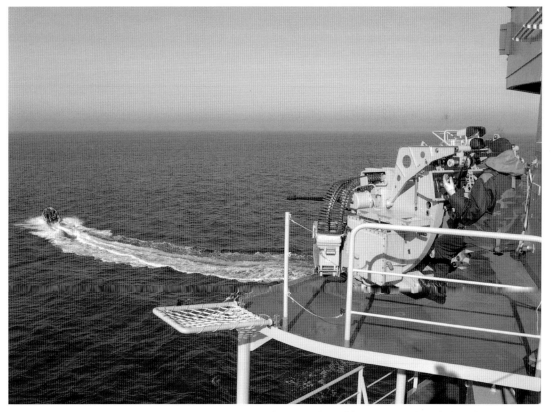

A light gun crew on the replenishment tanker *Etna* practises dealing with small boat attacks whilst deployed to the Indian Ocean in 2011. Anti-piracy operations off the Horn of Africa have been one of numerous missions the Italian Navy has been in engaged in since the early 1980s. *(NATO)*

The Italian Navy's 'Comandanti' class offshore patrol vessel *Comandante Foscari* on exercise with the US Navy in May 2010. The need to undertake ongoing fishery protection and humanitarian patrols in the Sicilian Narrows means Italy maintains a large force of minor warships for these missions. *(US Navy)*

The amphibious transport dock *San Giusto* pictured operating off Libya in March 2011. The *Marina Militare*'s response to the Libyan crisis was swift and extensive. *(NATO)*

patrol in the Sicilian Narrows, where there have been periodic clashes with Tunisian and Libyan ships. This work includes monitoring the clandestine immigration of desperate people – generally from Africa – calling for feats of seamanship and difficult rescue efforts on a weekly basis. The *Marina Militare*'s activities in this regard make it stand out in terms of its compliance with the duties imposed by treaty – and by humanity – in respect of the safeguarding of lives at sea.

The aforementioned missions have demonstrated the Italian Navy's overall efficiency, as well as that of its principal components. These include the battle groups, the air branch, the landing ships and marine corps (the navy's San Marco regiment and – after long training – related army landing and helicopter forces as well), as well as the more discreet, but often decisive, Special Forces and submarines. However, the ultimate proof of the *Marina Militare*'s development into an effective, balanced force was provided by its role in the recent NATO-led intervention in Libya's civil war.

THE PROOF: THE LIBYAN CAMPAIGN

On 15 February 2011, internet headlines announced 'Now Libya!': the latest in a series of international crises exacerbated by the so-called 'Arab Spring'. During the first week of this particular crisis the whole matter seemed just another of the many popular uprisings and putsches which, since January 1971, had vainly tested Gaddafi's iron grip on Libya's reins of power. On 21 February, however, the Italian foreign minister severely criticised the Colonel's regime. This statement reflected a correct appreciation of the situation: that the Americans, British and French had formed a secret alliance against Tripoli. The next day, the British Royal Navy frigate *Cumberland*, cruising in the Mediterranean, passed the Italian destroyer *Francesco Mimbelli*, which was already sailing off the Libyan coast. Some commented that this response was a typically Italian one of 'changing everything with the purpose of not changing anything', or in other words, safeguarding Rome's diverse and important economic interests in Libya against the West's developing coalition.

The *Marina Militare*'s answer to the developing situation was swift. The ELINT ship *Elettra*, the dock landing ship *San Giorgio*, the corvettes *Fenice* and *Comandante Bettica* and a submarine were all amongst vessels deployed off Libya's coast or adjacent seas by 24 February. As the likelihood of western intervention increased, the corvette *Libra* ferried humanitarian aid to Benghazi on 5 March. On 19 March, land-based French Rafale jets, followed shortly afterwards by a more effective barrage of cruise missiles from British and US submarines, as well as US surface ships, heralded the start of this involvement. The light carrier *Garibaldi* – fully prepared for operations – departed the naval base at Taranto on the same day, whilst the destroyer *Andrea Doria* and frigate *Euro* were also at sea in defence of Italy's national airspace. The Gaddafi regime endured the initial onslaught, with command of the intervention passing to NATO by the month's end. This heralded more active Italian participation in operations.

Italian Air Force aircraft had operated over Libya since 19 March and made seven airfields in Southern Italy available from the first for the allied air forces. Nonetheless, the government in Rome preferred not to allow strike missions before NATO assumed leadership, believing this would be the best way to protect its own interests. Later, it decided to bomb only targets outside towns and villages. The *Marina Militare* followed the same instructions and did not perform shore bombardments in the same manner as French and British Royal Navy warships. This was in spite of the availability of guided 127mm and 76mm shells, a technological field where Italian industry is in the forefront. The policy of restraint did not, however, prevent the Italian aircraft from conducting 10 per cent of the conflict's c.27,000 sorties, an equivalent figure to Canada, Norway and the United Kingdom. This was less only than France (33 per cent), the United States (16 per cent) and the pugnacious and very efficient Denmark (11 per cent).

The *Garibaldi*'s small complement of AV-8B Harriers flew 560 sorties. As she could sail close to the Libyan coast by virtue of her naval and submarine escort, the price of any sortie was roughly a fifth of the cost of equivalent missions conducted by the *Aeronautica Militare*'s land-based aircraft, which collectively made c.1,900 sorties. *Garibaldi*'s helicopters also performed some 399 missions.

NATO's Maritime Command in Naples, led by Admiral Rinaldo Veri, directed operations. Task Group 455.01, at first under the orders of Admiral Gualtiero Mattesi and later of Admiral Filippo Maria Foffi, was responsible for the naval blockade. During its 222-day duration, it checked over 3,100 merchant vessels, boarding around three hundred

The most recent ship to carry the *Andrea Doria* name – a 'Horizon' class air defence destroyer – was deployed in defence of Italy's national airspace at the start of the 2011 Libyan conflict. *(Italian Navy)*

and denying transit to eleven. The rebel traffic between Benghazi and Misrata (decisive for the latter's resistance) was also protected by these patrols.

The Special Forces (according to French sources Italy had on the ground around 150 men from the naval and army Special Forces branches) and submarines made significant contributions in their own right. However, despite some very long missions, the story of these activities is still secret and will be divulged, perhaps, only after many years. The ageing but effective *Garibaldi* did an excellent job. Even though that ship was due for an overhaul, she was tasked with remaining on station because of a shortage of operational naval aviation assets until returning to Taranto on 19 July 2011.

By the time operations finally wound down the *Marina Militare* could take satisfaction in its performance. Doctrine, personnel, ships, logistics, weapons, and materials had been tested and found satisfactory. The dogfight between former allies for Libyan markets that followed was not a matter of interest to the navy. As usual, it had provided – in conjunction with the other services – its politicians

and entrepreneurs with the chance to be present after the battle.

THE REAL CRISIS

It was, however, only after the end of Libyan operations that the real crisis began. The global economic crisis that had been developing since 2008 had Italy in its sights, and within a few weeks the Italian government had been swept up in the whirlwind, to be replaced by a new cabinet with a mandate for austerity. The new Minister of Defence, Admiral Giampaolo di Paola, had not returned from a visit to Afghanistan before a concentrated attack was launched against the Italian Navy's acquisitions, most notably the carrier *Cavour* and her future aircraft, the expensive F-35B Joint Strike Fighter.[7] The Italian Air Force, forgetting that it was the main beneficiary of plans to acquire over one hundred F-35s, joined the chorus against the *Marina Militare*'s luxury acquisition projects, with strong media support. Faced by such an orchestra, many leaders would have trembled and, most likely, capitulated. However, the new

Italy's new major unit, the carrier *Cavour* pictured with AV-8B Harriers and AW-101 helicopters on her flight deck. She is regarded as a major element of Italian influence within the Mediterranean. *(Italian Navy via Maurizio Brescia)*

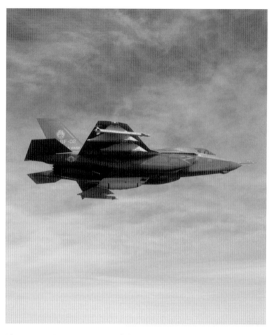

The F-35B STOVL variant of the Lightning II Joint Strike Fighter is scheduled to form the core of *Cavour*'s air group going forward. Planned Italian purchases of the F-35 were reduced in the 2012 defence review but the navy's plans to deploy the plane on *Cavour* remain intact. *(US Navy)*

minister at once accepted a series of television debates with the most aggressive and critical journalists. In these public forums he stood fast.

In the end, naval policy had, of course, to be modified in light of the economic crisis, although sacrifices were made by all services. Overall armed forces personnel will be reduced (by about a quarter of the current total), but it has been recognised that the navy's basic strategy is sound and it will be respected.[8] The service will drop from its present level of c.32,500 personnel to 27,000, whilst, organisationally, the *Dipartimenti Militari Marittimi* will be reduced to two to save money and personnel. The northern department, headquartered at La Spezia (where a programme of infrastructure improvements will continue without reduction) will span the area from Liguria to Tuscany and include Sardinia and the Adriatic coast from Trieste to the Abruzzi and Molise. The southern department based at Taranto (where a huge programme of infrastructural improvements was completed some years ago) will be responsible for the remainder of Italian territory.

The overall F-35 Joint Strike Fighter programme will be cut by forty aircraft to ninety. However, the reductions are focussed on the air force and the navy's allotment of twenty-two F-35B STOVL (short take-off and vertical landing) aircraft for *Cavour* seemingly remains largely untouched.[9] This decision has apparently settled the *Aeronautica Militare*'s latest effort to absorb the navy's fixed-wing air branch and prevented a similar outcome to that which befell Royal Navy air power after the merger of its own assets into Joint Force Harrier and the combined unit's neglect and eventual demise. What Minister di Paola has not been able to say – but which still seems to be a reasonable assumption – is the fact that the *Cavour* and the Italian fleet are effectively going to be a substitute American carrier battle group in the larger Mediterranean as the reduced US Navy carrier line-up is increasingly concentrated on the Pacific and Indian Oceans. This reinforces Italy's influence as a useful and long-tested friend in the Mediterranean, whose interests have coincided, geopolitically, with those of the United States since their respective wars of independence in the eighteenth and nineteenth centuries.

As outlined below, there will be fleet reductions, especially in the surface escort fleet. However, in the post-Libya environment there have been some positive developments as well, particularly in the co-operative field. One dividend is the fact that the 'new' Libyan navy will be trained and equipped by the *Marina Militare*. Using the auxiliary ships *Gorgona* and *Tremiti* and their specialised salvage personnel, it is recovering the wrecks of Gaddafi's warships sunk in their harbours, whilst helping the Libyans to recommission some small patrol vessels of the *Bigliani* class (former Italian custom guard boats) as the core of a new fleet.

Current principal units of the *Marina Militare* are set out in Table 2.4B.1.

THE FUTURE

Italian naval programmes inevitably remain work in progress during such times as the present. Nonetheless the *Marina Militare*'s basic operational model is little different than in 1950, as outlined by then Navy Chief of Staff Admiral Bruno Branciforte in a recent issue of the United States Naval Institute's *Proceedings* magazine.[10] The main goals remain:

■ To enhance the fleet's expeditionary role

Table 2.4B.1: MARINA MILITARE FLEET COMPOSITION – MID 2012

TYPE	CLASS	NUMBER	DATE	NOTES
Aircraft Carriers				
Aircraft Carrier – CV	CAVOUR	1	2008	One ship, *Cavour* (550). Typical air group of 8 x AV-8B jets and 12 x AW-101 helicopters.
Aircraft Carrier – CVS/LHA	GIUSEPPE GARIBALDI	1	1985	One ship, *Giuseppe Garibaldi* (551). Up to 18 jets & helicopters. To be converted as an LHA.
Principal Surface Escorts				
Destroyer – DDG	ANDREA DORIA ('Horizon')	2	2007-09	*Andrea Doria* (D553) & *Caio Duilio* (D554). Sisters to French *Forbin* class.
Destroyer – DDG	DE LA PENNE	2	1993	*Luigi Durand de la Penne* (D560) & *Francesco Mimbelli* (D560)
Frigate – FFG	MAESTRALE	8	1982-85	*Maestrale* (F570)*, *Grecale* (F571)*, *Libeccio* (F572), *Scirocco* (F573), *Aliseo* (F574)*, *Euro* (F575)*, *Espero* (F576) & *Zeffiro* (F577). Four un-modernised ships* to be withdrawn 2013-16.
Frigate – FFG	ARTIGLIERE	3	1995-96	*Aviere* (F583), *Bersagliere* (F584) & *Granatiere* (F585). *Lupo* derivatives originally built for Iraq. Lead ship paid off to reserve 2012. Rest to follow by 2015 or to be re-allocated to auxiliary duties.
Corvette – FS	MINERVA	8	1987-91	*Minerva* (F 551), *Urania* (F 552), *Danaide* (F 553), *Sfinge* (F 554), *Driade* (F 555), *Chimera* (F 556), *Fenice* (F 557) & *Sibilla* (F 558). Six to be withdrawn by 2016. Replacement light frigates planned.
Submarines				
Submarine – SSK	TODARO (Type 212A)	2 (2)	2006-07	*Salvatore Todaro* (S526) & *Sciré* (S257). German Type 212A class, locally built. Two more ordered.
Submarine – SSK	LONGOBARDO (SAURO IV)	2	1993-95	*Primo Longobardo* (S524) & *Gianfranco Gazzana Priaroggia* (S525). Enlarged *Sauro III* design.
Submarine – SSK	PELOSI (SAURO III)	2	1988-89	*Salvatore Pelosi* (S522) & *Giulano Prini* (S523)
Amphibious Ships				
Landing Platform Dock – LPD	SAN GIORGIO	3	1987-94	*San Giorgio* (L9892), *San Marco* (L9893) & *San Giusto* (L9894). Larger replacements planned.
Minor War Vessels				
Patrol Vessel – OPV	SIRIO ('Comandanti')	2	2003	*Sirio* (P409) & *Orione* (P410). More basic variants of earlier 'Comandanti' ships.
Patrol Vessel – OPV	FULGOSI ('Comandanti')	4	2001-02	*Comandante Cigala Fulgosi* (P 490), *Comandante Borsini* (P 491), *Comandante Bettica* (P 492), *Comandante Foscari* (P 493)
Patrol Vessel – OPV	CASSIOPEA	4	1989-91	*Cassiopea* (P401), *Libra* (P402), *Spica* (P403) & *Vega* (P404)
Minehunter – MCMV	LERICI	2	1985	*Milazzo* (M5552) & *Vieste* (M5553). *Lerici* & *Sapri* to pay off 2012.
Minehunter – MCMV	GAETA	8	1992-96	*Gaeta* (M5554), *Termoli* (M5555), *Alghero* (M5556), *Numana* (M5557), *Crotone* (M5558), *Viareggio* (M5559), *Chioggia* (M5560) & *Rimini* (M5561). Improved *Lerici* class.

Notes: Other vessels include four coastal patrol vessels; three replenishment tankers; a number of coastal transports, tankers and tenders; six survey and research ships; and various landing craft and tugs. Date refers to the commissioning of remaining ships in the class. *Cavour's* air group is effectively 'ad hoc' prior to the arrival of the F-35B: this note is therefore only indicative.

■ To use naval air power effectively
■ To achieve the ability to conduct brigade-level amphibious operations
■ To acquire multi-role platforms
■ To strengthen national defence and to promote maritime security

The key to achieving these goals is a balanced fleet. In support of this, *Cavour* will remain fully operational as an aircraft carrier, although *Garibaldi* will be converted into an amphibious assault ship. As noted above, procurement of the F-35B STOVL variant of the Lightning II Joint Strike Fighter is on schedule. Naval aviation will also be reinforced by new NH90 medium helicopters in both anti-submarine and utility versions, supplementing the existing, heavier AW-101s. Advanced studies are underway

The second Italian FREMM, *Virginio Fasan*, is one of four anti-submarine versions of the Italian design variant. She is pictured here at Fincantieri's shipyard in Muggiano in April 2012 prior to final outfitting. (*Giorgio Parodi via Maurizio Brescia*)

The first of Italy's new FREMM multi-mission frigates, *Carlo Bergamini,* is seen on preliminary trials in October 2011. Ten units were originally planned but it seems that budget reductions will result in only six ships being completed. They will replace the existing *Maestrale* and *Artigliere* classes. *(OCCAR)*

for a three-ship class of 20,000-ton multi-role landing vessels similar to but smaller than the US Navy's amphibious assault ships to replace *Garibaldi* and the *San Giorgio* class, although the first will not be ordered before 2015.

The navy's planned order of Franco-Italian FREMM multi-mission frigates will be reduced from ten to six units.[11] All will be fitted with the EMPAR (European Multi-function Phased Array Radar) found on the 'Horizon' class, giving a powerful air defence capability. Two will be the general purpose version and four anti-submarine variants, the latter being necessary to carry out the navy's new anti-submarine doctrine, which is quite different from Cold War practice. The first of these frigates, a general purpose type named *Carlo Bergamini*, started trials in 2011 and will be commissioned in 2013. The second ship, an anti-submarine variant named *Virginio Fasan,* was launched in April 2012, and will follow around six months after *Bergamini*. Work on a third, *Carlo Margottini*, is also well advanced. By way of contrast, the light frigate successors to the corvettes that will soon be withdrawn from service only constitute preliminary sketches. For the even longer term, once the amphibious modernisation programme is completed, the navy also anticipates developing a new multi-role offshore patrol vessel. This would also take modules to adapt it for mine warfare.

Two new modified Type 212A AIP-equipped submarines have already been financed, resulting in a four-boat underwater flotilla in the medium term. A support ship, which will also be used for survey missions, should materialise in the second half of this decade. Also planned within the same timescale is a new logistic vessel, which will be able to carry out (limited) sealift missions of materials and vehicles. She will replace the old and cramped tankers *Stromboli* and *Vesuvio*.

The navy's platforms are supported by an industrial base that has established a leading position in naval equipment, particularly in the anti-surface and electronic warfare domains. The main surface-to-surface missile is currently the Teseo Mk2/A (Mk2 Block IV). This can hit coastal as well as maritime targets through use of GPS, infrared (IR) imaging and a man-in-the-loop data-link. Notably, the Italian Navy developed this capability so as to be able to hit enemy vessels inside their harbours before the US and other NATO allies. A new supersonic (Mach 3) anti-ship missile named 'CVS 401 Perseus'

A new NFH-90 anti-submarine helicopter in *Marina Militare* colours. The Italian Navy has started to take delivery of forty-six NFH and ten transport variants of the NH90 to supplement its heavier EH-101 helicopters. (AgustaWestland)

A Teseo Mk2 surface-to-surface missile being fired from the destroyer *Luigi Durand de la Penne*. The Italian Navy is supported by a proficient armaments industry that has particularly strong positions in anti-surface warfare and electronics. *(MBDA)*

is under development by the European MBDA enterprise in which Italy's Finmeccanica has a significant stake. Meanwhile, the provision of ammunition of the new 'Vulcano' type for the Oto Melara 76/62 gun will appreciably add to the capabilities already provided by 'DART' guided shells to this long-standing weapons system, allowing engage-

ment of targets out to forty kilometres. The Oto Melara 127/54 IR sabot shell of the long range type uses the same technology. The related Italian electronic countermeasures system to counter this menace has also been successfully tested. Following the experience of the Second World War, the *Marina Militare* is more aware than most that main-

taining up-to-date aircraft, weapons systems, electronics and training are equally as important as deploying effective ships, strategy and doctrine if success is to be achieved.

In simple words the Italian Navy believes its doctrine, knows its story, and is aware of the fact that there is no alternative to a well-balanced fleet.

Notes:

1. An account of the navy's role in the 1943 armistice can be found in the authors' *Dark Navy: the Regia Marina and the Armistice of 8 September 1943* (Nimble Books, 2009).

2. Formed after the proclamation of the Kingdom of Italy in 1861, the *Regia Marina* ('Royal Navy') assumed its current title of the *Marina Militare* in 1946 after the abolition of the Italian monarchy.

3. The Italians' ultimately doomed attempts to retain their most modern battleships are documented in Erminio Bagnasco and Augusto de Toro's *The Littorio Class: Italy's Last and Largest Battleships 1937–1948* (Barnsley, Seaforth Publishing, 2011),

4. Other prohibited classes of warship included aircraft carriers, submarines, motor torpedo boats and assault craft, whilst new construction was prohibited before 1950. Many existing warships had either to be transferred to the allied powers as compensation or scrapped.

5. During this time, it is interesting to note that the

tradition of rivalry with the other European and Mediterranean powers continued, even if in a discreet way. For example, from spring 1945 until November 1948 – when the American government dictated a formal stop – the Italian navy and air force assisted the clandestine Jewish emigration into Palestine supplying even explosive boats of the 'MTM' type and training personnel to fight the British-supported Egyptian navy; this assistance culminated in the 22 October 1948 attack craft action off Gaza that sank the Egyptian sloop *El Amir Farouq*.

6. The new Italian aircraft carrier was described in detail in the authors' 'The Aircraft Carrier Cavour: Doctrine and Sea Power in the Italian Navy', *Seaforth World Naval Review 2010* (Barnsley, Seaforth Publishing, 2009), pp.116–31.

7. Admiral Giampaolo di Paola (born 15 August 1944) is an Italian career navy officer. A submariner by training, he also commanded the aircraft carrier *Giuseppe Garibaldi* and was the Italian military's chief of staff between 2004 and 2008. He was recalled from the chairmanship of NATO's military committee by new Italian Prime Minister Mario Monti in November 2011 to serve as Minister of

Defence in Italy's new technocratic administration.

8. The defence review, announced in February 2012, envisages a reduction in military personnel from c.190,000 to c.150,000, with civilian personnel falling from 30,000 to 20,000. The overall aim is to reduce personnel expenses from the current 70 per cent of the budget to around 50 per cent, thereby enabling the military to become more effective on the limited means available.

9. It appears that the Italian Air Force still wants the navy to share some of the pain, with Chief of the Air Force Lieutenant General Giuseppe Bernadis recently being reported as saying both forces would receive fifteen F-35Bs each, the remaining sixty aircraft being air force F-35As. This might even result in a pooled F-35B fleet.

10. See Admiral Bruno Branciforte, 'The Commanders Respond: Italian Navy', *Proceedings* – March 2012 (Annapolis MD, Naval Institute Press, 2012).

11. A full description of the distinct French anti-submarine FREMM variant is contained in Chapter 3.1.

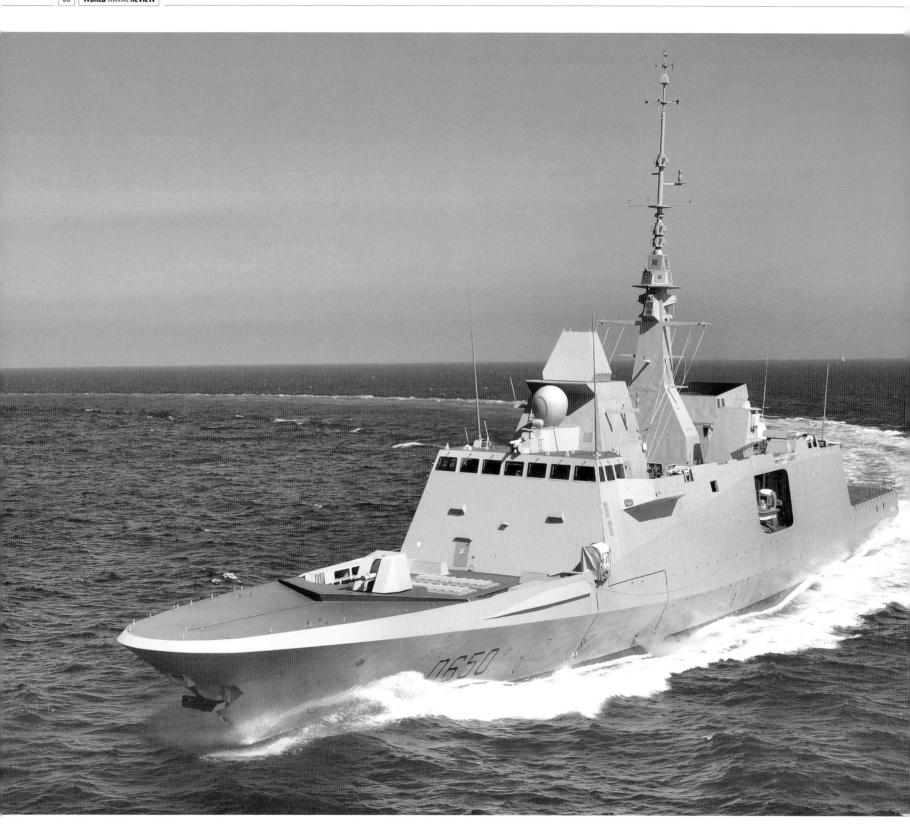

3.1 SIGNIFICANT SHIPS

Author:
Conrad Waters

FRANCE'S AQUITAINE

First French FREMM heralds a Renaissance for its Surface Fleet

Constituting the largest construction project for surface warships currently underway in Europe, the Franco-Italian FREMM (*Frégates Européennes Multi-Missions*) programme will steadily recapitalise the first line surface fleets of its two partner nations over the next decade. A key aim of the FREMM project has been to achieve a common, multi-role design framework that is flexible enough to permit variation dependent both on role and national preference, whilst still achieving economies of scale through shared design and procurement. So far as France's *Marine Nationale* is concerned, this will see the delivery of a distinctly French FREMM variant of separately specified anti-submarine and anti-air warfare frigates from 2012 onwards. Meanwhile Italy's *Marina Militare* will take ownership of anti-submarine and general purpose sub groups of its own FREMM variant that is also sometimes called the *Rinascimento* or 'Renaissance' class in Italian circles.

The first frigate completed under the FREMM programme, France's *Aquitaine,* commenced sea trials in April 2011 and will shortly be delivered to the *Marine Nationale.* She is one of nine French ships that will comprise the anti-submarine warfare

<hr>

Opposite: The new French FREMM multi-mission frigate *Aquitaine* pictured on sea trials in late April 2011. She is the first of nine anti-submarine optimised ships of the French FREMM variant being acquired by France's *Marine Nationale. (DCNS)*

(ASW) version of the French FREMM design. An additional ship is under construction for Morocco. Representing the latest thinking in ASW technology, it is *Aquitaine* and her anti-submarine optimised sisters of France's FREMM variant that form the principal subject of this chapter.

CLASS ORIGINS

The FREMM programme traces its origins to increasing concerns about the block obsolescence of both France and Italy's frigate forces that began to emerge in the late 1990s. At that time, both countries were engaged – along with, for a time, the United Kingdom – in plans to build a Common New Generation Frigate (CNGF) under Project 'Horizon'.[1] The two countries' generally successful collaboration on this project eventually resulted in a decision to extend co-operation to the design of a new class of surface ship. This was to be simpler, cheaper and thus more numerous than the 'high-end' air defence frigates that resulted from the Horizon programme. Initial plans envisaged a total of twenty-seven new multi-mission frigates based on a common hull, but ordered in anti-submarine and general purpose/land attack versions. At first, France was looking to procure as many as seventeen frigates to replace existing vessels of the *Tourville* (FASM-67), *Georges Leygues* (FASM-70) and *D'Estienne D'Orves* (A-69) classes on a near one-for-one basis. Italy's original requirement was for ten new ships to allow maintenance of a slightly reduced escort flotilla as its

existing four *Lupo* and eight *Maestrale* type frigates fell due for decommissioning.

Preliminary design studies for the new generation of frigates that was to become FREMM first commenced in France as a national effort around the turn of the new millennium. It was not until the second half of 2002 that the programme took on a multinational dimension, when collaboration between France and Italy was agreed. A co-operation accord between the two partner nations was signed in November of that year, with a formal framework agreement following in June 2003. This allowed common design work to begin in earnest.

At first, it was anticipated that the new ships would be delivered from 2008 onwards: a date that was to prove overly optimistic. Although the need to reconcile varying national requirements was part of the reason for the delay, it also proved difficult to stretch limited post Cold War defence budgets to accommodate such an ambitious commitment. For a period, France looked at leasing and deferred financing schemes to ease its share of the cost, whilst funding constraints in Italy even threatened its withdrawal from collaboration. As a result, it was not until October 2005 that a declaration of intent between the French and Italian governments at their 24th bilateral summit paved the way for construction orders to be signed. A design and development contract for the new ships was subsequently placed through OCCAR, Europe's Organisation for Joint Armament Cooperation, on 16 November 2005.[2]

Table 3.1.1: FRENCH FREMM DESIGN VARIANT: PLANNED & ACTUAL ORDERS

TYPE	ANTI-SUBMARINE (ASM)	LAND ATTACK (AVT)	ANTI-AIRCRAFT (FREDA)	TOTAL	NOTES
Planned (2002)	8	9	0	17	Orders planned in 3 batches
Actual (2012)	9	0	2	11	Plus 1 ASM for Morocco
Difference	+1	-9	+2	-6	

This included an agreement for completion of the first tranche of French ships, comprising eight frigates in total.

CONTRACT AND CONSTRUCTION

The contract for the detailed design and construction of France's FREMM units was awarded to Aramis, then a joint venture between French shipbuilder DCN and the electronics group Thales. Aramis was effectively assumed into the restructured DCNS, in which Thales took a 25 per cent (now 35 per cent) stake, in 2007. A similar alliance between Italy's Fincantieri and Finmeccanica – Orizzonte Sistemi Navali – is the overall prime contractor for the Italian part of the programme.

It was initially envisaged that the first eight French frigates would comprise six anti-submarine and two land attack versions. Orders for an additional two ASW and seven land attack oriented ships were to be placed in two follow-on batches at a later date, thereby completing the planned seventeen-strong class. However, termination of the preceding 'Horizon' programme at just two ships and cuts to France's surface fleet announced in the 2008 White

Left: An artist's impression of the French FREMM variant. The FREMM multi-mission frigate programme will deliver distinctively French and Italian variants to the respective countries' fleets. These will be further 'optimised' for various roles within the overall multi-mission design framework. *(DCNS)*

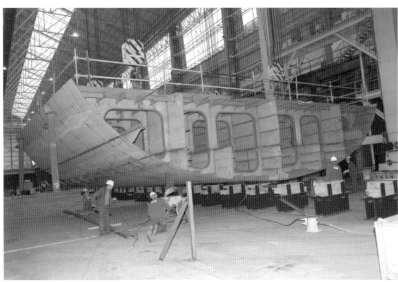

All France's FREMM type frigates are assembled in a covered dock at DCNS's shipyard in Lorient from blocks fabricated at Lorient or at other DCNS facilities. A greater level of pre-outfitting of the constituent blocks is envisaged as the programme progresses. *(DCNS)*

Aquitaine in the course of being floated out from DCNS's covered dock at Lorient on 29 April 2010. This was followed by a formal unveiling ceremony in front of French President Nicolas Sarkozy on 4 May 2010. *(DCNS)*

Paper on defence and national security resulted in a change of plan. It was decided to reduce France's FREMM order to just eleven units, of which nine would be optimised for ASW. The other two were to be built to a new air defence specification to replace a second pair of 'Horizon' vessels that were originally planned. This has resulted in all the first batch of eight French ships being built to the ASW specification. A follow-on order placed in October 2009 encompassed the air defence ships and the final anti-submarine unit. Table 3.1.1 summarises France's original and final FREMM acquisition plans.[3]

Construction of the French frigates is focused on DCNS's shipyard at Lorient in Brittany, where assembly of all the *Marine Nationale*'s front-line surface warships is now centred.[4] Located on both banks of the River Scorff, the historic Lorient facility has been extensively modernised to facilitate efficient delivery of the FREMM programme. It is capable of completing a FREMM-sized ship every seven months, the main capacity constraint being the covered shipbuilding dock on the east bank of the Scorff where the main assembly process takes place. On average, the French Navy is expected to receive one FREMM frigate every ten months so there is flexibility to encompass additional work on export contracts.

Fabrication of *Aquitaine* commenced early in 2007. Use of modern, modular techniques involves the manufacture and outfitting of each ship's constituent blocks on a production line that moves progressively towards the covered dock, where the completed blocks are assembled. Whilst there was a relatively low level of pre-outfitting of *Aquitaine*'s blocks, following ships will be completed to a much higher level. The modular nature of assembly also allows blocks to be allocated to other DCNS yards to spread workload. For example, many blocks for the second and third French units have been allocated to the group's facilities in Cherbourg and Brest. The latter yard has assembled the two ships' forward hulls from these modules, with the completed structures then being barged to Lorient to join other blocks in the final construction hall.

Aquitaine's construction progressed relatively rapidly after the first steel was cut, with propulsion

A key design influence on *Aquitaine's* design was the *La Fayette* stealth frigate class completed between 1996 and 2001 and which spawned several export derivatives. There is a particularly strong resemblance to the *Formidable* class built for the Republic of Singapore Navy, which also use the distinctive Herakles multi-function radar. *Steadfast* is pictured here on exercises with the US Navy. *(US Navy)*

new class, as evidenced by the principal ASW designation for nine out of the eleven planned ships.

It should be noted, however, that in spite of this anti-submarine optimisation, *Aquitaine* and her sisters are essentially modern, multi-mission surface combatants capable of deployment in a wide range of roles in line with the overall FREMM concept.[5] Displacing around 6,000 tons in full load condition, all the French ships will be built in accordance with a common hull design, propulsion system and general layout. Equally, each will be equipped with a range of anti-air, anti-surface and anti-submarine weaponry controlled by a generic DCNS SETIS combat management system. These weapons include Aster anti-air missiles, Exocet surface-to-surface missiles, anti-submarine torpedoes, a 76mm gun and an embarked helicopter. As such, the differences between the French ASW and FREDA (*frégate de défense aerienne*) anti air warfare equipped ships will largely be ones of detail incorporated to enhance capability in the chosen area.

WEAPONRY AND COMBAT SYSTEMS

Combat Management System: The heart of *Aquitaine*'s war fighting capability is provided by the new SETIS combat management system (CMS). This is designed to integrate the ship's defensive and offensive equipment to achieve maximum effect across all warfare domains. Evolved from the SENIT family of systems that have equipped previous generations of French warships, it follows current trends towards modularity, decentralisation and maximum use of 'off-the-shelf' commercial technology. A series of seventeen independent multifunction consoles are networked to the ship's weapons, sensors and communications systems. Each console is capable of being used to direct any of the command and control functions supported by the system. A key benefit of this approach is significant operational flexibility. For example, the system can be specifically configured to achieve the best match to the type of mission currently underway. SETIS was qualified on a land-based facility at Toulon before installation in *Aquitaine,* considerably simplifying subsequent testing during sea trials.

Anti-Submarine Warfare: *Aquitaine*'s ability to detect and track underwater targets is provided by a Thales-designed sonar suite. This comprises both hull-mounted and variable-depth elements. The hull-mounted sonar is Thales's UMS 4110, a low-

systems being installed from June 2008 and hull assembly being completed by the end of October 2009. Floating out on 29 April 2010 was followed by a formal unveiling ceremony in front of more than 1,200 guests on 4 May. The importance of the programme was reflected in the attendance of the then President of the Republic, Nicolas Sarkozy, at this event. Timely completion of final outfitting work allowed the first stage of an extensive schedule of sea trials to commence less than a year later on 18 April 2011. By the end of the year, Morocco's *Mohammed VI* had also been launched and a further three French members of the class were under construction.

OVERALL DESIGN: ANTECEDENTS AND FEATURES

The overall design of the French variant of the FREMM type draws heavily on DCNS's experience of surface escort construction for both domestic and overseas markets from the mid 1990s onwards. Overall structure, particularly the evident focus on

stealth design, is strongly influenced by the five *La Fayette* class light frigates, which first entered service between 1996 and 2001 and spawned several export derivatives. There is a strong family resemblance to Singapore's *Formidable* class which is also equipped with the pyramid-shaped Herakles multifunction radar used by *Aquitaine* and her sisters.

Other design influences include the preceding 'Horizon' air defence frigates that marked the start of Franco-Italian collaboration in warship construction. Interestingly, however, the 'Horizon' programme seems to have had a much more marked impact on the Italian FREMM variants, which share a common main radar system in the form of the Italian designed EMPAR (European Multi-function Phased Array Radar). *Aquitaine* has also benefited from previous DCNS experience in anti-submarine technology, gained in part from the group's almost unique involvement in both nuclear and diesel-electric submarine design. Protection of the strategic missile submarines of France's FOST (*Force Océanique Stratégique*) nuclear deterrent is a key mission for the

Right, top: The French 'Horizon' class air defence ship *Forbin* seen in April 2010. This previous example of Franco-Italian co-operation in warship design also influenced France's national variant of the FREMM design, although the family resemblance with Italy's distinctive FREMM subclass is more apparent. *(Conrad Waters)*

Right, middle: A picture of Italy's first FREMM-type frigate, the general purpose *Carlo Bergamini*, on trials during autumn 2011. Structurally very similar to the French FREMM variants, she incorporates a number of significant design features that are unique to the Italian ships, most notably the EMPAR radar housed in a spherical dome on top of the foremast. As a result, she is visually closer to the preceding 'Horizon' class than the French ships. *(OCCAR)*

frequency active and passive bow-mounted sonar suitable for medium to large platforms. It first entered service in France's existing FASM-70 frigates and also equips the Franco-Italian 'Horizon' class. Providing long-range detection irrespective of environmental conditions, it is particularly effective at detecting targets above the thermal layer and has been influenced by Mediterranean anti-submarine conditions. UMS 4110 is complemented by Thales's CAPTAS-4 variable depth sonar. This is another low-frequency active and passive device that is particularly well suited for detecting the quietest submarines at ultra-long ranges below the thermal layer. First entering service onboard the Royal Navy's Type 23 frigates as Sonar 2087, it is designated as UMS 4249 in French service. The various elements of the variable depth sonar are housed beneath the flight deck and deployed through openings in the stern. It is not clear at this stage whether CAPTAS will be fitted to the two air-defence optimised ships.

Prosecution of any submarines detected will largely be in the hands of the ship's embarked helicopter. The *Marine Nationale* is currently taking delivery of the NFH (NATO Frigate Helicopter) version of Eurocopter-lead NH Industries' new NH-90 design. This will be known as the Caiman in French service and will replace the smaller Lynx. Equipped with FLASH sonar, sonobuoys and 360-degree radar, as well as Link 11 communications and an ability to deploy anti-submarine torpedoes, depth charges and air-to-surface missiles, the NFH will be

Right: An excellent overhead view of *Aquitaine* taken during sea trials in the Atlantic during April 2011. In spite of her anti-submarine optimisation, she is essentially a modern, multi-mission surface combatant well capable of undertaking a wide variety of roles in line with the FREMM concept. *(DCNS)*

Left: *Aquitaine*'s foremast and Herakles multi-function radar in its distinctive pyramid-like housing. Capable of detecting and tracking a large number of air and surface targets simultaneously, Herakles also controls the ship's surface-to-air missiles. *(Conrad Waters)*

Above: An image of a French FREMM frigate's combat information centre, with the multi-function consoles for the SETIS combat management system featuring prominently. Each console is capable of being used to direct any of the command and control functions supported by the system. In air defence engagements, threats identified by the Herakles radar are co-ordinated with the overall operational 'picture' maintained by SETIS to facilitate their destruction with Aster surface-to-air missiles. *(DCNS)*

equally capable in anti-submarine and anti-surface roles. Initial trials of a Caiman were first carried out onboard *Aquitaine* in March 2012 and are said to have met with success. A ship stabilisation system and helicopter deck handling facilities provide for safe operation from the c.500m² flight deck in conditions up to Sea State 6. *Aquitaine* is also equipped with two twin fixed 324mm launchers for the MU-90 torpedoes deployed on the Caiman, providing a useful, fast-response backup.

Anti-Air Warfare: The core air defence capability of all the French FREMM variants will be provided by a combination of Thales's Herakles radar and MBDA's Aster surface-to-air missiles. A modern multi-function phased array, Herakles combines surveillance, target tracking and fire-control roles in a single system. Operating in the 2,000–4,000 MHz frequency E/F bands (USN S-band) as a compromise between the greater surveillance range obtainable from lower frequency systems and the enhanced tracking abilities of higher frequency arrays,

Herakles consists of a two-axis, rotating electronically scanned antenna.[6] It can detect air targets within a radius of c.250km and surface targets at distances of up to 80km. The manufacturer claims that over four hundred air and surface targets can be tracked simultaneously. Herakles is supported by Thales's Artemis passive panoramic surveillance system, which identifies and tracks the infrared signatures of low elevation air and surface threats. Three sensors are located on the mainmast to provide 360-degree coverage.

Air defence engagements are the primary responsibility of the Aster surface-to-air missile system, with which Herakles is integrated. Two eight-cell DCNS Sylver A43 vertical launch system (VLS) modules are located aft of *Aquitaine*'s main gun and can accommodate up to sixteen of the short range, Aster 15 variant of the missile. Potential aircraft and missile threats are identified and tracked by Herakles and co-ordinated with the overall picture maintained by the SETIS CMS. Hostile tracks can then be engaged with Aster missiles, which are guided

towards the target by Herakles uplink until the missile's active radar seeker takes over in the final stages of the engagement. Thales claims that all sixteen missiles can be provided with guidance support simultaneously. The two French air-defence optimised frigates will carry sixteen additional Aster missiles in their remaining VLS modules. These may be equipped with the longer range Aster 30 also used in the 'Horizon' class and the British Type 45.

In line with French operating doctrine, no provision is made for an additional close-in weapons system (CIWS) to supplement Aster. However, the Oto-Melara 76mm/62 Super Rapid medium calibre gun forward of the vertical launch modules can be used in an air-defence capacity as well as in an anti-surface role. A Sagem Vigy MM electro-optical fire control system is fitted above the bridge. Provision is also made for various light weapons for last ditch defence.

Anti-Surface Warfare: *Aquitaine*'s true multi-mission potential is probably best demonstrated by

Aquitaine's launch was followed by an extensive outfitting process, during which key systems that could not be fitted within the confines of the covered dock were installed. This early 2011 image shows the process close to completion, with the Herakles multi-function radar that forms the core of the ship's air defence capabilities now prominent on the foremast. Also evident is the tall mainmast, on which the Artemis passive surveillance system is fitted. *(DCNS)*

the provision made for prosecuting surface warfare. This extends beyond the normal outfit of anti-ship missiles typically installed in frigate-sized ships to encompass a land attack cruise missile capability. Provided by the new MdCN (*Missile de Croisière Naval*) naval variant of MBDA's air-launched SCALP/Storm Shadow, DCNS claim that this is the first time this functionality has been provided in a western surface ship built outside of the United States.

Three hundred SCALP Naval missiles were ordered from MBDA in December 2006. Two hundred and fifty of these are destined to enter service in the French anti-submarine FREMM variant from 2013 onwards.[7] Testing of the new missile is already well underway, with the first launch – using a FREMM frigate configuration – having been carried out in June 2010. The missiles will be housed in the extended-length, A70 version of the Sylver vertical launch system, which was purposely

designed with the MdCN in mind. Two eight-cell A70 modules are installed aft of the shorter A43 launchers. Capable of deploying a sizeable warhead with near pinpoint accuracy over distances in excess of a thousand kilometres, SCALP Naval will provide the *Marine Nationale* with a capacity similar – if somewhat shorter-ranged – to the Tomahawk cruise missile currently installed in the US Navy's *Arleigh Burke* (DDG-51) class destroyers.

SCALP Naval will be supplemented by the

MM40 Block 3 version of the well-established Exocet surface-to-surface missile. First fired operationally from the 'Horizon' class frigate *Chevalier Paul* in March 2010, the Block 3 variant has a range in excess of 180km and is claimed to have a coastal land attack capability in addition to its principal anti-ship role. Two quad launchers are fitted amidships, aft of the bridge. In addition, the embarked Caiman helicopter has the potential to play an important anti-ship role, particularly through use of the light air-to-surface missiles against fast attack craft and other small targets.

COUNTERMEASURES AND SURVIVABILITY

Aquitaine's weapon systems are supplemented by a comprehensive range of equipment providing electronic and other countermeasures. In addition, ship survivability is further enhanced both by stealth features and extensive provision for damage control. The principal electronic countermeasures suite is provided by the Sigen consortium which brings together the expertise of France's Thales and Italy's Elettronica. The suite encompasses passive Radar and Communications Electronic Support Measures (ESM) for early detection and warning of hostile aircraft, missile and ship transmissions, as well as

Table 3.1.2.

AQUITAINE PRINCIPAL PARTICULARS

Building Information:

Fabrication Commenced:	16 March 2007
Launched:	29 April 2010
Delivered:	Planned Summer 2012
Builders:	DCNS at its facility in Lorient, Brittany.

Dimensions:

Displacement:	5,200 tons standard displacement, 6,000 tons full load displacement.
Overall Hull Dimensions:	142.2m x 19.8m x 5.4m (7.3m maximum). Length between perpendiculars is 130.2m.

Weapons Systems:

Missiles:	2 x Sylver A43 8-cell VLS modules for a total of 16 Aster 15 surface-to-air missiles.
	2 x Sylver A70 8-cell VLS modules for a total of 16 SCALP Naval MdCN cruise missiles.
	2 x quad launchers for Exocet MM40 Block 3 surface-to-surface missiles.
Guns:	1 x 76mm Oto Melara Super Rapid. 2 x GIAT F2 20mm guns. Light machine guns.
Torpedoes:	2 x twin fixed 324mm anti-submarine torpedo tubes for MU-90 torpedoes.
Aircraft:	1 x NFH-90 Caiman helicopter.
Countermeasures:	Sigen Radar (RESM) and Communications (CESM) Electronic Support Measures. Sigen Radar Electronic Countermeasures (RECM) jammers.
	NGDS decoy launchers. SLAT torpedo defence system.
Principal Sensors:	1 x Herakles multifunction radar, including integrated IFF. Surface search and navigation radars.
	Artemis passive surveillance system. 1 x Thales UMS 4110 hull-mounted sonar. Thales UMS 4249 CAPTAS-4 towed-array.
Combat System:	DCNS SETIS combat management system.
	Fully Integrated Communications System (FICS) includes links 11 and 16 with provision for link 22.

Propulsion Systems:

Machinery:	CODLOG. 4 x MTU V16 4000 diesel generators each rated at 2.2MW linked to two Jeumont electric motors on each shaft.
	1 x GE/Avio LM2500+G4 gas turbine rated at 32MW. A retractable azimuth thruster can provide auxiliary propulsion.
Speed and Range:	Designed maximum speed 27 knots on gas turbine, 15 knots on electric motors. Range is 6,000 nautical miles at 15 knots.

Other Details:

Complement:	The core crew is 108, including 22 officers. Accommodation is provided for 145.
Class:	Nine ASW-optimised ships of the French FREMM variant have been ordered: *Aquitaine* (D650), *Normandie*, *Provence*, *Bretagne*, *Auvergne*, *Languedoc*, *Alsace*, *Lorraine* and one, as yet, unnamed ship. A further ship, *Mohammed VI*, is being built for Morocco.

active Radar Electronic Countermeasures (R-ECM) onboard jammers. The latter are mounted in specially designed stealth boxes located to the port and starboard of the mainmast. 'Soft kill' capabilities include a pair of NGDS decoy launchers, as well as the SLAT torpedo decoy system.

France has long been in the forefront of the development of maritime stealth technology. However, this is taken to new levels in the FREMM frigates.

Indeed, *Aquitaine*'s radar cross-section (RCS) is said to be considerably reduced from that of the much smaller *La Fayette* class that arguably heralded the current focus on stealth design in modern warships. In addition to the now well-established attention paid to hull and superstructure shaping and inclination, all the main working decks and boat handling areas are enclosed, missile launchers are integrated into the ship structure as far as possible and exten-

sive use is made of radar-absorbent materials and paints. Even the R-ECM onboard jammers are enclosed within their own stealth boxing, giving the ship a distinctive pair of 'ears'. Similar effort has been put into infrared and acoustic signature reduction. For example, diesel engine exhausts are located close to the waterline and can be cooled by seawater injection. Silent operation is, perhaps, even more important given *Aquitaine*'s anti-submarine optimi-

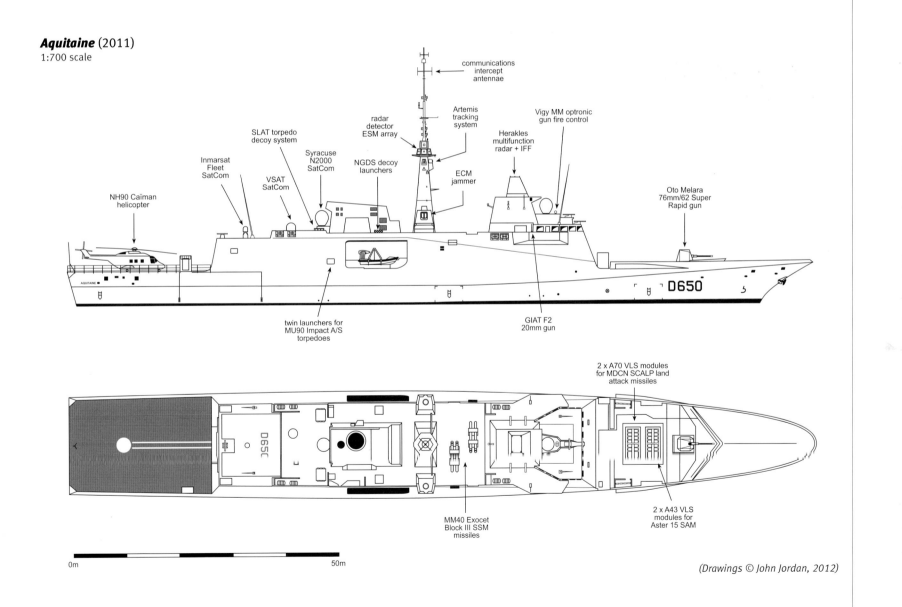

Aquitaine (2011)
1:700 scale

communications intercept antennae

radar detector ESM array

Artemis tracking system

Vigy MM optronic gun fire control

SLAT torpedo decoy system

Inmarsat Fleet SatCom

Syracuse N2000 SatCom

NGDS decoy launchers

Herakles multifunction radar + IFF

VSAT SatCom

ECM jammer

Oto Melara 76mm/62 Super Rapid gun

NH90 Caïman helicopter

twin launchers for MU90 Impact A/S torpedoes

GIAT F2 20mm gun

D650

2 x A70 VLS modules for MDCN SCALP land attack missiles

MM40 Exocet Block III SSM missiles

2 x A43 VLS modules for Aster 15 SAM

0m   50m

(Drawings © John Jordan, 2012)

A clear aerial image of *Aquitaine* early in 2011 showing close attention to stealth design, including enclosure of working decks, integration of missile cells into the structure and stealth boxing for the R-ECM jammers. *(DCNS)*

A stern view of *Aquitaine* in dry dock in Lorient in between sea trials during July 2011. Both hull and propulsion systems have been optimised for near silent operation. Details of the propellers, which are specifically designed for low acoustic operation during anti-submarine warfare, have been erased at DCNS's request. *(Conrad Waters)*

sation. In addition to the adoption of an ultra-quiet combined diesel-electric or gas (CODLOG) propulsion arrangement, this is achieved by close consideration of hull and propeller hydrodynamics. Extensive use is also made of noise dampening and elastic mountings to reduce the sound generated by ship systems.

Aquitaine has a total of seven decks, whilst its hull structure is divided into eleven sections separated by ten main watertight bulkheads. Press reports suggest that the ship can remain afloat with three adjacent hull sections flooded. Passage between the sections is principally by means of a central passageway at main deck level and there are technical galleries inboard of both sides of the hull carrying cabling and other services. Survivability is based around two self-sustaining damage control zones, each containing two vertical sub-divisions with independent ventilation and nuclear, biological and chemical filtration. The main damage control area is in the machinery control room, with propulsion and power generation systems also controllable from the bridge and the engineering spaces. Damage control panels located around the ship provide additional flexibility. Whilst details are inevitably restricted, it is believed that the most sensitive areas benefit from a degree of passive protection.

OTHER KEY DESIGN FEATURES
Another important design feature seen in *Aquitaine* is its CODLOG propulsion system. This is similar in concept to the arrangement adopted in the British Royal Navy's Type 23 frigates. Four sets of MTU 4000 series diesels are installed to generate electricity for both propulsion and 'hotel' services. In diesel-electric mode, the ship can be propelled up to a service speed of up to 16 knots by two Schneider Jeumont electric motors wrapped around the twin propulsion shafts. This covers around 65 per cent of mission profiles, including near-silent anti-submarine operations, and provides a maximum range of around 6,000 nautical miles. When higher speeds

A sunset view of *Aquitaine*. Her flexible CODLOG propulsion system – similar to that used in the British Royal Navy's Type 23 frigates – allows around two thirds of mission profiles to be completed on diesel-electric power alone. *(DCNS)*

are required, a single, mechanically connected GE/Avio LM2500+ G4 gas turbine takes over to achieve a top speed of 27 knots or more.[8] In effect, the hybrid arrangement offers much of the flexibility of all-electric propulsion without recourse to the larger motors and associated converters that would be required for high-speed electrical running.[9] A retractable azimuth thruster is provided to assist station-keeping and harbour manoeuvres, adding to the capability provided by the twin rudders. It can also serve in an emergency 'get you home' propulsion capacity at speeds of around 5 knots.

Machinery is controlled by a DCNS integrated platform management system, which is linked to around 7,000 monitoring devices distributed around the ship. It forms part of a broader package of platform management systems designed to reduce through-life costs by the maximum use of automation. In addition, a number of merchant marine practices not previously used by the *Marine Nationale*, most notably in bridge layout, have been introduced to allow ease of operation by a smaller ship's complement.

This overall design approach has been a key driver in reducing core crew size to just 108 core personnel: considerably less than half that found in the smaller FASM-70 type vessels which the class will replace. Accommodation standards are also significantly improved compared with previous ships: there are four spacious single-berth cabins and offices for the captain and senior officers, two-berth cabins for junior officers and senior ratings and four/six-berth cabins for junior ratings. Sufficient accommodation is provided for a total of 145 personnel to provide additional room to embark, for example, a command group or small military force. In addition, the modular nature of the cabins allows capacity to be expanded up to a maximum 180 crew: flexibility that is seen as important in facilitating export sales to nations with lower manning costs.

All communications are handled by a Thales fully integrated communications system (FICS). This is centred on a secure local network that allows more than 160 users to access the system through both voice and computer terminals located throughout the ship. The network provides access to a broad range of external communications. These include various radio frequencies, as well as both civilian and military satellite communications. NATO Links 11 and 16 will be supported from delivery, whilst provision for Link 22 is also incorporated. The system can be configured for specific needs by adapting, for example, user access or even the level of emissions.

TRIALS AND ENTRY INTO SERVICE

Aquitaine's maiden voyage on 18 April 2011 marked only the start of a comprehensive first-of-class trials programme that is planned to encompass a total of twenty weeks at-sea testing spread over nearly a year and a half. The programme has been supported by a *Marine Nationale* crew of around sixty personnel, who arrived at Lorient before

A picture of a NFH-90 Caiman helicopter during trials onboard *Aquitaine* during March 2012. The year and a half long trials programme has encompassed more and more core functions as testing has progressed. *(DCNS)*

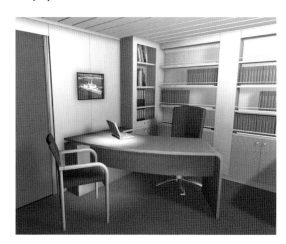

Aquitaine's crew is considerably reduced from previous *Marine Nationale* ships of comparable size as part of efforts to control through-life costs. This also allows much better accommodation standards: this image shows the Executive Officer's cabin. *(DCNS)*

Aquitaine first went to sea for training on a simulated ship management system.

The initial trials programme commenced with initial sea testing of the key platform systems, lasting approximately three weeks. Subsequent stages have seen independent sea trials of the main combat systems such as sonar before progression towards testing of 'total performance', extending to areas such as acoustic and magnetic signature. Deck landing operations with Lynx and NFH-90 Caiman helicopters have also been carried out to confirm the ship's suitability for the deployment of helicopters in, respectively, the 5- and 10-tonne classes.

The overall programme will conclude with official sea trials overseen by OCCAR on behalf of France's DGA (*Direction Générale de l'Armement*) procurement agency. These will encompass around 10 per cent of some 1,000 separate tests previously performed and confirm contractual conformity prior to formal handover. Delivery is currently planned for mid August 2012, although the contract makes allowance for a three-month grace period. It will still be some time thereafter before *Aquitaine* becomes fully operational, with an extensive period of post-delivery 'work-up' required to allow the *Marine Nationale* to make the most of its latest acquisition. It is envisaged that *Aquitaine* will be based at Brest to provide ASW support for France's strategic submarines. However, many of the ships that will follow her off the production line before construction concludes in around 2022 will be located at Toulon, the home of France's principal surface fleet.

A key objective behind DCNS's approach to *Aquitaine*'s design has been to maximise operational availability whilst minimising through-life support costs. Indeed, the initial construction agreement for the class included an option for a fixed price support contract to take effect from delivery in 2012. This encompasses the first six years of service life for the first six French ships. Considerable thought has been devoted to allow easy, cost effective maintenance to support performance of this agreement. This includes provision of improved clearances to aid in situ refurbishment, as well as improved removal routes to speed equipment replacement. Physical

Aquitaine in dry dock at Lorient. Key design objectives have been to maximise operational availability and reduce costs through a focus on ease of maintenance and the use of predictive support regimes. *(Conrad Waters)*

A computer generated graphic of a MdCN cruise missile, the naval variant of MBDA's air-launched SCALP/Storm Shadow. 250 of these weapons have been ordered to equip the anti-submarine optimised French FREMMs: they are likely to be installed in *Aquitaine* around a year after she is delivered in 2012. *(MBDA – Quadrimage)*

This page and opposite: *Aquitaine* set sail for her first set of sea trials on 18 April 2011, less than one year after launch. She is seen here in the Blavet River prior to entering the Atlantic. At this stage some key equipment has yet to be fitted, most notably the R-ECM jammers in their distinctive stealth 'ears'. The comprehensive first-of-class trials programme will encompass twenty weeks of 'at sea' tests spread over a year and a half. *(Bruno Huriet)*

design enhancements have also been supplemented by implementation of a broader maintenance philosophy. This incorporates greater attention to predictive maintenance, as well as a support cycle that integrates with reduced crew size through rationalisation of at-sea refurbishment needs. The overall approach is crucial to ensuring the project's affordability at a time when European defence budgets, particularly, are under pressure. It is noteworthy that around three-quarters of a modern major warship's through-life cost is accounted for by operating and maintenance costs.

CONCLUSION

Aquitaine has seemingly made good progress with her trials programme to date, with planned objectives achieved on – or even ahead of – schedule. Accordingly, she should be delivered to the *Marine Nationale*, as planned, during the second half of 2012. Her arrival will mark an important stage in the French Navy's modernisation, allowing a start to be made on replacing the increasingly obsolescent 1970s-era designs that comprise the heart of the current surface fleet. The multi-mission nature of the new frigate, providing a broad spectrum of capa-

bilities over and above the primary anti-submarine optimisation, will provide a major enhancement to the navy's operational flexibility. Equally importantly, the significant reduction in crew size and other operating efficiencies incorporated into the new design should provide material savings in ongoing costs at a time of tight financial constraints.

Of course, it has not all been plain sailing. The difficulties involved in securing co-operation with Italy which delayed the programme's initial launch have meant that existing ships have had to remain in service longer than first planned. In addition, project

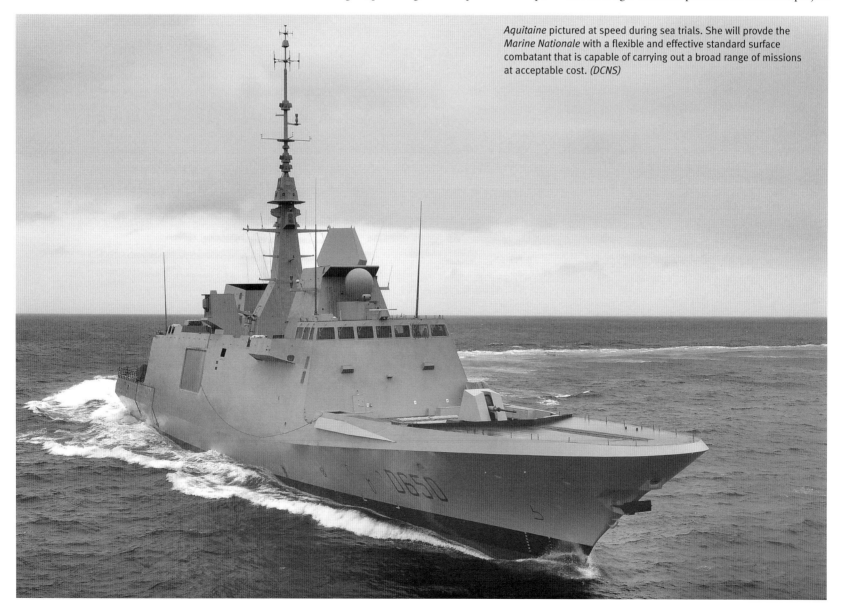

Aquitaine pictured at speed during sea trials. She will provde the *Marine Nationale* with a flexible and effective standard surface combatant that is capable of carrying out a broad range of missions at acceptable cost. *(DCNS)*

costs have been somewhat higher than originally envisaged. Whilst any accurate analysis of modern warship design and construction expense is fraught with difficulty, press reports during the FREMM project's preliminary design stage suggested France's then planned order for seventeen ships would account for c.€6.5bn of a total €11bn programme. The unit construction cost of each ship was said to be c.€280m at this time. The subsequent reduction in France's order, as well as the impact of variant changes, inflation and other cost increases has had a marked impact on these estimates. For example, figures quoted by France's national auditors, the *Cour des Comptes,* in 2010 suggested the total price of the reduced, eleven-ship project would be €7.8bn, with production expenses of c.€550m per unit.[10] Nevertheless, unit costs still compare well with those

of the preceding 'Horizon' class, as well as of the more highly specified Italian FREMM variants. This is a reflection of France's willingness – for example in its specification of the Herakles radar in preference to the more capable EMPAR – to select equipment sufficient to meet role requirements over more capable but costly alternatives. This pragmatism should enable France to maintain its first-line surface fleet at roughly current strength when most other major European navies are experiencing significant force reductions.

In conclusion, *Aquitaine* is a modern and effective surface combatant that will provide the *Marine Nationale* with the flexibility to carry out a broad range of missions at an acceptable cost. Her planned delivery during the summer of 2012 heralds a true renaissance in the capabilities of France's surface fleet.

A detail of the lettering spelling out *Aquitaine*'s name. Current plans envisage her being delivered to the *Marine Nationale* during summer 2012. *(Conrad Waters)*

Notes:

1. The Horizon project eventually resulted in the completion of two pairs of virtually identical destroyer-sized air defence ships for each of the French and Italian navies, respectively the *Forbin* and *Andrea Doria* classes. The United Kingdom withdrew from the project in April 1999, developing its own Type 45 *Daring* class. The Type 45 programme is described in detail in the editor's 'HMS *Daring*: The Royal Navy's Type 45 Air Defence Destroyer', *Seaforth World Naval Review 2010* (Barnsley, Seaforth Publishing, 2009) pp.132–49.

2. OCCAR (*Organisation Conjointe de Coopération en matière d'Armement*) was established by France, Germany, Italy and the UK in November 1996 to improve the management of pan-European armaments programmes. Headquartered in Germany, it is currently responsible for eight main defence projects, including the A400M transport aircraft and Boxer armoured vehicle as well as FREMM. Whilst OCCAR is officially responsible for overall management of FREMM procurement, in practice it works closely with France's DGA (*Direction Générale de l'Armement*) procurement agency to ensure project requirements are achieved.

3. Italy's original requirement for ten FREMM-type frigates was split between four anti-submarine and six general purpose ships. Orders for two prototype units were placed in 2006, followed by an agreement at the start of 2008 for the construction of a further three anti-submarine and one general purpose frigates. Italy's current financial situation makes it unlikely that any further ships will be built for the *Marina Militare*, leaving the final Italian total at just six units.

4. First established by the Companie des Indes, France's

rival to Britain's East India Company, the Lorient dockyard was acquired by the French government in 1778. It is one of ten DCNS sites in France, of which the main ones are at Brest, Cherbourg, Toulon and Lorient itself. The dockyard employs a workforce of around 2,000 employees, approaching 20 per cent of the DCNS total.

5. DCNS describes the FREMM type's core missions as encompassing:

– Protection of the FOST strategic ocean force.
– Contribution to France's standing risk prevention arrangements.
– Provision of intervention and rapid reaction capabilities for power projection missions.
– Contribution to force projections operations through protection of carrier and amphibious groups against air, sea and underwater threats.
– Participation in maritime safety and security missions.
– Command of a French or allied carrier or amphibious group.

6. Herakles use of the E/F band frequencies is mirrored by the UK 'Sampson' found on the Royal Navy's Type 45 destroyer and the earlier generation SPY-1 arrays associated with the US Navy's Aegis. *Seaforth World Naval Review* has also considered the subject of multifunction arrays in an earlier edition: please see Norman Friedman's 'Naval Multifunction Radars: An Overview of their Development', *Seaforth World Naval Review 2011* (London, Seaforth Publishing, 2010) pp.154–62.

7. The remaining fifty are destined for service in the new 'Barracuda' class nuclear-powered attack submarines currently under construction.

8. Over 28 knots was comfortably achieved during the first series of sea trials.

9. A good summary of the design considerations behind the *Aquitaine*'s propulsion system is contained in 'Innovative power and propulsion system proposed for FREMM', editor: David Foxwell, *Warship Technology* – October 2004 (London, RINA, 2004), pp.50–2.

10. Please see *La conduite des programmes d'armement* (Paris, Cour des Comptes, 2010) The document indicates that it is not just Anglo-Saxon defence programmes that suffer significant cost over-runs.

11. This chapter has drawn heavily on contemporary industry and other press releases to support its preparation. In addition, the following articles are recommended as a more structured source of information at various points in the French FREMM variant's development:

– Raphael Arnaud, 'FREMM: Les frégates de supériorité navale' *Marines & Forces Navales* – No 129 (Nantes, Marines Editions, 2010), pp.10–21.
– Bertrand Magueur, 'FREMM', *Navires & Histoire – Hors-série* No 09 (Outreau, Editions LELA Presse, 2008), pp.45–7.
– Guy Toremans, 'Common FREMM work for neighbours' frigate project', *Jane's Navy International* – October 2008 (Coulsdon, IHS Jane's, 2008), pp.18-31.

The considerable assistance of Vincent Martinot-Lagarde, FREMM programme manager at DCNS, as well as of Solen Dupy and Ludovic Colin from DCNS's press department, is acknowledged with gratitude.

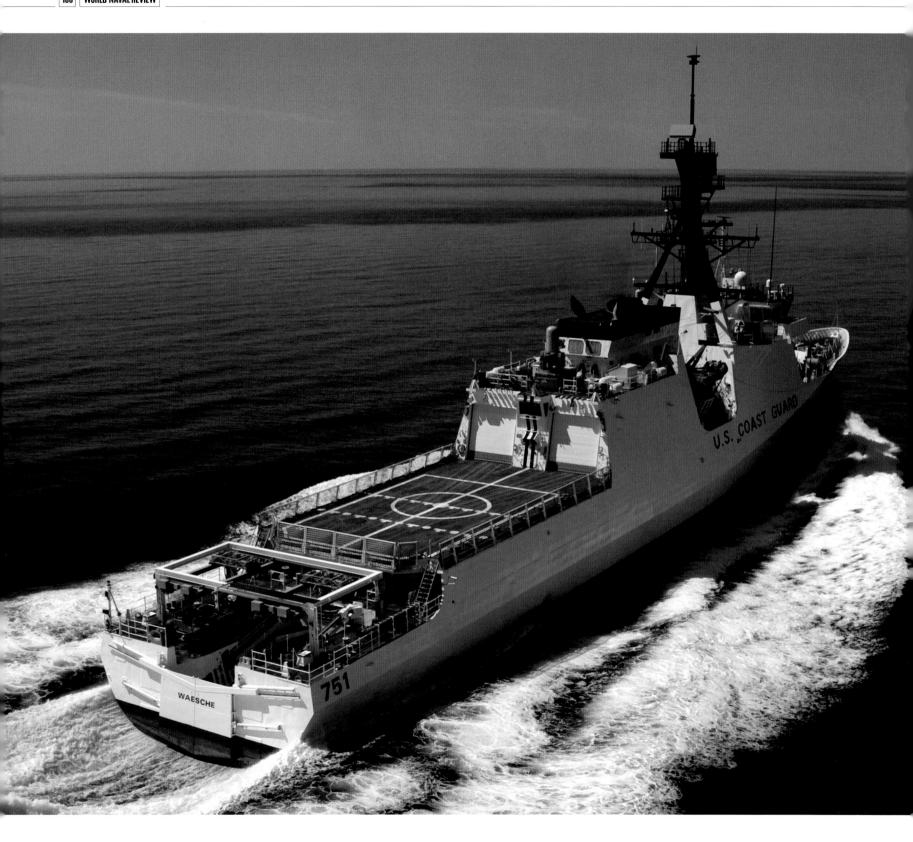

Author:
Scott Truver

3.2 SIGNIFICANT SHIPS

US COAST GUARD LEGEND CLASS CUTTERS

'Our Highest Priority for the Twenty-First Century'

The 'Legend' class national security cutters (NSCs) are the key nodes of the twenty-first century US Coast Guard (USCG), the fifth and smallest of America's Armed Services.[1] USCG Commandant, Admiral Robert J Papp, describes the first new major cutters constructed by US shipyards in more than twenty years as the service's 'highest priority for the Twenty-First Century'. Importantly, the NSCs are already 'proving to be a vital instrument for protecting American maritime security and prosperity', he underscored during his 23 February 2012 State of the Coast Guard address.

So it came as a surprise to many inside and outside government when the Secretary of the Department of Homeland Security (DHS) announced in February 2012 that the programme was being cut by 25 per cent, from eight to six NSCs, a decision clearly driven by near-term budgetary concerns at the expense of long-term strategic needs.[2] Although DHS Secretary Janet Napolitano held out a promise that the decision on NSCs Number 7 and 8 might be re-examined, doubters remained legion.

Opposite: The second 'Legend' class national security cutter, *Waesche* (WMSL-751), pictured whilst on builders' sea trials on 1 October 2009. Regarded as the United States Coast Guard's highest priority, 'flagship' programme, acquisition is still being reduced from eight to six units as a result of recent funding cuts. *(Huntington Ingalls Industries)*

'It seems to me that we are on a collision course with the Coast Guard about the need for some assets that look to me to be very important,' US Senator Thad Cochran remarked.[3] 'It seems that the Office of Management and Budget has probably tried to tamp down the requests or needs for shipbuilding against the recommendations of the Coast Guard leadership.'

CLASS ORIGINS – THE DEEPWATER PROGRAMME

Integral elements of the US Coast Guard's joint, inter-agency and global-partnership efforts, the eight NSCs in the original programme of record (and which, in mid 2012, remained the only programme of record) are intended to comprise the minimum level high-endurance cutter force needed to protect the nation's coastlines, safeguard the bounty of the seas and serve as America's maritime first responder. They provide unique capabilities to US defence at home and abroad; helping to protect US interests and friends worldwide. Indeed, the NSCs are designed and engineered to carry out a broad spectrum of homeland security, law and regulatory enforcement, national security, and defence tasks in support of the Coast Guard's 'prevent and respond' strategic concept: preventing potentially dangerous or illicit activities from occurring or, when prevention fails, responding quickly and effectively. This strategy is articulated more fully in

the *2011 DHS White Paper on the US Coast Guard*.[4]

The national security cutters have their roots in the ill-fated and now-defunct Integrated Deepwater System Programme that was commenced in the mid 1990s.[5] The programme envisaged replacing the US Coast Guard's ageing deep-water capable ships and aircraft with an integrated package of new aviation and maritime assets, as well as associated communications and logistical back-up, in a so-called 'system of systems' approach. The US president's 1999 Interagency Task Force on the Roles and Missions of the Coast Guard unequivocally underscored the compelling need for a multi-mission, military US Coast Guard capable of deep-water missions and recapitalised for the traditional and unconventional demands of the new century.[6] In short, the study concluded that if the US Coast Guard did not exist, it would have to be invented, paving the way for Deepwater to proceed.

Delivery of the Deepwater programme was entrusted to a private sector lead system integrator under a contract awarded to the Integrated Coast Guard Systems (ICGS) joint venture between Northrop Grumman and Lockheed Martin in June 2002. As of November 2006, the programme envisaged c.US$25bn of capital expenditure over twenty-five years, of which around US$15bn would be spent on surface assets. By this time, however, the programme was in serious trouble, with the US

Government Accountability Office (GAO) being just one of many organisations identifying serious management, funding, cost, schedule, design and technical shortcomings in several Deepwater asset classes. The upshot of these challenges was ultimately the dismissal of ICGS as lead systems integrator, a return to managing acquisitions on a system-by-system approach under a revamped Coast Guard Acquisition Directorate and the Coast Guard's assumption of the systems integration role.

The national security cutter is the largest and most technically advanced surface platform in this radically restructured recapitalisation programme. It is one of three classes of cutter (the 'Sentinel' class fast-response cutter and the offshore patrol cutter being the other two) that had their origins in Deepwater and are now being continued as separate acquisition projects. Along with other boats, new manned patrol aircraft, yet to be acquired unmanned aerial systems (UAS), and leading-edge command, control, communications, computers, intelligence, surveillance, and reconnaissance (C4ISR) equipment, they will significantly enhance Coast Guard operational effectiveness and interoperability.

The new national security cutters are capable of carrying out all of the US Coast Guard's missions, with the exception of specialist icebreaking and aids to navigation tasks. 'It takes a highly capable ship and crew, equipped with the right tools, command and control systems, onboard sensors, information exchange and weapons systems to meet our multi-mission demands,' Captain Kelly Hatfield, commanding officer of *Waesche* (WMSL-751), observed in several interviews. Hatfield, who previously served as the first executive officer of the lead national security cutter, *Bertholf* (WMSL-750), explained, 'the cutter must be able to get on scene quickly, maintain continuous presence for extended periods, monitor the areas with sensors and carry out the mission using a variety of tools such as small boats, helicopters and UASs [unmanned aerial systems]. And it must be able to do all these things in fair and foul weather, 24/7. Without a doubt, the NSCs are game-changers.'

'There was a real sense of urgency to get on with recapitalising the Coast Guard,' NSC programme officials said during several interviews at Coast Guard headquarters. 'And the NSC is a key factor in that recapitalisation.' However, that urgency seems to be muted in 2012. 'We are confronted with a no-

growth budget,' Admiral Papp said during a speech hosted by the Center for Strategic and International Studies in February 2012. 'There's only so much shipbuilding you can get in there.'[7]

CLASS REQUIREMENT AND MISSIONS

The NSCs are replacements for the twelve increasingly obsolescent and costly to maintain 378ft high-endurance *Hamilton* class cutters (WHEC-715 class) that have been in service since the 1960s. 'They are on average about forty-three years of age,' Admiral Papp noted in February 2012. 'They're obsolete; they're expensive to maintain; they're environmentally unsound. And oh, by the way, they are terrible for our people to live and work in. You have 60s designs, and I would suggest that the people who volunteer to step forward today deserve a little bit better working conditions than what you find on those ships.'

Accordingly, in May 2011, the Coast Guard decommissioned its first two '378' *Hamilton* class cutters, the *Hamilton* (WHEC-715) herself and *Chase* (WHEC-718), for transfer to the Philippines and Nigeria respectively. Additional withdrawals are being planned for mid 2012 and beyond. 'So, it's

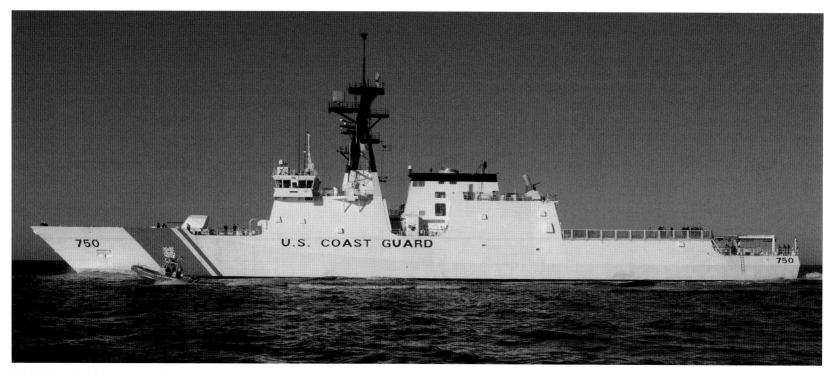

The US Coast Guard's new national security cutters are intended to be its largest and most technically advanced surface platforms. This image shows the first-of-class *Bertholf* (WMSL-750) in February 2008, some six months prior to delivery. *(US Coast Guard)*

National security cutter *Bertholf* (WMSL-750) is seen here operating with a new HC-144A Ocean Sentry maritime patrol aircraft and re-engined MH-65C Dolphin helicopter. Originally ordered as part of an integrated package of aviation and maritime assets under the ill-fated Integrated Deepwater System Programme, procurement of the national security cutters is now being progressed as a stand-alone project. *(US Coast Guard)*

vital we get all eight NSCs,' Admiral Papp testified in 2011, well before the decision to curtail the funding for just six cutters. 'Our nation needs them, our shipmates deserve them, and our service requires them to remain true to our motto, Always Ready.'[8] Three replacement national security cutters – *Bertholf*, *Waesche* and *Stratton* (WMSL-752) – were in the cutter force by June 2012 following *Stratton*'s commissioning on 31 March 2012. The contract for a new *Hamilton* (WMSL-753) was signed in 2010, whilst that for the fifth NSC, *Joshua James* (WMSL-754), was inked on 9 September 2011. Current plans call for the sixth – and possibly now final – vessel to be delivered by 2016. Although funding has been cut for NSCs 7 and 8, the official programme of record calls for eight 'Legend' class cutters.

The first three national security cutters are home-ported in Alameda, California. In early March 2012, Admiral Papp testified that the fourth and fifth cutters will be home-ported in Charleston, South Carolina; the sixth in Alameda; and the two final ships in Honolulu, Hawaii, if funding were to be restored. 'Even eight NSCs might not be enough,' Captain Hatfield said, 'as the "system-of-systems" modelling and analysis during the Deepwater phase arrived at eight NSCs supported by helicopters and UAS [as many as sixteen NSCs were identified in late-1990s requirements assessments]. If we don't get the unmanned aerial vehicles,' Hatfield continued, 'there might be a need for additional NSCs, but, for now, the programme of record remains at eight cutters', with funding in place for just six.

Other observers have commented that the national security cutter design would be ideal for the US Navy's growing maritime security/constabulary tasks under the National Fleet Policy approved by

The first and second national security cutters *Bertholf* (WMSL-750) and *Waesche* (WMSL-751) pictured together for the first time in February 2010 at the time of the latter ship's delivery. *Bertholf* commissioned on 4 August 2008 and *Waesche* followed her into service on 7 May 2010. *(US Coast Guard)*

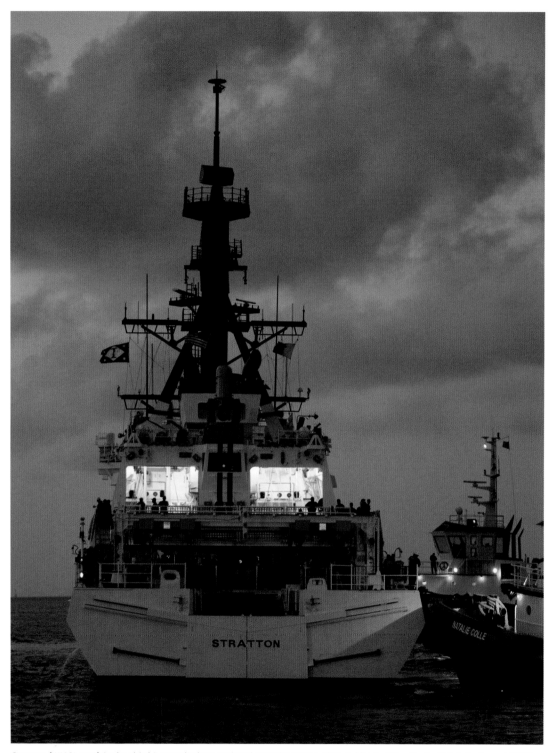

Stratton (WMSL-752) is the third 'Legend' class national security cutter. Pictured here at the start of trials in August 2011, she commissioned on 31 March 2012. Primarily intended for 'at distance' constabulary duties, the NSCs are also capable of acting as low-end, multi-mission warships. *(Huntington Ingalls Industries)*

the Coast Guard Commandant and the Chief of Naval Operations in 1998 and expanded in 2006. 'The national security cutter is a very good low-end multi-mission warship, in addition to its maritime homeland security capabilities,' Norman Polmar, author of the US Naval Institute's *Ships and Aircraft of the US Fleet*, noted in a March 2012 interview. 'Even with the white paint and orange "racing stripe", the NSC *looks* like a warship!' Indeed, in March 2012, the national security cutter's builder Huntington Ingalls Industries/Ingalls Shipbuilding unveiled a haze-grey 'patrol frigate' variant of the national security cutter that could complement the littoral combat ship (LCS) in US Navy plans.[9]

As Captain Michael Mohn, Coast Guard programme manager for Defense Operations and Counterterrorism, explained in early March 2012, 'Coast Guard major cutter demand by regional combatant commanders [COCOMs] is growing. Our ability to source that growing demand, unfortunately, has not kept pace. Cutters like the NSC possess unique attributes that are attractive to strengthening partnerships with foreign navies and coast guards, most of which are more similar to the US Coast Guard, than the Navy. Additionally,' he continued, 'many maritime agencies engaged by our COCOM Theatre Security Cooperation efforts align themselves with ministries outside of defence, thus more Homeland Security-centric.' Reflecting this, the summer of 2012 will mark two milestones for NSC defence operations, with participation in the RIMPAC (Rim of the Pacific) exercise off Hawaii and in CARAT (Cooperation Afloat Readiness Training) in Asia supplementing ongoing combined maritime security operations in the Arctic. 'These operations will underscore the national security cutter's viability as a unique maritime instrument of national security,' Mohn predicted.

'The NSCs *are* the Coast Guard's "battle-group deployers",' Commander Kevin Wirth, USCG, Deputy, Cutter Forces Division (CG751), said during a late 2011 interview. 'Although they are fully capable of "littoral" operations, NSC speed, range and endurance, and organic systems enable the cutters to provide persistent presence and long-distance power projection, in patrols ranging from the Bering Sea and Arctic Ocean to the maritime boundary line between Russia and the US, to Hawaii and Guam … hundreds of thousands of square miles of ocean space. This class of cutters will serve as the first line of a defence-in-depth for the homeland, which includes regions far overseas as well as near-US waters,' he added. 'Speed and endurance are critical,' as are sea-keeping and stability.

This was underscored by the Coast Guard's experience with the lead NSC during her initial deployment to Alaska waters. 'Greetings from the Bering Sea!' USCG Captain John Prince, first commanding officer of the *Bertholf*, exclaimed in May 2011.[10] 'We've been underway for more than a month on the first Alaska patrol for a national security cutter, and I can say it has been a truly impressive performance by the ship and our crew. We've experienced 20ft seas and winds in excess of sixty knots with temperatures below freezing, and despite these sea conditions the ship has remained within pitch and roll limits to launch our helicopter. We have been able to make a comfortable twelve to fifteen knots through the water in seas up to 14ft, validating the sea-keeping and stability of the NSC and our ability to respond quickly to any emergency.'

'The NSCs enable longer patrols in high-threat areas, e.g. the eastern Pacific west of the Galapagos Islands, where drug-runner "mother ships" support "go-fasts" and SPSS [self-propelled semi-submersible] vessels,' Captain Hatfield added. 'Our long-range C-130 MPAs [maritime patrol aircraft] can't remain on operationally significant station that far out. The surface forces, linked to national intelligence nodes and aviation assets, can provide the needed persistent presence to defeat the threat.'

Following *Waesche*'s ninety-day patrol to the eastern Pacific threat area in the fall of 2011, Hatfield explained, 'Tactical commanders should carefully consider NSC speed, endurance and inherent capabilities as they plan force lay-downs. The "Legend" class offers the ability to patrol well offshore, for longer periods of time, and with two helicopters the NSCs can patrol much larger areas of ocean. Additionally, the ability to sprint at higher speeds and higher sea states, compared to the 378s, means the NSC can quickly relocate and re-engage on a new target of interest without sacrificing time on station. In short, the "Legend" class cutters have the potential to be tactics- and game-changers.'

The US Coast Guard cutter *Waesche* (WMSL-751) refuelling from the Military Sealift Command oiler *Yukon* (T-AO-202) whilst operating in the Pacific in May 2011. The national security cutters are designed to be interoperable with other US military assets and are capable of long range deployment to provide defence-in-depth for the US homeland. *(US Coast Guard)*

Lead 'Legend' class national security cutter *Bertholf* (WMSL-750) operating with the Russian Boarder Guard Project 1135 'Krivak III' frigate *Vorovsky* in the Bering Sea in the spring of 2011. *Bertholf* was on her initial deployment to Alaskan waters at this time. *(US Coast Guard)*

'LEGEND' CLASS CHARACTERISTICS AND CAPABILITIES

'The NSCs were designed and engineered with two competing attributes,' Captain Hatfield noted. 'They are multi-mission ships that have long endurance but can go fast. The hull form has been optimised for speed, endurance and sea-keeping, such that the ship is quiet and smooth even at high speeds or in high seas.' Within that framework, since the late 1990s the NSC design has responded to increasingly challenging threats, requirements, missions and tasks. And, looking ahead, sufficient weight and volume growth margins have been designed in, to ensure the NSCs can meet projected Coast Guard missions of safety, security and stewardship during their expected thirty-year service lives.

Compared to the *Hamilton* class 378s, the 418ft NSC design provides better sea-keeping and higher sustained transit speeds; greater endurance and range; an improved ability to launch and recover small boats, helicopters and UAS; advanced C4ISR and ability to handle sensitive compartmented information; and significantly improved quality of life features: all key attributes enabling the Coast Guard to carry out, successfully and safely, its increased homeland security and national defence responsibilities. Table 3.2.1 lists principal national security cutter characteristics.

US Navy Interoperability: 'We have very close ties to the Navy,' NSC programme officials said, 'and the NSC is a key element of the Navy–Coast Guard

National Fleet policy and strategy.'[11] The policy calls for Navy and Coast Guard forces to 'be designed, wherever possible, around common command, control, and communications equipment and operational, weapon and engineering systems, and include co-ordinated operational planning, procurement, training and logistics.' Accordingly, national security cutter interoperability with US Navy platforms and systems is apparent, and there are direct commonalities with the *Freedom* and *Independence* LCS-1/2 classes and even the *Arleigh Burke* (DDG-51) guided-missile destroyers.[12] These commonalities include:

The NSC's Mk110, 57mm gun is identical to US Navy systems on the LCS. The 57mm has dual anti-air ('low and slow') and anti-surface capabilities and

---

Table 3.2.1.

BERTHOLF (WMSL-750) PRINCIPAL PARTICULARS

Building Information:

Laid Down:	29 March 2005
Launched:	29 September 2006
Commissioned:	4 August 2008
Builders:	Northrop Grumman Shipbuilding (now the Ingalls Shipbuilding division of Huntington Ingalls Industries) at its facility at Pascagoula, Mississippi.

Dimensions:

Displacement:	3,200 tons standard displacement, 4,500 tons full load displacement.
Overall Hull Dimensions:	127.4m x 16.5m x 6.8m.

Weapons Systems:

Guns:	1 x 57mm Mk110 gun, 1 x 20mm Vulcan Phalanx CIWS, Machine guns.
Aircraft:	Up to two MH-65C Dolphin or MH-60T Jayhawk helicopters. Unmanned aerial vehicles can also be operated.
Countermeasures:	SQL-32 electronic warfare suite. Mk53 decoy launching system. Ship's Signals Exploitation Equipment Increment E (SSEE-E).
Principal Sensors:	1 x EADS TRS-3D/16 air/surface search radar, 1 x SPQ-9B surface search and fire control radar, navigation arrays.
Communications:	Communications include HF, VHF and UHF radio links. Sensitive Compartmented Information Facility (SCIF).
Other:	1 x 11m LRI (Long Range Interceptor) and 2 x 7m OTH (Over The Horizon) boats for boarding/insertion. Stern launch ramp.

Propulsion Systems:

Machinery:	CODAG. 2 x MTU V20 1163 diesels each rated at 7.2MW. 1 x GE LM2500 gas turbine rated at 22MW. Two shaft propulsion.
Speed and Range:	Sprint speed is 30+ knots and 28 knots can be sustained. Range is 12,000 nautical miles at 12 knots.

Other Details:

Complement:	Typical crew size is c.110 personnel. Accommodation is provided for 148.
Class:	Current plans envisage six 'Legend' class national security cutters. Five ships have been ordered to date, viz. *Bertholf* (WMSL-750), *Waesche* (MMSL-751), *Stratton* (WMSL-752), *Hamilton* (WMSL-753) and *Joshua James* (WMSL-754).

Hunting: USCG Style.

I'm a long-time Montana deer and elk hunter, and I have a hunter analogy that applies to the Coast Guard.

When hunting the vast open country in Montana, you must study the animal's habits and its habitat to ensure you are in the best location possible. However, your success really depends on whether the animal happens to be there on any given day. If you return to the same spot daily, eventually you will be successful.

So it is for the Coast Guard. We have historic patterns, intelligence, and sensors that help us figure out where the bad guys are more likely to

be on our oceans and high-threat areas. Many of our op areas are thousands of miles offshore, far from home ports and support bases for our ships – the eastern Pacific west of the Galapagos Islands, US exclusive economic zones around our territories in the central Pacific, in the north Pacific and the Bering Sea.

This is further complicated by the fact that the bad guys dictate when they will be there. So we have to be able to be there day after day, for longer periods of time, through any weather and sea state, so that we will be successful in interdicting them when they arrive. That is

endurance. Knowing where the bad guys will be is great, but it's useless if you don't have the endurance to ensure you are there at the right time with the right capabilities.

The NSCs provide us much-needed endurance and capabilities to ensure we are successful in hunting bad guys who would do our nation and our international partners harm.

Captain Kelly Hatfield, USCG
Commanding Officer
USCGC *Waesche* (WMSL-751)
April 2012

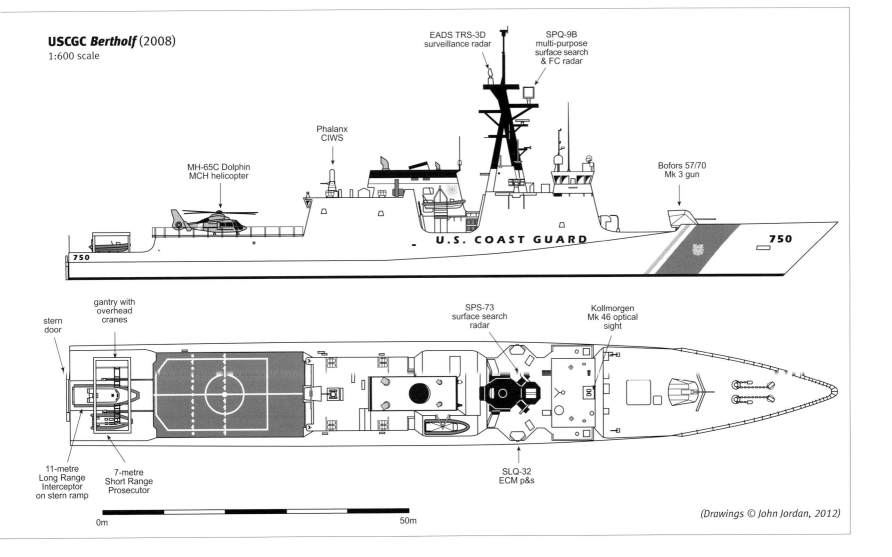

USCGC *Bertholf* (2008)
1:600 scale

(Drawings © John Jordan, 2012)

An overhead view of the lead national security cutter, *Bertholf* (WMSL-750). She shares many equipment commonalities with US Navy surface warships, including the 57mm main gun, Vulcan Phalanx CIWS, a similar mast to the DDG-51 design and several radar systems. *(Huntington Ingalls Industries)*

Pictures of *Bertholf*'s (WMSL-750) main Mk110 gun and Vulcan Phalanx close-in weapons system (CIWS) during combat system ship qualification trials in February 2009. The class's armament provides them with a range of capabilities against surface, aircraft and missile threats that are more than sufficient for their primary constabulary mission, reflecting a desire for broader interoperability with the US Navy. *(US Coast Guard)*

can be programmed for an air burst of a round some 7m above a surface target, making it an excellent weapon against go-fast boats. The Block 1B variant of the Close-In Weapon System (CIWS) is found on many US Navy warships and has an anti-surface as well as anti-air capability against aircraft and cruise missiles. The two services also operate the same .50-cal machine guns.

Other areas of inter-service commonality include TRS-3D air-search radars, X and S-band (NATO I/J and E/F bands respectively) surface-search and navigation radars, SPQ-9B fire-control radars, SLQ-32 electronic surveillance system, and Mk46 EO/IR systems.

The NSC has the same 'stealthy' mast as the current DDG-51 design and a similar gas turbine to the standard DDG-51 propulsion plant.

The Coast Guard trains its 57mm gun crews at the Navy schoolhouse, and the Navy trains its TRS-3D air-search radar operators at the Coast Guard school.

Although the national security cutter design was mature in 2000, the 9/11 tragedies prompted important requirements changes, including the need for chemical, biological, radiological, nuclear and enhanced explosive (CBRNE) defence and better interoperability with other military and Department of Homeland security forces. This included the addition of the Sensitive Compartmented Information Facility (SCIF), Ship's Signals Exploitation Equipment Increment E (SSEE-E), and secure C4ISR.

The national security cutters are the first US Coast Guard cutters to have a collective protection system (CPS) to protect against chemical, biological,

radiological and enhanced-explosive threats, and the first to have a dedicated SCIF/SSEE capability. 'One critical post-9/11 capability is the CPS,' Captain Hatfield noted. 'The NSCs can operate for up to ninety-six hours in a CBRNE environment, say from a "dirty bomb" in a crowded port/waterway. We'll be able to provide critical C4ISR capabilities to support federal and local first-responders.'

The SCIF/SSEE and secure C4ISR also mean that the national security cutters are fully capable of Navy strike group operations. The Coast Guard routinely provides dedicated 365 cutter-days per year to support navy and regional combatant commanders. Actual deployed days are determined annually through the Coast Guard's participation in the DOD Global Force Management process. 'For example, *Waesche* was scheduled to "chop" to the 7th Fleet for

Although many systems are shared with front-line US warships, the national security cutter's primary constabulary mission means that an ability to operate a range of small boats in adverse weather conditions is an essential requirement. This is assisted by provision of a stern ramp system and also of a side port door close to the waterline, both apparent in this October 2011 view of *Stratton* (WMSL-752). *(US Coast Guard)*

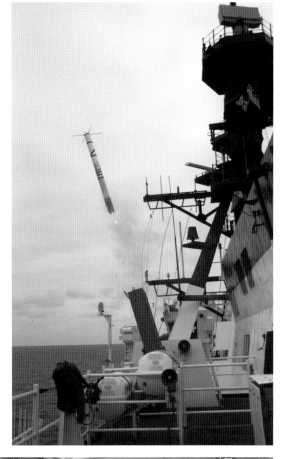

Above: A MH-65 Dolphin helicopter refuelling on *Bertholf* (WMSL-750) during its inaugural deployment to the Bering Sea between Russia and Alaska. The class has facilities for up to two helicopters, whilst unmanned aerial vehicles may also be used in future. *(US Coast Guard)*

Right: *Bertholf* (WMSL-750) launching a Nulka decoy round from her Mk53 decoy launching system. The national security cutter has unusually extensive provision for both electronic and physical countermeasures compared with many other offshore patrol vessel types. *(US Coast Guard)*

Crew (six-berth) and junior officer (two-berth) staterooms onboard the national security cutter *Bertholf* (WMSL-750). Accommodation for up to 148 people is provided in two-, four- and six-berth cabins, although normal crew is just over 110. Extensive provision for crew quality of life, including flexible, multi-gender configurations, is a key feature of the 'Legend' class design. *(US Coast Guard)*

CARAT 2012,' Captain Hatfield said. And, in national emergencies or war, all Coast Guard assets can be placed under the Secretary of the Navy. Thus, interoperability is an imperative, not a 'nice to have'. Moreover, the NSC is a key asset for Department of Homeland Security MOTR Plan responsibilities.[13] With its combination of US Code Title 14 and Title 10 authorities, the NSC fits perfectly at the seam of homeland security and homeland defence. Its size, endurance and C4ISR also allow support of other agencies exercising their authorities.

This was underscored by the *Bertholf*'s experience in the Northern Edge 2011 exercise conducted in June 2011. 'Clearly,' Commander David Ramassini, *Bertholf*'s executive officer, explained, 'our Navy partners possess significant and unique high-intensity capabilities that the national security cutter class does not, and we have a very real national security need for all of these arrows in our defence quiver. However,' he continued, 'with our smaller crew size and extended independent range, the national security cutter could offer the combatant commander a rather efficient way to extend the peace overseas in low intensity conflict and theatre security cooperation by expanding global maritime partnerships with the Coast Guard serving as an olive branch. Combatant commanders have traditionally liked the Coast Guard operating within their areas of responsibility; I would offer that once they see the national security cutter in action they'll not only like it, they'll love it and want some more of it!'[14]

Deployed Craft: The NSCs carry three boats: one 11m Long-Range Interceptor (LRI) and two 7m Over-the-Horizon (OTH) craft. The next iterations of these boats were under development in mid 2012. With a top speed of 35 knots and a range of 240 nautical miles at economic planing speed, the aluminium-hulled LRI-II will be an organic platform that greatly expands the national security cutter's tactical reach. Launched and recovered on the stern ramp and propelled by twin inboard diesels and water jets, the LRI can operate in Sea State 5 and survive through Sea State 6 (the stern launch or recovery evolutions generally take about three to five minutes at ship speeds of around 5 to 10 knots, depending on sea conditions). The craft are outfitted with the Scalable Integrated Navigation System (SINS), a standard communications package, and weapons include two M240 7.62mm general purpose machine guns. The aluminium-hulled

A view of *Bertholf*'s (WMSL-750) Long-Range Interceptor (LRI) being launched from the cutter's stern ramp. The 11m LRI is the largest of three small boats shipped on the national security cutters, which also carry two smaller, 7m Over-the-Horizon (OTH) craft. *(US Coast Guard)*

OTH boat is the national security cutter's quick-response surface asset and can be launched and recovered by the stern ramp or starboard davit. A single inboard diesel engine and water jet propulsion deliver a top speed of 40 knots and 200 nautical mile range at economical planing speeds. Capable of surviving through Sea State 5, the OTH boat is fitted with the same SINS and communications package as the LRI and has a single M240 7.62mm machine gun.

NSC design innovations include a starboard side port door, about three feet above waterline, which mitigates the need for a Jacob's ladder to get on board from small boats in a seaway. The door allows people to walk over and to load/offload stores and equipment in calm seas or pier side. The OTH boat davit is located on the starboard side, amidships, thus minimising pitch and roll and enabling boat operations in higher sea states. Organic aviation support is impressive, too. 'The NSC flight deck is huge,' Captain Hatfield said, 'which contributes to our ability to launch and recover helicopters – and when we get them, UAS – in higher sea states than the 378s.'

Propulsion System: Perhaps the most significant innovation is found in the ship's engineering spaces. The national security cutters are the first cutters to have combined diesel and gas turbine (CODAG) propulsion systems, meaning diesel and gas turbine 'prime movers' can be engaged simultaneously. The *Hamilton* 378s were the first large US military ships to have gas turbine (GT) propulsion, in this case CODOG propulsion, with the second 'O' indicating 'or'. The US Navy's GT-powered *Spruance* (DD-963) class only joined the fleet in 1975. [15] Two MTU diesels and one gas turbine drive the NSC's two shafts and twin contra-rotating propellers, an arrangement similar to the German Navy's F124 class warships, and the NSC gas turbine is very similar to the US Navy's DDG-51 plant. 'This is a "state-of-the-market" system, with very low risk,' NSC programme officials affirmed. That said, the arrangement results in superb endurance – 12,000 nautical miles' range at 12 knots and notional sixty-day patrol periods without replenishment – with more time on station and operational flexibility. And, the flexibility of the plant is significant.

'We can operate one or two diesels, or only the GT driving one or both shafts, while one diesel can drive both shafts with the ability to fix the shaft RPMs [revolutions per minute] while controlling each shaft's pitch, forward or astern, independent of the other shaft,' Captain Hatfield noted. 'For most economic "steaming", one diesel can drive one or both shafts; for high-speeds, greater than [the advertised] 28 knots, both diesels and the GT can be brought on line.'

'The overlapping power bands allow for economic efficiencies at all speed regimes,' NSC programme

Right: Pictures of the various blocks from which the second 'Legend' class national security cover *Waesche* (WMSL-751) was constructed at various stages in the assembly process. The number of blocks required to assemble each ship has been progressively reduced, allowing more of the early outfitting and testing to be conducted under cover and thus aiding efficiency. *(Huntington Ingalls Industries)*

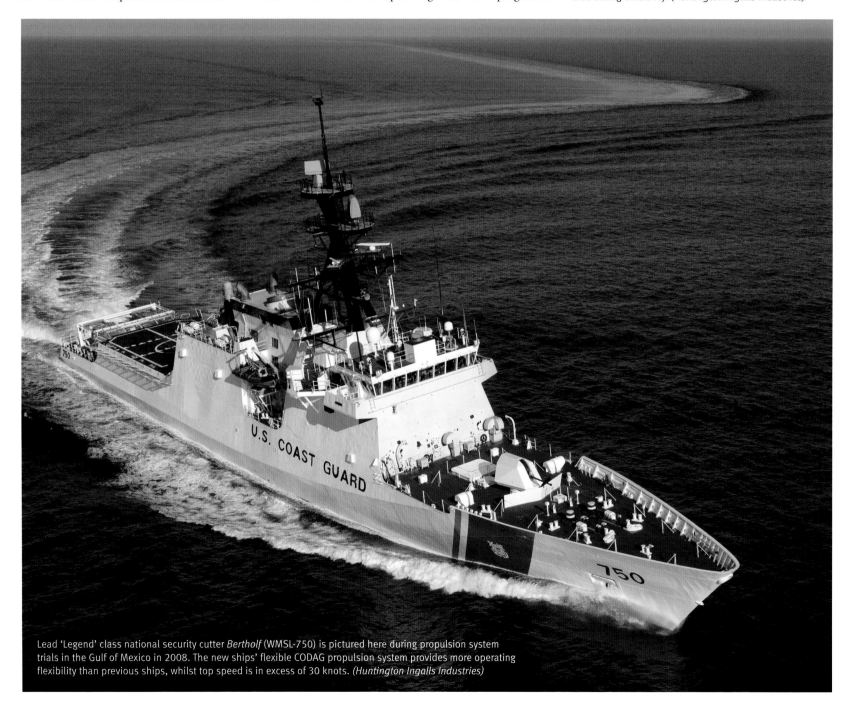

Lead 'Legend' class national security cutter *Bertholf* (WMSL-750) is pictured here during propulsion system trials in the Gulf of Mexico in 2008. The new ships' flexible CODAG propulsion system provides more operating flexibility than previous ships, whilst top speed is in excess of 30 knots. *(Huntington Ingalls Industries)*

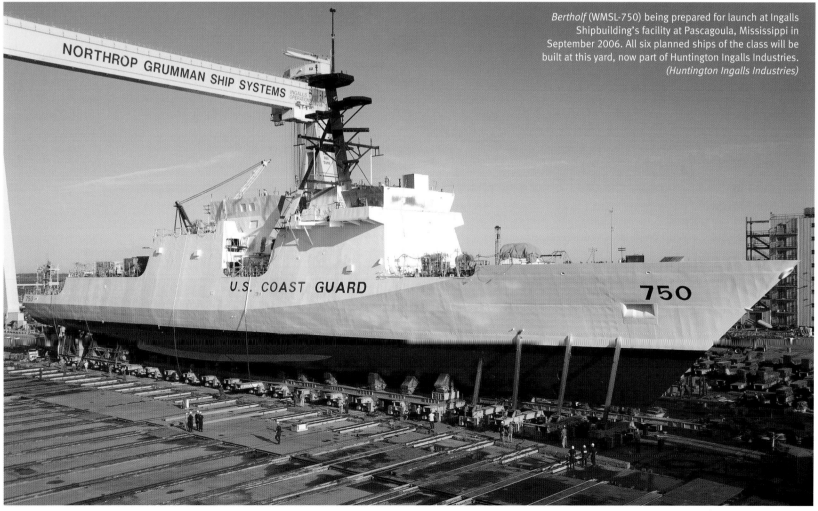

Bertholf (WMSL-750) being prepared for launch at Ingalls Shipbuilding's facility at Pascagoula, Mississippi in September 2006. All six planned ships of the class will be built at this yard, now part of Huntington Ingalls Industries. *(Huntington Ingalls Industries)*

officials noted, 'and the ship can operate at the "knee" of the speed/power curve for economic performance at all speeds: one diesel driving one shaft at lowest speeds to both diesels and GT powering both shafts for highest speeds.' The 'state-of-the-market' CODAG is more complicated than CODOG plants, the key being the combining gear that links one/some/all-three prime movers to each or both shafts. 'We can transfer power from one to the other quickly, another feature of the advanced machinery control system,' Captain Hatfield added. And, by having the ability to set one shaft forward and the other aft, the ship is highly manoeuvrable at low speeds and can berth alongside a pier or turn 180 degrees almost 'on a dime'. Another result is extremely good propulsion redundancy. 'It would take a catastrophic event for the NSC to lose power to the shafts,' he underlined.

The national security cutters also incorporate operational improvements that have environmental benefits. The 378s have no dedicated ballast tanks, so as they burn fuel they must add saltwater to their empty fuel tanks to maintain proper stability. When they return to home port, they need dedicated facilities to pump out remaining saltwater/fuel mixture and clean tanks before new fuel can be loaded: a time-consuming and potentially hazardous process. Instead, the NSCs have dedicated saltwater ballast tanks that enable maintaining operational trim without the side effect of contaminated fuel tanks. 'Our 12,000 nautical mile range at economical speed and 8,000 nautical-mile range at a speed of 14 knots has allowed us to remain at sea for more than twenty-four days at a time and cover large swaths of the ocean with our sensors and helicopter, while still maintaining a fuel reserve in the event of emergency,' Captain Prince noted. 'Keeping our stability well within safe limits without concern over low fuel levels, our installed ballast tanks help us to better preserve and protect the marine environment as we are not ballasting tanks that previously held fuel like on the 378s.'

The 'Human Element': The NSC's crew is 33 per cent smaller than a 378's crew, with the programme leveraging technologies and 'human-performance assessments' to reduce crewing requirements to optimal levels.

Mike Duthu, NSC programme manager at Ingalls Shipbuilding, a division of Huntington Ingalls Industries (formerly Northrop Grumman

A picture of the lead national security cutter *Bertholf* (WMSL-750) immediately after launch at Ingalls Shipbuilding, Pascagoula, Mississippi in September 2006. Defects – and construction costs – have reduced as experience has been gained in building the class. *(Huntington Ingalls Industries)*

Shipbuilding), said the focus on the human meant quality of life was emphasised right from the start of the design. 'NSC habitability and hotel features are excellent,' he noted in a telephone interview. 'We based quality of life features on the maximum crew size and have accommodation for 148 people in two-, four-, and six-person staterooms, each with its own facilities.' The notional crew is 114, so there's flexibility and margin to bring additional people on board.

'The commanding officer, executive officer, engineering officer and operations officer have single staterooms,' he added. Considerations regarding women at sea have resulted in highly flexible mixed-gender configurations, whilst each stateroom has computer connectivity to a ship-wide local area network and there is video entertainment on demand. There are dedicated living spaces for deployed law-enforcement, helicopter, UAS, and SCIF detachments, and a dedicated distant-learning facility doubles as a training room.

NSC crews are awash in fresh water. Two reverse-osmosis desalination units deliver 12,000 gallons of fresh water per day, some eighty-one gallons per day for each crew member. This is significantly greater than for US Navy surface ships and even aircraft carriers:[16] for example, a littoral combat ship supplies twenty-six gallons of water per day per person; a FFG-7 class frigate twenty-eight gallons per day and a DDG-51 destroyer some forty-four gallons per day. The next-generation CVN-21 nuclear-powered aircraft carrier will only produce in the order of thirty-six gallons per day per person. Only the optimally manned, 148-crew member, 15,300-ton DDG-1000 will provide the same potable water generation capability as the NSC.

'The design also has separate lounges for officers, chief petty officers and enlisted personnel,' Duthu noted. The centralised food services layout supports separate messes for officers, chiefs and enlisted men, which are all located on the same deck. There are sufficient consumables for sixty days away from port.

CONSTRUCTION PROGRAMME:

Despite the technological advances from the Coast Guard's perspective, this is a low-risk programme. 'We're not on the "bleeding-edge" of technology, here,' NSC programme officials admitted, 'but what we have produced is a very capable cutter. In some cases, we got much more than we bargained for.' Still, these sophisticated, multi-mission ships do not come cheap, and there have been the normal differences in costs between first-in-class and follow-on cutters.

Programme Costs: The first three cutters were procured through the Northrop Grumman and Lockheed Martin Deepwater Integrated Coast Guard Systems (ICGS) consortium under 'cost plus incentive fee' contracts. By contrast, the fourth and fifth ships are being procured from Huntington Ingalls Industries under 'fixed price incentive firm' contracts, which are more effective in controlling costs and schedules, whilst assuring quality.

Shipyard innovations and learning-curve efficiencies contributed to a significant reduction in the cost of WMSL-751 compared to the lead cutter. However, the following cutters *Stratton* and *Hamilton* also include the installation of structural enhancements to the design to improve fatigue life, contributing to an increase in cost compared to the first two NSCs. *Bertholf* and *Waesche* do not have these enhancements installed as of mid 2012 but will be completely retrofitted in the future. In addition, a three-year delay between *Stratton* and *Hamilton* and the award to a single prime contractor contributed to an increase in costs for the *Hamilton*. In mid 2012, the costs of the NSC programme were:[17]

- *Bertholf* (WMSL-750): US$413m production, US$106m LLTM (Long Lead Time Material)
- *Waesche* (WMSL-751): US$374m production, US$64m LLTM
- *Stratton* (WMSL-752): US$429m production, US$73m LLTM
- *Hamilton* (WMSL-753): US$480m production, US$100m LLTM
- *Joshua James* (WMSL-754): US$482m production, US$89.6M LLTM
- NSC#6 (WMSL-755): US$87.9m LLTM (production not awarded as of mid 2012)

Trials Experience: Compared to recent US ship-building experience, the first three NSCs were found

Waesche (WMSL-751) on trials in October 2009. *(Huntington Ingalls Industries)*

Table 3.2.2: 'LEGEND' CLASS: ACCEPTANCE TRIALS TRENDS

INSURV ASSESSMENT	NSC 1 BERTHOLF	NSC 2 WAESCHE	NSC 3 STRATTON	IMPROVEMENT (NSC 1 TO NSC 3)
Total Trial Cards	9,289	7,657	4,905	47%
Open Cards After Trials	4,030	2,166	2,649	34%
Starred Cards	8	3	2	75%
Priority I Safety Cards	78	54	41	47%

Source: US Coast Guard HQ (CG9): April 2012

to be remarkably 'clean' during their builders' and acceptance trials, and the Coast Guard shipyard team continues to capture lessons learned from the earlier ships in the class to put in place considerable efficiencies that wring costs out of the programme.

During the course of the acceptance process, the Navy's Board of Inspection and Survey (INSURV) conducted inspections and surveys of *Bertholf* and its systems to determine whether the ship was ready for delivery. INSURV observed and determined whether the contractor's equipment operated satisfactorily in accordance with contract requirements. Although several problems surfaced, e.g. in relation to the machinery control and monitoring system,

the INSURV Board concluded that *Bertholf* was a 'unique and very capable platform with great potential for future service.'

And, as Rear Admiral Ronald Rábago, then Assistant Commandant for Acquisition, testified on 11 March 2010, 'We capitalised on lessons learned from *Bertholf* during construction of the second NSC, *Waesche*, and took delivery in November 2009 of a cutter that had a higher level of quality and completeness than the first in class.'[18] Following her acceptance trials, INSURV reported *Waesche* was a 'very clean and capable platform' that met or exceeded all readiness expectations. Compared to *Bertholf*, Rábago continued, 'we saw significant

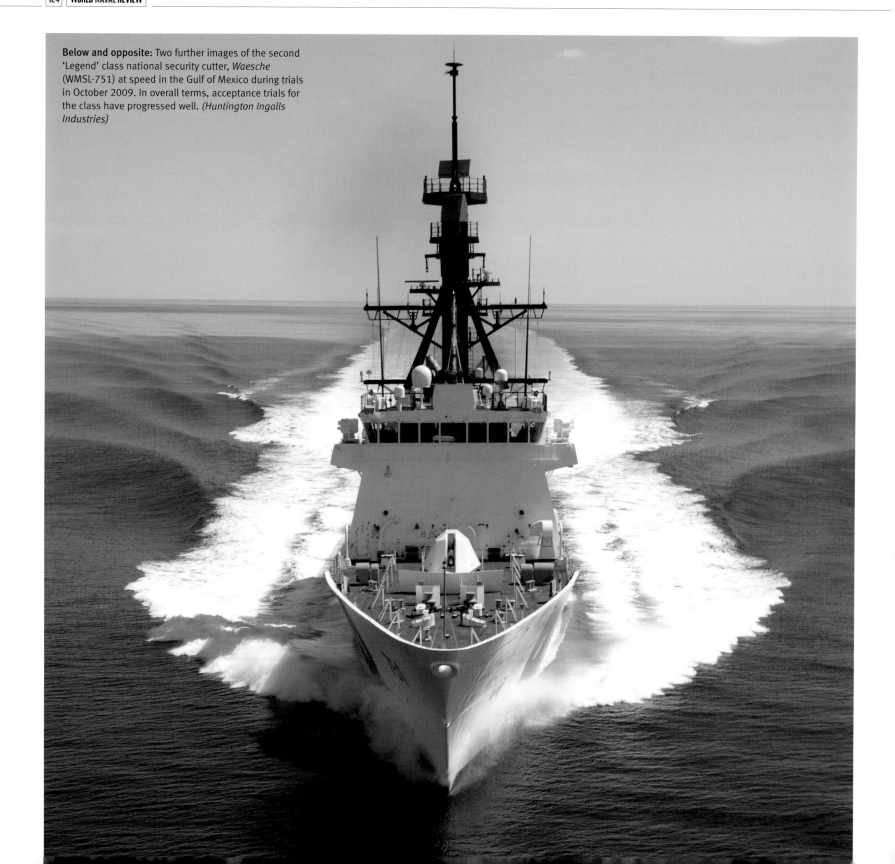

Below and opposite: Two further images of the second 'Legend' class national security cutter, *Waesche* (WMSL-751) at speed in the Gulf of Mexico during trials in October 2009. In overall terms, acceptance trials for the class have progressed well. *(Huntington Ingalls Industries)*

reductions in the number of trial cards, which identified discrepancies needing to be addressed to ensure the cutter met contractual requirements. While *Bertholf* had eight "starred" cards, which note major discrepancies that must be waived or corrected prior to delivery, *Waesche* had three.' Further, *Waesche* was granted the 'Authority to Operate' her classified networks only some two months after delivery, compared to a year for *Bertholf*. These positive trends continued with *Stratton*, as set out in Table 3.2.2.

During her August 2011 acceptance trials, items requiring additional work were far less for *Stratton* than for the first and second NSCs, a 'validation of stable technical requirements, effective project management, capable oversight by the USCG project office, and improved performance by the shipbuilder,' Captain James Knight, commanding officer of the NSC Gulf Coast Project Office, noted.[19] 'We starred just two of those cards, identifying work that must be accomplished prior to our taking delivery of the cutter early next month. As a

point of comparison, *Bertholf* had eight starred cards and *Waesche* had three … *Stratton*'s performance during her sea trials leaves no doubt that we will be delivering an exceptional ship to an even better crew.'

Design & Production Changes: Still, some changes will be needed, but that is not unusual for a new class of ships. During the Coast Guard's review of the NSC's design from 2002 to 2004, for example, concerns were raised about certain aspects of the ship's structure that could prevent it from achieving

With the great operational successes of the first three delivered 'Legend' class cutters, Huntingdon Ingalls Industries have high hopes for exports of a more heavily armed 'patrol frigate' variant to overseas markets. *(Huntington Ingalls Industries)*

its thirty-year expected service life. The question was whether some of the cutter's structural components would experience fatigue damage prior to the end-of-service-life objective, a critical consideration given anticipated extended, high-tempo operations. Following a US Navy/US Coast Guard assessment, the Coast Guard decided to increase the national security cutter's fatigue tolerance to ensure that the cutter's basic structure will meet its projected lifespan. Engineering changes to incorporate the needed structural enhancements were developed for *Stratton* and are incorporated up-front in the remaining new-construction cutters. As their schedules permit, *Bertholf* and *Waesche* will also have the modifications back-fitted.

Other improvements in the initial design include modifications to the stern launch and recovery gantry system and an enhanced replenishment at sea station, which incorporates a redesigned refuelling area that will be more efficient and ergonomic for cutter personnel. The Coast Guard and shipyard also improved the gas turbine removal route, which will make it easier to remove and repair the gas turbine module.

'We continue to build on lessons learned and are making significant improvements to the *Stratton*, including construction process efficiencies, enhanced functionality and improved sequencing,' Mike Duthu explained. 'There is an intense focus on achieving lessons learned, and we constantly ask ourselves: how can we do this better and more efficiently? This process involved all divisions of the yard and every functional department – ops, engineering, planning, and material experts.'

One of the most notable process improvements has been the significant reduction in the number of 'grand blocks' – multiple units stacked together in large assembly halls away from the waterfront – used to assemble the ship's hull. Entire sections of the NSC are built and outfitted on shore and then lifted into place, resulting in a significant reduction in wait times, as it allows for earlier outfitting completion and testing under cover. 'We used thirty-two grand block lifts to assemble *Bertholf* and twenty-nine lifts for *Waesche*, but needed only fourteen to assemble *Stratton*,' Duthu said. 'This enabled more sub-assembly work in each grand block in a controlled environment and led to fewer construction hours compared to the process for *Bertholf*.'

'The shipyard and the programme have also benefited from the mission/requirements stability,' Duthu said. 'There was not much churn in require-ments, although the post-9/11 environment did see some changes, including CPS for CBRN protection and the SCIF, in the *Bertholf* and following ships. Whilst concerns about hull strength and impact on service lives drove a design change in NSC3, the design has remained remarkably stable since the early 2000s. That's a good thing from the yard's perspective, as we can leverage the efficiencies associated with a stable design package.'

In that regard, acquisition stability is also critical, as it allows the yard to get close to a 'heel-to-toe' production schedule, ideally seeing a new ship award every year. 'We didn't see that in NSC1 to NSC3, but the USCG contract for NSC4 had an option for NSC5,' Duthu noted. The Coast Guard's acquisition practice of awarding one cutter every several years works against achieving greater efficiencies from serial production and subcontractors/materials buys. 'We'd be able to leverage everything – stable workload, stable funding, and a stable product funded at consistent and constant intervals – to wring even more efficiencies out of the programme,' Duthu offered. 'But without such stability, it's unlikely that the cost can come down much more than it already has.'

Even if additional efficiencies might not be obtained, the NSCs are bargains in today's squeaky-tight maritime security and defence fiscal environment. For that reason alone, the 2012 direction to zero funding for hulls seven and eight came as a surprise. Cutting the programme by 25 per cent would gut the learning-curve efficiencies at the shipyard, driving up the costs of any follow-on NSCs should the US Administration or Congress decide to reverse the projection. 'We take great pride in what we do,' Duthu underscored. 'We have third- and fourth-generation shipyard families, with some great-grandsons and granddaughters working on several projects, including the NSC. We know that what we build will someday go into harm's way, and that's something we don't take lightly.'

CONCLUSION: WHICH WAY AHEAD?

'I am often asked why the NSCs are so important,' Admiral Papp noted during February 2011 congressional testimony. 'The answer is simple. We must have ships with significant time, distance and endurance capabilities to meet America's security and disaster-response requirements. We are the maritime arm of the Department of Homeland Security. We need to have the tools to provide the American people what it has come to expect from the Coast Guard. The NSC provides us with just that: a versatile and adaptable platform that fully supports our military, maritime and multi-mission capabilities.' These cutters are thus at the fulcrum of US Coast Guard plans to sustain mission excellence, recapitalise and build capacity, and prepare for the future.

The NSC also serves as the surface (war)ship focal point for the Coast Guard's contribution to the nation's fleet. The US Navy might yet be asked to look at the 'Legend' class cutters as the cost-effective frigate-sized means to carry out 'low-end', but still critical, roles and missions, to complement the speedy, mission-tailored LCS. And interest from America's global maritime partners is growing. Ingalls Shipbuilding forecasts a global demand for as many as 215 frigate-sized ships during the next twenty years – hence the grey paint scheme for the patrol frigate variant.

'Coping plans' should the Service have to stay at just six NSCs are at best gap-fillers and merely kick the can further down the road. For example, the Coast Guard might have to retain four *Hamilton* class WHECs longer than projected, a bad decision all around: four obsolescent, technologically-constrained, and high maintenance 1960s-era ships compared with two state-of-the-art cutters. It boggles the mind.

One of America's greatest philosophers, Yogi Berra, advised: 'When you come to a fork in the road, take it!'[20] The US Coast Guard in 2012 contemplated numerous 'forks' in its way forward, not least the direction for the highest-priority 'Legend' class cutters. Although Captain Hatfield suggested, 'eight might not be enough', six might prove to be all that the United States will afford.

Notes:

1. Tracing its origins to the Revenue Cutter Service founded in 1790 and constituted in its current form in 1915, the US Coast Guard has formed part of the US Department of Homeland Security from 1 March 2003. There are provisions for it to be transferred to Department of the Navy control, particularly during wartime. The National Security Cutter designation is unique to the Coast Guard but broadly corresponds to the constabulary-orientated oceanic patrol vessels found in other fleets.

2. See Christopher P Cavas, '2 Cutters Removed from FY13 Coast Guard Budget', *Navy Times* – 24 February 2012 (Springfield VA, Garnett Government Media, 2012).

3. The Senator was quoted by Maria Recio in 'Cochran Questions Coast Guard Budget', *Sun Herald* – 9 March 2012 (Gulfport MS, The McClatchy Company, 2012).

4. See Director of Strategic Management and Doctrine, *Safety, Security and Stewardship: 2011 DHS White Paper on the US Coast Guard* (Washington DC, US Coast Guard, 2011). A copy can be found at http://www.uscg.mil/strategy/docs/WP/DHS_CGWP.pdf

5. For background on the Deepwater Programme, see Ronald O'Rourke, *Coast Guard Deepwater Acquisition Programs: Background, Oversight Issues, and Options for Congress* (Washington DC, Congressional Research Service, RL33753, 20 January 2012).

6. See *The US Coast Guard of the 21st Century* (Washington DC, US Coast Guard, 2000) and Joint Interagency Task Force on Roles and Missions of the United States Coast Guard (Washington DC, Department of Transportation, 10 February 2000). An internet based copy of the former document can be located at http://www.uscg.mil/history/articles/21stcentury.pdf

7. Admiral Robert J Papp, 'Confronting New & Non-Traditional Challenges in the Age of Austerity' (Transcript:

Washington DC, Center for Strategic and International Studies, 13 February 2012), p.15.

8. See Admiral Robert J Papp, Jr, 'Recapitalizing and Building Capacity: The National Security Cutters', in *Coast Guard Compass: Official Blog of the US Coast Guard* – 22 February 2011. This can be found online at http://coastguard.dodlive.mil/index.php/2011/02/recapitalizing-and-building-capacity-the-national-security-cutters/#

9. See Philip Ewing, 'H-I Pitches "Patrol Frigate" as Cheaper Alternative to LCS', and the same author's 'Industry View: Why the Navy Needs a "Patrol Frigate"', both in the *DoDBuzz – Online Defense & Acquisition Journal* of 28 March 2012. They can be found by searching at http://www.dodbuzz.com/

10. These remarks are taken from Captain Prince's blog 'From the Bridge of the *Bertholf*: A Word from the Commanding Officer', in *Coast Guard Compass* – 9 May 2011. See also Captain Prince's interview, 'Full Speed Ahead: Underway in Alaska, *Bertholf* impresses Crew, Allies and Adversaries', *Seapower* – July 2011 (Arlington VA, Navy League of the United States, 2011), pp.36–40.

11. Admiral Michael G Mullen, Chief of Naval Operations, and Admiral Thomas H Collins, Commandant of the Coast Guard, *National Fleet: A Joint Navy/Coast Guard Policy Statement* (Washington DC, Department of the Navy/US Coast Guard, 3 March 2006), p.2.

12. Captain Joe Vojvodich, USCG, Acquisition Directorate (CG9), 'USCG National Security Cutter Combat System Architecture', briefing presented at ASNE Naval Warfare Systems Symposium, 18 June 2009.

13. MOTR (Maritime Operational Threat Response) of the National Strategy for Maritime Security (October 2006) assigns the Department of Homeland Security (DHS) and the US Coast Guard as the lead MOTR agency for the

interdiction of maritime threats in waters where they normally operate.

14. Cdr David Ramassini, USCG, 'From the Bridge of the *Bertholf*: Northern Edge 2011', *Coast Guard Compass* – 29 June 2011.

15. Norman Polmar, *Ships and Aircraft of the US Fleet*, 18th ed (Annapolis MD, Naval Institute Press, 2005), pp.577–9.

16. Ian Peek, NSWCCD-SSES (Code 985), 'Current Navy Desalination Capability', briefing presented at the US Office of Naval Research, Industry/Applied Researchers Day, BAA 11-010: Demonstration System Development for Advanced Shipboard Desalination [Future Naval Capability], Long Beach, CA, 31 March 2011, p.18. Data for ship crew from Polmar, *op. cit.* For DDG-1000, see Captain George V Galdorisi and Scott C Truver, 'From Minimal to Optimal', US Naval Institute *Proceedings* – July 2011 (Annapolis MD, Naval Institute Press, 2011), pp.26ff.

17. Cost data for WMSL750-755 provided by Brian R Olexy, Programme Analyst (CG925), Acquisition Directorate, US Coast Guard headquarters in mid 2012.

18. Testimony of Rear Admiral Ronald Rábago, Assistant Commandant for Acquisition, 'Coast Guard Acquisition Status Update', before the House Subcommittee on Coast Guard and Maritime Transportation, 11 March 2010, p.5.

19. Captain James Knight, 'NSC Stratton Performs Exceptionally at Sea Trials', *Coast Guard Compass* – 18 August 2011.

20. *Editor's Note:* Lawrence Peter 'Yogi' Berra (born 12 May 1925) is a renowned former US baseball player and manager, spending most of his playing career with the New York Yankees. He is almost equally well known for his tautological and contradictory witticisms, perhaps most famously, 'It's déjà vu all over again.'

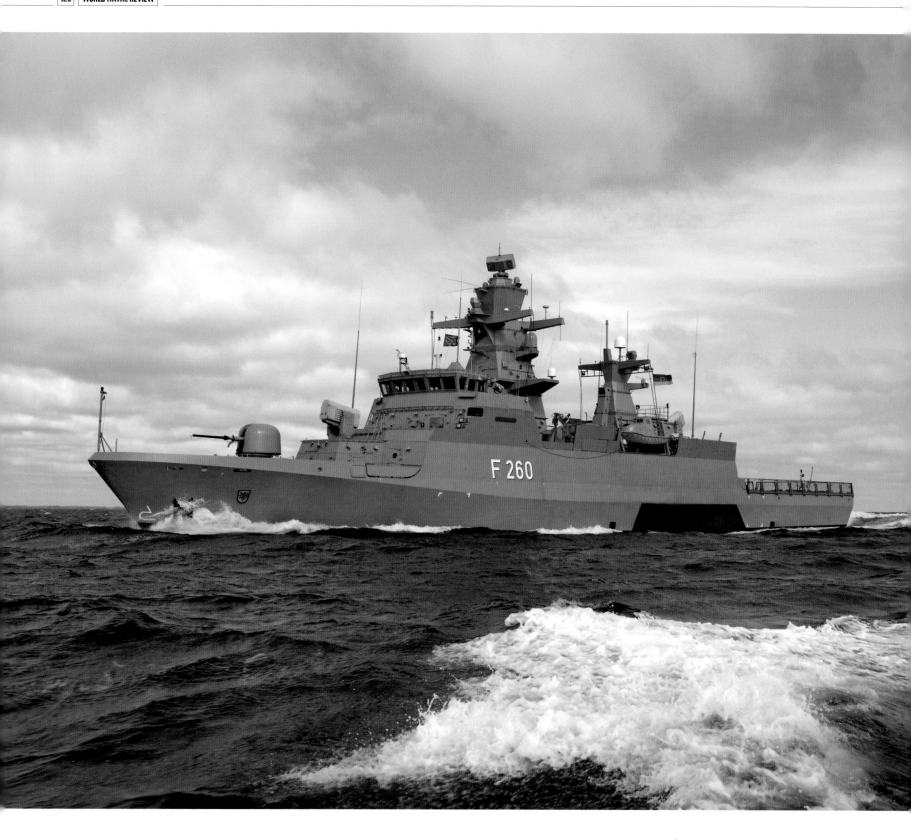

Author:
Guy Toremans

3.3 SIGNIFICANT SHIPS

BRAUNSCHWEIG CLASS CORVETTES

Eagerly awaited by the German Navy

During the past decade the German Navy has become, more than ever, a key instrument of the country's foreign and security policy. The new and extended task spectrum associated with the resultant enlargement in the navy's geographical responsibilities has placed new demands on its capabilities, necessitating a reorientation in terms both of organisation and equipment. The forthcoming completion of the K-130 *Braunschweig* corvette programme will mark an important step in this process.

CONCEPT PROVENANCE

It became clear in the years following the end of the Cold War that the restricted mission profiles of the German Navy's missile-equipped *Tiger* (Type 148), *Albatros* (Type 143B) and *Gepard* (Type 143A) class fast patrol boats did not meet evolving navy requirements. Designed for operations in the Baltic, these fast attack craft had been an indispensable component of the Cold War era German fleet, forming a major anti-invasion component tasked with

Opposite: The lead German K-130 type corvette, *Braunschweig,* on builders' sea trials in September 2007 before delivery to the German Navy. The programme's imminent completion marks an important step in the transition of the *Deutsche Marine*'s force structure to a fleet of more globally deployable assets. *(Blohm & Voss, TKMS)*

preventing the Warsaw Pact nations from attacking NATO territories from the sea. The one-watch boats had a very limited endurance by nature of their limited seaworthiness and the fatigue factor impacting their crews. At the same time, the patrol boats continued to prove their high value in respect of surveillance tasks. The units were regularly deployed 'out-of-area', for example to participate in Strait of Gibraltar counter-terrorism patrols in 2003 and, up to the present date, in support of UNIFIL MTF-448, the maritime element of the United Nation's Lebanese peacekeeping deployment.

As such, when the Germany Navy announced a requirement to replace the ageing Type 148 and Type 143B fast attack craft in the mid 1990s, a key objective was to overcome these deficiencies. It therefore opted to acquire larger, more survivable ships that would have much greater flexibility, with an ability to be deployed and sustained over prolonged periods. They would be capable of undertaking extended national and international tasks in line with enlarged European aspirations, being suited for deployment on worldwide operations (excluding the Polar seas) throughout the navy's entire spectrum of missions. The German Navy's key-user stipulations for these new platforms inevitably called for capabilities over and above those provided by the fast patrol boats. They encompassed:

- Sufficient stability for worldwide missions.
- Suitability for sustained operations in both open-ocean and littoral environments. Surveillance and protection capabilities in littoral waters.
- Ability to control sea lines of communication (SLOC).
- Tactical co-ordination and command of task groups.
- Engagement of surface targets on the high seas and close to the shore, and of land targets.
- Presence during crisis operations.

Analysis of these requirements led to an official conceptual design that considerably exceeded the cost limits laid down in the defence budget. To adhere to cost limitations, the principal of 'design-to-requirement' was shifted towards a 'design-to-cost' strategy. The use of specific construction principles – including application of the 'Rules & Regulations for the Construction of German Naval Ships' – was kept to a minimum. This gave way to a focus on innovative solutions and economical production procedures. As a result, industry could select the best solution from various technical alternatives.

CONTRACT & CONSTRUCTION

The project definition phase for what became known as the Korvette 130 (K-130) project started in 1998. Bidders were invited to propose innovative

An image of Germany's Type 143A fast attack craft *Zobel* on deployment in the Mediterranean. The K-130 class are intended to offer a more effective means of carrying out lengthy deployments in littoral areas away from home waters. *(German Navy)*

The contract for the K-130 programme was awarded to the ARGE K130 consortium of German shipyards. An early artist's impression of their winning design is depicted here. *(Blohm & Voss, TKMS)*

solutions and production procedures to satisfy the navy's functional specification requirements within the limited budget. Two bidder groups submitted proposals: the ARGE K130 consortium – comprising the Blohm & Voss GmbH, Nordseewerke Emden GmbH and Friedrich Lürssen Werft GmbH shipyards – and the HDW Project Group K130. On 17 July 2000, the German Ministry of Defence selected the ARGE K130 Consortium as their preferred supplier. The Federal Office of Defence Technology and Procurement (BWB) subsequently awarded the consortium a €880m (c.US$1bn at then current exchange rates) construction contract for an initial batch of five ships on 13 December 2001.[1]

The contract award not only stipulated the design, production and delivery of five K-130 corvettes. It also encompassed the integration of all systems and equipment, as well as the development, adaptation, integration and testing of the operational software for the combat direction system (CDS) and the message handling system. Detailed design of the ships started in January 2003. The construction work was split up among the three shipyards in the ARGE consortium, with each yard constructing the same sections of each of the five units. Final assembly of the various ships was also spread out across the yards, with final outfitting completed by the shipyard assigned to deliver the particular vessel. The forward sections were built by Nordseewerke at its Emden shipyard; the aft sections were built by Lürssen in Bremen, whilst the superstructure modules were the responsibility of Blohm & Voss in Hamburg.

Construction on the first of class, which was to be christened *Braunschweig*, kicked off at the Blohm & Voss yard on 19 July 2004. Units two and three began construction at, respectively, Lürssen Werft and ThyssenKrupp Nordseewerke (TNSW) before the end of 2005. Units four and five followed during 2006 at Blohm & Voss and Lürssen Werft. Table 3.3.1 provides a class list.

OVERALL DESIGN

Table 3.3.2 sets out a summary of the K-130's key characteristics. Based on the Blohm & Voss MEKO A-100 design, the K-130 *Braunschweig* class corvettes have an overall length of 89.1m, a beam of 13.3m, a draught of 3.4m and a full load displacement of c.1,850 tons (with a growth margin of approximately 150 tons). This is approximately four

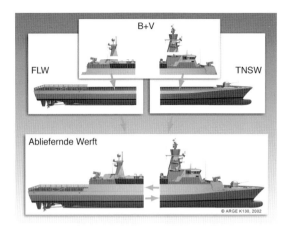

Construction of the new corvettes was split between the ARGE K130 consortium's yards, with each yard – Lürssen (FLW), Blohm & Voss (B&V) and Nordseewerke (TNSW) building the same modules, as depicted here. Final assembly of each ship was allocated to one of the three as a delivery yard (*abliefernde werft*). *(Blohm & Voss, TKMS)*

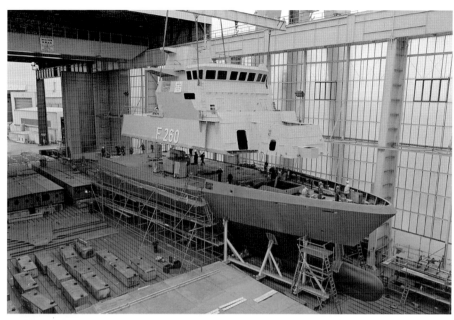

A picture of *Braunschweig* in the course of construction at Blohm & Voss, Hamburg early in 2005. *(Blohm & Voss, TKMS)*

A diagrammatic representation of the K-130 class's X-form design, under which the ship's hull and structure are inclined at different angles to reduce radar cross section. *(Blohm & Voss, TKMS)*

times the size of the former fast attack craft that they have replaced. The principles of the original MEKO concept are adhered to. Masts and weapons are laid out as modules, whilst the combat information centre (CIC) and other key equipment compartments feature modular foundation systems, facilitating the installation of complete equipment packages into confined spaces.

Stealth Features: Reflecting the latest progress in radar cross section (RCS) and infrared (IR) suppression, a prime design feature of the K-130 class is their use of the so-called X-shape, where the hull and superstructure are inclined at different angles and the sides of the ship broken up. This significantly reduces and scatters radar echoes across the complete height and length of the vessel. The avoidance of angled reflectors and small equipment on the decks also materially reduces the class's radar signature, both horizontally and vertically.

The strongest thermal (infrared) radiation sources of a ship are the exhaust outlets, its plume, and ship surfaces heated by exhaust gases. The corvettes' infrared signature is kept to an absolute minimum thanks to an innovative cooling system. By injecting seawater into the exhaust piping, diesel propulsion engines, and electric generator, exhaust gases are cooled down from 500°C to approximately 60°C: a level not achievable by air cooling. The exhaust outlets, arranged horizontally along the ship's sides

Table 3.3.1: K-130 *BRAUNSCHWEIG* CLASS – CLASS LIST

NAME	PENNANT	LAID DOWN	LAUNCHED[1]	COMMISSIONED	BUILDER[2]
Braunschweig	F260	19 July 2004 [3]	19 April 2006	16 April 2008	Blohm & Voss, Hamburg
Magdeburg	F261	19 May 2005	6 September 2006	22 September 2008	Lürssen, Bremen
Erfurt	F262	22 September 2005	29 March 2007	[Scheduled 2012]	Thyssen Nordseewerke, Emden
Oldenburg	F263	19 January 2006	28 June 2007	[Scheduled 2012]	Blohm & Voss, Hamburg
Ludwigshafen[4]	F264	14 April 2006	26 September 2007	[Scheduled 2012]	Lürssen, Bremen

Notes:

1 Relates to date of christening. This does not necessarily coincide with technical launch.

2 Yard of final assembly. Each of the three yards in the ARGE K130 Consortium constructed the same modules for all ships but final assembly was allocated between them.

3 Refers to start of fabrication.   4 Full name is *Ludwigshafen am Rhein*.

and just above the waterline, are fitted with jets that create a water veil to reduce the infrared signature even further. A spin-off from this new technology is that there are no funnels, allowing a better arrangement of the weapons and sensors on and below deck.

In order to reduce noise radiation and create the acoustic conditions necessary for the installation of a sonar-supported torpedo defence system, relevant equipment is comprehensively shock-mounted and can be considered as virtually vibration-proof. The corvettes are also equipped with a degaussing system to generate a mirrored magnetic field in order to reduce the danger from magnetic mines.

Survivability: The ships are divided into twelve water- and gastight sections. No double bulkheads have been installed but active damage limitation has been a key area of focus. In case of major damage, the ship can be divided into two damage control zones with self-sufficient ventilation. Two air locks with integrated cleansing stations permit access to the deck areas under NBC conditions. The engine room is equipped with integrated modular air plants that provide independent hyperbaric pressure outputs in order to avoid contaminated air inlets. The galley and sickbay areas are also self-contained from a ventilation perspective. A spray system wets the ship with a film of water in order to avoid the permanent contact with NBC agents on the upper decks.

Survivability is also assisted by dispersion of key facilities, with the CIC, the communications room and the platform/machinery control room all distributed throughout the ship. The K-130's designers also took strict environmental protection regulations into account and incorporated the latest waste-water processing and treatment technology. Fresh water is produced by means of two reverse-osmosis units, with a daily capability of 4.8m³.

Sea-keeping and Ship Operation: A noteworthy feature of the *Braunschweig* class is their excellent seaworthiness and manoeuvrability. Very stable in high seas and strong winds, the corvettes turn well and accelerate quickly, while their slender, bulbous bow allows for higher speeds whilst reducing fuel consumption. However, *Braunschweig's* sea trials

The first German K-130-type corvette, *Braunschweig*, seen during her christening ceremony at Blohm & Voss on 19 April 2006. The slender, bulbous bow allows for higher speeds whilst reducing fuel consumption. *(Blohm & Voss, TKMS)*

An excellent overhead image of *Braunschweig* at sea in July 2008, shortly after commissioning into the German Navy. The modular nature of the design and attention to overall stealth are apparent. Note also the absence of funnels due to the use of waterline exhaust outlets, facilitating topside arraangements. A Schiebel S-100 Camcopter UAV is undergoing trials from the spacious flight deck. *(German Navy)*

A stern view of *Magdeburg* taken in September 2011 showing the large flight deck and X-form stealth inclination of hull and superstructure to good effect. Exhaust outlets, positioned just above the waterline, are fitted with jets that create a water veil to reduce IR signature. *(Guy Toremans)*

revealed that the combination of its substantial superstructure and small draught meant that the corvettes tend to drift very quickly at low speeds, which made going alongside tricky. Subsequently, the German Navy has decided to retrofit a bow thruster to all five units.

As one of the design goals was to achieve and maintain a full operational capability up to Sea State 5, the corvettes have been fitted with two semi-balanced rudders and a Rudder Roll System (RSS). Introduced for the first time in the *Sachsen* class (F-124 type) frigates, the RRS principle combines information about the ship's course and rudder dampening signals into control signals for the rudder drive. Using a rudder angle margin of +/–20° up to a cruising speed of approximately twenty knots and a maximum permissible rudder rate of eight to ten times the minimum value of 2.4° per second compensates for the ship's rolling and yawing movements, giving the ships almost unprecedented stability.

The aft section of the K-130 class is dominated by a 24m-long flight deck. Due to its limited size (24m x 12.6 m) this has been designed as a multifunctional deck, fitted with retractable, submarine-like bollards to ensure a clear, uncluttered area. Nevertheless its dimensions and strength allow the

Table 3.3.2.

BRAUNSCHWEIG PRINCIPAL PARTICULARS

Building Information:

Fabrication Commenced:	19 July 2004
Launched:	19 April 2006
Commissioned:	16 April 2008
Builders:	Blohm & Voss at its Hamburg facility. Constituent modules were also constructed by Lürssen Werft and Nordseewerke.[1]

Dimensions:

Displacement:	1,850 tons full load displacement.
Overall Hull Dimensions:	89.1m x 13.3m x 3.4m (4.6m maximum). Length between perpendiculars is 82.8m.

Weapons Systems:

Missiles:	2 x twin launchers for Saab RBS15 Mk3 surface-to-surface missiles.
	2 x 21–cell RAM Mk49 launchers for RIM-116B rolling airframe missiles.
Guns:	1 x 76mm Oto Melara Compact. 2 x Mauser MLG 27mm guns. Light machine guns.
Other:	The class has a mine-laying capability.
Aircraft:	Landing facilities for one helicopter up to Sea King size. Up to two UAVs such as the Schiebel S-100 Campcopter can be stored.
Countermeasures:	UL 5000K electronic warfare suite. Rheinmetall MASS decoy launchers.
Principal Sensors:	1 x EADS TRS-3D/16 air/surface search/target acquisition radar, including integrated IFF. Navigation radars.
Combat System:	Thales SEWACO
	Integrated Communications System includes links 11 and 16 with provision for link 22.

Propulsion Systems:

Machinery:	Diesel. 2 x Tognum MTU 20V 1163 TB93 diesels each rated at 7.4MW. Two shaft arrangement with cross connected gearbox. Bow thruster.
Speed and Range:	Designed maximum speed is 26knots. Range is over 4,000 nautical miles at 15 knots.

Other Details:

Complement:	The core crew is 58, including 8 officers. Accommodation is provided for 65.
Class:	There are five members of the class: *Braunschweig*, *Magdeburg*, *Erfurt*, *Oldenburg* and *Ludwigshafen am Rhein*.

1 Both the Blohm & Voss and Nordseewerke yards were part of the ThyssenKrupp group, forming constituents of ThyssenKrupp Marine Systems when HDW was acquired in 2005. The division has been restructured and only Blohm & Voss Naval, a system house for naval ships, and submarine builder HDW remain within the ThyssenKrupp group.

operation of a medium-sized helicopter of up to 12.5 tons, such as the new NH-90 helicopter. Alternatively, unmanned aerial vehicles (UAV) such as the Schiebel S-100 Camcopter type can be deployed for air reconnaissance and over-the-horizon targeting. UAVs can be stored in the 53m² hangar space. In addition to motor lifeboats, the corvettes also mount a 7m RHIB, which is operated by a crane equipped with a swell compensator.

WEAPONS SUITE

Carrying a suite of highly automated weapons and defence systems, the *Braunschweig* class corvettes can conduct both anti-surface (ASuW) and anti-air (AAW) warfare operations. They have good self-defence capabilities against land and seaborne missiles, as well as against aircraft and helicopter attacks. Anti-submarine warfare (ASW) capabilities are more limited.

The corvettes' main ASuW capability is provided by four Saab Bofors Dynamic RBS15 Mk3 surface-to-surface missiles. With a range of more than 200km, these are capable of engaging targets at sea or on land at medium and long distances. A true 'fire and forget' sea-skimming cruise missile, the RBS15 Mk3 incorporates an active radar target seeker, a fully digital autopilot and GPS-supported naviga-tion, as well as using an advanced missile engage-

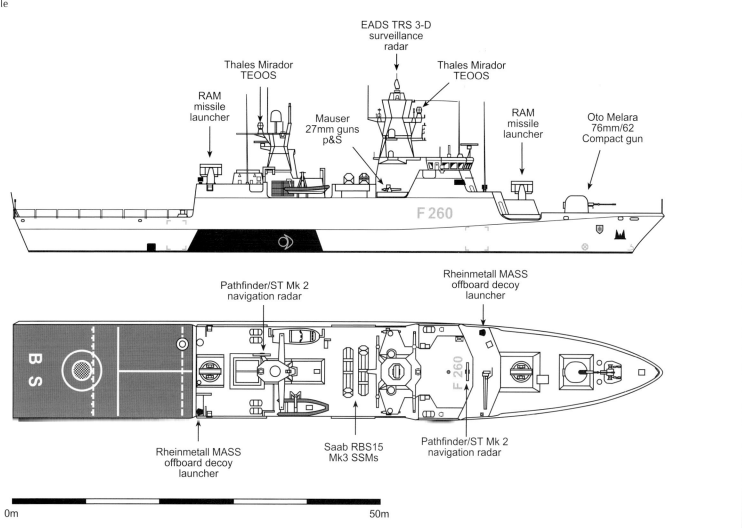

Braunschweig (2011)
1:500 scale

RAM missile launcher

Thales Mirador TEOOS

EADS TRS 3-D surveillance radar

Thales Mirador TEOOS

Mauser 27mm guns p&S

RAM missile launcher

Oto Melara 76mm/62 Compact gun

F 260

Pathfinder/ST Mk 2 navigation radar

Rheinmetall MASS offboard decoy launcher

F 260

Rheinmetall MASS offboard decoy launcher

Saab RBS15 Mk3 SSMs

Pathfinder/ST Mk 2 navigation radar

0m   50m

(Drawings © John Jordan, 2012)

A German Navy Lynx helicopter landing on *Magdeburg* during landing trials in August 2011. The flight deck is large enough to take helicopters up to Sea King size but the hangar only has space to store smaller UAVs. *(German Navy)*

A forward view of *Magdeburg* showing the 76mm Oto Melara Compact gun and forward Mk49 RAM launcher that are key components of her armament. *(Guy Toremans)*

The K-130 class ships two Mauser MLG 27mm cannon for close range defence against asymmetric threats, such as speedboats and floating mines. This picture shows one of the weapons on *Braunschweig*. (Conrad Waters)

ment planning system. The flexible, pre-launch programmable Ku-band seeker can select priority targets when faced with multiple choices and is said to have outstanding electronic countermeasures resistance, employing home-on-jam or chaff discrimination against soft-kill defences. The missile has a maximum speed in excess of 0.8 Mach and can fly as low as 1m in its terminal phase, combining this low trajectory with a vast set of evasive manoeuvres to minimise warning time and confuse enemy defences. A large, 200kg HE blast and pre-fragmented warhead is capable of causing severe damage to vessels of up to major surface combatant size.[2]

An Oto Melara 76mm/62 Compact gun provides the vessels with a surface-target and shore-bombardment capability. The 7.5 ton cannon has a rate of fire between ten and seventy-five rounds per minute and has a range of 8.6 nautical miles with standard ammunition and 10.8 nautical miles with extended range ammunition. The gun can fire high explosive, pre-formed, multi-role, and semi-armour piercing extended range Oto munitions.

For self defence, the K-130 units ship two Rheinmetall DeTec Mauser MLG 27mm guns. These are designed as remotely controlled, fully autonomous weapons with two-axis stabilisation, covering +/–170° traverse and –15° to +60° in elevation. They significantly improve the ships' self-defence capabilities against terrorist attacks and are of particular relevance with regard to peacekeeping operations. A dedicated gun control panel and a monitor in the CIC display all the information from an on-the-mount sensor package. The c.800kg mounting has an automatic target track mode using a daylight or IR-camera together with a high repetition eye-safe laser rangefinder. With an ammunition capacity of ninety ready-to-fire rounds (optionally 135 rounds), the gun is capable of eight engagements (optionally twelve) – each with a burst of eleven rounds – before reloading. Rate of fire is between 200 and 1700 rounds per minute, which allows for effective deployment against air, shore and surface targets, including fast incoming attack craft and even floating mines. All-purpose Frangible Armour Piercing Discarding Sabot (FAPDS) ammunition increases engagement distance as a result of its high muzzle velocity and flat trajectory. It is effective up to ranges of 2.5km against aircraft and light sea targets but up to distances of 4km against larger surface vessels and coastal targets.

The *Braunschweig* class's principal AAW capability is limited to two, twenty-one-cell Raytheon/RAMSYS Mk49 Rolling Airframe Missile (RAM) launchers for RIM-116B RF/IR Block 1A missiles. RAM was initially designed to serve primarily for defence against incoming missiles but the Block 1A upgrade allows the engagement of helicopters, slow aerial targets and surface targets at close ranges. Launchers are currently positioned fore and aft, although there is a possibility that the aft launcher will be replaced by a torpedo defence system in the future.

The K-130 class does not feature an anti-submarine suite, although an embarked NH-90 or Super Lynx helicopter could provide ASW capabilities.

A picture of *Braunschweig*'s rather cluttered midships section, including two of the Saab RBS15 Mk3 missile launchers that provide her principal strike weaponry. *(Conrad Waters)*

Schiebel's S-100 Camcopter UAV typically carries a 25kg payload for six hours, with a maximum payload of 50kg, and has been tested with the Thales UK Lightweight Multi-role Missile. Its 55hp rotary engine gives a dash speed of 120 knots.

The K-130 also carries two Rheinmetall Multi-Ammunition Soft-Kill System (MASS) launchers for radar and IR decoys. This stealthy, fully-trainable, stabilised, lightweight carbon fibre chaff launching system is claimed to be the only self-protection system to generate ship-like decoy patterns and full ship screening. Based on thirty-two identical, omni-spectral munitions per launcher, MASS is efficient in ultraviolet, electro-optical, infrared, radar and laser spectrums.

SENSOR SUITE

The K-130 class's main sensor is the mechanically stabilised EADS TRS-3D/16 air/surface surveillance radar (with an integrated IFF MSSR/STR 2000i system) for the detection, identification and tracking

A close-up view of *Magdeburg*'s foremast, showing the EADS TRS-3D/16 radar that it is used for surveillance and target indication purposes. Immediately below is one of the ship's two Mirador TEOOS electro-optical sensors that have surface surveillance and fire control capabilities. *(Guy Toremans)*

of targets. Operating in the 4,000-5,000 MHz G Band (US C Band) and optimised for conditions in the littoral, the radar is able to process more than four hundred air and sea targets simultaneously.

Sea surveillance is provided by two Thales Mirador electro-optical sensors, each equipped with two TV cameras for short and long ranges, an IR camera, and a laser rangefinder. The Mirador TEOOS (Trainable Electrical-Optical Observation System) sensor is capable of automatic and autonomous 3D target acquisition and tracking. Its role is to support the crew in detecting, observing and identifying surface and aerial targets, day and night, and in poor visibility. Due to their ability to automatically track targets, the Miradors can also be used for fire control purposes.

The K-130 corvettes feature very advanced navigation equipment, including two Pathfinder/ST Mk2 navigation radars to ensure safe navigation and the detection of surface targets at close range. The incorporation of an automatic radar plotting aid function in these radars means that they can also be used to detect helicopters at close range and support them when they are heading for the ship. Other navigating equipment includes an electronic sea chart system, a weather satellite system, an automatic manoeuvring system and an Automatic Identification System (AIS). Navigation data is passed straight to the CMS via two bus interface units, each containing a navigation computer, thus giving 100 per cent redundancy in case of failure or battle damage.

The UL 5000K electronic warfare suite consists of both electronic countermeasures and electronic support measures modules. The suite is capable of deceiving hostile radar units, in particular the radar search heads of approaching missiles, with strong jamming signals and detecting and identifying electronic emitters. The suite can also be used for creating a passive situation map. Radiation sources can be quickly allocated by means of extensive databases in which all known radiation sources are systematically recorded.

COMBAT INFORMATION CENTRE (CIC)

Under the overall responsibility of ET Marine Systems (a subsidiary of EADS and Thales Nederland), the K-130 design introduced an innovative operations centre. For the first time ever on a German naval vessel, the combat information centre (CIC) is operated under normal lighting conditions.

This necessitated a special lighting concept, developed to ensure glare-free monitors. Console colours are of a comfortable CORIAN™ Turkish blue, mixed with cream.

The modular combat direction system (CDS) is an example of the increasingly popular decentralised computer arrangements seen in the new generation of warships. There are a total of seven multi-purpose consoles, each with two 21in large daylight monitors. These are supplemented by four auxiliary workstation consoles, a large screen display for briefing purposes and for the display of status information and a number of consoles dedicated to specific tasks such as electronic warfare and 27mm gun operation. Horizontal display arrangements ensure a free and unhindered view to every console operator. If the CIC should be taken out of action, a multifunction console on the bridge allows continued operation of the ship's weaponry.

COMBAT AND PLATFORM MANAGEMENT SYSTEMS

Integrated Combat Direction System: The integrated combat direction system is a scaled down version of the Thales Naval Nederland SEWACO series installed on the F-124 *Sachsen* class frigates, incorporating both reused and newly developed software. The system has the capacity to handle up to 1,200 tracks simultaneously. Sensors and weapons can be linked to form functional chains and allow automatic operation.[3] In addition, access to communications such as Links 11 and 16 allows the exchange of target data with other units. The integration of data received from Link 11 and Link 16 with NATO's Maritime Command & Control Information System (MCCIS) also allows the preparation of a worldwide situation map. Additionally data about airports, air traffic routes, ship types and geographical features can be called up online and used for tactical evaluation. There is scope for upgrading the K-130 class with Link 22 in due course.

A key aspect of the K-130 class's CDS is its integration with the platform management system to achieve a total ship control capability. All monitoring and control system information can be displayed on the CDS workstations, allowing operators immediate access to the status of systems that are critical to them. Upon confirmation that the ship is transitioning to combat-ready status, automatic sequences are launched, for example to bring all

An early graphic of the K-130 class's combat information centre – including the twin screen multifunction consoles used to fight the ship – and a photograph of the realised concept onboard *Magdeburg*. The K-130 class is the first German warship with a combat information centre that operates in normal lighting conditions. *(Blohm & Voss, TKMS/ Guy Toremans)*

generators online or to prepare damage control auxiliaries such as the main fire system. In case of damage to systems critical to the overall CDS, the CDS operator can set the repair priority assigned to various equipment, which will then be used by the damage control function to direct the dispatch of the necessary repair teams.

Integrated Monitoring and Control System (IMCS): The K-130 corvettes are equipped with an L-3 MAPPS Integrated Monitoring and Control System (IMCS), which has been tailored to the class's specific requirements. The distributed, open-architecture nature of the system is the same as that used in the *Sachsen* class, providing a comprehensive range of user interfaces that allow the crew to monitor and control the ship's propulsion plant, electrical systems, air conditioning, closure status and damage control facilities. There are around 7,000 separate signals associated with the IMCS, of which only 2,500 are hardwired. The remaining 4,500 are received through links interfacing with the local controllers of various ship machinery. All system elements share a common database, which is constantly updated on every change in sensor data or operator-initiated process. Short-term data storage for the last twenty-four hours is available at each console, whereas long-term data storage is provided

A view of *Magdeburg*'s machinery control room, with a prominent bank of screens for the L-3 MAPPS Integrated Monitoring and Control System (IMCS). *(Guy Toremans)*

Above and opposite: A series of images of the second K-130 corvette *Magdeburg* coming alongside a fleet replenishment ship during Exercise Danex/Northern Coasts 2011, the first time one of the class had participated in an international exercise. The high level of automation provided by the ship's Integrated Bridge System (IBS) facilitates such manoeuvres. *(Guy Toremans)*

by a USB-connected removable storage device. Some 7,000 different sensors are distributed through the ship, providing a flexible, effective approach to data acquisition and control.

ICMS consoles are equipped with generously sized monitors, keyboards and trackballs, allowing comfortable control and operation. Small details such as cup holders and item stowage compartments are provided as well. The high-resolution colour LCD monitors display ergonomically designed graphical pages of the platform machinery and systems. Drawn deck plans selectively show all important systems, technical equipment, piping and cable runs. The system translates the relevant status of all important events, for example the activation of temperature or water sensors, into process images that are displayed on screen. The operating mode of any of the multi-purpose consoles can be selected to fit the crew member's assigned role, providing significant flexibility in respect of the organisation and set-up of groups for sharing mission work.

To support manpower reduction, the IMCS features an integrated closed-circuit digital television system, with over a dozen web-based colour CCD cameras. It provides video monitoring of the ships' machinery spaces and other locations. The cameras are connected to the platform management system consoles using an independent network that allows the screens to display the video image in a window that can be maximised to the extent of the full screen area. To provide the most flexibility, any camera can be selected for display on any console. An elaborate alarm processing subsystem (fire and flooding alarms) triggers the automatic display of the relevant camera images at specific consoles.

The redundancy inherent in the IMCS's design, as well as a battery backed-up power supply, ensures a high fault tolerance. All stations have the same database and perform a continuous synchronisation between each other. A unique feature is an ability to link the control systems of several ships with each other or to a shore-based station. This allows just one machinery control room to be manned, leaving the crew of the remaining ships free for other duties. The IMCS also includes an onboard training system that permits training activities at any time on a single or several consoles. The system can be set to simulate any conceivable malfunction or damage scenario. A German Navy requirement was that it should be possible to switch from training mode to real mode within one second.

Integrated Bridge System (IBS): The corvettes feature an ergonomically designed Raytheon Integrated Bridge System (IBS), sub-contracted to Raytheon Anschütz GmbH. The concept is based on the one-man bridge of modern merchant ships, with an innovative design and growth potential for different outfitting variants. The K-130's IBS has three working stations: one for the officer on duty, one for the helmsman and, at the port side, one for multi-purpose usage. The high level of automation allows a ship to be conned by a single watch officer and it can be operated during transit cruising with a crew of three on the bridge. Besides pure navigational data, engineering control information and the complete naval tactical data situational picture is displayed.

Integrated Battle Damage Control System (IBDCS): An integral part of the platform management system is the Integrated Battle Damage & Control System (IBDCS). This provides operators with a graphical interface to identify ship emergencies or casualties quickly. It records, processes and reports specific information to the damage control teams, which is retrievable from any console at each damage control station. The system presents information as a two-dimensional overlay to the general arrangement plan, with subsidiary windows providing additional views and data. By increasing the zoom factor, detailed information, such as room numbers or section markings, becomes visible. Again, any imaginable problem or damage scenario can be simulated for crew training purposes.

As a further damage control mechanism, online 'kill cards' have been implemented to assist the crew in taking decisions and to indicate possible corrective actions. These cards provide detailed information on the ships' systems, equipment, materials, disconnecting devices, valves and show a list of mechanical and electric systems running through a selected compartment or room.

The basic safety concept for detecting and fighting fires, fumes and flooding on *Braunschweig* and her sisters is based on isolating the rooms subjected to these hazards and providing redundant controls for the relevant installations, thus minimising the risk of any potential spread of smoke and heat.[4] It is anticipated that only a few compartments would therefore be impacted by any particular hazard, with other compartments – including their ventilation – remaining intact. To increase

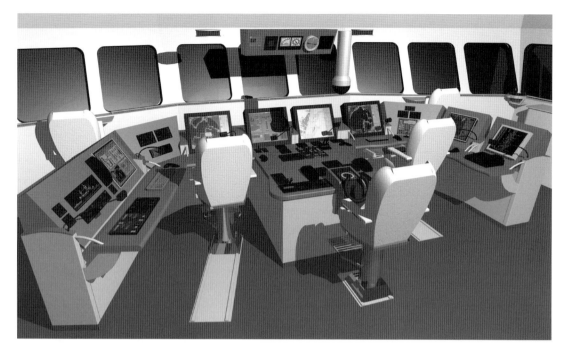

The K-130 class's Integrated Bridge System (IBS) is based on commercial 'lean manning practices' and can be operated with just three crew on the bridge during transit. There are three principal workstations, as shown here in these concept and 'real life' images. *(Blohm & Voss, TKMS / Guy Toremans)*

survivability, important systems such as the electrical and ventilation plants and the fire extinguishing system are arranged so as to give rise to a high degree of compartment independence. Given the fact that the K-130 corvettes have a small crew, the officer assigned to damage control duties needs the platform management systems to provide a comprehensive picture of the damage situation in the most effective way possible. Damage control is normally directed from the machinery control room – from where all key systems can be operated – backed up by the ICMS sub-station consoles distributed elsewhere in the ship.

Integrated Communication System (ICS): The EADS-supplied Integrated Communications Suite (ICS) ensures the security and effectiveness of both external and internal communications. For external communications, the K-130 class is equipped to operate over the VLF, LF, MF, HF, VHF and UHF frequency bands. In addition, the corvettes mount UHF military Satcom, Inmarsat 'B' and 'M' commercial systems and German Army radio connectivity for contacting army forces ashore. If required, a SHF-Satcom system could be back-fitted. The heart of the internal communication system is a digital communication network, with a total of forty-eight extensions, allowing onboard communications via the public address or radio-telephone systems. The software allows the automatic evaluation and distribution of incoming messages and, through an interface to the IMCS, extensive ship system data is sent to the CDS and evaluated. This modern communication suite allows the K-130s to be employed as command platforms, for example, for national or international mine-countermeasure or fast patrol-boat task groups.

HABITABILITY

The K-130 class corvettes can accommodate up to sixty-five personnel. However, a crew of only fifty-eight is required to achieve a continuous manning policy. With seven spare bunks, the ships can embark a small staff and act as a command platform for a task group of fast attack craft or mine-countermeasure vessels. The corvettes are also fitted 'for-but-not-with' a planning room for this purpose.

To ensure the crew performs well under stressful working conditions, high demands have been placed on habitability. The corvettes are said to offer almost cruise-ship-like accommodation, with six-berth

A damage control post in one of *Magdeburg*'s two damage control zones, each with self-sufficient ventilation. The console is used to access the ship's Integrated Battle Damage Control System (IBDCS). *(Guy Toremans)*

cabins being the most 'crowded' ones. Ratings are accommodated in compartments for four or six persons, with toilets and washrooms in close proximity. Chief Petty Officers (CPO) and Petty Officers (PO) enjoy two- or four-berth cabins with private lavatories and showers, while officers have two-berth cabins with private lavatories. The commanding officer has his own living/office space, bedroom and private bathroom. Each crew member has his/her own locker, as well as stowage bins underneath the berths, whilst every cabin features a writing desk and a place to sit. The accommodation concept satisfies mixed-gender crewing requirements. The major part of the accommodation is located in the forward area of the ship. Furniture, wall and ceiling systems have a low weight but high shock resistance, are easy to remove and to reinstall, and feature good noise reduction qualities and high durability. The mess rooms are multifunctional and located next to the galley. By moving the room dividers the officers' and CPO mess rooms can be turned into one consolidated mess that can function as a briefing or presentation area.

PROPULSION

The propulsion plant comprises two Tognum MTU 20V 1163 TB93 diesel engines, each of which is provided with its own shaft line and controlled pitch propeller. The two 7.4MW, water-cooled, 20-cylinder, four-stroke diesel engines produce a total power output of 14.8MW via a cross-connected gearbox, enabling a maximum speed in excess of 26 knots to be achieved. Operational range is 4,100 nautical miles at 15 knots. Under single shaft propulsion, the corvettes can cruise at 20 knots. The gearboxes are equipped with independent programmable logic control systems to cover all gearbox monitoring and safety functions. Even in the case of a total IMCS breakdown, the main machinery could be controlled and monitored from independent local control stations. The main electrical power supply system is fed by four generator sets, each providing a power output of 570kW via two switchboard panels. These provide a redundancy level of 100 per cent. The operation, control and monitoring of the electrical plant is mostly automated, ensuring that a sufficient number of genera-

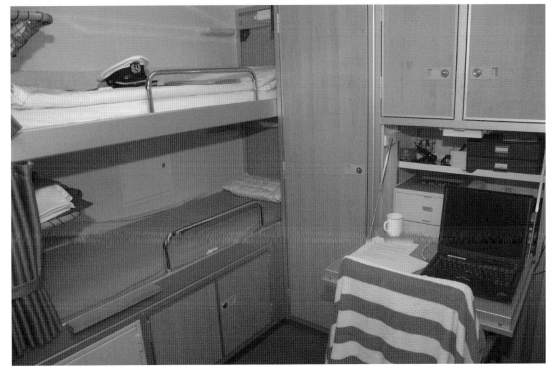

This photo of an officer's cabin on *Magdeburg* reveals good standards of accommodation in spite of the class's small size. *(Guy Toremans)*

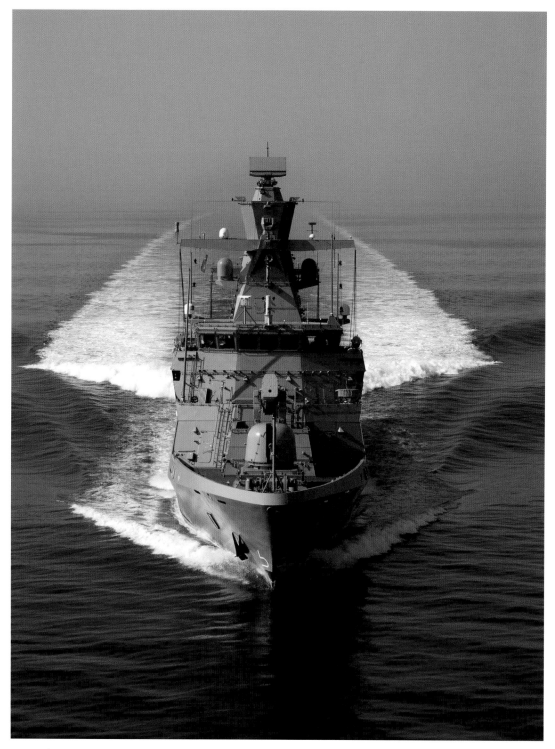

Braunschweig pictured at speed during propulsion trials in the autumn of 2007. A twin-diesel, twin-shaft arrangement with cross-connected gearbox provides a maximum speed in excess of 26 knots and a range of over 4,000 nautical miles at economical speeds. *(Blohm & Voss, TKMS)*

tors is always available for both manual requirements and automatic processes. Fuel and provision requirements have been calculated to allow the ship to remain at sea for at least seven days without having to resupply. With a supply ship available, a K-130 class corvette can remain at sea for up to twenty-one days. Two replenishment stations are provided to transfer fuel and water, either alongside or from the stern.

THE K-130 CLASS OPERATIONAL EXPERIENCE TO DATE

FGS *Braunschweig* (F 260): The lead ship of the K-130 class, *Braunschweig,* was commissioned on 16 April 2008. Being the first of her class, she was required to undergo extensive post-delivery tests. The integration and trials period revealed a number of technical problems and issues that had to be rectified. As a result, she spent additional time in dry dock, alongside and undergoing further trials. In May 2008, the corvette deployed to the Mediterranean to take part in the Italian Navy sponsored multinational Exercise 'Mare Aperto 2008'. This was followed by a period of warm-water trials in the Red Sea. Upon her return home she also carried out tests with the Schiebel S-100 Camcopter unmanned aerial vehicle.

In the meantime, during a trial run with *Oldenburg,* the fourth of class to be launched, significant problems with the gearing system were identified. The gearbox's screws loosened and fell into the gears, causing material damage. The shipyard, subcontractors, the Federal Office for Defence Technology & Procurement, the German Ministry of Defence, and the German Navy, all put a lot of effort into the challenging process of identifying and solving the underlying problem. The gearboxes, produced by MAAG in Switzerland, presented well-known Swiss precision work. However, they also contained some deficiencies that were not apparent from early trials and only revealed themselves after a period of operation. The German Naval Staff ultimately decided to remove the gearboxes of all the ships in the class, causing the enforced lay-up of the class until rectification work was complete. Another issue discovered during early operations was an alignment problem when firing the RAM missiles from the CIC, with the weapons jittering around the target. This problem was solved after a revision to the contracted specification by early 2012.

Braunschweig has now recommenced her test

programme and will deploy again to the Mediterranean in the early summer of 2012 to carry out a second warm-water trial period, followed by live firings with her RAM system in the North Sea. After summer leave she is scheduled to take part in the Danex/Northern Coasts 2012 exercise (31 August to 14 September 2012). Upon successfully passing her German Operational Sea Test (GOST) at the end of September 2012, *Braunschweig* should finally be declared fully operational. She will probably subsequently be deployed to the Eastern Mediterranean in support of UNIFIL Operation MTF 448 off Lebanon.

FGS *Magdeburg* (F 261): The second of the K-130 series, *Magdeburg* commissioned on 22 September 2008. However, due to the gearbox problems mentioned above, it was effectively not until November 2010 that she started her post-delivery trials in the North and Baltic Seas. The corvette was initially taken through a series of tests to see whether the platform and systems were working according to specification. These sea-readiness checks were followed by cold-weather trials off Hammerfest in Norway in February 2011. Immediately afterwards, *Magdeburg* underwent extensive compliance tests on the integrated weapon and sensor suites in order to assess the ship's combat capability, validate the combat system and sensor suites, check combat data gathering capabilities, and conduct target acquisition and tracking tests to calibrate the systems, and measure radiation levels against a variety of targets.

Subsequently, *Magdeburg* successfully conducted landing trials with a Sea Lynx and Mk41 Sea King helicopter.

In September 2011 the corvette took part in Exercise Danex/Northern Coasts 2011, the first large scale exercise in which a K-130 class unit participated. It was an excellent tool for enhancing the ship's war-fighting skills and a good opportunity to assess her combat capability in a wide variety of situations. Upon completion of the German Navy's annual fast attack craft exercise, *Magdeburg* successfully concluded her cold-water trials off Norway and Sweden in the winter of 2011. After a brief dockyard period early in 2012, she underwent her GOST in March/April, followed by a five-week work-up period with Flag Officer Sea Training (FOST) in the United Kingdom. The corvette is scheduled to deploy in support of the UNIFIL MTF-448 off Lebanon by the end of summer 2012.

A rare view of *Oldenburg* on sea trials off Heligoland during June 2008. The failure of a gearbox during trials has delayed completion of the K-130 programme by around three years. *(Blohm & Voss, TKMS)*

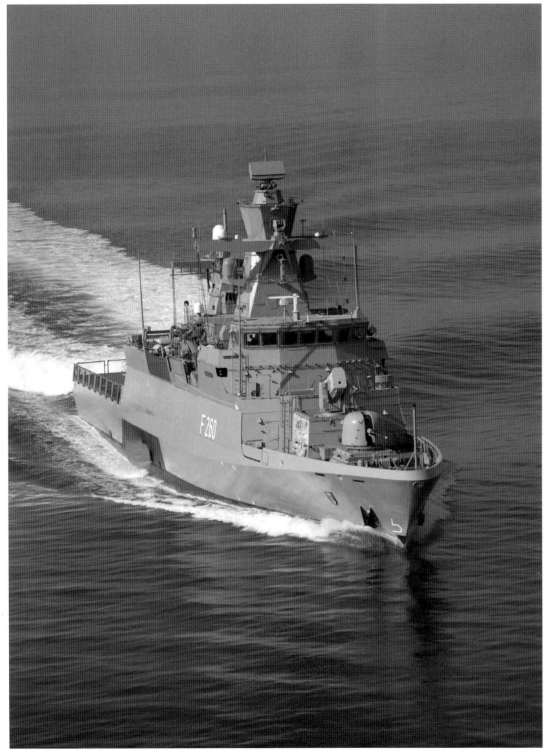

Another view of *Braunschweig* on 2007 propulsion trials. Completion of the K-130 programme will provide the German Navy with a class of new ships optimised to meet evolving tactical and operational requirements. *(Blohm & Voss, TKMS)*

FGS *Erfurt* (F262): *Erfurt* commenced her sea acceptance trials in March 2012. Her official commissioning is expected by the end of 2012.[5]

FGS *Oldenburg* (F263) and FGS *Ludwigshafen* (F264): *Oldenburg* and *Ludwigshafen* should finish their sea acceptance trials during the summer of 2012 and are scheduled to enter service in the autumn of the same year.

The three last-mentioned corvettes are scheduled to start operational work-up post-commissioning. They will take part in both national and international exercises before embarking on their maiden operational deployments.

Fregattenkapitän Andreas Kutsch – Staff Officer of *Einsatzflottille* 1 in Kiel – has confirmed that all the K-130 class's problems have been solved: 'I am not able to predict the exact dates when the K-130 corvettes will reach their full operational capability but we anticipate having all five *Braunschweig* class corvettes fully operational end 2012. We are keen to deploy FGS *Magdeburg* in support of the UNIFIL Maritime Task Force 448 off Lebanon within the running year [2012].'

He added, 'As for the exact commissioning dates for the remaining platforms [*Erfurt, Oldenburg* and *Ludwigshafen*], subsequent training, full operational capability and potential deployment periods, these are still open, but we are confident that by end 2012 all corvettes will be in service.'

Clearly, completion of the K-130 corvette programme will give the German Navy the ability to deploy innovative platforms outfitted with appropriate equipment for their intended roles. Optimised to meet the German Navy's tactical and operational requirements, the five *Braunschweig* class ships will be despatched worldwide to undertake surveillance missions, embargo and counter-drug operations, as well as, potentially, to participate in combat missions either alone or within national or multinational task groups. One should certainly not be surprised to see the corvettes taking part in counter-piracy operations off the Horn of Africa in the near future.

THE WAY AHEAD

Faced with a need to replace its ten remaining fast attack craft of the *Gepard* class (Type 143A), the Germany Navy began conceptual work on a second batch of corvettes back in 2007. Initially code named the K-131 project, this has now been renamed the multi-role combat ship or *Mehrzweckkampfschiff* 180 (MKS-180) in German terminology. It encompasses the acquisition of a medium-sized surface warship with a primary role of crisis-response operations and surveillance tasks worldwide.

One of the lessons already learned from the K-130 programme was that, although significantly larger than the fast patrol boats, the new corvettes have still proved to be a bit too small to operate comfortably and effectively in support of some of the German Navy's growing mission requirements around the globe. The new ships will therefore be significantly larger.

Details currently released about the new MKS-180 project suggest that it may involve up to six units in the range of 2,500 tons with core anti-air warfare (AAW) and anti-surface warfare (ASuW) capabilities and the potential for addition mission-specific modules to be shipped. A construction contract may be allocated before 2020 to follow on from the current F-125 stabilisation frigate programme, with all six units likely to be in service by 2027/28.

Notes:

1. The BWB is Germany's defence procurement agency. It was originally envisaged that further batches of the class would be ordered, with an ultimate total of around fifteen units. In the event, no further contracts have been placed.

2. It was initially planned to equip the K-130 class with eight Polyphem-S missiles. These wire-guided, surface-to-surface missiles, with a range of more than 60km and equipped with an IR-camera in the search head, would have been housed in vertical launchers arranged below the flight deck. The overall Polyphem missile programme was cancelled in 2003.

3. The K-130's various sensors, weapons, equipment and missile workstations are linked for a network that is based on a fast Ethernet infrastructure in a redundant configuration.

4. A fixed pressurised water/foam extinguishing plant can also be remotely activated in the machinery room.

5. The delivery and commissioning of all the three final members of the K-130 class was delayed until the gearbox problem could be rectified and builders' trials completed. The overall delay to the programme is probably in the order of three years.

Braunschweig pictured during post-delivery trials in 2008. With gearbox repairs now completed on all five vessels, the entire class should be operational before the end of 2012. *(German Navy)*

A September 2011 view of *Braunschweig*, with RBS15 missiles installed. The planned, follow-on, MKS-180 class will be larger still, encompassing lessons learned to date from *Braunschweig* and her sisters. *(German Navy)*

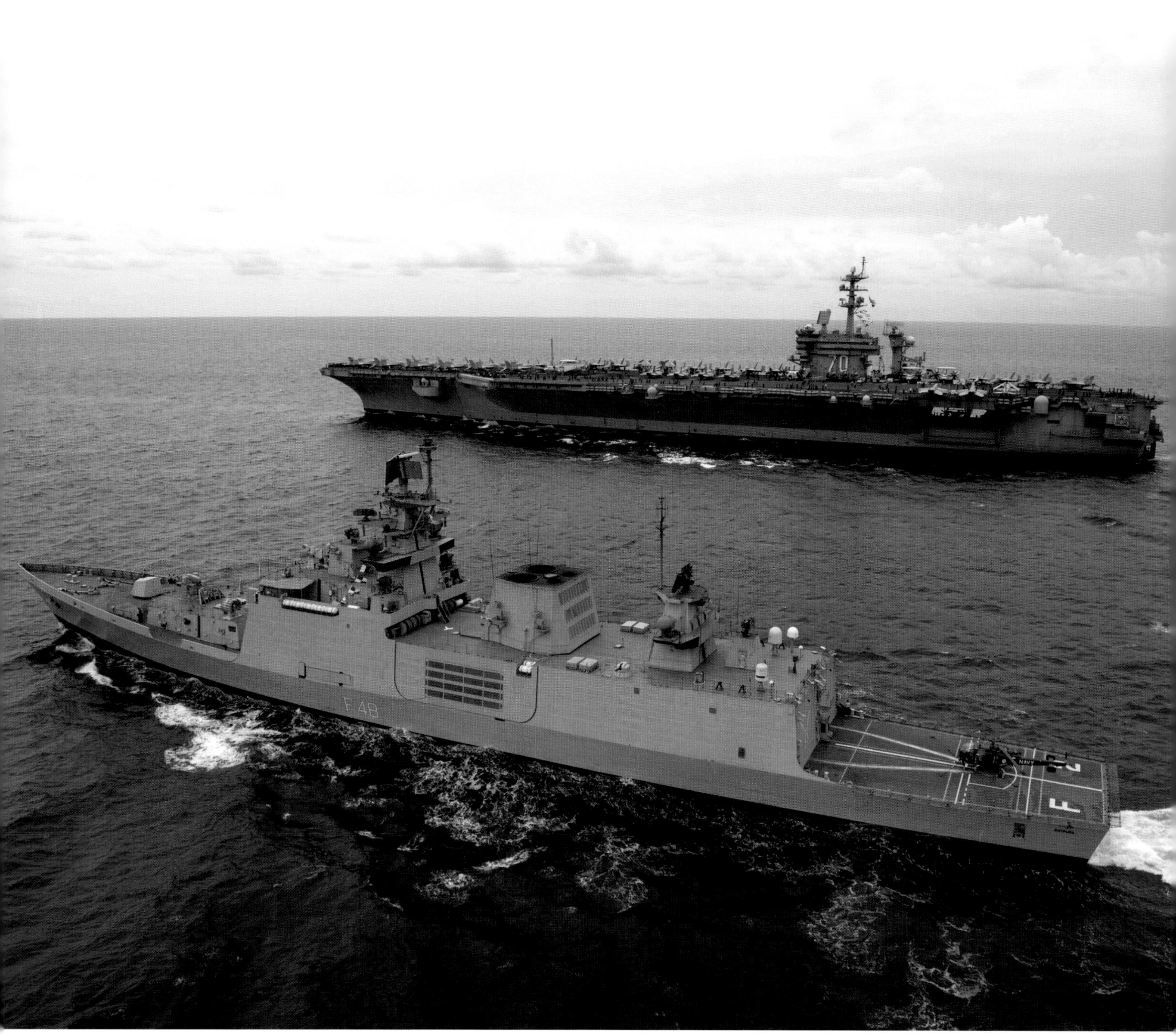
F 48
70
F

3.4 SIGNIFICANT SHIPS

Author:
Mrityunjoy Mazumdar

SHIVALIK CLASS FRIGATES

An Overview of India's Project 17 and Project 17A Stealth Frigates

The much delayed commissioning of India's *Shivalik*, the first of three Project 17 (P17) stealthy frigates built by Mazagon Docks Ltd (MDL), at Naval Dockyard, Mumbai, on 29 April 2010 heralded a new era for India's naval shipbuilding industry and the Indian Navy's in-house design bureau, the Directorate of Naval Design (DND). Addressing the media during the commissioning ceremony, the ship's commanding officer, Captain M D Suresh remarked that he was very satisfied with the ship. Crucially, he added, 'this frigate opens up new tactical exploitation possibilities for the Indian Navy', as its stealth capabilities are both a generation ahead of other warships in the Indian fleet and also comparable to other stealth warships elsewhere. Captain Suresh's words embody the significance of these frigates, which represent a step change in features and indigenous naval shipbuilding capabilities over previous DND designs such as the P15 *Delhi* class destroyers and P16/16A series frigates.[1]

Costing around Rs. 2,800 crores (US$525m)

Opposite: India's Project 17 *Shivalik class* frigate *Satpura* operating alongside the US aircraft carrier *Carl Vinson* (CVN-70) in the Bay of Bengal in April 2012. The stealthy Project 17 class offers a step change in Indian naval capabilities compared with previous indigenous warship designs. *(US Navy)*

each, these ships represent many 'firsts' for the DND.[2] These include:

- The DND's first design with enhanced 'stealth' features, notably reduced Radar Cross Section (RCS), Infrared (IR) and Radiated Noise signatures.
- Its first design to allow helicopter operations up to Sea State 6 due to improved sea-keeping.
- Its first design to incorporate CODOG (COmbined Diesel Or Gas) turbine propulsion.
- Optimised hull and propeller design to allow exceptionally high cavitation inception speeds in excess of 22 knots.
- Increased automation and reliability through use of an Integrated Platform Management System (IPMS).
- Enhanced battle damage survivability through zoning of weapon, power and ventilation systems, including a Total Atmospheric Control System (TACS) which allows for prolonged operations in a nuclear, biological and chemical (NBC) environment.
- Its first ship with a powerful ATM switch based fibre-optic local area network system, AISDN-17, integrating voice, ship data and tactical data in real time to present a comprehensive situational awareness for ship and weapons system operators.
- Improved habitability, including facilities for two

female officers, through use of Korean-designed modular accommodation.

According to Rear Admiral K N Vaidyanathan, who heads the DND, *Shivalik* 'heralds a paradigm shift in the design of future surface combatants for the Indian Navy', because of these new features that now serve as key design drivers going forward. In the *Shivalik* class, the DND took the bold step of designing a contemporary, stealthy surface combatant with a distinctive, home-grown appearance. By doing so, India joined a select group of nations – France, Germany, Italy, Japan, South Korea, Netherlands, Sweden, the United Kingdom and the United States (as well as China, to a growing extent) – that have developed these state of the art warships.

DESIGN HISTORY

The Project 17 design was conceived in c.1992–93 around Naval Staff Requirements (NSR) calling for a state-of-the-art, multi-role, CODOG-powered platform capable of performing anti-air and anti-submarine warfare missions. The ship was to have low observable (stealth features) and enhanced sea-keeping performance (to allow weapon and helicopter operations in Sea State 6), as well as good endurance and survivability, high levels of automation and excellent habitability.

Discarding a low-risk proposal to convert the steam-powered P16 *Godavari* hull form into a CODOG-powered frigate, DND chose to go with a higher risk approach of designing a new, modern hull form incorporating stealth and enhanced performance over existing frigates in Indian service. The then Director General, Naval Design (DGND), Vice Admiral Rajeshwer Nath, chose to acquire stealth technologies from overseas, whilst carrying out design work in-house to the maximum extent possible. This decision set the groundwork for creating a design group specialising in various aspects of stealth design.[3]

Concept studies commenced in 1993 and various concept designs were presented to Indian Naval Headquarters in early 1994. Approval was obtained shortly thereafter. Initial concept studies were carried out by a small 'Gas Turbine Frigate' group under then Commander K N Vaidyanathan. The frigate was initially named Frigate 2000, then Frigate 2001, and finally Project 17. The ship's basic design – the hull form, structure, internal arrangements, stealth, propulsion, weapons and overall configuration – commenced in 1994. Unlike previous warship projects, a separate funding stream to conduct model testing and significant other design work, as well as propulsion system integration, was obtained by 1995. After the preliminary hull design and propeller shapes were evolved, model testing – at MARIN (Maritime Research Institute Netherlands), the Dutch hydrodynamics and maritime technology research institute – commenced in July 1995. Test results closely matched DND predictions – to within 2.5 per cent according to Vaidyanathan. In parallel, other design studies into signature management – RCS, IR and underwater radiated noise – as well as wind tunnel tests and propulsion systems integration – were concluded. All these were completed by 1997.

Tests and design studies were carried out both by the DND and by consultants at various establishments at home and overseas. For example, the UK's DERA was appointed to carry out underwater noise studies, whilst Germany's IABG was consulted for RCS reduction studies. Having achieved desired RCS levels on the bare hull – in the order of less than 1 per cent of the ship's RCS – using specialised software packages such as the German RAMSES, DND specialists focused on the weapon and sensors to achieve RCS reductions with exposed equipment. While the team was successful in reducing the RCS

of the Oto Melara Super Rapid mount, they were not so successful with Russian suppliers. While the bulk of the design was done at DND, the shipbuilder, MDL, also carried out detail design under the technical guidance of DND. MDL produced the bulk of the production drawings for the ship.

CONTRACT AND CONSTRUCTION

By January 1998, India's high level Cabinet Committee on Security had sanctioned the construction of three P17 frigates at a projected cost of Rs. 2,250 crores (c.US$600m at prevailing exchange rates) with deliveries to commence from December 2005. MDL, in turn, received a letter of intent in February 1998. The plan was for MDL to commence fabrication sometime during July/August of 1999. However, a switch from the specified British steel (which was no longer available) to an alternative based on Russian D-40S specification, as well as incomplete design data for the weapons suite, resulted in production being postponed by seventeen months. As such, construction of the first ship,

Yard 12617, only commenced on 20 December 2000. Formal keel laying followed on 11 July 2001 and the hull – without superstructure – was launched as *Shivalik* on 18 April 2003. Subsequently, a series of design-related delays – as well as a deferment of GE LM2500 gas turbine commissioning due to US support being withheld following a paperwork mix up – meant that it took nearly six years to complete construction and outfitting. Sea trials ultimately commenced early in 2009 and the first full power was achieved on 24 August of that year. MDL finally delivered *Shivalik* to the Indian Navy on 30 March 2010 and the ship was commissioned on 29 April 2010.

Keel-laying for the next two ships, Yard numbers 12727 and 12637, took place on 31 October 2002 and 30 September 2003 respectively. Yard 12727 was launched as *Satpura* on 4 June 2004 and delivered to the Indian Navy on 9 July 2011. This was followed by commissioning on 20 August 2011; several months later than the planned November 2010 delivery date. Similarly, delivery of Yard 12737,

An archive photograph of the first Indian Project 17 frigate, *Shivalik*, at Mazagon Dock Ltd in Mumbai on her launch day, 18 April 2003. Significant construction delays meant that it was to be another seven years before she finally commissioned. *(Mrityunjoy Mazumdar/ Mazagon Dock Ltd)*

which was launched as *Sahyadri* on 27 May 2005, is also currently running more than a year behind a schedule that has already been significantly revised. She should have been handed over by 31 March 2012 but this did not happen. However, MDL finally achieved delivery on 25 June 2012.

Although protracted construction of complex warships is an endemic global problem, the extent of the delays with the Project 17 class is worthy of further discussion.[4] The reasons for these, which amounted to around five years in total, can be summarised as follows:

■ Commencement of construction was delayed, as already referenced above, by around seventeen months due to delays in completing structural drawings and steel sourcing issues. Alternative D-40S specification steel could only be obtained once a procurement agreement was reached with the Russian producer.[5]

■ Significant delays also arose from designs not being frozen prior to start of production, deferred decisions on main systems, and late receipt of binding design and interface data from suppliers. The P17 was primarily designed around Russian weapon systems and the breakdown of the centralised Soviet-era supply chain caused particular problems. In addition, there were some significant systems changes; for example the substitution of a combined Barak 1 and AK630M anti-missile defence complex for the planned 'Kashtan' system following a poor experience with the latter on the first Russian-built Project 1136.6 frigate, *Talwar*. The substitute system was only ready for installation when *Shivalik* was 87 per cent complete, necessitating major structural and electrical reworking. The net result of evolving changes to weapons and other systems, as well as to accommodation layouts, meant that *Shivalik* went through as many as 758 modifications post launching.

■ The indigenous supply chain – primarily small- and medium-sized enterprises – initially struggled to deliver components and equipment that met

Right: Two views of the third and final Project 17 frigate, *Sahyadri*, under construction at Mazagon Dock Ltd in Mumbai. The photos indicate the inadequate infrastructure at the shipyard which was one of the factors behind protracted completion times. *Sahyadri* had yet to be delivered at the time of writing. *(Ajai Shulka / Mrityunjoy Mazumdar)*

the stringent quality standards established for the project. Procuring machinery that achieved demanding vibration and airborne noise specifications was a particular challenge. Although teams from the Indian Navy's Directorate of Quality Assurance did much to help firms develop robust quality systems, the learning curve was steep and delays resulted.

■ There was lack of support from certain overseas original equipment manufacturers. For instance, the paperwork mix up by GE mentioned above with respect to technical assistance approval from the US State Department meant that its technicians could not support post-installation pre-commissioning activities on *Shivalik* for a time. Italy's Avio had to be used to provide a workaround for four months until the issue was resolved.

■ To an extent, inadequate infrastructure at MDL led to capacity issues as well as inefficient material flow.

These factors also resulted in major cost escalation, amounting to c.260 per cent over the initial estimate, reportedly more according to some sources. An additional problem was that the initial cost estimates were not very good to begin with, being based on less complex ships, on 1994 rather than 1998 prices, and encompassing unrealistic exchange rate assumptions. The overall picture was examined by India's Comptroller and Auditor General (CAG) in a report on India's indigenous warship building programmes published in 2011, which looked at the increases in P17 production costs between the origi-

Two views of the first Project 17 stealth frigate *Shivalik* on sea trials off Mumbai during the first half of 2009. She was finally delivered to the Indian Navy on 30 March 2010, commissioning on 29 April of the same year. There were multiple reasons for her prolonged construction time. *(Indian Navy via S Aroor/Livefist)*

nally approved price in January 2008 and a revised price sanctioned in March 2006 in some detail.[6] These are set out in Table 3.4.1.

The CAG explained the principal reasons for the extensive cost overrun as follows: 'The sharp increase in costs was mainly due to the increase in cost of weapons and equipment. This was primarily due to change in weapons and equipment from the originally envisaged choices. The initial estimates of Russian equipment were based on Russian supplies made for P16A and P15 warship projects in the 1980s and early 1990s. The commercialisation of the military hardware industry of Russia, which replaced the State controlled regime, also pushed up purchase prices. Additionally, costs rose because of the effort to indigenise various equipment. Another major issue was the increase in labour man days to be used in construction which increased by 40 per cent from an estimated 1.5 million to 2.1 million man days. This increase, coupled with the wage revision in MDL in 1998, contributed to the higher total costs. Other factors included costs incurred for hiring installation specialists, increase in sub-contracting impacting costs, and increase in material overheads.'

Table 3.4.1: PROJECT 17 COST INFLATION[1]

COST CATEGORY[2]	ORIGINAL SANCTION (JAN 1998)	REVISED SANCTION (MARCH 2006)	PERCENTAGE INCREASE
Major Equipment & Material	1,414.34	4,062.75	187.25%
Shipyard Cost	506.44	2,373.27	368.62%
Sub Total 1: Basic Shipbuilding Cost	**1,920.78**	**6,436.02**	**235.07%**
Shipyard Profit	137.22	482.70	251.77%
Sub Total 2: Total Shipbuilding Cost	**2,058.00**	**6,919.00**	**236.20%**
Base & Depot Spares	192.00	965.00	402.6%
MDL Modernisation	Nil	217.00	n/a
Total Programme Costs[3]	**2,250.00**	**8,101.00**	**260.04%**

Notes:

1. Data from the Indian Comptroller & Auditor General's *Report No 32 of 2010-11 for the period ended March 2010, Performance Audit of Indigenous Construction of Indian Naval Warships*.

2. Figures are expressed in Indian crore. 1 crore is 10m or 0.01bn rupees. So Rs. 2250 crores is the equivalent of Rs. 22.5bn. Rs. 100 crores also is currently the equivalent of c.US$18.5m.

3. One recent report in *The Hindu* has suggested total programme cost is closer to Rs. 10,000 crores.

The CAG also noted problems in concluding shipbuilding contracts, which – in the case of the P17 class – only finally took place in June 2008, well after the original date estimated for delivery. As such, the rights and responsibilities of the contracting parties remained undefined and a large part of the construction period was without an effective control framework. This situation largely arose due to a failure to reach agreement between the Navy and MDL on two counts: an assessment of required labour effort – 'man days' – and the revised delivery schedule. Although efforts were made to introduce a fixed price element into the P17 programme – *Shivalik* was to be built on a cost plus basis, but the expectation was for the two follow-on ships to be constructed on the 'frozen' cost of the first ship – the delay in agreeing contracts merely formalised the extensive cost growth that had already occurred.

However, to be fair, this was the first time a complex programme of this magnitude and complexity had been undertaken by the DND, MDL and Indian industry. As such, the learning curve was much steeper and took much longer to assimilate than anticipated. Valuable lessons have been learned from the overall P17 construction process that should assist the successful execution of subsequent shipbuilding programmes.

OVERALL SHIP DESCRIPTION

A summary of principal P17 design characteristics is set out in Table 3.4.2. The class has an overall length of 142.5m, a length between perpendiculars of 132m, a beam of 16.9m, a moulded depth of 9.2m, a design draught of 4.5m and a maximum

A photograph of the second Project 17 stealth frigate, *Satpura*, on 20 August 2011, her commissioning day. The original plan was for her construction contract to be based on the frozen cost of the first ship but delays in agreeing contracts meant this did not work out as planned. *(Kapil Chadni)*

draught of 7.1m. Standard displacement is over 5,000 tons, while full load displacement is c.6,200 tons. The hull has a high waterplane area, as well as a relatively sharp turn to the hull sections around the bilge for improved roll damping and improved sea-keeping, while the relatively large rudders give the ship excellent manoeuvring performance. Roll resistance and sea-keeping performance have been found to be exceptionally good during sea trials, surpassing those of larger designs like the P15 *Delhi* class destroyers. Flow resistance has been reduced by minimising the effects of appendages through optimising the rake of the propeller shafting, the flow adapted orientation of the A-frames (shaft brackets) and careful placement of rudders and stabilisers.

To lower its RCS, *Shivalik* has a flared hull and what appears to be a continuous superstructure block with sloped walls à la the French *La Fayette* class frigates, but is actually a visually integrated, three-piece superstructure. This features a middle section (with enclosed curtains for the ship's boats) that is physically disconnected from the rest of the superstructure, being supported by internal bulkheads and the funnel. This serves as an expansion joint. There are eight deck levels – four above the main deck, four below. Internal layout features wide alleyways and overall spaciousness. The large bridge is well designed with ergonomic consoles. The ship sets hitherto unprecedented standards for habitability. Spacious modular accommodation designed in Korea and supplied by Godrej Boyce is a complete departure from existing Indian Navy warships.

Table 3.4.2.

SHIVALIK PRINCIPAL PARTICULARS

Building Information:

Fabrication Commenced:	20 December 2000
Launched:	18 April 2003
Delivered:	30 March 2010
Builders:	Mazagon Dock Ltd, Mumbai, India

Dimensions:

Displacement:	6,200 tons full load displacement.
Overall Hull Dimensions:	142.5m x 16.9m x 4.5m (7.1m maximum). Length between perpendiculars is 132.0m.

Weapons Systems:

Missiles:	1 x single S3-90 launcher for 24 Shtil 1 (SA-N-12 Grizzly) surface-to-air missiles. 4 x 8-cell Barak 1 PDMS.
	1 x 3R-14N-17 8-cell launcher for 3M-54 Klub-N (SS-N-27 Sizzler) missile system. Includes surface-to-surface, anti-submarine and land attack cruise missiles.
Guns:	1 x 76mm Oto Melara Super Rapid. 2 x AK-630M guns as part of CIWS. Light machine guns.
ASW Systems:	2 x 12-tube RBU 6000 A/S rocket launchers.
Aircraft:	2 x AgustaWestland Sea King Mk42B helicopters or equivalent.
Countermeasures:	BEL Ellora electronic warfare suite. CSN-56 Kavach decoy launching system. Mareech torpedo decoys and towed noisemakers.
Principal Sensors:	1 x MR-760 M2EM Fregat (Top Plate) 3D search/target designation radar and 4 x 3R-90 (Front Dome) illuminators for Shtil 1 system.
	1 x Elta EL/M-2238 ER search/target designation radar. 2 x Elta EL/M-2221 fire control radars for PDMS/CIWS.
	1 x 3Ts-25E Garpun Bal (Plank Shave) target designation/fire control radar for Klub-N system.
	Surface search and navigation radars. MkXI IFF integrated with search radars. HUMSA-NG hull sonar. Towed array to be fitted.
Combat System:	BEL CMS-17/CAIO-17. BEL CCS Mk2 communications system and data links. Rukmani satellite communications.

Propulsion Systems:

Machinery:	CODOG. 2 x Pielstick 16 PA6 STC diesels each rated at 5.7MW. 2 x GE LM2500 gas turbines each rated at 18MW. Two shafts.
Speed and Range:	Designed maximum speed is 30+ knots. Range is 5,000 nautical miles at 18 knots.

Other Details:

Complement:	Typical core crew is c.255, including c.35 officers. An embarked air wing would add another c.15-20 personnel.
Class:	Three Project 17 class vessels have been ordered: *Shivalik* (F47) commissioned on 29 April 2010, *Satpura* (F48) commissioned on 20 August 2011 and the yet to be delivered *Sahyadri* (F49).

Certainly, officers' quarters are well appointed. In another first, the ship also has bespoke quarters for two female officers.

Ship's complement is c.255 including approximately thirty-five officers, plus an aviation group of between fourteen and twenty-two depending on number and type of embarked helicopters. While crew size could be reduced, manpower costs are low and the Indian Navy likes to operate ships with adequate manning so that all combat systems are fully manned at all times. Navy officers also contend

there is no substitute for having adequate numbers of personnel to conduct effective damage control operations should the need arise. The galley can prepare meals for four hundred at a time. Key equipment includes a rotary *dosa* maker and a stabilised chapatti maker. Getting these to work within the specified pitch and roll requirements (roll +/–30º and pitch 0 +/–15º) necessitated special roller bearings that posed some unique design and procurement challenges.

A centre-line passage between the two helicopter

hangars provides a clear lobby between the helicopter deck and the inside of the ship. The Larsen and Toubro supplied flush deck helicopter traversing system, besides lowering RCS, gives the ship much improved operational flexibility for the helicopter.

At a first glance, *Shivalik*'s appearance is similar to the Project 1135.6 *Talwar* class frigates from Russia's Severnoye Design Bureau, leading many observers to conclude, erroneously, that the Indian ship drew upon *Talwar*'s design. In fact, P17 is a wholly indigenous design, created 'from scratch' by

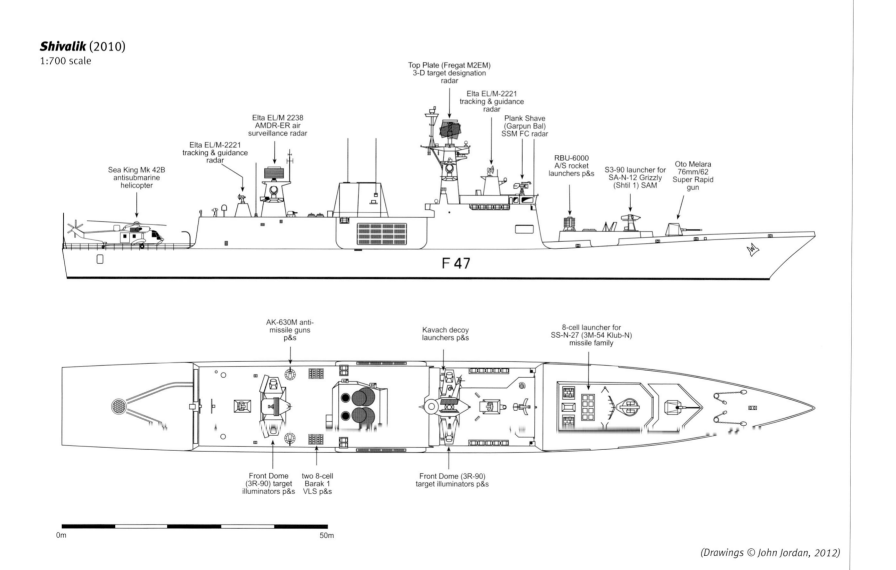

Shivalik (2010)
1:700 scale

Top Plate (Fregat M2EM) 3-D target designation radar

Elta EL/M-2221 tracking & guidance radar

Elta EL/M 2238 AMDR-ER air surveillance radar

Plank Shave (Garpun Bal) SSM FC radar

Elta EL/M-2221 tracking & guidance radar

RBU-6000 A/S rocket launchers p&s

Sea King Mk 42B antisubmarine helicopter

S3-90 launcher for SA-N-12 Grizzly (Shtil 1) SAM

Oto Melara 76mm/62 Super Rapid gun

F 47

AK-630M anti-missile guns p&s

Kavach decoy launchers p&s

8-cell launcher for SS-N-27 (3M-54 Klub-N) missile family

Front Dome (3R-90) target illuminators p&s

two 8-cell Barak 1 VLS p&s

Front Dome (3R-90) target illuminators p&s

0m   50m

(Drawings © John Jordan, 2012)

With an overall length of 142.5m and a full load displacement of c.6,200 tons, *Shivalik* is a relatively large frigate. While certain aspects – particularly forward arrangements – are smilar to the smaller Russian-built Project 1135.6 *Talwar* class, there are also significant differences. This photograph was taken during sea trials in 2009, when her F47 pennant number was still painted in black. *(Indian Navy via S Aroor/Livefist)*

Indian naval designers. Indeed, P17's concept design and hull form was completed over two years *prior* to concluding the contract for the Project 1135.6 ships. The reasons for the similarity between the *Shivalik* and *Talwar* are two-fold. Around the time *Shivalik*'s design was being developed, discussions were underway with Russia for the acquisition of the *Talwar* class frigates. 'It was as a result of our comments and reviews on the 1135.6 that the Russians evolved a shape for *Talwar* which looks somewhat similar to P17', according to Rear Admiral Vaidyanathan. Additionally, since both ships have similar weapons packages, it is logical, for example, that the forward arrangements are nearly identical. However, as set out in Table 3.4.3, the two types also reveal significant differences.

WEAPONRY & COMBAT SYSTEMS

The P17 weapons suite reflects the class's multi-role specification. They have been designed for anti-air warfare (AAW), anti-submarine warfare (ASW) and anti-surface warfare (ASuW) missions in a network-centric war-fighting environment.

The primary AAW weapon is the medium range Shtil 1 (NATO: SA-N-12 Grizzly) surface-to-air system with the semi-active radar homing 9M317E surface-to-air missile (SAM). These missiles are fired

from a single arm 3S-90E launcher. Twenty-four rounds are carried in a below decks rotary launcher. The missiles are directed by four MR-90/3R-90 Orekh (NATO: Front Dome) illuminators to engage up to four targets simultaneously. Two M-22E gyro-stabilised telesights mounted atop the bridge are also thought to provide an electro-optical backup to the MR-90 illuminators. The 9M317E has a much improved engagement zone over the earlier version of the Shtil/Kashmir (NATO: SA-N-7 Gadfly) system with the 9M38 missile that is installed on the Indian Navy's P15 class. The 9M317 has a minimum range of 3.5km, a maximum range of 42km (possibly as much as 50km) and an effective altitude of 5m to 15,000m against aircraft. The missile can engage inbound anti-ship cruise missiles flying at altitudes of 5m to 10,000m at ranges

between 3.5km and12km. The missile also has an advertised anti-surface capability at ranges of 3.5km to 25km. It has a length of 5.55m, a diameter of 0.4m, a span of 0.86m with fins extended and a weight of around 715kg. It can engage targets flying at 1200m/s and manoeuvre at up to 24Gs.

Point defence against aircraft and anti-ship missiles is primarily by thirty-two Barak 1 missiles and two AK-630M gun mounts. The Barak 1 missiles are mounted in two clusters of twin, eight-cell vertical launch units. They have a maximum range of c.10–12km. The AK-630M guns, with a 4,000–5,000 rounds per minute rate of fire, are there to take care of 'leakers' that get past the outer screen of Baraks. The 76.2mm Oto Melara Super Rapid gun, which fires a variety of ammunition types at up to 120 rounds per minute, can also be

Table 3.4.3: PROJECT 17 *SHIVALIK* & PROJECT 1135.6 *TALWAR* COMPARISON

CLASS	PROJECT 17 *SHIVALIK*	PROJECT 1135.6 *TALWAR*
Design Inception	1994	1997
Full Load Displacement:	6,200 tons	4,000 tons
Principal Dimensions:	142.5m x 16.9m x 4.5m (7.1m maximum)	124.8m x 15.2m x 4.5m
Propulsion:	CODOG, 30+ knots maximum	COGAG, 30+ knots maximum
	2 x LM2500 turbines, 2 x 16 PA6 STC diesels	2 x DS-71 cruise and 2 x DT-59 boost turbines
Aircraft:	2 x Mk42B Sea King helicopters	1 x Ka-31 helicopter
Crew:	c.255	c.180

Two unusual aerial views of the lead Project 1135.6 frigate, *Talwar*, during an Indian Presidential Fleet Review in 2006. Although there have been claims that the Project 17 design was influenced by these Russian-built ships, *Shivalik* and her sisters were actually conceived before *Talwar* and her sisters were ordered. *(Mrityunjoy Mazumdar)*

Shivalik's principal air defence capability is provided by the Russian Shtil 1 (NATO SA-N-12 Grizzly) surface-to-air missile system. These photographs show the Fregat (Top Plate) surveillance and target indication radar, 3R-90 Orekh (Front Dome) illuminators and 3S-90 launcher that form the system's principal components. Note also the M-22E telesights below the illuminator that provide an electro-optical backup. *(Mrityunjoy Mazumdar)*

used in the anti-cruise missile role, engaging targets at ranges of over 5km. Two Elta EL/M-2221 fire control directors control the Barak 1 missiles and guns, complemented by a mast mounted EON-51 electro-optic director.

Long-range ASuW strike capability is provided by the 3M-54 Klub-N (NATO: SS-N-27 Sizzler) missile system, with one eight-cell 3R-14N-17 missile launcher. Klub-N comprises a family of missiles that includes two anti-ship variants – the 3M54E with a supersonic kill stage, a 200kg warhead and a range of 200km, and the 3M54E1 with a 400kg warhead and a range of 300km. The family also extends to the 91RE2 ASW missile that can deliver a MPT-1ME torpedo out to a maximum range of 40km – much like the US Navy's ASROC – and the 3M14E land attack cruise missile. A 3Ts-25E Garpun Bal (NATO: Plank Shave) radar uses both active and passive channels to provide long-range surface target designation for the Klub system.

ASW weapons comprise the aforementioned 91RE2 rocket and two, twelve-barrel RBU 6000 ASW rocket launchers using the Purga fire control system. The Indians say that the RBUs are 'very effective' in the ASW role. Curiously, there are no organic torpedo launchers. Instead, the concept of operations uses ASW helicopters for this purpose, although DND designers say that torpedo tubes can be fitted if necessary. Two large helicopters, such as the AgustaWestland Sea King Mk42B, can be embarked for both ASW and ASuW roles.

Search radars include a Salyut-built MR 760 M2EM Fregat (NATO: Top Plate) 3D search radar operating in the E band (US S band), providing target indication to the Shtil 1 system. According to Salyut literature, the radar has a minimum range of 2km, a maximum range of 300km, an altitude of 30km and an elevation of 45–55° depending on the number of active radar channels. However, advertised detection ranges are much less. For instance, a jet can be detected at 230km, a stealth jet at 100km and a cruise missile at 50km. Targeting data – against low flying missiles – for the Barak 1 surface-to-air missiles is provided by an extended range version of Elta's 3D EL/M 2238 anti-missile defence radar, which also operates in the E band. This has an instrumented range of 350km, can detect fighter-sized targets at 250km and provides automated threat alerts against missiles at 28km. MkXI Interrogation Friend or Foe (IFF) sets are integrated with both arrays.

This picture of *Satpura* provides a good overview of the Project 17 class's overall weapons systems, notably the 76mm gun, Shtil 1 surface-to-air missile system, and point defence complex. *(US Navy)*

The sonar system includes a hull-mounted HUMSA-NG sonar and an unspecified active towed array sonar system. All indications suggest the ships were delivered without the towed array, with recent reports suggesting that Bharat Electronics Ltd (BEL) will be supplying a licence-built LFATS (low frequency active towed array sonar) from L-3 Ocean Systems in due course.

Countermeasures include the BEL-built Ellora electronic warfare system, with both active and passive functionality. Constructed from components largely sourced from Israel, it includes two electronic support measures (ESM) antenna head units, two multi-beam array transmitter jammers, two millimetre wave jammers for use against millimetric wave monopulse seekers commonly found on cruise missiles, and a communications intercept module. Other countermeasures encompass the Indian-developed CSN-56 Kavach decoy system, consisting of a pair of short-range and a pair of medium/long-range launchers. In common with other Indian warships, anti-torpedo defences would appear to comprise the local Mareech torpedo decoy system, along with towed noise makers.

Shivalik's various weapons systems and sensors are linked to the class's CMS-17 combat management system by a dual redundant, fibre-optic network known as AISDN-17 (ATM – Asynchronous Transfer Mode – Integrated Ship Data Network). Data from AISDN-17 is displayed on several multi-function versatile consoles distributed around the ship. Details are sparse on the combat management system/combat action information organisation, although it has a federated, flexible system architecture with the ability to add more systems. It would appear that it has potential in the area of network centric operations, possibly extending to a co-operative engagement capability to control weapons on other fleet ships in due course.[7] The class is certainly equipped with tactical data links – including BEL's Link II – and satellite communications to assist network-based warfare, whilst both external and internal communications are facilitated by the BEL-supplied CCS Mk2 communications system. Both AISDN-17 and the combat management system were designed by the Indian Navy's Weapons and

A view of *Shivalik*'s point defence complex, including the Elta EL/M 2238 surveillance radar, two eight-cell Barak 1 launchers forward of the mast and an AK-630M CIWS. The Elta EL/M-2221 fire control radars that provide tracking and guidance are not shown in this picture. *(Mrityunjoy Mazumdar)*

Electronics Systems Engineering Establishment (WESEE) in New Delhi in collaboration with the Centre for Development of Telematics (C-DOT), the Indian government's telecommunications research and development centre, as well as BEL and a 'foreign expert company', believed to be Russia's Meridian.

STEALTH DESIGN

The DND says that *Shivalik*'s stealth features, along with other design elements, translate into a number of operational advantages. By far the greatest is the ship's much reduced vulnerability to detection and tracking, as well as reduced lock-on ranges for hostile anti-ship missiles and underwater weapons. In addition, the ship can achieve higher speeds over longer ranges at significantly lower life cycle operating costs, besides having superior damaged stability and greater operational availability in high sea states.

Every warship has a set of 'signatures' that uniquely identify the vessel and impact its vulnerability to various weapons. These include its pressure signature, its RCS, the IR signature, underwater noise (acoustics) and extra-low-frequency emissions. To avoid sea mines, for example, pressure signature needs to be minimised. To avoid anti-ship missiles, RCS and IR signatures need to be minimised.

Shivalik test firing her RBU 6000 anti-submarine rocket launchers during trials. The Indian Navy believes that this system remains very effective in the anti-submarine role. However, they provide less stealth than many of the Project 17's design features. *(Indian Navy)*

Similarly, acoustic, magnetic and extra-low-frequency emission signatures need to be reduced to counter the threat from homing torpedoes.

A detailed explanation of the various stealth measures incorporated in *Shivalik* has been provided by the DND's former Director General, Vice Admiral Nath.[8] He noted that RCS reduction and prediction are generally performed in the 2–40GHZ frequency range, adding that a good balance between RCS contribution from a ship's bare hull and its weapons/equipment is required to evolve an overall stealth design. A very stealthy ship will have a RCS of more than 1,000m² (28dBm²) with the bare hull contributing only around 1 per cent of the RCS (the rest being weapons and equipment). By contrast, a conventional ship might have a RCS of 40,000m² (46dBm²), with 80 per cent of the RCS coming from the bare hull. For comparison, warships with a sloped superstructure and bulwarks have a 5 per cent contribution to the RCS signature from the hull, while those with only a sloped superstructure might have a 10 per cent RCS contribution from the hull.

Specific RCS reduction measures on the *Shivalik* class include a stealthy gun turret, use of vertical launchers where possible, a full beam superstructure sloped at about ten degrees, sloped bulwarks and flush deck rails for the helicopter traversing gear. Another is the use of radar-transparent materials – components made out of composite materials with an inherently low RCS – for equipment such as stanchions, railings, guardrails, radar-transparent ladders, Radar Suppressed Side Screens (RSSS), helicopter deck safety net frames and pipes. In addition,

Shivalik pictured at speed during trials shortly before delivery in early 2010. RCS features apparent include the stealthy gun turret, a full beam superstructure sloped at about ten degrees and some use of vertical launchers. *(Indian Navy)*

coatings such as radar-absorbent paint and radar-absorbent material, as well as ROOT (Radar Opaque Optically Transparent) windows – essentially frequency selective windows – have been used. Several of these composite items and coatings items were indigenously developed. Reducing the ships' RCS required time-consuming, iterative optimisation studies using a variety of prediction and modelling software. For example, the RSSS, covering the gas turbine air intakes, posed a particular challenge as designers sought to balance RCS against airflow requirements in defining the optimal mesh size.

The principal IR signatures are from the ship's hot exhaust gas plumes, as well as from hot surface temperatures such as uptakes in the funnel stack. The emitted electromagnetic radiation from the above sources lies primarily in two infrared band widths: the 3–5µm (medium IR) band and the 8–12µm (far IR band). As might be expected, IR seekers on missiles and other detection devices operate in these bands too.

Engine exhaust IR signature can be reduced by approximately 95 per cent in the 3–5µm band through IR signature suppression measures such as a plume cooling device. Besides exhaust gas cooling, hot metal is also cooled, thus offering a good measure of 'look-down protection' from hostile IR sensors. The engine room ventilation system, with

Satpura on exercises with the US Navy. The overall impression of stealth is somewhat marred by some of the imported Russian weapons and sensors. *(US Navy)*

seawater coolers and acoustic enclosures for the diesel alternators, helps to reduce hull contrast temperatures. Davis Engineering supplied 'eductor diffuser' IR signature suppression devices, as well as the LM2500 gas turbine intakes/uptakes, for all three ships. India's Naval Science Technological

Laboratory claims it 'developed' (reverse engineered) these devices for use on the diesel engine exhausts. Full scale operational conditions conducted at engine builder Kirloskar Oil Engines Ltd's (KOEL) Nasik facility showed a 90 per cent signature reduction in IR bands, with minimum back pressure.

One of *Shivalik*'s gangways, flush mounted into the hull, as part of efforts to minimise the ship's radar cross section (RCS). *(Mrityunjoy Mazumdar)*

A view of *Shivalik*'s midships section, including one of the Radar Suppressed Side Screens (RSSS) that cover the gas turbine air intakes. These also enclose the ship's boats. *(Mrityunjoy Mazumdar)*

The extent of indigenous content within the three *Shivalik* class frigates depends on how the term is defined. Some equipment, such as the Oto Melara Super Rapid main gun, is produced under licence whilst others, including the Larsen and Toubro helicopter traversing system, are entirely of Indian origin. *(Kapil Chadni)*

Acoustic signature management measures were directed mainly at minimising or suppressing the sources of underwater radiated noise from machinery – both propulsion and auxiliary – as well as from fluids flowing in the distributed pipe line systems and from propeller cavitation. *Shivalik* incorporates resilient mounts, double mounts, rafts, flexible couplings, quiet propellers and acoustic enclosures for machinery. In particular, the relatively large, inward turning propellers were specially designed for low noise and high cavitation inception speeds of over 22 knots, besides having a narrow wake. As mentioned earlier, designers focused on achieving very low hull appendage resistance to minimise flow noise and vibrations by careful placement of components. In another example of attention to detail, the seawater suction arrangement required carefully designed sea chests to avoid radiation of fluid-borne noises due to pump impulses.

OTHER KEY DESIGN FEATURES

Shivalik's CODOG propulsion plant features two licence-built Kirloskar Pielstick 16 PA6 STC diesel engines each rated at 5700kW and two Hindustan Aeronautics-assembled General Electric LM2500 gas turbines, each rated at approximately 18MW

with L-3 MAPPS digital engine control modules. The diesels are used for cruising speeds, with the gas turbines used for rapid acceleration and higher speeds. By using the CODOG plant, the Indian Navy estimates life cycle operating costs will be at least 50 per cent less than that of a comparable COGOG (COmbined Gas Or Gas) plant.

The engines drive two Wärtsilä-LIPS controllable pitch propellers through two Renk BGS 192.5 Lo double helical reduction gearboxes. These gearboxes, which weigh almost 54 tons each, can transmit up to 22.4MW of power. They reduce the gas turbines' output from 3,600rpm to 215rpm and the diesel engines' output from 1,050rpm to 136rpm at the propellers. Licence-built by Elecon in India, they are designed to reduce structure-borne noise levels and set new standards for Indian-manufactured marine gearboxes. Other key propulsion system equipment includes the LIPS supplied shafting that was assembled by Goa Shipyard Ltd. Each frigate also has four locally-assembled diesel generator sets that provide up to 4MW of electrical power in total.

The Integrated Platform Management System (IPMS) – for automating shipboard machinery and equipment operations – was initially envisaged as a completely integrated system. However, a decision by India's Directorates of Marine Engineering and

Electrical Engineering (DEE) to pursue separate paths meant that the IPMS installed in the *Shivalik* class is not actually fully integrated. Instead, it has two modules – an Integrated Machinery Control System (IMCS) and a Battle Damage Control System (BDCS) – that are supplied by L-3 MAPPS and a separate, stand-alone Automated Power Management System (APMS) module from General Electric India. Nevertheless, *Shivalik* is still the first Indian warship to be fitted with this level of automation.

The IMCS is used to monitor and control *Shivalik*'s platform machinery, including its propulsion, electrical, damage control and auxiliary machinery systems. It also provides advanced functionality such as onboard embedded team training and equipment health monitoring. The October 2011 award of a contract by MDL to L-3 MAPPS (then CAE of Canada) to act as the overall platform functional integrator and supplier of the IMCS was a landmark decision in Indian naval procurement, since it was the first time a Western company had been put in charge of such a vital Indian Navy project. According to Rangesh Kasturi, Vice President of Sales at L-3 MAPPS, the resulting 'unprecedented level of automation implemented on this ship provides the Indian Navy with several benefits including reduced manning and better exploitation of the ship's platform machinery and systems while maintaining the highest levels of ship safety and survivability.'

Besides the main control panels in the machinery control room, system operators – especially Damage Control Parties – can access the IMCS using a number of distributed remote terminal units placed in each damage control zone to monitor and control the ship's BDCS, as well as propulsion and auxiliary systems. The system can also be accessed by a computer laptop at several access points throughout the ship. Damage control hardware includes the Russian supplied Ladoga-ME firefighting system.

To ensure stability and retain a degree of operational capability in case of damage, shipboard fires or water ingress, the ship is divided into five independent gastight/watertight citadels and fire zones. Each zone has independent smoke clearance arrangements, as well as electrical power from an energy distribution system. The ship's heating, ventilation and air conditioning system – known as the Total Atmospheric Control System (TACS) – maintains a continuous positive air pressure inside the ship and the separate citadel zones to enable operations in a nuclear, biological, chemical (NBC) environment. The system was largely supplied by Denmark's York Novenco and included seventy-five air treatment units, 111 heat exchangers/fan coils and thirty air filtration units.[9] The last-mentioned came in two sizes with flow rates of 900m³/h and 1800m³/h respectively and supply filtered air to the citadels when operating in NBC conditions.

INDIGENOUS CONTENT

While India likes to say that sixty per cent of the *Shivalik* is indigenous, the accuracy of this figure really depends on interpretation of the term. In any project of this magnitude, it is helpful to keep in mind that the process of indigenisation is a gradual one and, certainly, dependent on how one defines 'Indian-made equipment'. Adhering to a definition of indigenous equipment as 'designed and made in India', would mean that very little equipment would qualify as such. Nevertheless, several critical components have either been reverse engineered – 'indigenised' as the Indian Navy prefers to call it – or assembled in India. By that definition, the class can be said to be largely indigenous.

Some key locally-produced items include the helicopter traversing system from Larsen and Toubro, stabilisers and steering gear from Veljan Hydrair, a

number of the previously-mentioned stealth coatings and radar transparent materials, as well the IR signature suppression systems, fittings, pipes, modular accommodation. Locally-built weapons include Kavach decoy launchers, Mareech torpedo decoy systems in addition to the licence-built 76mm Oto Melara Super Rapid main gun and AK-630M guns. Equally importantly, extensive experience of complex systems engineering and system integration has been gained though the development of AISDN-17, the combat management system and state-of-the-art electronic warfare equipment.

It is also clear that considerable effort has been made to absorb technologies from foreign partners into Indian companies. Crucially, much system integration knowledge has been gained. In the long run, this is much more crucial than a numbers game as Indian companies gain the know-how and competence to build upon their knowledge base. The dividends from these efforts will pay off as an increasing number of Indian companies field locally-developed versions of hitherto imported systems on new warship projects

OPERATIONAL

When *Shivalik* was commissioned, she was already combat-capable in almost all respects. Almost all weapons had been test-fired except the missiles, which could not be tested until the ship was

A generic image of a L-3 MAPPS local control panel. The Project 17 class features integrated machinery and battle damage control systems provided by the company, including remote terminals in each of the five damage control zones. (*L-3 Communications MAPPS Inc.*)

Shivalik and her sisters form part of India's Eastern Fleet and are based at Visakhapatnam. This picture shows *Shivalik* arriving at her new home port for the first time in March 2011. (*Indian Navy*)

commissioned. MDL had also worked hard to minimise the number of open issues and rectify defects – the so-called D-448 shipyard liabilities – prior to commissioning.[10] *Shivalik* subsequently had to complete evaluation by India's Flag Officer Sea Training followed by a work-up period with the Western Fleet to attain full operational status.

The Project 17 class ships are being based with India's Eastern Fleet in Visakhapatnam (Vizag). This is very much in tune with the emphasis on the development of India's Eastern Fleet as part of India's 'Look East' drive. This is thought to be in response to a growing threat perception in respect of China's increasingly capable People's Liberation Army Navy. Since their induction, the two ships already in commission have taken part in several exercises. For example, *Shivalik* took part in the Indian-Sri Lanka exercise SLINEX II in September 2011. In April 2012, *Satpura* exercised with the US Navy in Exercise Malabar. In May, *Shivalik* sailed with two other warships and a fleet tanker participating in the Indian Navy's annual Southeast Asia deployment.

As previously indicated, *Sahyadri,* the third ship should have been handed over by 31 March 2012. Whilst this did not happen on time, delivery was finally achieved on 25 June 2012, with commissioning scheduled for late July.

Judging by the comments of commissioning commanding officers, the DND has been very successful in realising the Project 17 design requirements. Going forward, lessons learnt from the programme will serve as the basis for future surface combatants of the Indian Navy. Operationally, the Indian Navy will have to learn to fully exploit the inherent 'stealth characteristics' to achieve tactical superiority over potential adversaries.

While these frigates may not quite be on par with other state-of-the-art ships in terms of battle damage control systems or fully integrated combat management system or long-range air defences, their stealth features are certainly on par. In addition, *Shivalik* and her sisters are certainly far more capable ships than most potential adversaries, such as the Pakistani F-22P *Zulfiqar* class frigates.

Satpura pictured on joint exercises involving US and Indian Navy ships as part of the annual Malabar training programme. The two Project 17 frigates that have commissioned so far have been kept busy with a number of deployments as far as China and Japan. They should be joined by *Sahyadri,* the final member of the class, before year end. *(US Navy)*

PROJECT 17A

The Project 17 programme will end when MDL delivers the last of class, *Sahyadri*. The class will be superseded by the more advanced Project 17A. The programme calls for seven ships – four to be built at MDL and three at Garden Reach Shipbuilders and Engineers (GRSE) at Kolkata. Total project cost, including the cost of modernised infrastructure at the shipyards, is reported to be worth more than Rs. 45,000 crores (over US$8bn). The anticipated cost for each vessel is above Rs. 4,000 crores (c.US$750m). Earlier estimates of first-of-class delivery by 2016 are entirely unrealistic given that construction contracts are yet to be awarded.

The P17A ships will be stealthier than their predecessors, including a cleaner topside arrangement, a covered mooring deck and flush deck mounted vertical launch missile launchers. The number of antennae on the ship will be reduced by use of a multifunction radar system. The design will also explore better options for roll stabilisation of the platform.

According to the DND, the P17A frigate will use the P17 hull form but it will be slightly larger and heavier than the preceding class – perhaps by as much as 5 per cent. This suggests its length and tonnage could be around 154m and 6,500 tons respectively.

Graphics released by the Indian Navy offer some clues to combat systems planned for the new class. Gone are the single arm launchers for surface-to-air missiles. Instead, vertical launch units for a variety of missiles are fitted. Significantly, a partially integrated mast fitted with what looks like the Elta EL/M-2248 MF-STAR radar suggests that Barak 8 long-range surface-to-air missiles are planned. BrahMos supersonic cruise missiles jointly developed by India and Russia are also likely. Like the P17, a combination of Barak 1 missiles and AK-630M guns will be fitted for point defence. A Thales Smart-L radar is a possibility, as is a Garpun Bal radar for BrahMos targeting data. ASW weapons include two RBU 6000 launchers and torpedo tubes.

It has also been recently reported that the Indian Navy is interested in acquiring the US Navy's Aegis anti-air warfare system – including the SPY-1F radar and Standard SM-3 missiles – for the P17A. If selected, it could have major implications for the Barak 8 long range surface-to-air missile project.

In order to reduce build time and improve productivity, the Project 17A class will be designed for modular construction in large, pre-outfitted blocks. MDL says that ships are to be built from twelve large blocks with a planned build time of thirty-six months. Ships will be laid down at six month intervals. Production at GRSE is likely to commence six months after MDL starts the project.

The design, project management and life cycle will be supported by a more comprehensive use of computer engineering tools. To this end, Italy's Fincantieri won a tender for providing design support and technical assistance in modularising the design.

Shipbuilding contract awards for the P17A class are slated for 2012. MDL is to be lead shipyard since they have more experience in building bigger ships. It remains to be seen if MDL and GRSE can come reasonably close to delivering these ships within the planned timelines.

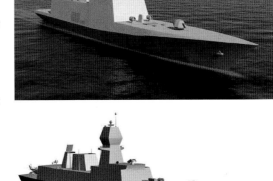

Two computer-generated images of the Project 17A design, which will replace the Project 17 class in production. They will feature further improvements in both stealth and weapons systems over their predecessors. *(Indian Navy)*

Notes:

1. The author's previous overview of the Project 15 series can be found in 'Delhi Class Destroyers: An Overview of India's Project 15, Project 15A and Project 15B Series', *Seaforth World Naval Review 2011* (Barnsley, Seaforth Publishing, 2010), pp.102–19.

2. This information is derived from Commander K K Varma's *Naval Construction in India: 50 years of the Corps of Constructors, Indian Navy*. This is self published and can be found at http://www.scribd.com/doc/6346892/Naval-Construction-in-India

3. The involvement of Rear Admiral Vaidyanathan in this process is further covered in the late Vice Admiral G M Hirandani's *Transition to Guardianship, The Indian Navy 1991–2000* (New Delhi, Lancer Publishers, 2010).

4. The P17 class's complexity is illustrated by the fact that each ship required c.4,000 tons of D-40S steel, over 10km of pipe work and more than 500km of cables.

5. Some sources state that the P17 class were ultimately constructed from licence-produced steel, manufactured in India to D-40S specification. However, these are probably not accurate. The Indian developed equivalent – DMR 249A/B – has been used in other ships, notably the P15A destroyers, P28 anti-submarine corvettes and P71 indigenous aircraft carrier.

6. See *Report No 32 of 2010–11 for the period ended March 2010, Performance Audit of Indigenous Construction of Indian Naval Warships* (New Delhi, Comptroller & Auditor General of India, 2011).

7. The Indian Navy is actively focused on improving network-centric capabilities and aims to integrate data from Indian Air Force AWACS aircraft, as well as from reconnaissance satellites, in order to assist engagement of targets at long ranges.

8. Vice Admiral Rajeshwer Nath, 'Shivalik: India's New Generation Warship', *Indian Defence Review* – Volume 25.2 (New Delhi, Lancer Publishers, 2010). The online version is at: http://www.indiandefencereview.com/defence-industry/SHIVALIK-Indias-New-Generation-Warship.html

9. As *Shivalik*'s hull and superstructure was already built when ventilation equipment was delivered, it all had to be sized or be capable of easy disassembly so as to get through doors and hatches with a maximum size of 800 x 600mm for mounting on board.

10. *Shivalik* had 140 D448 items on handover. In third of class *Sahyadri* this figure had fallen to less than fifty, which are to be corrected by MDL within one year of delivery.

11. In addition to the sources listed above, this chapter has also benefited from publicity material issued by the DND and Indian Navy, whilst the relevant pages of the Bharat Rakshak (http://www.bharat-rakshak.com/) website and of Ajai Shulka's informative Broadsword blog (http://ajaishukla.blogspot.co.uk/) are useful for additional information.

4.1 TECHNOLOGICAL REVIEW

Author: **David Hobbs**

WORLD NAVAL AVIATION

An Overview of Recent Developments

INTRODUCTION

The last year has seen the F-35 Lightning II Joint Strike Fighter continue to dominate news flow in respect of fixed wing naval aviation. The protracted problems which have marked the aircraft's development have combined with significant budget reductions to produce a slowdown in United States orders, whilst the United Kingdom has continued to vacillate over which variant of the F-35 to buy. More widely, the flexibility provided by amphibious aviation is resulting in significant investment and, accordingly, this chapter incorporates an extended overview of current capabilities in this field.

CARRIER AVIATION

The US Navy's core fleet of eleven aircraft carriers and ten carrier air wings has survived the significant cuts in defence spending that were laid out in the FY2013 budget request in February 2012. However, there will be a drop to ten ships between 2013 when the *Enterprise* (CVN-65) is withdrawn from service and 2015 when *Gerald R Ford* (CVN-78) is completed. The 2013 budget requests 192 aircraft for the Navy and Marine Corps, slightly less than the 221 funded in 2012. These include twenty-six F/A-18 E/F Super Hornet strike fighters and twelve EA-18 G Growlers but only six F-35B and four F-35C Lightning II Joint Strike Fighters. Funding continues for the X-47B unmanned combat aircraft system demonstrator, UCAS-D, which is to carry out the world's first deck landing by an unmanned aircraft during carrier compatibility trials in 2013. However, the derivative unmanned carrier-launched airborne strike and surveillance aircraft, UCLASS, has had its projected initial operational capability put back from 2018 to 2020. This will save money in the short term, although the decision probably also reflects the realisation that the original date was too optimistic. Further savings will be achieved by postponing the procurement of a number of production aircraft for up to five years including sixty-nine F-35B and C Lightning IIs. In addition to offering

A Lockheed Martin F-35B Lightning II Joint Strike Fighter landing on the US Navy's amphibious assault ship *Wasp* (LHD-1) during initial ship suitability testing in October 2011. The F-35 programme has continued to dominate news relating to fixed wing aviation over the past twelve months. *(Lockheed Martin)*

Right: The US Navy's first nuclear-powered aircraft carrier *Enterprise* (CVN-65) pictured operating in the Atlantic in March 2012 during her last deployment. There will be a temporary fall in the US carrier fleet to ten ships after the fifty-year-old carrier decommissions. *(US Navy)*

A US Navy F/A-18F Super Hornet from Naval Air Station Patuxent River in Maryland conducting flight testing of an AGM-88E Advanced Anti-Radiation Guided Missile (AARGM). The Super Hornet is still being purchased in significant numbers, although production is due to end in FY2014. *(US Navy)*

short-term cost reductions, the USN also hopes this will save more money in the longer term by not having to rectify defects that continue to emerge during the aircraft's protracted development phase. Table 4.1.1 summarises overall USN aircraft procurement plans.

Meanwhile, aircraft from US Navy carriers have flown about forty per cent of the close air support missions over NATO forces in Afghanistan, where the F/A-18 Super Hornet has proved to be a most effective strike fighter. Its stable-mate, the EA-18 G Growler electronic attack aircraft, is replacing the

Table 4.1.1: US NAVY PLANNED AIRCRAFT PROCUREMENT: FY2012-FY2017

TYPE	MISSION	FY2012[1]	FY2013	FY2014	FY2015	FY2016	FY2017	FYDP (2013-17)
Fixed Wing (Carrier Based)								
F-35B Lightning II JSF	Strike Fighter (STOVL)	6	6	6	6	9	14	41
F-35C Lightning II JSF	Strike Fighter (CV)	7	4	4	6	9	14	37
F/A-18E/F Super Hornet	Strike Fighter	28	26	13	–	–	–	39
EA-18G Growler	Electronic Warfare	12	12	–	–	–	–	12
E-2D Advanced Hawkeye	Surveillance/Control	5	5	5	7	6	7	30
Fixed Wing (Land Based)								
P-8A Poseidon	Maritime Patrol	11	13	17	20	20	13	83
C-40A Clipper	Transport	–	–	–	–	–	1	1
KC-130J Hercules	Tanker	1	0	2	2	2	2	8
Rotary Wing								
AH-1Z/UH-1Y Viper/Venom	Attack/Utility	31	28	27	27	26	31	139
CH-53K Super Stallion	Heavy Lift	–	–	–	–	2	2	4
MV-22B Osprey	Transport	30	17	18	19	19	18	91
MH-60R Seahawk	Sea Control	24	19	19	31	38	–	107
MH-60S Seahawk	Multi-Mission	18	18	18	8	–	–	44
Unmanned Aerial Vehicles								
MQ-8 Fire Scout/Fire-X	Reconnaissance	12	6	7	7	8	8	54
MQ-4 BAMS Global Hawk	Maritime Patrol	0	0	3	4	4	5	16
STUAS[2]	Tactical reconnaissance	0	5	5	5	0	0	15
Training								
T-6A/B Texan II	Training	36	33	31	0	0	0	64
Totals:		**221**	**192**	**175**	**142**	**143**	**113**	**765**[3]

Notes:
1 FY2012 relates to previously approved procurement; numbers for 2013-17 relate to FY2013 budget plans
2 Small Tactical Unmanned Aircraft System
3 Represents a 77 airframe reduction over the 842 aircraft envisaged in previous procurement plans.

MiG-29K single seat and MiG-29KUB tandem seat fighter aircraft in Russian and Indian markings are pictured onboard the Russian aircraft carrier *Admiral Kuznetsov* in this file photograph. Russia has recently ordered twenty-four of the aircraft, whilst India is looking forward to operating the type when *Vikramaditya* is delivered towards the end of 2012. *(Russian Aircraft Company MiG)*

EA-6 B at the rate of about two squadrons a year and is proving to be equally effective and popular with its crews.

The French Navy will operate a second Rafale M equipped *Flotille* in 2013, 11F having joined 12F at NAS Landivisiau in 2012. The latest version is referred to as an omni-role fighter and achieved conspicuous success over Libya while embarked in *Charles de Gaulle* during 2011. 17F is the last Super Etendard (Modernised), SEM, unit and will continue to operate the type until 2015 when it, too, will transition to the Rafale M, giving the French Navy an impressive strike fighter force. The carrier air wing comprises a flexible mix of fighters, E-2C battle-space management aircraft and helicopters. French naval aircrew are trained by the USN and their aircraft are not only fully capable of operating from US carriers but do so during exercises. French naval aviation in 2013 is an excellent example of what can be achieved at reasonable cost when a carefully considered long-term plan is followed.

The Russian aircraft carrier *Admiral Kuznetsov* provides the Northern Fleet with a deployment capability which it demonstrated in 2012. The 279th Independent Ship Fighter Naval Aviation Regiment embarked Sukhoi Su-33 fighters and Su-25 UTG trainers which flew a combined total of about one hundred sorties during a three-month deployment into the Mediterranean during which one pilot made his hundredth deck landing, making him the regiment's fourth 'centurion'. The air

group's Kamov Ka-27 helicopters flew a further 200 sorties, eighty of which were at night. These numbers show that the *Kuznetsov* is employed largely to 'keep the art alive' but the Russian Navy is believed to be studying ways to build new aircraft carriers and has recently ordered twenty new MiG-29Ks and four MiG-29KUBs similar to those in production for the Indian Navy. They are to be delivered between 2013 and 2015.

India operates its remaining Sea Harrier FRS 51s from *Viraat* (the former British Royal Navy *Hermes*), which will be fifty-four years old in 2013. However, attention is focusing increasingly on the much larger *Vikramaditya* (once the Soviet *Admiral Gorshkov*) which carried out sea trials in 2012 and is due to work up with MiG-29Ks embarked from 2013. The indigenous new *Vikrant* is reaching an advanced stage of construction but is still some years away from completion. The MiG-29K is now the Indian Navy's primary fighter but the Service has also stated a requirement for forty-six indigenous Tejas lightweight fighters, which are being developed by Hindustan Aeronautics Limited (HAL). The initial naval prototype Tejas flew for the first time on 27 April 2012, powered by a General Electric F404 engine. After testing by HAL it will go to INAS Hansa for carrier compatibility trials. Deck landing trials are scheduled for 2013 but the main production run for this aircraft is expected to comprise a Mark 2 version with more powerful General Electric F414 engines. The Indian Air Force

version of the Mark 1 was cleared for operational service in 2012.

The new Chinese aircraft carrier, named *Shi Lang* in some reports but unnamed in others, carried out what were described as 'scientific research and experiments' at sea in 2012 but reports persist that the Chinese are having difficulty procuring arrester gear from Russia. Deck landing trials will not begin until these are fitted and tested but meanwhile pilots are practising 'dummy deck landings' ashore with Sukhoi Su-33 fighter derivitives similar to those used by the Russian Navy.

Italy and Spain both operate versions of the AV-8B Harrier. The Spanish Navy has not announced plans for a replacement but must decide soon as its present aircraft are likely to reach the end of their useful lives at the end of the decade. The Italian Government had plans to procure 131 F-35 Lightning IIs provisionally split between sixty-nine F-35As and sixty-two F-35Bs, with the Navy receiving twenty-two of the latter to replace its sixteen AV-8B Harriers. Although the defence budget was cut as an austerity measure in 2012 and the number of F-35s to be procured was reduced to a total of ninety, it appears that the *Marina Militare*'s tranche remains largely intact.[1]

Brazil, too, demonstrates a small but efficient carrier-based naval air arm with US Navy support. The Brazilian Navy is the largest in South America and although its single carrier, *São Paulo*, is elderly, it has been extensively refurbished and can operate a variety of aircraft types up to a maximum of thirty-nine. In 2013 the air wing includes twelve A-4KU Skyhawks, which provide a viable strike capability and a sound basis from which to expand. Eight redundant C-1A Trader aircraft have been purchased from the USN and at least four are being upgraded by Embraer to operate in the air-to-air refuelling tanker and carrier-onboard delivery roles. Their original Wright R-1820 piston engines are being replaced by Honeywell TP331-14GR turboprops.

The British Royal Navy (RN) responded positively after the loss of *Ark Royal* and its Harriers in 2010, signing an agreement with the US Navy which provided funding for pilots, operations teams, air traffic control officers, engineers, aircraft handlers, weapons supply teams and meteorological staff to serve at sea in USN aircraft carriers. Their numbers were scheduled to grow significantly from 2013 as they acquired and then maintained the knowledge and skills needed to man and operate

Spot the difference! Concerns over the cost of converting one of the new *Queen Elizabeth* class carriers to CATOBAR operation, as determined by the 2010 Strategic Defence and Security Review, resulted in the United Kingdom considering a reversion to STOVL operation during 2012. These images show the alternative configurations; the top STOVOL variant eventually won out. *(BAE Systems)*

ships of the *Queen Elizabeth* class when completed. The pilots were to fly F/A-18Es and, indeed, the first completed a combat tour in the US Navy's *John C Stennis* (CVN-74) in 2012. By 2013 the RN would have had more fighter pilots at sea than it would have had with Joint Force Harrier, with pilots also flying Rafales with the French Navy in addition to those serving with the USN. The decision to fit catapults and arrester wires to at least one of the *Queen Elizabeth* class was the most sensible to emerge from the 2010 Strategic Defence and Security Review (SDSR) and was intended to capitalise on the design specification that they were to be easily fitted with them if required. Installation should be a relatively simple operation but outrageous costs for the work were bandied about in early 2012, leading the UK to consider reverting to STOVL F-35B variant of the Joint Strike Fighter to save the short-term cost of modification. US Navy experts who saw the figures expressed surprise, being unable to understand how such large numbers were derived.[2]

Catapults and arrester wires would allow the British ships to operate a wider range of more effective aircraft at a significantly lower through-life cost, to cross-deck and embark USN and French aircraft in accordance with treaty obligations, and to operate unmanned aerial vehicles (UAVs) such as the X-47B and its derivatives in the medium and long term. Procurement of the F-35B would save the short-term cost of fitting catapults and arrester wires but add cost in every other way and throw away the advantages including, possibly, the close co-operation just begun with the USN and France, which might no longer see the RN as a viable maritime partner. The downstream effect on attempts to market British designs such as the Type 26 frigate could be significant. The F-35B variant suffers from the known inability to land vertically with a significant weapon load and would have to either jettison expensive precision guided munitions before landing at high weights or undergo UK-funded development to achieve a 'rolling vertical landing' for which there is no time-scale or cost. However, on 10 May 2012, it was announced that the UK was, after all, to revert

The initial UK F-35 Lightning II – a 'B' STOVL variant – made its first flight on 13 April 2012. *(Lockheed Martin)*

to the pre-SDSR plan to operate the F-35B, the justification being the higher than anticipated costs of carrier conversion; a likely delay to 2023 in being able to field the F-35C; and a greater likelihood of being able to afford to operate both carriers without conversion costs. Under the new plan, production F-35B aircraft will be delivered from 2016 and undertake trials on *Queen Elizabeth* from 2018 prior to restoration of an operational fixed-wing British carrier capability in 2020.

Meanwhile, development problems continue to cast a shadow over the whole F-35 programme and arguments in Washington over unit costs are difficult for international customers to understand as different departments use different accounting methods. Vice Admiral David Venlet, USN, the Programme Manager, brought some clarity to the subject early in 2012 when he stated that the major problem was building production airframes before the development phase was complete or even fully understood. 'Concurrent production' has meant that production airframes cannot be used until they are modified to set right deficiencies found in testing, some of which are already known to be structural weaknesses that require substantial rectification work. On a positive note he stated that for him the question was not 'F-35 or not' but 'how many and how soon' and, indeed, Defence Secretary Leon Panetta has removed the F-35B probation order put in place by his predecessor. The delayed procurement reflected in the 2013 USN budget proposals show that the US Navy is prepared to wait for the answers and – potentially – build more F/A-18s to fill the short term gap, operating them into the 2030s.[3]

On the negative side, Venlet ordered a 'Quick Look Review', or QLR, which highlighted more than a dozen critical design problems which need to be resolved before any variant of the F-35 can be declared fit for service use, even in training units. These include major problems with the pilot's helmet-mounted display system; failure of the fuel dumping system; failure of the integrated power package which typically breaks down after thirteen hours of use instead of the designed 2,200; excessive buffet at high angles of attack and problems with the

The E-2D Advanced Hawkeye continues to move closer towards initial operating capability. This image shows the type's first landing on *Harry S Truman* (CVN-75) early in 2011. *(Northrop Grumman)*

arrester hook design in the F-35C. International customers will have to decide at what level of design maturity they are prepared to commit to making firm orders and how many aircraft they can afford to buy when a meaningful unit price is calculated.

AIRBORNE SURVEILLANCE AND CONTROL

2013 will see the E-2D Advanced Hawkeye closer to initial operational capability with the US Navy after a series of evaluations which included a period embarked in the *Enterprise* during 2012 and participation in several war games. The USN plans to procure seventy-five airframes, which will gradually replace the E-2C over the next decade. However, the procurement of nine E-2Ds has been delayed by five years as a cost-saving measure. The E-2C is also operated by the French Navy which has signed a contract with Northrop Grumman for a fourth aircraft and upgrades to the latest standard for the earlier three. The fourth aircraft will be a refurbished ex-USN E-2C since the production line at St Augustine in Florida has already changed over to E-2D production tooling. The UK and Spain both operate versions of the venerable Sea King but Italy uses a new variant of the AW101 Merlin, which was finally cleared for operational use in 2012. The main sensor is Selex Galileo's HEW-784 radar, characterised by an enlarged radome. It has demonstrated the ability to detect surface vessels at 162 nautical miles and has an 'Alarm' mode which is activated when high-speed sea-skimming missiles are detected. Development was extended to incorporate high-resolution inverse synthetic aperture radar imaging for the stand-off classification and identification of surface targets. Russia also operates an AEW helicopter, the Kamov Ka-31 RLD fitted with a solid-state Oko E-801 surveillance radar under the fuselage. Nine export versions of this type have been acquired by the Indian Navy and China is also reported to have purchased the type.

The British Royal Navy has amassed considerable experience with the Sea King ASaC7 and continues to base one of the two operational squadrons in Afghanistan, where the Searchwater radar has proved capable of detecting small, moving objects over land, including people and animals as well as vehicles. On present plans it is due to be withdrawn in 2014. The other operational unit is tasked with embarkation in support of fleet operations. The Sea King is due out of service in 2016. For over a decade

A British Royal Navy Sea King ASaC7 helicopter pictured while deployed in Afghanistan during 2011. *(UK/MoD Crown Copyright 2012)*

An Italian *Marina Militare* 'HEW' airborne early warning variant of the AgustaWestland AW101, which is recognisable by its enlarged radar housing. The type has now been cleared for full operational use. *(AgustaWestland)*

Production of the modernised Merlin HM2, showing few external differences to the previous HM1 version but a vastly upgraded mission system is well advanced. The first production models should be delivered during 2013. (*Agusta Westland*)

the MOD has studied replacement options under the maritime surveillance and control, or MASC, project at significant expense but with no obvious result. However, the requirement – now named 'Crowsnest' – was confirmed as part of the UK's ten-year defence procurement programme on 14 May 2012, with Lockheed Martin's 'Vigilance' pod-mounted system subsequently reported as being the favoured solution.

SEA CONTROL HELICOPTERS

France, the Netherlands and Italy continue to move towards full operational capability with their NH-90 sea control helicopters in 2013, but the Royal Australian Navy's (RAN's) purchase of SH-60R Seahawks in 2011 shows the wisdom, for a medium-sized navy, of procuring a fully developed, contemporary type that can be operational soon after deliveries commence. The RAN will receive twenty-four Seahawks as part of Project Air 9000 Phase 8 to replace the existing sixteen Seahawk S-70B2 helicopters and the failed Seasprite. The first two aircraft are due to arrive in 2014 and will be used to introduce the type into service. Operational deployments are due to commence in 2015 and the twenty-four aircraft will eventually be able to provide at least eight warships with a combat helicopter concurrently, including ANZAC class frigates and the new air warfare destroyers. The remainder will be based at RANAS Nowra where they will be used for training, work-up and regular maintenance cycles. In RAN service the aircraft will be armed with Hellfire air-to-surface missiles, flexibly mounted machine guns and Mark 54 torpedoes. The latter will be acquired as a new weapon system for the RAN specifically for use on Seahawks.

The new RN AgustaWestland Wildcat should achieve a deck-landing clearance in 2013 after successful sea trials carried out in the Type 23 frigate *Iron Duke* by the prototype ZZ 402 during 2012. A total of 390 deck landings were made, of which 148 were at night, seventy-six of these using night-vision goggles. The first production aircraft from the twenty-eight on order are expected to arrive with 700W Naval Air Squadron at RNAS Yeovilton during 2013 and operational evaluation will continue throughout 2014 to achieve initial operational capability in 2015. The first two production Merlin HM2 helicopters will be flying with the RN in 2013 with up to ten aircraft at a time on the 'pulse line' and 'new' aircraft delivered to the RN every six weeks. Modification of each airframe takes eight months and the thirtieth and last airframe to the new standard will be completed in December 2014. Although front line squadrons will be flying with the HM2 in 2013, initial operational capability will not be achieved until early in 2014.

In what was intended to be a transformational step, a detachment of MQ-8B Fire Scouts from HSL-60 embarked in the US Navy's frigate *Simpson* (FFG-56) for an operational patrol off Africa in early 2012. The MQ-8 is operated in flight by two people, an air vehicle operator, AVO, and a mission payload operator, MPO, who sit at adjacent consoles in the ship's command centre. The AVO is responsible for the safety of the airframe, its navigation and recovery to the deck. The MPO directs the aircraft's mission systems and distributes the real-time intelligence, surveillance and reconnaissance information gathered from it to the command and to other network-enabled platforms including those of allies.

The detachment in *Simpson* comprised two air vehicles with four AVOs, three MPOs and fifteen technical sailors. Each airframe had an endurance of eight hours and with the operators divided into watches, the detachment had the ability to provide non-stop coverage of large areas of sea or land for considerable periods without a break. Other MQ-8B detachments were operating ashore at the same time in support of the US Marine Corps in Afghanistan but, unfortunately, both deployments suffered incidents in the first half of 2012 that led to an 'operational pause for the indefinite future', which grounded all Fire Scouts shortly before this chapter was completed. The first occurred on 30 March 2012 at night off West Africa when one of *Simpson*'s air vehicles failed to lock onto the ship's automated recovery beacon. After a number of approaches and attempts to troubleshoot the problem, the MQ-8 reached its minimum fuel level ꞏꞏꞏꞏ ꞏꞏꞏ ꞏꞏꞏꞏꞏꞏꞏꞏꞏꞏ ꞏꞏ ꞏ ꞏꞏꞏ ꞏꞏꞏꞏꞏꞏ ꞏꞏꞏꞏ ꞏꞏ ꞏꞏꞏꞏ and deliberately ditched to terminate the flight. It was subsequently recovered 'relatively intact' by *Simpson* and will now be the subject of a searching enquiry.

The new AW159 Wildcat helicopter commenced sea trials onboard the British Royal Navy Type 23 frigate *Iron Duke* in early 2012. This November 2011 photograph shows earlier 'at-sea' tests onboard the larger RFA *Argus*. (AgustaWestland)

A MQ-8B Fire Scout unmanned aerial vehicle being prepared for night operations off the West African coast on 8 February 2012 whilst deployed on the frigate *Simpson* (FFG-56). The ditching of one of *Simpson*'s two aircraft during night operations on 30 March 2012, followed closely after by the crash of another MQ-8B in Afghanistan, resulted in the type being grounded. A third aircraft was shot down over Libya in June 2011. (US Navy)

The second incident occurred in Afghanistan when an MQ-8 crashed on 6 April 2012; sources say that enemy action was unlikely to be a factor and the indefinite grounding will apply until the causes of both incidents are known and understood. Apart from the second air vehicle in *Simpson* and others in Afghanistan, a planned deployment to the USS *Klakring* (FFG-42) later in 2012 was disrupted. The failure of the automatic recovery system, from whatever cause, poses questions about the safe and economical operation of UAVs from warship platforms which will need to be addressed before detachments become widespread.

The USN is developing an improved version of the air vehicle, designated the MQ-8C, which uses the same avionics in a larger airframe based on the Bell 407 to give greater endurance and payload. The projected medium-range maritime unmanned air system, MRMUAS, has been cancelled by the USN, therefore, partly to save US$200 million in its 2013 budget but principally because it now believes that the MQ-8C can be developed incrementally to meet the same requirement.

The US Navy is developing an improved unmanned aerial vehicle, the MQ-8C Fire-X, which is based on a Bell 407 airframe. A US$262m contract to develop two test models and six production airframes was awarded to Northrop Grumman on 23 April 2012. *(Northrop Grumman)*

MARITIME PATROL AIRCRAFT

The first production P-8A Poseidon, BuAir number 168428, was delivered to the US Navy's VP-30, 'the Pro's Nest' at NAS Jacksonville in Florida during 2012 for training while the prototype aircraft continued to fly at NAS Patuxent River in Maryland. Initial operational capability is planned for 2013 with new aircraft being delivered at the rate of about one a month until the 'programme of record' total of 117 is reached. The Indian Navy has twelve P-8Is on order, the first of which flew in 2011 for delivery in 2013. In due course the IN plans to order twelve more for an eventual total of twenty-four. In addition to these aircraft, the IN has issued a request for information from nine separate companies seeking input for six medium-range maritime reconnaissance (MRMR) aircraft with options on three more which will form the middle layer of a three-tier maritime surveillance system. The outer layer will be patrolled by the P-8; the middle by the MRMR and the inner by existing Dornier 228s and, potentially, small UAVs. MRMR

The first flight of the Indian P-8I variant of the US P-8 Poseidon maritime patrol aircraft took place in September 2011, with deliveries of the twelve aircraft currently on order scheduled to commence in 2013. *(Boeing)*

is not required to have an anti-submarine capability and will focus on maritime surveillance with the capability to carry anti-ship missiles. The aircraft selected will replace the IN's twelve Britten-Norman Islanders. Boeing is one of the nine companies and may submit a lightened P-8 derivative with simplified avionics.

The US Navy's P-8A force will operate with the MQ-4C as its partner in the broad area maritime surveillance, BAMS, role. The first MQ-4C will fly in 2012 and its multifunction active sensor, MFAS, has been tested in a Gulfstream II test-bed. After a further series of evaluations during 2013, the type is expected to enter operational service from 2015 when four aircraft will commence a single 'orbit'. The US Navy hopes eventually to build up to a five 'orbit' inventory and will require sixty-eight MQ-4Cs to sustain them over the life of the project.

Australia has already announced that it intends to procure the P-8A as a P-3 replacement at the end of this decade and a number of other P-3 operators are likely to follow. The Russian Navy took delivery of an upgraded Il-38 N 'May' in 2012 which went to the Northern Fleet's 7050th Naval Aviation Base at Severomorsk. The upgrade included the Novella sensor suite which comprises a new high-resolution thermal imaging system, improved radar, a new magnetic anomaly detector together with optical detection and tracking equipment. The Russian Navy is believed to have about forty Mays in service and plans to modify them all to the new standard.

AMPHIBIOUS WARFARE
Big-deck ships capable of using helicopters to land amphibious forces from the sea continue to be built in significant numbers. They offer the ability to travel long distances, poise off a potentially hostile coast and, if and when necessary, to land marines at specific targets, potentially well inland; provide them with close air support and to act as a focal point for their logistical support. They also provide command and communication centres and tactical control for land-based aircraft.

UNITED STATES:
The US Navy and its Marine Corps have an operational amphibious capability that exceeds that of the rest of the world combined, currently operating nine LHA/LHD type amphibious assault ships and an inventory of aircraft and helicopters that do not

An unusual image of the first MQ-4C unmanned aerial vehicle, which will partner US Navy P-8A Poseidons in the broad area maritime surveillance (BAMS) mission, in the final stages of assembly early in 2012. Its first flight was scheduled for later in the same year. *(Northrop Grumman)*

A picture of the 'large deck' USN LHD type amphibious assault ship *Iwo Jima* (LHD-7) with a full air group embarked whilst operating in the Atlantic in April 2012. Aircraft pictured include AV-8B Harriers, MV-22B Osprey tilt rotors and CH-53E Super Stallions. The way the MV-22Bs forward are stowed for storage is particularly interesting. *(US Navy)*

require joint forces to augment them. The eight LHDs of the *Wasp* (LHD-1) class form the core of the US Navy's amphibious ready groups (ARGs). Typically they embark a Marine Air Wing of six AV-8B Harriers; twelve MV-22B Ospreys or CH-46E Sea Knights; four CH-53E Super Stallions; three UH-1Y Hueys and four AH-1Z Cobras. Alternative mission-specific air wings can be embarked that could, for example, comprise up to forty MV-22Bs or twenty AV-8Bs with appropriate support and weapons supplies, the latter giving a better strike capability than some nations' aircraft carriers and further demonstrating the 'crossover' potential of these large warships. Vehicles, including tanks, can be landed by landing craft utility (LCU) or hovercraft type landing craft air cushion (LCAC) from the dock aft and the embarked expeditionary force has a total of up to c.1,900 men. Extensive medical facilities include six fully-equipped operating theatres and the ability to treat up to six hundred casualties give these ships an important role in humanitarian operations, especially when combined with the ability to operate large numbers of helicopters for long periods. *Peleliu* (LHA-5) of the older *Tarawa* (LHA-1) class remains in service but

Although Harrier aviation in the British Royal Navy is a thing of the past, the US Marine Corps continues to make extensive use of the type. This image shows a pair of AV-8B Harriers from Marine Attack Squadron (VMA) 542 approaching the amphibious assault ship *Kearsarge* (LHD-3). *(US Navy)*

Table 4.1.2: US AMPHIBIOUS WARFARE AIRCRAFT

AIRCRAFT [1]	AV-8B HARRIER II	F-35B LIGHTNING II	MV-22B OSPREY	CH-46E SEA KNIGHT	CH-53E SUPER STALLION	AH-1Z VIPER
Manufacturer:	Boeing	Lockheed Martin	Bell/Boeing	Boeing	Sikorsky	Bell Helicopter
Role:	Close Air Support	Close Air Support	Assault/Transport	Assault/Transport	Heavy Lift	Attack
Type:	Fixed Wing Jet	Fixed Wing Jet	Tilt-rotor	Rotary	Rotary	Rotary
Length:	14.1m	15.6m	19.2m	25.7m (rotors)	30.3m (rotors)	17.8m (rotors)
Wing/Rotor span:	9.2m	10.7m	11.6m (25.8m width)	15.5m	24.1m	14.6m
Maximum Take-off Weight:	14,100kg	27,000kg	27,400kg	11,000kg	33,400kg	8,400kg
Engine:	1 x RR F402-RR408 105kN thrust	1 x PW F-135[2] 191kN thrust	2 x RR AE-1107 4,600kW each	2 x T85-16 1,400kW each	3 x GE T64-GE416 3,300kW each	2 x GET700-GE-401C 1,300kW each
Maximum Speed:	585 knots	Mach 1.6	305 knots	145 knots	150 knots	220 knots
Combat Radius:	300 nautical miles	›400 nautical miles	›250 nautical miles	›130 nautical miles	50 nautical miles [3]	125 nautical miles
Combat Radar:	AN/APG-65(AV-8B+)	AN/APG-81	–	–	–	AN/APG-78 Longbow
Weapons/Load:	7 x weapon stations Optional 25mm cannon Range of munitions	11 x weapons stations Optional 25mm cannon Range of munitions Optional machine guns	24 marines (seated) 9,000kg internal load 6,000kg external load Optional machine guns	25 marines (seated) [14 combat equipped] 4,000kg useful load Optional machine guns	1 x armoured vehicle 1 x M-198 howitzer c.14,000kg useful load	1 x 20mm M197 cannon 6 x weapon stations Range of munitions
Crew:	1 pilot	1 pilot	2 pilots, 1-3 crew	2 pilots, 3 crew	2 pilots, 1-3 crew	2 pilots

Notes:

1 Data has been compiled from manufacturers' documentation and other publicly available information. Due to considerable variations in published information, data should be regarded as indicative only

2 Also 1 x RR Lift System.

3 At maximum take off weight.

America (LHA-6), first of a new class of LHAs, will not now be delivered in 2013 because of the need to incorporate changes into her design. When complete, *America* will have considerably enhanced aviation facilities to exploit the capabilities of the US Marine Corps' (USMC's) new generation of aircraft. A second ship of this class, *Tripoli* (LHA-7), was contracted for in 2010 but a contract for the third, LHA-8, has been delayed until FY2017 as a savings measure.

Current US amphibious warfare aircraft are summarised in Table 4.1.2. The USMC continues to place great emphasis on the F-35B and, while its STOVL capability has relevance in amphibious assault scenarios, it is difficult to see how its expensive fifth-generation stealth characteristics can be justified for the role in which it will be used. Opening strikes against enemy command and air defence systems would be better undertaken by SSN-launched Tomahawks and EA-18G electronic attack aircraft in the short term and UCAVs after 2020. The six F-35Bs in an LHD would, in any case, be insufficient to achieve the necessary effect against any but the most basic opposition. In their primary close air support role they would be operating with non-stealthy helicopters and tilt-rotors and would need pylon-mounted external ordnance that would negate their own stealth. However, the USMC sees the aircraft as the only STOVL project in development and, therefore, must have it despite its unnecessary complexity and cost. Regrettably, the original advanced-STOVL project from which it evolved became entangled with so many other 'silver bullet' political fighter projects over the past two decades.

Delays in developing the F-35B mean that the USMC will have to maintain the AV-8B in operational service beyond 2020 but it has been helped by the procurement of the entire British force of seventy-two Harrier GR9s at a fraction of their cost in the British taxpayer. Some may be modified to AV-8B standard to replace older USMC aircraft in operational squadrons and others will be used as spares. Meanwhile, F-35B ship suitability testing commenced in the autumn of 2011 with the deployment of two test aircraft, BF-2 and BF-4 onboard *Wasp*. Subsequently, the first F-35B arrived with USMC training squadron VMAT-501 at Eglin Air Force Base in Florida during 2012 and training is expected to have begun by 2013.

The MV-22B will continue to replace the CH-46

A picture of the first F-35B landing on the amphibious assault ship *Wasp* (LHD-1) on 3 October 2011. The US Marine Corps continues to place great emphasis on the F-35B and its STOVL capability. *(Lockheed Martin)*

A US Marine Corps MV-22B Osprey tilt-rotor pictured whilst supporting training operations in Iraq prior to the withdrawal of American troops. The huge Rolls Royce AE-1107 powered rotors are shown to good effect. *(Boeing)*

during 2013 although orders for twenty-four MV-22s will be delayed beyond 2013 as a savings measure. Both new and refurbished AH-1Z and UH-1Y helicopters are replacing earlier models in operational squadrons.

The CH-53K is a 'clean-sheet' design under development by Sikorsky to replace the CH-53E. It will incorporate 'fly-by-wire' control and be powered by three General Electric GE38-1B turboshafts, each rated at 5,600kW. The first of two development aircraft is expected to fly in 2014 and – later in the year – the USMC test and evaluation unit, VMX-22, is to verify that the new helicopter can lift an under-slung load of 12,300kg while operating in hot and high conditions. The 'Kilo', as it is known, is seen as fundamental to the USMC's future capability to fly an expeditionary force, including artillery, vehicles and logistic support, into a remote landing site in a single night and subsequently sustain it in action.

UNITED KINGDOM:

The United Kingdom's Amphibious Ready Group (ARG), now subsumed into the broader UK Response Force Task Group (RFTG) concept, suffered under the 2010 defence review and will have only limited capability in 2013. The helicopter

Two AH-1Z Viper helicopters on a training flight display their capability to ship a heavy armament to good effect. The type is replacing earlier models in operational squadrons. *(Bell Helicopter)*

Table 4.1.3: UK AMPHIBIOUS WARFARE AIRCRAFT

AIRCRAFT [1]	SEA KING HC4	MERLIN HC4	LYNX AH9A	CHINOOK HC2-4	APACHE AH1
Manufacturer:	AgustaWestland	AgustaWestland	AgustaWestland	Boeing	AgustaWestland
Service:	Royal Navy	Royal Navy [2]	Royal Navy/Army Air Corps	Royal Air Force	Army Air Corps
Role:	Assault/Transport	Assault/Transport	Attack/Assault	Assault/Transport/Lift	Attack
Type:	Rotary	Rotary	Rotary	Rotary	Rotary
Length:	22.2m (rotors)	22.8m (rotors)	15.2m (rotors)	30.2m (rotors)	17.8m (rotors)
Wing/Rotor span:	18.9m	18.6m	12.8m	18.3m	14.6m
Maximum Take-off Weight:	9,700kg	14,600kg	6,000kg	22,700kg	8,200kg
Engine:	2 x RR Gnome H-1400 1,200kW each	3 x RR/Turbomeca RTM322 1,700kW each	2 x LHTEC CTS800-4N 1,000kW each	2 x Lycoming T-55-L-712 2,800kW each	2 x RR/T RTM322 1,700kW each
Maximum Speed:	125 knots	165 knots	160 knots	160 knots	150 knots
Combat Radius:	>250 nautical miles	>250 nautical miles	290 nautical miles	>300 nautical miles	>120 nautical miles
Weapons/Load:	20 marines 3,000kg external load Optional machine guns	24 marines 4,000kg external load Optional machine guns Machine guns	9 marines 1,000kg external load 4 x weapons stations	c.50 marines 10,000kg external load Optional machine guns	1 x 30mm chain gun 4 x weapons stations Range of munitions
Crew:	1-2 pilots, 1-2 crew	1-2 pilots, 1-2 crew	1-2 pilots, 1-2 crew	2 pilots, 1-2 crew	2 pilots

Notes:

1 Data has been compiled from manufacturers' documentation and other publicly available information. Due to considerable variations in published information, data should be regarded as indicative only

2 Currently operated in earlier versions by Royal Air Force – to be transferred to the Royal Navy after modification.

carrier *Ocean* will be in refit leaving the re-rolled *Illustrious* as the operational LPH type helicopter assault ship, backed up by the LPD type amphibious transport dock *Bulwark* and three Royal Fleet Auxiliary-manned 'Bay' class auxiliary LPDs. A fourth member of the latter class was sold to Australia and has become HMAS *Choules*. *Illustrious* will be decommissioned when *Ocean* rejoins the fleet.

Current UK amphibious warfare aircraft are summarised in Table 4.1.3. The venerable Sea King HC4 has served with the RN Commando Helicopter Force (CHF) since 1981 but is due to be withdrawn from service in 2016. The CHF itself forms part of the UK Joint Helicopter Force (JHF). The Ministry of Defence plans to replace the Royal Air Force (RAF) Merlin HC3 currently serving in JHF with a new production batch of Boeing CH-47 Chinook helicopters; the Merlins will then be transferred to the CHF as Sea King replacements.

Unfortunately, their limited RAF specification prevents them operating at sea and considerable modification will be required before they can do so safely. The airframes are ten years old and the opportunity will be taken to implement a life-sustainment upgrade intended to keep them in service until 2025. They will be fitted with a 'glass cockpit' based on the design for the Merlin HM2 and the same type of power-folding main rotor-head and tail pylon. Other necessary modifications include the

The British Royal Navy's last remaining aircraft carrier, *Illustrious,* is now serving as an amphibious helicopter carrier prior to her planned withdrawal in 2014. *(Conrad Waters)*

An artist's impression of one of the new Chinook HC6 heavy lift helicopters recently ordered from Boeing for the Royal Air Force. Delivery of the type will release Merlin transport helicopters for Royal Navy use, whilst Chinooks can also be embarked on Royal Navy helicopter carriers as part of JHF (joint helicopter force) assets. (Boeing)

OTHER NATIONS:

France is arguably second in amphibious capability to the United States, operating three 20,000-ton *Mistral* class LHDs, a type known as a *Batiment de Projection et de Commandement* or 'BPC' in French circles. These are about half the size of their US contemporaries. Each is capable of embarking sixteen NH-90 helicopters, 450 troops (900 in austere conditions) and has stowage for sixty armoured fighting vehicles, including thirteen main battle tanks. These can be landed from the dock by LCU or LCAC. The single 27,000-ton Spanish LHD *Juan Carlos I* provides a capability somewhere between the French and American designs and two very similar ships are being built for the Royal Australian Navy as the *Canberra* class; the first due to enter service in 2014.[4] South Korea operates a LHD slightly smaller than *Mistral* and a number of other navies' own aircraft carriers which could be used for amphibious operations in an emergency. Many nations also operate amphibious shipping with more limited aviation capabilities than those provided by the 'large deck' amphibious assault ships, relying to a greater or lesser extent on joint forces to provide close air support and helicopters for assault and tactical transport. Most also have

fitting of flotation gear, telebrief, a radar transponder and lashing points. Once modified, the aircraft will be designated Merlin HC4 and will share support and training with the HM2. During 2012 twelve Royal Navy and Royal Marine pilots and thirty-five aircraft engineers and technicians underwent training on the un-modified Merlin HC3 but the MOD has not yet announced a timescale for HC4 conversion and a gap in capability after 2016 is beginning to appear possible.

The Lynx AH9 is operated by the Royal Marines as a battlefield reconnaissance and light attack heli- copter with the useful ability to carry a small number of men in tactical moves. The RN lacks heavy lift and attack helicopters, and therefore other JHF assets are embarked for these tasks. RAF Chinooks lack folding blades and are too big to fit the lifts in *Illustrious* and *Ocean*, making them diffi- cult to operate. The side lifts in *Queen Elizabeth* will be big enough to strike them down with rotors spread in due course. The Army Air Corps has prac- tised embarking AH1 Apaches since 2010 and the type operated successfully during missions over Libya during 2011.

Table 4.1.4: REPRESENTATIVE AMPHIBIOUS WARFARE AIRCRAFT – REST OF WORLD

AIRCRAFT:[1]	MRH-90[2]	S-70A BLACKHAWK	EC 725 COUGAR	KA-29 'HELIX' B	KA-52K 'HOKUM' B
Manufacturer:	NH Industries	Sikorsky	Eurocopter	Kamov	Kamov
Country:[3]	Australia	Australia	France	Russia	Russia
Role:	Assault/Transport	Assault/Transport	SAR/Transport	Assault/Transport	Attack
Type:	Rotary	Rotary	Rotary	Rotary	Rotary
Length:	19.6m (rotors)	19.8m (rotors)	19.5m (rotors)	11.3m	14.2m/16m (rotors)
Wing/Rotor span:	16.3m	16.4m	16.2m	15.9m	14.5m
Maximum Take-off Weight:	10,600kg	11,100kg	11,000kg	12,000kg	10,800kg
Engine:	2 x RR/Turbomeca RTM322	2 x GE T700-GE-701C	2 x Turbomeca Makila 2A1	2 x Istov TV3-117	2 x Kilimov VK-2500
	1,700kW each	1,400kW each	1,800kW each	1,700kW each	2,400kW each
Maximum Speed:	160 knots	195 knots	170 knots	145 knots	195 knots
Combat Radius:	>300 nautical miles	>125 nautical miles	300 nautical miles	250 nautical miles	200 nautical miles
Weapons/Load:	20 troops	10-15 troops	Up to 29 troops	Up to 16 troops	1 x 30mm cannon
	2,500kg internal load	4,700kg internal load	4,700kg external load	4,000kg external load	4 x weapons stations
	4,000kg external load	4,100kg external load	Optional machine guns	Optional machine guns/cannon	Range of munitions
	Optional machine guns/cannon	Optional machine guns	External weapons stations		
Crew:	2 pilots, 1 crew	2 pilots, 1 crew	2 pilots, 1-3 crew	2 pilots, up to 2 crew	2 pilots

Notes:

1 Data has been compiled from manufacturers' documentation and other publicly available information. Due to considerable variations in published information, data should be regarded as indicative only;

2 The MRH-90 is the Australian produced version of NH Industries' TTH variant of the NH-90 helicopter (produced in Australia by Eurocopter subsidiary Australian Aerospace).

3 Country to which specimen data relates – many types listed are operated by a number of countries.

A picture of Spain's new amphibious assault ship, *Juan Carlos I*, at sea. Two sister ships are building for the Royal Australian Navy, giving both fleets a powerful amphibious capability. *(Navantia)*

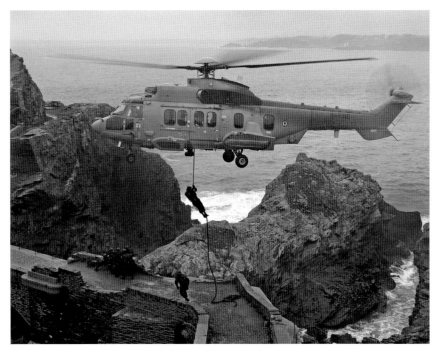

A French EC 725 Cougar transport helicopter involved in Special Forces training on the French coast in December 2011. The type is used for a number of specialised transportation and search and rescue tasks. *(Eurocopter)*

A Eurocopter Tiger attack helicopter and a NH Industries NH-90 tactical transport helicopter pictured operating in company. Both types have been deployed in amphibious roles. *(Eurocopter)*

marines in some form to act as specialised amphibious troops.

The Australian Defence Force eagerly awaits its new LHDs and General David Morrison, Chief of Army, talked at the 2012 RAN Sea Power Conference about how the ships will form an integral part of a combat system with unprecedented command, control and sustainment capabilities. He added that the weapons system of the new ships will be the embarked forces and their full capability will be the joint effect delivered by army, navy and air force elements within the amphibious task group. The Chief of Air Force, Air Marshal Geoff Brown added that the Royal Australian Air Force (RAAF) was committed to supporting the full range of Australian naval activities. Australia has no marines but an Army battle-group, based on the Second Battalion, Royal Australian Regiment, and including a cross-section of combat and enabling capabilities, will be trained and committed to the development of a truly amphibious capability. This rapidly-deployable group will be reinforced by a follow-on, multi-role combat brigade.

Russia is also making plans for the enormous increase in capability that will follow the entry into service of its four planned *Mistral* class ships. The Russian Navy's Commander-in-Chief, Admiral Vladimir Vysotsky, stated in 2012 that the first two ships, now under construction in France, will be named *Sevastopol* and *Vladivostok*. Technology will be transferred during their construction and the third and fourth, as yet unnamed, ships will be built in Russian shipyards. All four will have a version of the French SENIT-9 tactical data system. Their air wing will comprise eight Kamov Ka-52K and eight Ka-29 helicopters.

A table of representative amphibious warfare aircraft operated by other navies is set out in Table 4.1.4. Australia will have an impressive amphibious capability after 2014 as the *Canberra* class become operational. By then the MRH-90 will be in service with the RAN and Australian Army Aviation Corps (AAC) as their principal assault helicopter, with both services providing embarked helicopters on a regular basis. The RAN will recommission 808 Naval Air Squadron in the second half of 2012 to operate the MRH-90 and to act as the specialised amphibious helicopter unit responsible for the development of best embarked practice. The MRH-90 is a derivative of the Tactical Transport

Helicopter (TTH) variant of the Eurocopter-led NH Industries NH-90 helicopter being produced for the French, Italian and other air arms and is built under licence by Australian Aerospace. AAC Chinooks, similar to those in the UK's JHF will also embark to provide heavy lift, whilst the AAC will still operate S-70A Blackhawks in 2014 and this type is also shown for comparison; other nations operate Blackhawk or Seahawk helicopters from their amphibious ships and their details are similar.

The French Eurocopter EC 725 Cougar is operated by specialised French armed forces squadrons which regularly embark detachments on naval operations and its details are representative of other French assault helicopters that can embark as part of an amphibious force. The *Mistral* class will also operate the TTH variant of the NH-90 similar to the RAN MRH-90, as well as Eurocopter EC 665 Tiger attack helicopters. Both Russian types are operated in small numbers at present but new orders and an enlarged training programme are expected to expand their complement before the first new amphibious assault ship enters service after 2015.

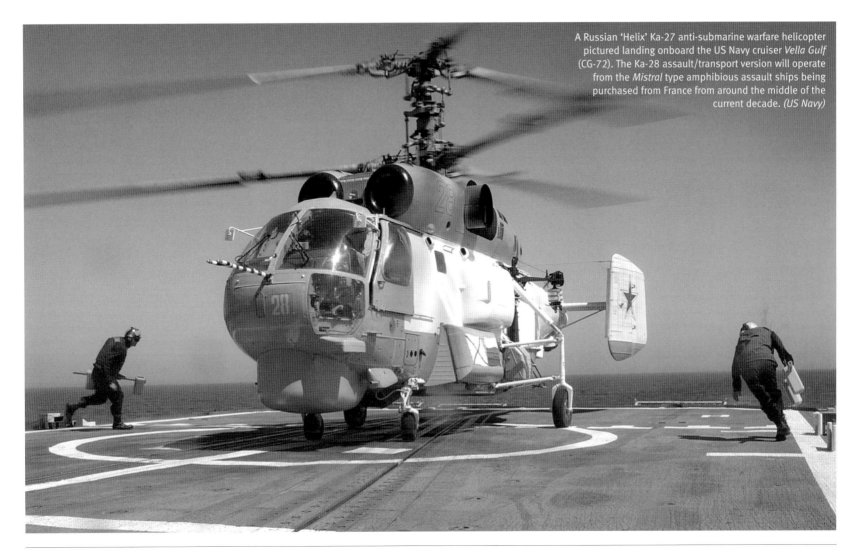

A Russian 'Helix' Ka-27 anti-submarine warfare helicopter pictured landing onboard the US Navy cruiser *Vella Gulf* (CG-72). The Ka-28 assault/transport version will operate from the *Mistral* type amphibious assault ships being purchased from France from around the middle of the current decade. *(US Navy)*

Notes:

1. A review of Italy's *Marina Militare* is contained in chapter 2.4B. There have been reports that the Italian Air Force has been successful in reducing the Italian Navy's allotment of a smaller order from twenty-two to fifteen airframes, which may share base facilities with its own F-35Bs.

2. Press articles reported that the cost of converting the second *Queen Elizabeth* class carrier, *Prince of Wales,* to Catapult Assisted Take Off and Barrier Assisted Recovery (CATOBAR) using the new US Electro-Magnetic Aircraft Launch System (EMALS) could amount to as much as £2bn, a figure confirmed by British Secretary of State for Defence, Philip Hammond, on announcing termination of the plan on 10 May 2012. However, an article by the *Daily Telegraph's* defence correspondent, Thomas Harding – 'Aircraft carrier costs will be half what you think, US tells ministers', *The Daily Telegraph* (London, Telegraph Media

Group Ltd, 24 March 2012) suggested that equipment costs were just £458m, with installation amounting to approximately another £400m.

3. In an interesting development, press reports during April 2012 disclosed that the US Navy had issued a request for information for a new carrier-based aircraft to replace the Super Hornet and Growler in the 2030 timeframe. Some analysts have suggested that this indicates a desire to have a fall-back 'Plan B' if F-35 problems cannot be satisfactorily resolved. However, the US administration continues to remain firmly committed to F-35.

4. A full review of the *Mistral* and *Juan Carlos I* designs is contained in the editor's 'Modern European Amphibious Assault Ships', *Warship 2011* (London, Anova Books, 2011), pp.80–93.

5. This chapter has been compiled from a wide range of periodicals, of which *Air International, Flight, Jane's Defence Weekly, Warship World* and *The Navy* (the journal of the Navy League of Australia) provide particularly good sources of further reading. Reference should also be made to the following publications, as well as to the websites of relevant aircraft manufacturers and navies:

Gunter Endres and Michael J Gething, *Jane's Aircraft Recognition Guide* – fifth edition (London, Collins-Jane's, 2007)

Norman Friedman, *The Naval Institute Guide to World Naval Weapon Systems* – fifth edition (Annapolis, MD, Naval Institute Press, 2006)

Jane's Fighting Ships – various editions (Couldson, Surrey, IHS Jane's)

BALLISTIC MISSILE DEFENCE AND THE USN

INTRODUCTION

For the past two decades the United States Navy has been developing a radically new capability, unique among the world's navies: the ability to intercept and destroy ballistic missiles in flight. It seems to

have been a fortunate accident that this new capability reached maturity at just about the time the Chinese announced a new ballistic anti-ship missile. The US programme was inspired by the proliferation of ballistic missiles around the world. Even

when they cannot target moving ships, they can certainly affect naval operations because, to influence events ashore, navies often have to set up and use fixed port or port-like facilities.

This system has been successful, not only against test targets but also against an unpredictable real-life one. On 20 February 2008 a single Standard SM-3 missile launched from the cruiser *Lake Erie* (CG-70) destroyed a tumbling defunct US reconnaissance satellite at an altitude slightly greater than 150 miles. This was no arranged demonstration for publicity. The satellite was destroyed because toxic fuel on board was expected to survive re-entry into the atmosphere and thus to endanger anyone in its impact area. Although the satellite was far larger than a missile re-entry vehicle, it was a more difficult target due to its unpredictable motion. The SM-3 was designed to hit its target directly, because any kind of stand-off destruction would be difficult or impossible in space. Thus it had to manoeuvre to destroy the target. Closing speed, about 22,000mph, was greater than that SM-3 would have encountered when dealing with a ballistic missile. The Aegis ballistic missile defence system (Aegis BMD system) subsequently became operational on 1 November 2008 with its first fleet firing during Fleet Exercise Pacific Blitz.

On one level, Aegis BMD is a straightforward extension of fleet air defence, which has always had the mission of protecting not only the fleet at sea but also critical (if limited) areas ashore, such as amphibious objective areas. Ballistic missiles such as

The US Navy has developed a capability to intercept and destroy ballistic missiles in flight through leveraging the potential inherent in the Aegis combat system and Standard missile. This image shows the *Arleigh Burke* (DDG-51) class destroyer *Hopper* (DDG-70) firing a Standard SM-3 Block IA missile during a 2009 test. *(US Missile Defense Agency)*

the widely-used Scud can threaten such areas, as well as forward port facilities.[1] On another – and probably far more significant level – Aegis BMD and comparable systems provide an area or strategic defensive capability which complements the long-standing area *offensive* capability of the fleet. That is, since the advent of carriers, fleets have been able to strike at the territory of an enemy, not just at his fleet. Now ships offshore can protect the territory of a country against the threat of missile attack. Fleet air defence missiles never offered anything like that, because their range was very limited. Even fleet fighters could not protect the land area of a country under threat. However, attacking missiles must often pass within range of an interceptor ship offshore.

This is not just a matter of protecting allies. Ships standing offshore in neutral waters can now intercept missiles fired by one country at another. For more and more governments, ballistic missiles are preferable to aircraft as an instrument of attack. They require fewer personnel, and they are much more difficult to counter. It may often be in the interest of the United States (or of its allies) to turn off a missile offensive against some other country without intervening directly. That is not a new issue. In the 1980s the United States and the United Kingdom placed ships in the Gulf in hopes of stopping the tanker war then being waged by Iran and Iraq as part of their larger war. Both countries were targeting tankers operated by third parties – carrying oil vital to the Western world – in hopes of forcing the major Western powers to intervene on their side. It would not be difficult to imagine a similar war waged now in which ballistic missiles were fired at the oil fields or other resources of third parties as a means of bringing pressure to bear on the Western powers. Similarly, if it is possible to turn off a ballistic missile offensive without direct presence on anyone's territory, it may be possible to draw down a local war. Any other form of missile defence would have to be imposed by the United States by placing weapons on the territory of one combatant or the other – which might well be difficult if both combatants were friends of the United States.

HISTORIC ORIGINS

The current US Navy programme is a distant consequence of the Reagan-era Strategic Defense Initiative ('star wars'), which was largely an army programme. After the end of the Cold War, US interest in strategic defence (i.e. defence against ballistic

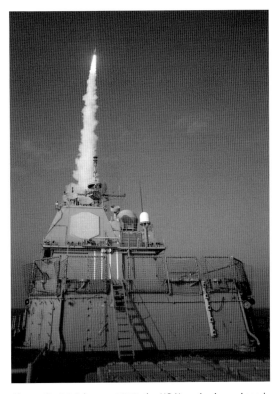

Above: On 20 February 2008, the US Navy Aegis-equipped cruiser *Lake Erie* (CG-70) launched a single Standard SM-3 missile to destroy a non-functioning reconnaissance satellite that threatened to release hazardous fuel over populated areas as it returned to earth. The missile successfully impacted the satellite's fuel tank some 133 nautical miles over the Pacific, validating the Aegis BMD concept in a 'real life' scenario. *(US Navy)*

Above and below: Images of a Russian Scud missile launcher and its support vehicles. The Scud series of tactical ballistic missiles has been widely exported and has become synonymous with the numerous similar missile systems that they have spawned. Iraq's use of Scud missiles in the Gulf War had a significant impact on the US Navy's development of an Aegis-based ballistic missile defence system. *(US Department of Defense)*

The Aegis BMD-capable cruiser *Shiloh* (CG-67) on exercise with Japanese Maritime Self Defence Force (JMSDF) units in September 2009. The US Navy's missile defence programme has probably succeeded because it has been developed as an adjunct to the existing fleet air defence systems built around Aegis and the Standard missile rather than as an entirely separate capability. *(US Navy)*

missiles) moved towards the defence of forward-deployed US forces and of allies. Reflecting that change, the Strategic Defense Initiative Organization was renamed the Ballistic Missile Defense Organization (it is now the Missile Defense Agency). The then director of the programme, Ambassador Henry Cooper, had language inserted into the 1991 Missile Defense Bill requiring navy and air force participation. He reasoned that both services could contribute a great deal to any forward-deployed anti-missile system. Not long after Ambassador Cooper began to press the navy to join the strategic defence programme, the United States found itself at war against Iraq.

Many in the navy saw little point in adding yet another mission when money was already tight due to post Cold War cuts. Supporters of a navy programme pointed out that the navy could not evade the ballistic missile problem. As in many previous wars, sea power was the vital but often neglected dimension of the Gulf War. The war was fought largely on land (though carrier air power was

vital), but about 90 per cent of what was used to fight came by sea. Iraq presented no threat to the seaborne traffic, but the sea link to the battle area included a single crucial port in Saudi Arabia: Jubayl.

That just one port, and often just one container pier in that port, could be crucial to the successful conduct of a campaign is an often-unappreciated fact of modern shipping life. Shippers turned to containers because they provided so much more efficiency than the earlier break-bulk form of shipping. Container operation requires very specialised infrastructure, in the form of the gantries and truck facilities, which are now so familiar (and which have moved shipping activity away from major cities). The sheer cost of such facilities has concentrated seaborne trade in a few very efficient ports. In turn, the protection of these few key ports is an inescapable part of shipping protection – and missiles like the Scuds and their longer-range relatives clearly threaten critical port facilities in a theatre of operations.

In the case of the Gulf War, navy supporters of

missile defence pointed to an Iraqi Scud which crashed into the sea near the pier when ships carrying (among other things) the Marine Corps aviation maintenance facility were tied up alongside. The Scud missed the ships, but had it carried a chemical warhead, which the Iraqis had, it could have wiped them out and also put the pier and the container facility out of action pending decontamination – a lengthy process. Had the pier been put out of action altogether, the entire attack on Iraq might have been jeopardised.

SYSTEM DEVELOPMENT

The US Navy programme has probably been successful because it has never been permitted to push aside other core naval missions. Resources were always limited. For example, the navy could not afford to build specialised missile defence ships, because it knew that it would not receive enough extra money for the new mission. Proponents of naval ballistic missile defence therefore took the position that missile defence ships should retain their other naval capabilities. They should be integrated into the fleet just like other warships. This incidentally contrasted with the navy's previous foray into missile defence, a proposal to build special missile defence cruisers as part of the Johnson- and Nixon-era national missile defence programme. It followed that naval missile defence would be an extension of the existing fleet air defence programme – the Aegis system and the Standard missile – rather than an entirely new system. That ballistic missile defence had to piggyback on existing fleet air defence systems imposed what turned out to be a valuable discipline. Piggybacking was an option both because of the way the existing ballistic missile defence programme evolved and because of the flexibility inherent in the navy's Aegis air defence system.

The Reagan-era Strategic Defense Initiative began as a largely nuclear programme, the hope being that nuclear lasers in space could deal with the large number of missiles the Soviets could be expected to launch in a nuclear attack. This approach failed. The nuclear-pumped X-ray laser was, apparently, unexpectedly difficult to develop. In addition, the US government was reluctant to withdraw from the treaty prohibiting nuclear weapons in space. Initially, it seemed that a nuclear missile defence system could be developed despite the treaty, the idea being to launch the anti-missile weapons into

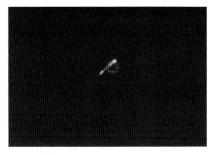 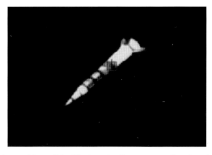 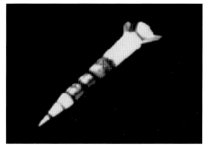 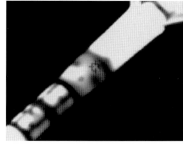

Although it was clear at an early stage that Aegis could track ballistic missile targets, the development of a version of the Standard missile the could intercept such targets was equally important. This included a different type of guidance. The sensor on board the SM-3 missile's kinetic energy warhead creates an image of the target, so that the warhead can choose its point of impact. Shown here are a series of actual sensor images taken during a test interception on 25 January 2002. *(US Missile Defense Agency)*

space as soon as the Soviets began a mass attack. That idea, incidentally, inspired the major navy proposal for involvement in the Strategic Defense Program, to launch missiles from submarines. It was soon obvious that it would be impossible to launch large numbers of nuclear anti-missile weapons into space in time to beat off a massive attack. Some alternative had to be found.

There had long been interest in an alternative: a device which would manoeuvre itself into colliding with a warhead. In one version of the strategic defence programme, missiles carrying such devices would be launched to pursue the cloud of Soviet missile warheads flying towards the United States. The problem of detecting, tracking, and intercepting the warheads would be somewhat simplified because the pursuing interceptors would close their targets at relatively low speeds. When the Cold War ended, the Strategic Defense Program was reoriented, for a time, towards an attempt to deal with ballistic missile warheads wherever in the world they were fired. The problem was simplified in that it no longer seemed likely that anyone would be firing masses of ballistic missiles on a Soviet scale.

Even if vast numbers of missiles did not have to be intercepted, the defence had to be everywhere at the same time, which meant that it had to be placed in space on a very distributed basis. By this time microelectronics had made it possible to shrink the necessary homing mechanism (using infrared). The US microelectronics industry was so productive that such devices could be mass produced at a reasonable cost. Advocates of global missile defence therefore proposed that large numbers of satellites be orbited, each carrying several of the small self-homing anti-missile devices. This concept was called Brilliant Pebbles; the sensor activating the

devices was a network of missile launch detection satellites (Brilliant Eyes).

Within a short time this idea was dead, because even relatively cheap anti-missile devices would be expensive to deploy in the numbers envisaged. With the Cold War over, there was no longer an imminent threat to the United States which could justify the level of expenditure envisaged. However, there was clearly still a missile threat to American allies and to US forces deployed in forward areas. The missile defence programme therefore shifted towards ground-based systems, which would use the new self-homing devices as their warheads. It was at that stage that Ambassador Cooper called for US Navy participation.

The first tentative stage of navy involvement was to see whether it was feasible in the first place. During the 1991 Gulf War, Aegis cruisers in the Gulf and in the Red Sea had taped whatever they detected with their SPY-1 phased array radars. The existing treaty against national ballistic missile defence included detailed prohibitions against radars powerful enough to support such a defence, and SPY-1 had therefore been deliberately limited to avoid conflict with these treaty provisions. No one expected it to track Iraqi Scuds fired at Israel and at Saudi Arabia. Yet examination of tapes from the ships in the Gulf allowed that they had detected Scuds and that they could have tracked the missiles. Moreover, because SPY-1 was a software-based radar, it might be relatively easy to modify it to the extent that it could track a distant fast target. It would be more difficult to modify the radar to acquire the missile target, but an Aegis ship could certainly be cued by other sensors. That was already being done in the 1991 Gulf War: US satellite systems cued the Patriot missile batteries which fired at the incoming Scuds.

The other aspect of feasibility was to decide whether an Aegis ship could be modified to accommodate a useful interceptor. The launcher cells on board the ship handled the Standard missile, the product of a long evolutionary process stretching back to the 1940s. In 1991 the US Navy was about to retire the two-stage version of the missile, SM-2 Extended Range (which could not be fired from a vertical launcher), but at the same time it was about to field a new two-stage version with similar performance, using a massive new finless booster. The key perception was that the two-stage Standard missile could be adapted to launch the homing vehicle

The SM-3 missile's kinetic-energy warhead, or KW, uses an imaging infrared sensor to guide the warhead onto its target in the final stages of an engagement. In this view, taken at a Navy League show, the sensor is at the right, facing the viewer. Around the body of the warhead are the nozzles of the rocket (the Divert and Control System) used to manoeuvre the warhead into position to strike the target. *(Raymond Cheung)*

which the Ballistic Missile Defense Organization was developing. To do that it needed a new powered upper stage and a different kind of guidance.

In the Aegis system, the Standard missile is command-guided on an intermittent basis. The Aegis system tracks both the target and the missile it controls. It orders the autopilot of the missile to manoeuvre it into a homing 'basket'. Once the missile is in that basket, the Aegis system turns on a separate illuminator, and the missile homes onto radar energy reflected from the target. This would not suffice for a very distant target in space, as the Standard missile relied on its tail surfaces for control.[2] Moreover, it was unlikely that the shipboard illuminators could produce anything like enough power for homing at the distances envisaged. That was why it was assumed that the final stage of the anti-missile system would have to home independently on the incoming missile.

However, the basic Aegis concept was clearly appropriate. The homing anti-missile device had to be placed in a position from which it could lock onto its target. The core of the Aegis system is a picture of the tactical situation. Normally, that picture is developed based on what the SPY-1 radar detects, but there is no reason that inputs must be limited to that particular radar. Given the core picture, Aegis produces the appropriate commands.

TERRIER LEAP

To see what could be done, a navy science experiment was conducted. The term 'science experiment' indicated a relatively informal effort which could be conducted quickly. A few existing SM-2 Extended Range missiles were given upper stages carrying a homing vehicle known as LEAP – the Lightweight Exo-Atmospheric Projectile – which had already been developed by the Ballistic Missile Defense Organization. The upper stages were fitted with GPS locators, so that they could know their positions in space, reporting down to the launching ship. The missile cruiser *Richmond K Turner* (CG-20) was selected for the experiments. She had an Aegis-like system (without SPY-1) called the New Threat Upgrade. On the first flight on 24 September 1992, with an unpowered third stage, the modified Terrier SM-2 missile reached an apogee of about 104km (about 50 nautical miles). A second series of shots used a powered third stage, albeit with hypergolic propellant which would have been unacceptable in an operational missile. Trial shots continued into 1995, by which time Terrier LEAP was formally a Risk Reduction Flight Demonstration Program, i.e. a test to see what had to be done to produce a usable anti-missile weapon. It included two shots against live targets. About halfway through the programme, however, it was decided that all the New Threat Upgrade ships would be decommissioned, so Terrier LEAP could not be turned into an operational weapon. However, it was still able to demonstrate what Aegis and the long-range version of the SM-2 missile could do, since the big booster gave SM-2 the same performance as the missile that the cruiser fired.

The Terrier LEAP shots proved that a navy BMD system was feasible. At the same time, they were

A Standard SM-3 missile being launched from the cruiser *Lake Erie* (CG-70) during an early test of the Aegis BMD system in February 2005. The image gives a good idea of overall missile size driven by the big booster also used in the vertically launched Standard SM-2 missile. The challenge throughout Aegis BMD development was to compress the warhead and the new upper stage into the space normally occupied by the Mk115 warhead and guidance sensor in a SM-2 Standard missile. *(US Navy)*

A 1988 view of the US Navy cruiser *Richmond K Turner* (CG-20). The cruiser was used in the Terrier LEAP trials that were the forerunners to an Aegis-based ballistic missile defence system. *(US Navy)*

never entirely successful because of particular problems, such as data handling errors. The series was limited because the ship was retiring, and because only two LEAP vehicles were available. In the last test the LEAP died due either to a dead battery or a bad connector. Even so, as an inert slug it got to within 170m of the target – close enough to have hit had it been live.

The road beyond the Terrier LEAP experiments was rocky. For much of the time, the Ballistic Missile Defense Organization took the position that the naval programme was no more than a minor supplement to ground-based systems, particularly after the Bush Administration decided to develop a national ballistic missile defence system in 2003. It turned out, however, that the navy system proved far more reliable than its ground-based rivals.[3]

AEGIS BMD

The reason why goes back to the navy's insistence that it would develop the new ballistic missile defence system out of existing elements, viz. the Aegis combat system and the Standard missile. All ballistic missile defence systems have a core command and control element. In the 1990s Aegis was already reliable and well-developed, and it was not difficult to extend its capabilities beyond the

Table 4.2.1: AEGIS BALLISTIC MISSILE DEFENCE TEST TRACK RECORD

DATE	DESIGNATION	SHIP	TARGET	HIT	NOTES
2002 Jan 25	FM-2	Lake Erie (CG-70)	Unitary Target Test Vehicle – Short Range	Yes	SM-3 Block 0
2002 Jun 13	FM-3	Lake Erie (CG-70)	Unitary Target Test Vehicle – Short Range	Yes	
2002 Nov 21	FM-4	Lake Erie (CG-70)	Unitary Target Test Vehicle – Short Range	Yes	
2003 Jun 18	FM-5	Lake Erie (CG-70)	Unitary Target Test Vehicle – Short Range	No	Guidance problem during final interception stage
2003 Dec 11	FM-6	Lake Erie (CG-70)	Unitary Target Test Vehicle – Medium Range	Yes	
2005 Feb 24	FM-7/FTM-04-1	Lake Erie (CG-70)	Unitary Target Test Vehicle – Short Range	Yes	First firing with operational SM-3 Block 1 variant
2005 Nov 17	FM-8/FTM-04-2	Lake Erie (CG-70)	Separating Target – Medium Range	Yes	First test against separating target.
2006 May 24	Pacific Phoenix	Lake Erie (CG-70)	Unitary Target – Short Range	Yes	Carried out with SM-2 Block IV interceptor
2006 Jun 22	FTM-10	Shiloh (CG-67)	Separating Target – Medium Range	Yes	First engagement with SM-3 Block 1A
2006 Dec 07	FTM-11	Lake Erie (CG-70)	Unitary Target Test Vehicle – Short Range	No	No launch. Aegis incorrectly set to engage target
2007 Apr 26	FTM-11 Event 4	Lake Erie (CG-70)	Unitary ARAV-A Target – Short Range	Yes	
2007 Jun 22	FTM-12	Decatur (DDG-73)	Separating Target – Medium Range	Yes	Fist use of a DDG-51 type destroyer for launch
2007 Aug 31	FTM-11a	Classified	Classified	Yes	
2007 Nov 06	FTM-13	Lake Erie (CG-70)	Unitary ARAV-A Target – Short Range x 2	Yes	Two successful interceptions of two targets
2007 Dec 17	JFTM-1	Kongou (DDG-173)	Separating Target – Medium Range	Yes	First JMSDF test interception
2008 Feb 20	Burnt Frost	Lake Erie (CG-70)	Satellite US193	Yes	Operational interception of failed satellite
2008 Jun 05	FTM-14	Lake Erie (CG-70)	Unitary Target – Short Range	Yes	Carried out with SM-2 Block IV interceptor
2008 Nov 01	Pacific Blitz	Hamilton/Hopper	Missile Targets – Short Range x 2	Yes/No	One hit, one miss. First Fleet Firing
2008 Nov 19	JFTM-2	Chokai (DDG-176)	Separating Target – Medium Range	No	Guidance problem during final interception stage
2009 Mar 26	Stellar Daggers	Benfold (DDG-65)	Ballistic Missile Target – Short Range	Yes	Carried out with SM-2 Block IV interceptor
2009 Jul 30	FTM-17	Hopper (DDG-70)	Unitary ARAV-A Target – Short Range	Yes	
2009 Oct 27	JFTM-3	Myoko (DDG-175)	Separating Target – Medium Range	Yes	
2010 Oct 28	JFTM-4	Kirishima (DDG-174)	Separating Target – Medium Range	Yes	
2011 Apr 15	FTM-15	O'Kane (DDG 77)	IRBM Target – Intermediate Range	Yes	
2011 Sep 01	FTM-16	Lake Erie (CG-70)	Ballistic Missile Target – Short Range	No	First test of SM-3 Block 1B. Rocket motor failure
2012 May 09	FTM-16 Event 2a	Lake Erie (CG-70)	Unitary ARAV-A Target – Short Range	Yes	First successful test of SM-3 Block 1B.
2012 June 26	FTM-18	Lake Erie (CG-70)	Separating Target – Medium Range	Yes	

Notes:

1 ARAV is an Aegis Readiness Assessment Vehicle;

2 Unitary targets simulate missiles where the warhead remains attached to the booster record, as in Scud type technology;

3 Separating Targets simulate missiles where the warhead separates from the booster rocket, as in North Korean No-Dong type technology. Interestingly, all JMSDF tests have been against this latter missile technology;

4 SM-2 Block IV engagements rely on fragmentation rather than 'hit to kill' interception. Source: US Missile Defense Agency data with notes supplemented by additional sources.

atmosphere. Similarly, the booster and the Standard missile were well-known quantities. Aegis could command the aerodynamically-controlled Standard missile perfectly well.

The only new elements of the Aegis BMD system were a higher-powered version of the SPY-1 radar, the powered upper stage, and the LEAP vehicle – and the latter benefited from the fact that the Ballistic Missile Defense Organization wanted a common LEAP for all its missiles. Effort could be concentrated on a small part of the overall system. By way of contrast, the other US BMD systems were entirely new, so their developers had to deal with a

much greater variety of problems. This is not to minimise the effort involved. For example, the Ballistic Missile Defense Organization tolerated a LEAP motor (the Divert and Control System) using toxic propellants, and it did not envisage the typical shipboard environment of shock and vibration. The field of view of the LEAP seeker was, at least at first, poorly matched to the beam-width of the SPY-1 radar, and the vehicle was not designed to search through the whole beam-width to find its target. US Navy advocates of ballistic missile defence had to overcome considerable scepticism.

The adapted Standard missile was designated SM-3 (RIM-161).

On 25 January 2002 USS *Lake Erie* fired the first wholly successful Aegis BMD shot, making a direct hit on the target equivalent to a Scud. In November 2005 the same ship hit a target equivalent to longer-range Third World missiles. Formal deployment of the Aegis BMD missile was approved on 17 December 2002, to begin in 2004. That year the first Aegis BMD ship was deployed.[4]

The US Navy's philosophy has been to develop

the system in blocks, never opting for a completely new missile but rather improving one element at a time. The initial capability was effective against missiles like the Chinese M-9, which was fired into the sea near Taiwan in 1996. It was understood that it did not offer anything like the ultimate potential of the system, but it could be put into place quickly; and it worked. Aegis LEAP offered a real and vital capability from the outset plus great growth potential without a massive concurrent investment in entirely new systems. Improvements included the ability to fire based on remote data, which is essential for long-range missile defence. The key point is that an Aegis system placed closer to a threat and provided with data by remote sensors can defend a large area. In 2009 President Barack Obama announced that the United States would deploy Aegis BMD to Europe under a Phased Adaptive Approach (PAA) to missile defence. PAA provided immediate protection because Aegis BMD ships could at once be deployed to southern European waters. Ultimately PAA includes separate sensors, such as a big land-

The SPY-1 radar associated with the Aegis combat system was not conceived for ballistic missile defence and, ideally, ships should have a more capable one. The US Navy has developed a dual-frequency AMDR (Air and Missile Defense Radar), which was originally to have equipped *Zumwalt* (DDG-1000) class destroyers. AMDR combines a Raytheon SPY-3 X band (NATO I/J band) array with a Lockheed Martin S band (E/F band) VSR (volume search radar), both front ends sharing a single back end. In theory the VSR would acquire missile targets and the SPY-3 element would guarantee precision tracking compatible with the characteristics of the kinetic energy warhead seeker. This Raytheon model shows how the arrays of an AMDR could be fitted to a later-flight *Arleigh Burke* class destroyer. *(Norman Friedman)*

The JMSDF Aegis-equipped destroyer *Atago* (DDG-177) operating with other JMSDF ships in October 2011. Japan has been a keen supporter of the Aegis BMD concept and *Atago* and sister ship *Ashigara* (DDG-178) will be modified in line with Japan's earlier *Kongou* (DDG-173) class to become BMD-capable. *(US Navy)*

based radar, to cue the deployed Aegis systems (including systems on land).

Several allied navies have shown considerable interest in Aegis BMD, the most active being the Japanese Maritime Self-Defence Force (JMSDF), whose destroyers have been upgraded as required (and have fired Aegis BMD missiles). The first Japanese engagement was by the destroyer *Kongou* (DDG-173), in 2004. The Dutch *Tromp* and the Spanish *Méndez Núñez* have also tracked targets during Aegis BMD exercises, but they have not fired SM-3 anti-missile weapons.[5] In addition to operating SM-3 ships, Japan is engaged in co-operative development of the SM-3 missile, looking to future blocks which may, for example, make fuller use of the volume of the vertical launch cell, to achieve higher performance.

Aegis BMD was developed because of threats to land targets presented by growing numbers of ballistic missiles in countries which may be hostile to the United States and to her allies. However, the system matured just as the Chinese began advertising their Dong-Feng DF-21D 'carrier-killing' ballistic missile (which had not, at the time of writing, yet been fired at a moving ship target). This would seem to be a fortunate coincidence for the US Navy, as the ability to deal with the emerging Chinese missile is already in existence, in a form well adapted to further development.

Although naval ballistic missile defence has been built around the Aegis system, other ships are capable of acquiring BMD capabilities. The Netherlands will modify its four *De Zeven Provinciën* class frigates to track – but not intercept – ballistic missiles through upgrades to their SMART-L surveillance radars. This picture shows *Tromp* on 24 March 2012. *(US Navy)*

Notes:

1. First developed in the 1950s, the Scud series of tactical ballistic missiles was widely exported and has become synonymous with all missiles of this type in the public mindset. According to the US Missile Defense Agency, around 6,000 ballistic missiles – the vast majority in the 300–1,000km range spectrum – existed outside of the arsenals of the US, NATO, Russia and China as of 2010.

2. The missile cannot use its tail surfaces to steer it outside the atmosphere, since they depend on the movement of air over them to have any effect.

3. As of June 2012, the US Missile Defense Agency claimed twenty-two successful intercepts from twenty-seven flight test attempts for the Aegis BMD programme, not including Satellite US193's destruction. This represents a success rate of slightly over 80 per cent.

4. In addition to trials with SM-3, tests have also been carried out with a variant of the SM-2 Block IV missile as a low-level interceptor. Blast-fragmentation warheads, like

that of SM-2 Block IV, are ineffective outside the atmosphere, because they depend on the air to carry their shock wave. Originally, the US Navy envisaged a two-tier system in which SM-2 Block IVA intercepted missiles and warheads inside the atmosphere, and SM-3 intercepted those outside. SM-2 Block IVA combined a semi-active seeker with an infrared (IR) adjunct, the idea being that semi-active would not be able to discriminate between the target and decoys or fragments accompanying the missile warhead. SM-2 Block IVA was cancelled due to overruns (some blame the politics of the Ballistic Missile Defense Organization). Later, the navy developed SM-6, a version of SM-2 with an active seeker. SM-6 is usually associated with the need to intercept cruise missiles beyond the horizon, where it is impossible for a ship to illuminate them for semi-active interception. However, it also replaces SM-2 Block IVA as the lower-tier interceptor. In general, SM-3 cannot intercept a low-altitude target because its kill vehicle will not function properly inside the atmosphere. SM-2 cannot intercept a target outside the atmosphere because it cannot manoeuvre there (as it relies entirely on

aerodynamic surfaces). SM-3 relies on a passive IR seeker because IR offers the necessary precision for a hit-to-kill projectile; radar beam-widths are apparently too great for that, given the limited ability of the kinetic energy interceptor to manoeuvre in the end-game of SM-3.

5. The Dutch *De Zeven Provinciën* class frigates, of which *Tromp* is one, are not equipped with SPY-1 or Aegis. Instead, *Tromp*'s Thales SMART-L long range search radar was modified to allow tracking of ballistic missile targets prior to live exercises with the US Navy in 2006. In September 2011 the Netherlands announced that it would equip all four ships to operate this Extended Long-Range radar variant. There are currently no Dutch plans to integrate SM-3 missiles with the radar – the intention being that missile targets will be passed to other sea or land-based interceptors for engagement – but Germany is reportedly considering the possibility with respect to its similar F-124 *Sachsen* class frigates. Other navies are also investigating the possibility of developing ballistic missile defence capabilities from existing air defence systems.

Contributors

Richard Beedall: Born in England, Richard is an IT Consultant with a long standing interest in the Royal Navy and naval affairs in general. He served for fourteen years in the Royal Naval Reserve as a rating and officer, working with the USN and local naval forces in the Middle East and around the world. In 1999 he founded one of the earliest naval websites on the Royal Navy – now called *Navy Matters*. He has contributed to *Seaforth Naval Review* since the initial 2010 edition, and has written extensively on naval developments for many other organisations and publications, including *AMI International*, *Naval Forces*, *Defence Management* and *Warships IFR*. He currently lives in Ireland with his wife and two young daughters.

Enrico Cernuschi & Vincent P O'Hara: Enrico Cernuschi and Vincent P O'Hara have co-authored articles for British, Italian and American publications including *Warship, World War II Quarterly*, and *World War II*. Mr O'Hara is the author of six books, including most recently *In Passage Perilous: Malta and the Convoy Battles of June 1942* published by Indiana University Press. He resides outside San Diego, California. Mr Cernuschi, based in Pavia, Italy, is a frequent contributor to *Storia Militare* and *Rivista Marittima* and has nearly four hundred articles as well as twenty books to his credit, including the definitive *Le navi da guerra italiane 1940–1945*.

Norman Friedman: Norman Friedman is one of the best-known naval analysts and historians in the US and the author of over thirty-five books. He has written on broad issues of modern military interest, including an award-winning history of the Cold War, whilst in the field of warship development his greatest sustained achievement is probably an eight-volume series on the design of different US warship types. A specialist in the intersection of technology and national strategy, his acclaimed *Network Centric-Warfare* was

published in 2009 by the US Naval Institute Press. The holder of a PhD in theoretical physics from Columbia, Dr Friedman is a regular guest commentator on television and lectures widely on professional defence issues. He is a resident of New York.

David Hobbs: David Hobbs is a well-known author and naval historian. He has written eight books and co-authored eight more. He writes for several journals and magazines and in 2005 won the Aerospace Journalist of the Year, Best Defence Submission. He lectures on naval subjects worldwide and has been on radio and TV in several countries. He served in the Royal Navy from 1964 until 1997 and retired with the rank of Commander. He qualified as both a fixed and rotary wing pilot and his log book contains 2,300 hours with over 800 carrier landings, 150 of which were at night.

Mrityunjoy Mazumdar: Mr Mazumdar, whose father served in the Indian Navy, has been writing on naval matters since 1999. His words and pictures have appeared in many naval and aircraft publications including several of the *Jane's* family, *Ships of the World* and the Royal Institution of Naval Architects' *Warship Technology*. He is also a regular contributor to several naval annuals including *Combat Fleets of the World, Flottes de Combat, Jane's Fighting Ships, Seaforth World Naval Review* and *Weyers Flotten Taschenbuch*. Besides his writing, he maintains a comprehensive website on the Indian Navy at www.bharat-rakshak.com. Mr Mazumdar lives in Alameda, California with his wife.

Guy Toremans: Guy Toremans is a Belgium-based maritime freelance correspondent and a member of the Association of Belgian & Foreign Journalists, an association accredited by NATO and the UN. His reports, ship profiles and interviews are published in the English language naval magazines *Jane's Navy International, Naval Forces* and *Warships IFR*, as well

as in the French *Marines & Forces Navales* and the Japanese *J-Ships*. Since 1990, he has regularly embarked on NATO, Asian, South African and Pacific-based warships, including aircraft carriers, destroyers, frigates, mine-countermeasures vessels and support ships.

Scott Truver: Dr Scott C Truver is Director, Team Blue, at Gryphon Technologies LC, specialising in national and homeland security, and naval and maritime strategies, programmes and operations. Since 1972 Dr Truver has participated in numerous studies and assessments – most notably supporting the inter-agency task force drafting the US *National Strategy for Maritime Security* (2005) – and has also written extensively for US and foreign publications. He has lectured at the US Naval Academy, Naval War College and Naval Postgraduate School, among other venues. His further qualifications include a Doctor of Philosophy degree in Marine Policy Studies and an MA in Political Science/International Relations from the University of Delaware.

Conrad Waters: A lawyer by training but a banker by profession, Conrad Waters was educated at Liverpool University prior to being called to the bar at Gray's Inn in 1989. His interest in maritime affairs was first stimulated by a long family history of officers in merchant navy service and he has been writing articles on historical and current naval affairs for over twenty years. This included six years producing the 'World Navies in Review' chapter of the influential annual *Warship* before assuming responsibility for *Seaforth World Naval Review* as founding editor in 2009. When not combating the ongoing impact of the Eurozone crisis in his role as Managing Director for Credit Analysis at the European arm of one of the world's largest banks, Conrad lives with wife Susan and children Emma, Alexander and Imogen in Haslemere, Surrey.

Jacket images:
Front, main: *Aquitaine (DCNS)*, **top, left to right:** Exocet MM40 Block 3 surface-to-surface missile *(MBDA – Michel Hans)*; Indian P-8I variant of US P-8 Poseidon maritime patrol aircraft *(Boeing)*; *Fort Worth* (LCS-3) *(Lockheed Martin)*; *Thor (Rolls-Royce)*; *Vikramaditya (Sevmash via Cmde S K Grewal, IN)*.

Back, main: *Shimakaze* (DDG-172) and *McCampbell* (DDG-85) *(Royal Australian Navy)*; **insets, top to bottom:** *Satpura (US Navy)*; *Defender (BAE Systems)*; *Niamh*, Presidential Fleet Review, April 2012 *(Defence Forces Ireland)*.